The International Library of Sociology

VOLUNTARY SOCIETIES
AND SOCIAL POLICY

Founded by KARL MANNHEIM

The International Library of Sociology

PUBLIC POLICY, WELFARE AND SOCIAL WORK
In 18 Volumes

I	The Church in Social Work	*Hall and Howes*
II	Creative Demobilisation (Part One)	*Gutkind*
III	Creative Demobilisation (Part Two)	*Gutkind*
IV	Higher Civil Servants in Britain	*Kelsall*
V	Housing Needs and Planning Policy	*Cullingworth*
VI	Penelope Hall's Social Services of England and Wales	*Forder*
	(The above title is not available through Routledge in North America)	
VII	The Price of Social Security	*Williams*
VIII	The Professional Task in Welfare Practice	*Nokes*
IX	Social Casework	*Timms*
X	Social Policies for Old Age	*Shenfield*
XI	Social Security: Beveridge and After	*George*
XII	Social Services in British Industry	*Young*
XIII	Social Services of Modern England	*Hall*
XIV	The Sociology of Housing	*Morris and Mogey*
XV	Voluntary Social Services since 1918	*Mess*
XVI	Voluntary Societies and Social Policy	*Rooff*
XVII	Voluntary Work and the Welfare State	*Morris*
XVIII	Working with Community Groups	*Goetschius*

VOLUNTARY SOCIETIES AND SOCIAL POLICY

by
MADELINE ROOFF

First published in 1957 by
Routledge and Kegan Paul Ltd

Reprinted 1998, 1999 (Twice), 2001, 2002
by Routledge
11 New Fetter Lane, London EC4P 4EE

Routledge is an imprint of the Taylor & Francis Group

Printed and bound in Great Britain

© 1957 Madeline Rooff

All rights reserved. No part of this book may be reprinted or reproduced or utilized in any form or by any electronic, mechanical, or other means, now known or hereafter invented, including photocopying and recording, or in any information storage or retrieval system, without permission in writing from the publishers.

The publishers have made every effort to contact authors/copyright holders of the works reprinted in *The International Library of Sociology*. This has not been possible in every case, however, and we would welcome correspondence from those individuals/companies we have been unable to trace.

British Library Cataloguing in Publication Data
A CIP catalogue record for this book
is available from the British Library

Voluntary Societies and Social Policy
ISBN 0-415-17728-6
Public Policy, Welfare and Social Work: 18 Volumes
ISBN 0-415-17831-2
The International Library of Sociology: 274 Volumes
ISBN 0-415-17838-X

CONTENTS

Acknowledgments	*page*	ix
Introduction		xi

PART ONE
SOME ASPECTS OF THEORY AND PRACTICE IN THE 19TH AND EARLY 20TH CENTURIES

I	Influences affecting Social Policy and Voluntary Action	3
II	New Forms of Partnership	17

PART TWO
THE MATERNITY AND CHILD WELFARE MOVEMENT

	Introduction: The Position To-day: Some Unsolved Problems	29
III	The Pioneer Phase	31
IV	The Pioneer Phase (*cont.*)	41
V	Developments between the Two World Wars	50
VI	The Second World War and the Post-War Transition Period	66

PART THREE
THE MENTAL HEALTH SERVICES

	Introduction: The Position To-day: Pressure from the Past	79
VII	First Phase in the Development of Social Policy	83
VIII	Private Enterprise: Pioneer Work for the Insane	90
IX	Private Enterprise (*cont.*): Pioneer Work for the Mentally Defective	99
X	Expansion between the Two World Wars	112
XI	Expansion between the Two World Wars (*cont.*)	123
XII	The Relation between Voluntary Action and Social Policy	136
XIII	The Response to the Emergency. The War and Post-War Developments	149
XIV	Changes in Social Policy: Effect on Voluntary Organisations	159

CONTENTS

PART FOUR
THE WELFARE OF THE BLIND

	Introduction: The Position To-day: Outstanding Problems	173
XV	Voluntary Action in the Pioneer Phase	176
XVI	Social Policy in the Pioneer Phase	194
XVII	Expansion of Social Policy between the Two World Wars	206
XVIII	Voluntary Organisations and their Relations with Statutory Authorities between the Two World Wars	216
XIX	Developments during the Second World War: The Post-War Period	234

PART FIVE
REFLECTIONS ON THE CHANGING ROLE OF VOLUNTARY ORGANISATIONS AND THEIR RELATIONS WITH STATUTORY BODIES

XX	Persistence and Change in Social Attitudes and their Effect on Social Relations	253
XXI	Influences affecting the Relationship	270
	Bibliography	296
	Voluntary Societies and Professional Organisations	303
	Index	308

TABLES

		Page
Table I	Number of Cases (Mental Illness) dealt with by M.A.C.A., 1887–1918	96–97
Table II	Number of Cases (Mental Illness) dealt with by M.A.C.A., 1919–39	119
Table III	Occupation Centres etc. for the Mentally Defective: Statutory and Voluntary, 1921–50	126
Table IV	Mental Deficiency Service. Improvement in Backward Areas, 1922–39	141
Table V	Number of Cases (Mental Illness) dealt with by M.A.C.A., 1939–50	157
Table VI	M.A.C.A. Average Income, 1890–1954	166
Table VII	Developments in Community Care by the C.A.M.W. (later by N.A.M.H.), 1915–54	167–168
Table VIII	Number of Defectives reported to Local Authorities and how they were dealt with, 1924–54	169
Table IX	L.C.C. Total Expenditure on Welfare of the Blind and Grants to Charities, 1924–39	212
Table X	L.C.C. Payments to Voluntary Associations for the Welfare of the Blind, 1937–38	213
Diagram	Total Income of Charities for the Blind Registered with the L.C.C., 1924–37	232
Table XI	L.C.C. Total Expenditure on Welfare of the Blind and Grants to Charities, 1939–55	249
Table XII	Southern Regional Association for the Blind, Annual Income, 1940–55	250
Table XIII	L.C.C. Expenditure on Services for Mothers and Children, 1948–55	293
Table XIV	L.C.C. Expenditure on the Mental Health Services, 1948–55	294
Table XV	L.C.C. Expenditure on Services for the Welfare of Handicapped Persons, 1948–55: Directly and through Voluntary Associations	295

ACKNOWLEDGMENTS

I am greatly indebted to the many voluntary and statutory bodies without whose help this study would have been impossible. I should like in particular to thank the senior officers of voluntary societies who not only lent reports and journals and discussed problems with me, but who also read the relevant sections of the manuscript: they include members of the staff of the National Association for Mental Health, the Royal National Institute for the Blind, the National Association for Maternal and Child Welfare, the Family Welfare Association and the National Council of Social Service. The secretaries of the Mental After-Care Association, of the National Baby Welfare Council and of the Southern Regional Association for the Blind also gave most helpful interviews and lent documentary material. I received valuable suggestions from officers of the Ministry of Health in the Departments of Maternity and Child Welfare, Mental Health and the Welfare of the Blind, who read parts of the manuscript and discussed questions arising, and from officers in the Department of the Comptroller of the London County Council who supplied statistics not generally available and took great trouble in checking figures submitted to them.

I may perhaps be allowed to mention two distinguished public servants by name since they are both retired: Dr. McCleary read the section on maternity and child welfare, and Miss Bramhall that on the welfare of the blind. Their friendly criticism was much appreciated.

I should like also to thank my colleagues at Bedford College, especially Dr. Wootton, who, with the help of a small research grant, started me off on this enterprise; Professor Lady Williams who took a continued interest in the progress of the study and encouraged me when circumstances seemed adverse; Dr. Pinchbeck who most kindly read the script in its later stages; Mrs. Jefferys who helped to prepare the tables and diagram; and the library staff for their co-operation at all times.

Finally I should like to record my gratitude to my friend, Miss Dorothy Trollope, who not only read the first drafts of the manuscript, but also volunteered to correct the proofs.

I must add that, although I received much valuable criticism and advice, those I have mentioned are in no way responsible for the use I have made of the material.

MADELINE ROOFF

Bedford College,
Regent's Park, London, N.W.1.
September 1956

INTRODUCTION

My main purpose is to throw some light on the changing role of voluntary organisations and their relation with statutory bodies in the provision of the British social services.

The great experiments in social welfare in the mid-20th century have stimulated interest in the social services. Overseas visitors are constantly enquiring 'how things began', while sociologists are aware of the need for more detailed research into origins and development if the problems of to-day are to be fully understood.

This country has built up a unique partnership of voluntary and statutory action but, so far, there has been little investigation into the nature of the relationship.[1] An Official History[2] may acclaim voluntary action as 'characteristic of the British Social services', and social legislation may embody the principle of co-operation between statutory and voluntary agencies, but there is still some uncertainty about the function of voluntary organisations in a community which has achieved a reasonable measure of social security and welfare.

Co-operation and co-ordination have become vital issues in the complex society of to-day. The achievement of satisfactory relations between individuals and groups is one of the outstanding problems of social administration. It is not always easy to understand the varying attitudes of local authorities towards public and private enterprise in the provision of the social services. The rapidity with which changes have occurred in social policy and social structure have made it difficult to see the pattern as a whole. It is clear, however, that the influence of the past is still strong. For this reason special attention is paid, in this study, to origins and development, in the attempt to analyse the causes of friction and the conditions which make for co-operation, and to discover the reasons for persistence and change.

---

[1] There have been several general studies of voluntary action, e.g. those by H. Mess, and by the Nuffield Foundation, and later, that by Lord Beveridge. The official report on *Law and Practice Relating to Charitable Trusts* has thrown light on important aspects of the question.

As my study was nearing completion an enquiry was undertaken by Mr. Mencher, a Fulbright scholar, into the relationship between voluntary and statutory agencies in a few selected areas. This has now been published as a pamphlet by the F.W.A. When my manuscript was completed a forthcoming publication by Young and Ashton on *British Social Work in the 19th Century* was announced.

[2] See the official *History of the Second World War: Civilian Health and Medical Services*.

INTRODUCTION

It has been decided to select a few services for intensive study, concentrating, for the most part, upon Mental Health, Maternity and Child Welfare, and the Welfare of the Blind. No attempt has been made to cover the whole range of services within each field: for the purpose of illustration, the main emphasis has been upon 'community care' as distinct from residential care, although it is recognised that voluntary organisations have done, and are still doing, valuable work in the provision of homes, hostels and other institutions. Even though most hospitals and some convalescent homes were taken over as a statutory service after the introduction of the National Health Service, voluntary bodies such as the British Red Cross Society and the W.V.S. continued to play a welcome part in the provision of many new welfare services, giving what officials liked to call the 'personal touch'.

I have purposely excluded the hospital service, although this provides a valuable example of voluntary-statutory co-operation for maternity and child welfare, mental health and blind welfare, since soon after I had begun my study, the National Council of Social Service and King Edward's Hospital Fund sponsored an enquiry into the needs of the hospital service. The Report has since been published under the title *Voluntary Service and the State* (J. Trevelyan).

In all three services, Mental Health, Maternity and Child Welfare and the Welfare of the Blind, the main development has taken place in the 20th century, although the influences which determined their origin and growth can be traced much further back. While there are certain characteristics common to all three, their structure has been variously affected by economic and social influence, by the impact of two world wars and by the popularity of their appeal.

For several reasons a fuller study has been made of the Mental Health Service, particularly of the mental deficiency branch. This accounts for the otherwise disproportionate attention given in Part III to the Mental Deficiency Service. In the first place it is a service which has received less public attention,[1] and one in which many problems are still outstanding. It is also one in which experiments in community care by voluntary organisations have been considerable, and where the combination of public and private enterprise in the face of repeated setbacks affords an excellent illustration of a partnership in social service.

It is regretted that so little published material was available for a study of the financial aspects of the partnership, and for an investigation of the committee structure at the local level. The device of the grant, and payments for agency services, have given considerable impetus to co-operation, but official information is seldom disclosed about the finance of particular services. A series of enquiries in local areas would be necessary to complete the study of the financial relationship and of

[1] Since this section was written the Government has appointed a Royal Commission on the Law relating to Mental Illness and Mental Deficiency (1954).

committee representation and other forms of co-operation at the local level. The annual reports of voluntary societies have supplied some details, but the method of presentation of accounts has not been uniform, and it has sometimes been impossible to distinguish between statutory and voluntary sources of income. I have tried to indicate, however, from material gathered from various sources, what have been the main changes in the financial position of the voluntary organisations, and to show the increasing dependence upon statutory payments. Much of the material available on organisation and structure and on finance has been included in the main body of the text, and not, as originally intended, brought together in one section.[1]

Part I deals with some aspects of theory and practice in the 19th and early 20th centuries against which the development of voluntary organisations may be seen in perspective. This is followed by more detailed studies, in Parts II, III and IV, of the three selected services: in each case the legislative framework has been sketched in, in order to relate the development of voluntary enterprise to the limitations and opportunities of the statutory system. Part V summarises the pattern of development, the main forms of relationship between voluntary and statutory bodies, and the contribution which may be expected from combined action in the development of the social services.

Notes on Use of Terms

The terms 'voluntary organisation', 'voluntary society', 'voluntary agency' or 'voluntary association', in the context of the social services, are used interchangeably to cover those bodies which provide some form of social service, which control their own policy, and which depend, in part at least, upon financial support from voluntary sources. To a greater or less degree they receive personal help from voluntary, that is unpaid, workers but many of them, to-day, have salaried officers in key positions.

When we speak of statutory authorities and their functions we have in mind those bodies, central, regional or local, which have powers and duties bounded by statutes and administrative regulations. They, too, depend largely on voluntary service. Not only are local councillors unpaid, but advisory committees, at all levels, have relied upon experienced voluntary members. We may note, too, that while many civil servants and local government officers are administrators, social workers have been added to their ranks, particularly since the new legislation of 1948, most of whom have had experience of both voluntary and statutory social service. Two characteristics which particularly distinguish statutory bodies from voluntary organisations are the requirement that they work within legally authorised limits, and that they are strictly accountable for the expenditure of public money.

[1] A detailed analysis is given in the index.

INTRODUCTION

Partnership between voluntary and statutory bodies may involve the voluntary organisation in action as agent of a statutory authority in carrying out a power or a duty, or in supplementing a service already provided by the authority, or in providing a service which the authority has no power to give but which, nevertheless, it welcomes as ancillary to its own schemes.

In recent years it is becoming customary to speak of governmental and non-governmental organisations, particularly in the international sphere. Similarly, reference is often made to public and private action within the field of social service. Generally, the older and more familiar terms, voluntary and statutory, are used in this study, but occasionally the newer ones have seemed more apt.

PART I

Some Aspects of Theory and Practice in the 19th and early 20th Centuries

I

INFLUENCES AFFECTING SOCIAL POLICY AND VOLUNTARY ACTION

Tradition of Combined Action: the Force of Political and Economic Theory: the Pressure of Events

A WIDESPREAD partnership between statutory and voluntary agencies is a modern conception, but some combination of public and private action has its roots deep in the history of the English social services. We need go no further back than the Elizabethan Statute of Poor Relief issued together with the Statute of Charitable Uses in 1601, to see that, while statutory responsibility was accepted for the relief of the poor, charity continued to offer assistance to 'aged, impotent and poor people'. There was no clear distinction between public and private sources of help. The difference was largely one of range and scope, the voluntary funds serving a greater variety of purposes, whether meeting disastrous situations,[1] providing dowries for poor maids or promoting the education of scholars.

Charity and the Poor Law continued to function side by side, with fluctuating strength, during succeeding generations, The 18th century saw many private benefactions to hospitals, orphanages and other institutions, but it was during the 19th that new forms of partnership between voluntary organisations and statutory bodies were evolved. It was left to the 20th century to develop a comprehensive social policy in which public and private action were combined.

Before this stage was reached, however, a period of confusion reigned, when humanists and philanthropists were caught up in controversy, when charity was uncertain of its aims, and the Poor Law, dominated by the Malthusian theory of population, was administered as a disciplinary measure rather than as an instrument for relief.[2] For a great part of the

[1] These included the preferment of orphans, help to 'persons decayed', and the repair of bridges, havens, seabanks and highways.
[2] As a result the Poor Law was so hated that, generations after, its traditional bad name made even a reformed scheme of public assistance unacceptable.

SOME ASPECTS OF THEORY AND PRACTICE

19th century the prevailing social philosophy denied the responsibility of the community for the welfare of its adult citizens. In spite of the challenge of a variety of political, economic and scientific theories, the transition from the Philosophic Radicalism of Bentham and his followers[1] to the Idealism of Green and Bosanquet was slow and cautious. Until the 1870's Individualism dominated thought, and Laissez-Faire was widely accepted as the proper role of the State.

Nevertheless, some practical results were achieved as Radicals and Evangelicals organised national support for State action in strictly limited spheres, or philanthropists banded together to found voluntary societies for special purposes, while industrial workers, with little sympathy from the rest of the community,[2] gradually built up schemes of mutual aid to meet the hazards of the changing economic system. The two conflicting forces, a political theory which seemed to support the natural inclination of men to busy themselves with their own affairs and let others be, and the stress of circumstances which called for spontaneous activity on behalf of those in need, had a strong influence on the development of voluntary organisations and social policy in the 19th century, and on the relation between private and public action in the 20th. The diversity and experimental nature of charitable effort and the halting advance of legislative action must be seen in the light of a slowly changing philosophy and a rapidly changing economic and social structure.

This is not the place to discuss at any length the many forces which helped to shape the social history of the 19th century. We need only refer briefly to certain issues which have a special bearing on the development of voluntary organisations and social policy. We may note first the pressure of events as industrial and commercial expansion gathered strength, as increased production and the development of transport brought opportunity to the rising middle classes, and later, to the artisans. The importance of these classes in relation to the economic wealth of the country was reflected in measures for electoral reform. The demand for skilled workers led to a corresponding insistence on more democratic control of political institutions: the new Franchise Act was followed by the first Education Acts. Experience in large-scale business operations pointed to the need for greater efficiency in public administration: local government was reformed and the Civil

---

[1] J. S. Mill's fine conception of liberty allowed room for limited statutory intervention to secure the conditions of freedom. The Idealists took a further step in their recognition of the close relation between the individual and the community: it was necessary to remove abuses in order to secure the good life. The Socialists were to give a more positive and dynamic interpretation in their advance from Collectivism towards the 'Welfare State'.

[2] In the first half of the century there had been great hostility to the workers' movements for Co-operation, Trade Unionism and Chartism. Even later, when tempers were less frayed, and self-help a much prized virtue, there was some fear of the growing strength of the Friendly Societies.

SOCIAL POLICY AND VOLUNTARY ACTION

Service freed from corruption. One result of the extension of statutory responsibility, relevant to our study, was the appointment of an increasing number of experienced inspectors. They were to play an important part in raising the standard of service, both of voluntary and statutory agencies, as they spread knowledge of experiments, and gave guidance for future needs.

From one point of view social policy and voluntary action may be seen as the response to vast economic and social changes: changes which compelled attention as the rapidly growing population was concentrated in factories and towns. Looked at from another angle we see reforms as the achievement of a persistent minority against almost overwhelming odds. The problems which resulted from large-scale urbanisation, and the break-up of families as an economic unit, brought to light new pressures and strains at a time when the community was ill-prepared to deal with them. The influential middle classes were, for the most part, too absorbed in seeking to maintain and improve their own social and economic status to give over-much thought to those who failed: prosperity seldom induces sympathy. It seemed to the successful that progress was assured. The prevailing optimism was reinforced by the advances of science: physics and chemistry had opened up new fields of experiment in industry and transport; discoveries in biology were stimulating ideas in a variety of related studies; while medicine and engineering were making valuable contributions to public welfare.

There were, however, some misgivings with the threat of foreign competition and recurrent fluctuations in trade. In the economic depressions of the 1880's poverty amongst the unskilled workers became insistent. Infant mortality was heavy and the general death rate high. Uncontrolled urbanisation, with its overcrowding and its back-to-back houses, was little affected by the meagre attempts to improve housing conditions. The findings of Charles Booth[1] came as something of a shock, but no frontal attack was made, nor was the discredited Poor Law effectively challenged, until the 20th century. Individualism was sufficiently strong to prevent any fundamental legislative action for social reform.

How difficult it was to break down hostility to statutory intervention in the 19th century is illustrated by the long struggle to secure lunacy reform, in spite of many official enquiries and unofficial revelations of brutal restraint.[2] Again, a century of effort was needed to establish a comprehensive system of industrial health and welfare, although the movement for factory reform was strongly organised. Social reformers were to find that the publicity given to abuses, whether in mine, factory or lunatic asylum, was their most effective weapon. But they were not content with harrowing the emotions; they were also careful to insist

[1] Charles Booth published his *Life and Labour of the People of London* in a series of volumes between 1889 and 1902.
[2] See K. Jones, *Lunacy, Law and Conscience, 1744–1845*.

that no violation of the principle of Individualism would result from legislation: pauper apprentices might be excepted by virtue of their immaturity; the addition of women and young persons to the category of protected persons could be supported on the grounds that they were of less than adult status; when the first grants were made towards the education of poor children, statutory intervention was defended largely as a matter of expediency.[1] It was a series of epidemics, particularly the devastating cholera of the 1840's, which prepared the way for the acceptance of the first Public Health Act. In every instance opposition was strong, and the very minimum of public responsibility admitted. In the endless 19th-century debates advocates of Laissez-Faire showed considerable aptitude for quoting from the authorities, particularly from political economists, but others could be pressed into service. Utilitarianism was readily interpreted as the pursuit of self-interest, although Bentham had applied his principles to work out a series of reforms in education, health and penal law. He could easily be misquoted to support the equation of success with morality, leaving the poor as weaklings in both spheres. If further proof were needed of the inadvisability of intervention, the findings of Darwin could be misapplied to give an ethical interpretation to 'the survival of the fittest'.

Contrasts in Theory and Practice

As we look back over the 19th century it appears as an age of sharp contrasts. The indifference of a society dominated by Laissez-Faire was broken into by the vigorous and persistent enterprise of the few. It was a prosperous era, yet the 'Condition of England' question appeared to be more urgent than ever. Class distinctions were intensified, and the chaotic development of towns emphasised extremes of poverty and wealth: the massing of the 'lower orders' in congested areas, and the flight of the 'upper classes' to the more salubrious quarters, widened the gulf. Such division of the classes was to create many problems of economic, social and psychological import for social reformers in the 20th century.

The 19th century was also an age of fierce conflicts in many other spheres of thought and action, conflicts which persisted into the 20th century. Such were the political and religious controversies which raged with bitterness, and had severe repercussions upon social policy and the role of voluntary organisations. The feeling of insecurity in an age of rapid change called up strong emotional reactions, leading to violent resistance to the enlightened minority struggling for social, political or religious reforms.

Yet it was an age of increasing interest in social questions as journalists followed eagerly the reports of Royal Commissions and Select

[1] The inculcation of order and obedience, when parental discipline was suspect, was a matter of urgency in the turbulent 30's and 40's.

Committees. The official collection of vital statistics and, later, the extension of scientific method to the conduct of social surveys, marked an important stage in knowledge of social conditions. The readiness to discuss problems and to institute enquiries was illustrated by the growth of learned societies.[1] One founded in the late 1850's was particularly concerned with social questions: the *Association for the Promotion of Social Science*,[2] in its thirty-odd years of existence, was successful in focusing attention on a variety of important issues. Its achievements were to be judged, not only in terms of practical results, although it took part in several investigations in the field of public health which helped to influence legislation, but also in relation to the opportunity it gave to men and women of widely varying interests and experience to bring their ideas before a larger public. It was there that Mary Carpenter argued that children ought never to be considered as paupers or delinquents, but as boys and girls in need of education and training. It was before this body that Dr. Brodie gave his paper on the care and training of the mentally defective, pointing to the more enlightened practice overseas. We find eugenists, medical officers, social reformers, philosophers and various practitioners in the field of social work, all anxious to hear and discuss the many efforts being tried out at home and abroad to improve social conditions.[3] At the same time, several voluntary organisations were paying particular attention to the needs of the handicapped, and a number of enquiries were set on foot. Accurate knowledge was gradually being accumulated from both voluntary and official sources.

Meanwhile, a wider reading public had been made aware of social conditions through pamphlets, registers and journals of writers like Owen, Cobbett and Carlyle. Even more popular were the new 'novels with a social purpose'.[4] As Mrs. Gaskell, Kingsley, Dickens, Disraeli and a number of lesser artists like Mark Rutherford portrayed the wretched conditions of the labouring poor and helped to lighten the darkness which hid 'the other nation', their readers gradually became more sensitive to the sufferings of the oppressed.

Whatever doubts may be cast on the existence of 'a humanitarian movement',[5] there was certainly a new spirit abroad in the late 18th century which gathered strength in the 19th, and prepared the way for the extension of the social services in the 20th. It showed itself in a gradual widening of sympathy for the less fortunate members of the

[1] Note, too, the popularity of such discussions in local debating societies and workmen's clubs, and the use of such material for articles in the press, e.g. the *Morning Chronicle* series, 1844–49, 'London Labour and the London Poor'.
[2] See B. Rogers, *The Social Science Association, 1857–1886*.
[3] The Association kept a close watch on experiments overseas.
[4] See K. Tillotson, *Novels of the Eighteen-Forties*.
[5] See D. George, *England in Transition*, for an account of 'the rising tide of humanitarianism' ... when 'the age of Reason merged into the age of Feeling'; e.g. p. 66 and pp. 74–5.

community. Not all had the vision to see the fundamental need for social reform: few had the constructive energy of Robert Owen, whose welfare schemes for his mill workers in Lanark had been so successful[1]; hardly any were conscious of the magnitude of the problems facing a society passing from an agricultural to an industrial economy. Yet men and women in increasing numbers were to be found with a genuine concern for those in distress.

In spite, however, of much apparent interest, those who were concerned with questions of social welfare, whether associated with political reform, charitable effort or mutual aid, were in a minority. For the most part, the public became aware of particular needs only at moments of crisis, while statutory intervention was generally accepted from fear of catastrophe. At the same time, many of the labouring poor themselves, after the collapse of the earlier efforts for Trade Unionism, Co-operation and Chartism, were said to be 'sunk in apathy', unresponsive to the endeavours made to improve their lot. Until the broader movements for social and political reform had gathered strength, and a higher standard of living had reached the whole community, the lowest wage earners were forced to live under conditions of wretchedness beyond their power to control.

It was in such an atmosphere that voluntary organisations sought to make themselves acceptable. It is no wonder that for many years private enterprise in philanthropy found itself confused and uncertain as it met new and baffling problems in its effort to help the poor and the handicapped. Only as strong local societies were formed and contact was made with like-minded agencies,[2] was it possible to speak with confidence again.

Signs of a Changing Attitude: the Religious Influence and Experiments in Social Service

A striking example of the changing attitude to social questions is found in the relationship between Church and State, progressing from hostility or indifference to social reform, through a period of confusion to a final policy of co-operation. Although the Established Church had had a long tradition of association with charity, and religion had inspired many public-spirited men and women to voluntary action, the Church as an institution[3] stood aloof from most of the great social issues of the 19th century.[4] Early in the century the bishops had, in fact,

---

[1] Owen's welfare schemes for his mill workers in Lanark were more successful than his schemes for co-operation in New Lanark. The former became models and achieved world fame.

[2] National organisations sometimes developed 'from below upwards' in this way.

[3] It must be remembered that the Established Church had long been deprived of its Houses of Convocation, and it was in no position to speak with one voice.

[4] Education was an exception. See S. C. Carpenter, *Church and People,* for a full discussion.

SOCIAL POLICY AND VOLUNTARY ACTION

been closely allied with the Government in support of repressive measures, thereby earning the bitter hostility of the working classes. The Evangelical Revival[1] and the Oxford Movement[2] did much to recall the Established Church to a recognition of its spiritual function. For a great part of the century it was absorbed in trying to recover from long years of neglect by absentee clergy or indifferent congregations, while growing industrial centres called for strenuous effort by a new generation of hard-working vicars and curates. At the same time the Church was faced with the challenge of science, first of geology, then of biology, and its bishops entered into violent controversy with the secularists. Most of its energy was now devoted to ecclesiastical and theological questions and the restoration of discipline and order in its worship. Both the Anglican and the Nonconformist churches were deeply involved in questions of faith and order, and of schism within their ranks.

Yet, in spite of much 'shortness of thought',[3] a new outlook was gradually achieved. By the end of the century Archbishop Davidson could speak of the Church's dual role, 'both temporal and spiritual', and of the duty of bishops to devote themselves not only to the spiritual but to the social welfare of the nation.[4]

As the 20th century advanced, leaders of the Church, of all denominations, were to take an interest in a wider range of questions and to combine with laymen in practical efforts to strengthen the relation between voluntary action and social policy.[5]

Throughout the previous century, however, while the Church was otherwise engaged, men and women of religion were moved to organise voluntary action on behalf of their neighbours. The majority of the voluntary societies founded in the 19th century had a religious basis, while much social legislation was carried through in response to religious conviction or humanitarian principles. Any study of voluntary organisations and social policy must take note of the influence of religion in directing and sustaining reformers in both spheres of activity. Lord Shaftesbury, whose long life spanned a great part of the 19th century,

---

[1] Essentially other-worldly, Evangelicalism had yet inspired many of its followers to devote themselves to voluntary service.

[2] See W. G. Peck, *The Social Effects of the Oxford Movement*.

[3] An apt phrase coined by Dean Church, one of the enlightened thinkers within the Anglican Church, who refused to accept the prevailing theories of the relation between religion and science. See *Life and Letters of Dean Church*. Note his correspondence with Dr. Asa Grey, the American botanist.

[4] See *Randall Davidson*, by G. K. A. Bell, for the Archbishop's reply to Augustine Birrell. Davidson believed the Church's duty to be ' to inculcate large principles but not to take the place of statesmen as regards their practical working out' (*op. cit.*, p. 542). He himself had taken an active part in the House of Lords and elsewhere in helping to guide social policy. Cf. Davidson's charge to his clergy when he was Bishop of Rochester (*op. cit.*, p. 227). In 1899 the Archbishop once more made this principle clear in his charge to his bishops (*op. cit.*, p. 318).

[5] Note especially the activities of William Temple, the campaign for C.O.P.E.C. and the close concern with national and international questions.

SOME ASPECTS OF THEORY AND PRACTICE

is an outstanding example, since his influence was felt both as a parliamentarian and as chairman, president or patron of many new voluntary organisations connected with his interests in factories and mines, in lunacy reform, public health, ragged schools or the welfare of chimney-sweep boys. Shaftesbury stands apart from his contemporaries, however, both in the breadth of his interests and the narrowness of his vision. The effect of Evangelicalism on a boy of his reserved temperament and aristocratic background was to drive him to untiring effort in selected fields of social reform, of which agricultural reform was not one. (This omission is emphasised by those historians who are most critical of Shaftesbury's contribution.) He remained to the end an opponent of democracy, and, as a staunch Protestant and anti-ritualist, was to become a source of embarrassment to the Anglican Church, where his intolerance helped to prolong a regrettable controversy. But, in spite of acknowledged limitations, Shaftesbury had made a valuable contribution to the development of voluntary societies and to social reform.

While Shaftesbury was mainly concerned with developments at a national level, others were grappling with urgent local problems. The century was remarkable for the foundation of numerous local voluntary societies, of which the following may be noted in illustration of their variety in method and aim.

The work of the Domestic Mission in Liverpool[1] throws light on the struggle of men of goodwill to bring their religion to bear upon a bewildering situation. They made a conscious effort to organise neighbourliness, and to create a better understanding between the classes. They were faced, however, with an intolerable situation as they strove to reconcile their desire to bring friendship and spiritual comfort with their realisation of the depth of misery into which their neighbours were plunged. After a generation they were driven to change the order of approach: 'First that which is natural; afterwards that which is spiritual', seemed to be the only way out of their dilemma.[2] Others, too, were struggling to resolve the difficulties imposed by current assumptions, as they tried to meet immediate and urgent needs: 'how could the poor be assisted without encouraging dependency', 'how could the unemployed be helped and yet remain 'less eligible' than the respectable workman?', 'to what extent could poor children be educated without undermining parental responsibility or raising them above their station?'. Many of these questions were still being asked in the early 20th century, and both social legislation and voluntary action were affected by the answers.

[1] See M. B. Simey, *Charitable Work in Liverpool*, pp. 37–45. The mission was one with which the Rathbone family was closely associated.
[2] This decision was taken in 1848. See Annual Report, 1850, *op. cit.*, p. 45. Their heroic first missioner, John Johns, who gave his life nursing his neighbours in the cholera epidemic, had put spiritual matters above all else, but he had insisted that common humanity demanded the decencies of civilised life, which should be taken for granted.

SOCIAL POLICY AND VOLUNTARY ACTION

Other ventures in organised neighbourliness, many of which have persisted to modern times, are worth noting as indications of the variety to be found within the field of voluntary endeavour, and as examples of the preoccupation of many 19th-century philanthropists with the question of personal relationships.

Little will be said of Christian Socialism[1] since as a movement it did not survive, but the indirect influence of F. D. Maurice, Kingsley and their partners in the experiment in co-operative production was far-reaching, and the Working Men's College lived on as a memorial to some of the ideals of these men of deep religious experience, who combined intellectual gifts with warm humanity.

The Settlement movement had some affinity with Christian Socialism in its stress on the responsibilities of neighbourliness. The residential settlements to be found in the poorest parts of some of the large industrial centres brought together men of widely different experience,[2] and proved to be a social and educational experiment of considerable interest. Though the settlements were few in number, they led to a better understanding of the effects on the lives of individuals of changing economic and social conditions in a rapidly industrialised society, and they offered a useful training ground for future social reformers.[3] Their contribution, like those of other charities, reflected the dependence for financial stability mainly upon the donations of the more affluent. Not until the approach of the mid-20th century were they to become community centres, with the members taking a more responsible part in the conduct of affairs. But within the limitations imposed by the exigencies of the time, the settlements came near to solving the difficulties involved in a 'help relationship', where one group is thought of as socially superior to the other. The residents knew that they had much to learn as well as something to give. The settlements are of particular interest to our study of the relation between voluntary organisations and statutory bodies since many of the residents were active in both fields, serving on Boards of Guardians, or on local councils, and associating closely with many voluntary societies in their neighbourhood. They did much to foster a spirit of co-operation between public and private agencies.

A response far more colourful and resounding was made by men like William Booth and Dr. Barnardo, both of somewhat autocratic temper and outstanding vigour, who built up vast voluntary organisations which acquired international fame. These pioneers were products of an age when the challenge to religious principles threw up from the ranks men of character and personality. Dr. Barnardo combined a simple but

---

[1] See C. E. Raven, *Christian Socialism*, for a sympathetic account of this movement.
[2] Women were to play a more active part in the subsequent development of settlements, e.g. Elizabeth Macadam and Hilda Cashmore. Most wardens of settlements to-day are women.
[3] Men like William Temple and Clement Attlee, as well as many humbler social workers, were glad to acknowledge their debt.

intense religious faith with a strong practical bent as he conducted his campaign on behalf of deprived children.[1] William Booth broke from Methodism as he went into 'Darkest England'[2] with trumpet and cymbal, to build up his Salvation Army. He, too, found that men also need bread if salvation is to be effective, and his combination of philanthropy and religion won many converts. His strident propaganda helped to rouse the people of England to some awareness of the social consequences of extreme poverty. It was not only 'Darkest Africa' which cried out for zealous effort, but 'these sinking classes' in the heart of London[3] and other built-up areas.

Many other examples of responsible neighbourliness were to be found amongst men and women of religious faith, whatever the denomination.[4] The charitable work of the Jewish Board of Guardians was notable in several respects. It was concerned not only to give assistance to needy families, but to bind its members together in a strong community of interest. Since much of their work was done on behalf of the immigrant who needed help to settle in a new land, they respected his capacity for managing his own affairs, once the initial difficulties had been met. For this reason careful investigation to see the full extent of the need, followed by adequate assistance, helped to establish a method which is now recognised as fundamental to social case work.

The Quakers, similarly, were amongst those groups which successfully preserved a relationship devoid of superiority as between giver and receiver. They had much in common with the Unitarians. They were, like them, a small sect, yet they produced some outstanding experiments in voluntary organisation, some of which had an effective influence on social reform. The work of Elizabeth Fry and of the Tuke family achieved an international reputation. The many who supported the Adult School Union, the Educational Settlements and schools of various kinds are, perhaps, less well known. Others combined sound business capacity with charitable intent as they developed schemes to improve industrial relations, or set up day continuation schools for their young workers.

One other significant feature, common to many voluntary societies whatever their denomination, was the strong interest in the provision of residential accommodation. Funds were raised to establish hospitals and convalescent homes for the sick, almshouses for the aged, refuges for

---

[1] Other national organisations also did excellent work in the same field, e.g. the Waifs and Strays Society, afterwards 'The Church of England Children's Society', and the National Children's Homes. Dr. Barnardo's Homes are cited for the purpose of illustrating the variety of response.

[2] *In Darkest England*, the title of his book published in 1890.

[3] *Op. cit.*, Preface.

[4] Nothing has been said, for example, of the work of the increasingly numerous religious communities, both Roman and Anglican. Many of these devoted themselves to charitable work. Cf. P. F. Anson, *The Call of the Cloister*, for a recent account of Anglican Communities.

SOCIAL POLICY AND VOLUNTARY ACTION

young girls, asylums for the mentally handicapped, a variety of homes for the disabled and orphanages for deprived children. Many local societies seem to have been formed for the express purpose of selecting suitable applicants.[1] One of the merits of the majority of these homes was their small size; they were more 'homelike' than the large institutions: good personal relations were important if they were to fulfil the aims of their founders.

Other ventures, which resulted in the establishment of numerous voluntary societies to meet a local need, or to fulfil the special interests of their members, can only be referred to briefly. No national survey has been made of their number, and it is often only by chance that they acquired fame beyond their own borders.[2] From those which have come to light one feature seems to be characteristic: whether societies were formed for visiting the poor, for providing homes for old people, or for pioneering in schemes for maternity and child welfare, all had a strong moral purpose.[3] Many of the visiting societies, founded in increasing numbers in the 19th century, were, in fact, run in connection with local churches. Some were highly organised on a regional basis, linking together a group of parishes, as in London and Liverpool. At the same time, moral welfare work in its more specialised form was being encouraged in the dioceses throughout the country.

The essential humanity and the readiness to learn from experience, common to many of these pioneers in social service, is nowhere more apparent than in the progress from the condemnatory tone of some of the early organisations, such as those to suppress mendicity or vice, to the constructive schemes worked out in practice: schemes which contained some of the elements of the process to be known in the mid-20th century as 'rehabilitation'. Amongst these the Temperance Societies, which achieved national fame and enrolled members in their thousands, made a strong impression as they challenged the conditions which led to drunkenness, and proved that positive action gave better returns than moral exhortation. It was these organisations which prepared the way for statutory action by their appointment of police-court missionaries, the forerunners of the 20th-century probation officers.

Similarly, the pioneer work of voluntary organisations providing clubs for boys and girls, so often begun as preventive or remedial work,

[1] We must note, too, the now discredited system of 'letters' distributed to patrons according to the amount of their contribution.
[2] Cf. charitable trusts; the Nathan Committee reported, as late as 1952, that no one—not even the Charity Commissioners—knows how many charitable trusts there are... (*Report of the Committee on the Law Relating to Charitable Trusts*, p. 37).
[3] In the choice of titles, no other age could have produced societies 'for the Betterment of the Poor', or the 'League of Well-doers'. This latter group, founded originally as 'The Liverpool Food Association' in 1893, became 'The Food and Betterment Association in 1898' and 'The League of Well-doers' in 1909 (M. B. Simey, *op. cit.*, p. 121).

came to include a wide range of recreational activities, available for any who wished to participate.[1] Not until the threat of a second world war, however, were they officially recognised and invited to share in a statutory scheme for the 'Service of Youth'. On the other hand, the 19th-century voluntary organisations concerned mainly with adults which set out 'to bring joy into dull lives' were sometimes matched by the efforts of municipalities to provide parks, museums and libraries,[2] or by the workers' own schemes to share opportunities for mutual enjoyment. All three strands were to unite in the 20th century when the Council for the Encouragement of Music and the Arts[3] was founded under the auspices of a charitable trust and a Government Department distributing grant aid to help private ventures which showed initiative and enterprise in providing for 'common enjoyment'.

The Emancipation of Women

Charitable effort on so large a scale,[4] and the extension of local government activities, would not have been possible without the service of vast numbers of unpaid workers. Many of those who staffed voluntary organisations were women. The Women's Movement had released many of them from the frustration of a narrow social round. They took their place as part-time social workers in voluntary societies, and helped to create a demand for statutory measures, particularly for those related to the care of mothers and children or to services for the handicapped.

The emancipation of women was, in fact, one of the important influences in the advance of social welfare. Although the first concern of those who worked for 'Emancipation' had been to secure opportunities for women's paid employment, which in turn required further opportunities for education, it was part of a larger demand for equality and freedom. As women sought to widen their horizon and to take a more responsible part in the life of the community, they found in social service a vast field in which to work. Middle-class women, in particular, had an

[1] See the report of a survey made under the auspices of the Carnegie United Kingdom Trust, 1935, *Youth and Leisure*, Madeline Rooff.
[2] Some libraries were started by philanthropists, others by industrialists for their workers, but by the mid-19th century several large towns had established public libraries.
[3] The C.E.M.A., 1940–45, founded to meet a war-time need, was to go on as a permanent organisation, an autonomous body, leaving the shelter of the Ministry of Education with a grant-in-aid directly from the Treasury. In August 1946 the 'Arts Council of Great Britain' received the Royal Charter. See the First Report of the Arts Council for the statement of the principles on which the arts were to be supported. It is characteristic of the new public interest that the Local Government Act, 1948, enjoined local authorities to devote up to a sixpenny rate on entertainment and the arts.
[4] The number of charitable trusts alone increased from 9,154 in 1880, to 22,607 in 1900. This leaves out of account all charities known by the Charity Commissioners to have been in existence before 1837, and it omits all collecting societies. See Nathan Report, *op. cit.*, p. 80.

opening for their talents at a time when the changing family structure and the new pattern of society had taken from them the older household responsibilities. As some of them welcomed the chance to give personal service they found themselves obliged to work out new ways of assistance appropriate to urban life in an industrial society. Visiting the poor had long been a recognised form of charity but it had developed in an agricultural community. Visiting was still an important part of philanthropic work, but conditions were more exacting and results less easy to see.

Women had now to learn to take a larger share of the organisation and administration of voluntary societies, and to co-operate with officials of statutory bodies. Sometimes, like Florence Nightingale, they had to fight their way into entrenched strongholds of conservatism, or, like Louisa Twining,[1] to endure vulgar opprobrium, before they could win their cause. Public speaking required courage of no mean order, as Josephine Butler discovered as she campaigned for the repeal of the Contagious Diseases Acts. That practical ability and business methods might be combined with friendliness and understanding were proved by women like Mary Carpenter and Octavia Hill.[2] As the century advanced, women were playing an increasing part in public life as members of Boards of Guardians,[3] while others were offering help to medical officers of health as they built up a service of infant welfare. The joint contribution of men and women was to prove of value in broadening the field of service. At first the learning process proceeded mainly by trial and error; it had needed vision beyond the normal to discover in the changing conditions of the age, not only 'Who is my neighbour?' but, 'What kind of help does my neighbour want?' The further question, 'What is the fundamental cause of distress?' was often left unasked. Not until later were working women to take a larger share in voluntary organisations and local government. The experience of Women's Co-operative Guilds in the towns or of Women's Institutes in the rural areas was for many the first step towards public service. Two world wars gave further opportunities, and organisations like the British Red Cross Society and the Women's Voluntary Services were to recruit workers from all sections of the community.

In the late 19th and early 20th centuries, however, the demand was for 'educated women', and a number were beginning to ask for training

[1] Louisa Twining did much to improve workhouses, and to modify the attitude of Poor Law Guardians.
[2] Octavia Hill, the pioneer of 'Housing Management'. See Moberly Bell, *Life of Octavia Hill*.
[3] Objections to the appointment of women guardians had been made in 1850 on the grounds of public policy. The first woman was elected to the Kensington Board in 1875, and after ten years the number had increased to 50. When the Local Government Act, 1894, abolished the rating qualification, women stormed the citadel and in twelve months increased the number to 839. See S. and B. Webb, *English Local Government*, Vol. VIII, p. 234.

SOME ASPECTS OF THEORY AND PRACTICE

on scientific lines. As the social services developed in scope and range there was need for full-time professional workers.[1] Amongst the first to be appointed to paid posts were women housing managers and hospital almoners. They found that they had to keep in close touch with both local authorities and voluntary bodies if adequate help were to be given to the families for whom they were concerned.

[1] See p. 19, below.

II

NEW FORMS OF PARTNERSHIP

IN considering those aspects of social policy and voluntary organisation which were to influence the development of the social services in the 20th century, two spheres of activity are worthy of special notice since they illustrate new forms of partnership; these are the education service and the relief of poverty and distress.

Co-operation in the Education Service

In 1833 the first grant from public funds was made to two religious organisations[1] which had been experimenting for some twenty-five years in the provision of elementary education for the children of the poor. This tentative recognition of statutory responsibility resulted in a peculiar combination of private and public effort which has left its mark on the education service to this day. There is no doubt that the motives for this departure from the policy of non-intervention were mixed. A genuine desire to offer Christian teaching to 'children of the ignorant poor' was strengthened by the belief that discipline and obedience were urgent necessities in a revolutionary age. But while fear of a disorderly and discontented mob might secure a minimum of Government support, the temper of the times precluded the possibility of a State system of education, while religous opposition foiled several attempts to get public provision of teachers' training colleges. Opposition to statutory provision came from all sides: religious organisations were suspicious of radical secularist tendencies, and individualists were still convinced of the propriety of voluntary effort.[2] The situation was further complicated by the rivalry between the Anglicans and the Nonconformists. It is arguable that the bitterness engendered by this conflict held up, at least

[1] The British Society, a Nonconformist body, and the National Society, an Anglican body, with Lancaster and Bell, respectively, as their notable leaders in establishing the monitorial system, at a time when teachers were untrained and few in number.
[2] It is interesting to find Jeremy Bentham, an agnostic, giving his approval to the work of these schools.

for a time, the main line of advance towards a national system of education. However, in spite of some hostility, voluntary organisations continued to receive public support throughout the 19th century, even though the emphasis was upon 'cheap and elementary education'.[1]

When, at length, the first Education Act, of 1870, made possible the provision of schools out of public funds, voluntary organisations were still acknowledged to be the senior partners in the scheme.[2] By the early 20th century the pattern of statutory–voluntary co-operation was an accepted tradition in the public system of education in this country, although increasing demands reversed the standing of the two partners.[3] The great Education Act, 1902, was, however, nearly wrecked as the hostility between the Established Church and the Nonconformists flared up again. Eventually a compromise was reached,[4] and the bitterness gradually died down. During the Second World War the churches were to combine with considerable effect as they secured further provision for religious education in the Act of 1944. A national system of education was eventually established but dual control continued to be a characteristic feature.

'Spheres of Influence' in the Relief of Poverty and Distress. Co-operation in Infant Welfare

A partnership of a different kind had resulted from the attempt to relieve poverty and distress. The scope of public and private assistance was a matter of increasing concern, both to the Poor Law Board as it tried to grapple with the problem of destitution and 'pauperism', and to the voluntary organisations as they tried to substitute constructive help for indiscriminate almsgiving. A joint answer was sought in the strict administration of the Poor Law, and the scientific organisation of charitable aid, while an understanding was reached on the respective spheres of influence of voluntary and statutory bodies. It resulted, in 1869, in the issue of the famous Goschen Minute, and in the same year, in the formation of the Charity Organisation Society.[5]

---

[1] Note this phrase in the terms of reference of the Newcastle Commission, 1857.

[2] In the initial period the new School Boards were to provide schools only when the religious organisations were unable to meet the need. Generous financial aid was extended until, finally, the State assumed full responsibility for the maintenance of voluntary schools and for the salaries of their teachers.

[3] Religious organisations had only to raise money for buildings and their maintenance, and, even there, an allowance was made for 'fair wear and tear'. But voluntary bodies could no longer provide sufficient schools to meet the needs of the growing population of the towns, although they continued for many years to offer the only available education in many country villages.

[4] See, *Randall Davidson*, G. C. K. Bell, *op. cit.*, for some illuminating chapters on the prolonged struggle for agreement on the education issue.

[5] Its first title was 'The Society for the Organisation of Charitable Relief and Repressing Mendicity'. It should be noted that an earlier attempt to organise charity had been successfully carried through in Liverpool when several overlapping societies were amalgamated to form the Central Relief Society in 1863.

NEW FORMS OF PARTNERSHIP

The oft-quoted Goschen Minute ruled, in effect, that the Poor Law should be concerned with the wholly destitute, while charity should be reserved for those who had some but insufficient means.[1] Unfortunately for the recipients, this solution of the relation between charitable effort and public responsibility was generally interpreted as a distinction between the deserving and the undeserving,[2] the reformable and the unrepentant, or the helpable and the hopeless. Nearly twenty years later,[3] an extension of the Local Government Board's policy of co-operation with voluntary agencies was made when the municipalities were encouraged to provide work for wages, out of funds collected by voluntary appeal. Such work was to be reserved for the respectable unemployed, as distinct from the less desirable jobs found for casual workmen in the labour yards under Poor Law auspices.[4]

Meanwhile the C.O.S. was trying to co-ordinate charitable aid in London; at the same time it respected rigorously the spirit of the Goschen rule, as it kept in close touch with the Poor Law Guardians and concentrated on helping only the helpable. Though the Society acknowledged that the springs of charity were sympathy, religion and science,[5] onlookers might be excused if they failed sometimes to recognise the more human qualities in the early stages of C.O.S. case work.[6] Its methods had the merit, however, of emphasising the need for adequate assistance adjusted to the needs of the individual, with the family as the unit, if constructive work was to be achieved. Moreover, it was among the first to insist that voluntary workers should take a responsible and regular place in the organisation if their services were to be acceptable. In addition, it made a contribution to the training of social workers which has continued to rank high to the present day.[7] The C.O.S. also took an active part at a national level as it organised enquiries, conducted propaganda, and exerted pressure on government departments in such spheres as education, the welfare of children, housing, blind welfare or mental health. It did much to encourage new ventures such as the

---

[1] See the Nathan Report on Charitable Trusts for a fuller discussion of this point. It was suggested that the most likely form which charity might take would be in the provision of 'once and for all articles'.

[2] C. S. Loch, in *3,000 Years of Social Service*, gives a clear exposition of the ideas of the C.O.S. on the relation between charity and the Poor Law (Ch. XXXVII). He argues that the question was not whether a person was deserving or not but 'whether, granted the fact, the distress can be stayed and self-support attained'.

[3] Chamberlain's famous circular of 1886.

[4] In 1905, under the Unemployed Workmen Act, Distress Committees were set up in all towns, financed by local rates and an Exchequer grant; their function was to help 'capable workers'.

[5] C. S. Loch, *op. cit.*, p. 396.

[6] Its case work became more flexible, particularly as it learned from America, and from the experience of psychiatric social workers.

[7] Its co-operation in practical training for students is sought by all the Social Science Departments of the universities. (*N.B.:* C.O.S. is now the F.W.A., i.e. the Family Welfare Association. See p. 255, below.)

appointment of hospital almoners, and the formation of the Invalid Children's Aid Association.[1]

But the Society's strong individualism brought it into violent conflict with the advocates of Collectivism. It was anathema to the Fabians and the new left-wing political groups,[2] and it aroused the bitter hostility of a number of voluntary organisations for its ruthlessness in opposing any weakness in administration. This policy led it into conflict with established organisations of repute, as well as with more questionable and ephemeral societies. Its criticism of the methods of Dr. Barnardo's, of the Salvation Army and of the N.S.P.C.C. roused much ill-feeling. It succeeded, however, by its publicity, in putting charitable organisations on their mettle, and it undoubtedly helped to reduce the number of bogus societies. Its strong belief in the need to encourage self-help and to avoid 'injurious dependency'[3] was in line with the generally accepted doctrine of the age. It continued, throughout, to co-operate closely with the Boards of Guardians to ensure that no overlapping occurred, but its effort to establish a 'mutual register', supported by all agencies, both voluntary and statutory, was not successful. In spite of the increasing demands for statutory action in the late 19th and early 20th centuries, the old philosophy lingered on. Had the signatories of the Majority Report of the Royal Commission on the Poor Laws[4] had their way, C.O.S. principles would have triumphed: voluntary committees would have been set up to play the more constructive role of registration, interviewing and deciding upon appropriate treatment.

But the role of the State as junior partner was not acceptable to a vigorous Liberal Government. The changing political theory, the rising standard of living, the advance in knowledge of social problems and their causes,[5] the vitality of some of the municipalities and, perhaps most potent of all, the shocks of the Boer War[6] had combined to make

[1] It also supported Octavia Hill in her pioneer work for housing management.
[2] The assumption that voluntary organisations should play a major role was criticised, not only as a matter of principle, but from accumulated evidence of the inadequacy of voluntary action in relation to total needs.
[3] C. S. Loch, *op. cit.*, p. 406. It was for this reason that the C.O.S. opposed the giving of outdoor relief, save only in emergency. Instead, the workhouse should, if properly conducted, be the means to the full reinstatement of the family. It would be the role of the Society to help re-establish them, once family responsibility was accepted.
[4] The Royal Commission on the Poor Laws, 1905–09. The persistence of the 19th-century attitude towards the unemployed was illustrated during the inter-war years, when the 'dole' was the contemptuous name for extended insurance benefits during periods of heavy unemployment. The unemployed were often accused by a thoughtless public of being workshy, until the chronic situation in the 'special areas' forced the issue. The establishment of the Unemployment Assistance Board followed, in 1934.
[5] The accumulated evidence of official committees, the Booth Surveys and Fabian Research all contributed to a better understanding of social questions.
[6] Particularly the findings of the Committee on the Physical Deterioration of the Race.

the demand for statutory services more urgent. Old age pensions, measures for the education, health and welfare of children, the establishment of Trades Boards and Labour Exchanges, and improvements in Poor Law administration laid the foundations for the development of new statutory social services. In 1911 a new principle was introduced into social policy with the inauguration of the social insurance schemes. After a stormy beginning these schemes were to secure general approval, not least in their acceptance of self-help as one of the three contributory elements. Some of the reforms, however, caused considerable misgiving. The C.O.S., carrying their philosophy to its logical conclusion, opposed school meals to necessitous children[1] as tempting a mother to neglect her family, and old age pensions as undermining self-respect and discouraging thrift. It was to argue that the provision of municipal hospitals, like the provision of pensions was 'a stereotyped form of relief to large numbers of persons whose needs are very varying and only capable of being met by individual attention'.[2]

In spite of much new social legislation the Government had had no clear policy for the development of a comprehensive system of social services. Instead, statutory intervention was made haltingly, step by step, as immediate demands made reform expedient, while voluntary enterprise was carried on, with varying degrees of strength, according to individual or local interest and enthusiasm.

Meanwhile, some of the more vigorous local authorities were not only developing their public health services along generally accepted lines of sanitation, but were experimenting in new forms of personal service outside the hated Poor Law. They were to be pioneers in combining with voluntary bodies to build up a maternity and child welfare service under the guise of sanitary reform; they were also to show that it was possible, as local education authorities, to interpret their powers sufficiently widely to include various forms of welfare, some in close co-operation with voluntary societies. But the relief of the poor was for long to remain an 'omnibus' service, outside their jurisdiction.[3]

[1] A number of voluntary societies had already been organising such meals in various parts of the country, and statutory provision was made in 1906.
[2] Quoted Beveridge, *Voluntary Action*, p. 148. In the inter-war years the C.O.S. gradually modified this attitude. Its more flexible case work brought it into greater sympathy with social policy. While preserving the basic principles of self-help and family responsibility, it recognised the value of the social security services, and sought to work closely with statutory authorities on a new reciprocal basis. The change of name, in 1947, to the Family Welfare Association, was more in keeping with the Society's aims.
[3] It was not until 1930 that local authorities took over responsibility from the Poor Law Guardians and had power to give assistance to certain groups outside the Poor Law. See Local Government Act, 1929, Section 1, which provided that on the appointed day the functions of Poor Law Guardians should be transferred to the councils of counties or county boroughs. In the same Act, Section 5, it was provided that 'A council... shall have regard to the desirability of securing that, as soon as circumstances permit, all assistance which can lawfully be provided otherwise than by way of poor relief, shall be so provided.' The Acts to which a declaration might

SOME ASPECTS OF THEORY AND PRACTICE

Experiments in Co-ordination, Local and National. Financial Relationship

The development of a close relationship between statutory authorities and voluntary societies was still rare. Some organised attempts to secure combined action during the haphazard growth of the social services in the early 20th century were made as Guilds of Help, Councils of Social Service and similar local bodies were formed for the express purpose of bringing together members of public and private organisations in their area.[1] The general advantage of extending such schemes was recognised when, in 1914, the report of a special committee, chaired by the President of the Local Government Board, was followed by the first of a series of official recommendations on the prevention and relief of distress.[2] A conference sponsored jointly by the C.O.S. and Guilds of Help had immediate success, and resulted in the foundation, after the First World War, of the National Council of Social Service. This great co-ordinating organisation has, since its inception, taken a prominent part in fostering a partnership between government departments, local authorities and voluntary societies. It has become the recognised channel for the distribution of a number of grants from both public and private sources, and, like the C.O.S., has thrown up experiments and sponsored new ventures in social welfare.[3]

Another partnership of particular interest was the recognition by a powerful local authority of the desirability of combined statutory–voluntary action: the London County Council in establishing its Care Committee scheme early in the century, appointed experienced social workers in key positions on the understanding that they would recruit and train voluntary workers to form school care committees, and to keep in close touch with teachers, parents and children. Although this was part of the new School Medical Service, it was intended that organisers should be concerned not only with the child's health but with his welfare. With that in mind they were expected to co-operate with any agency, voluntary or statutory, available for the purpose: another opportunity was given for the development of a co-ordinated service.

Before we go on to consider forms of co-operation worked out in the three selected services something should be said of the financial relationship. In the 19th century the voluntary organisations were mainly dependent on money derived from appeals to the charitable public, or from the legacies and bequests which formed a surprisingly large pro-

---

apply included: the Public Health Act, 1875, the Local Government Act, 1888, the Mental Deficiency Act, 1913, the Maternity and Child Welfare Act, 1918, the Blind Persons Act, 1920, the Public Health (Tuberculosis) Act, 1921, and the Education Act, 1921.

[1] A number of them affiliated with the C.O.S.

[2] P.R.D.I. recommended that such committees might represent local authorities, Boards of Guardians, distress committees, trades unions and philanthropic organisations such as S. and S.F.A.

[3] See p. 260 and pp. 265-6, below.

portion of their income. In a few spheres, notably that of education, public money was increasingly available for the extension of the work of voluntary bodies. To a lesser extent, payments were made by Poor Law authorities for services rendered by voluntary societies, but their powers were limited and the amounts were small.[1] Occasionally progressive municipalities made 'donations' to organisations for special services, e.g. the provision of Braille books. Sometimes a local authority, though having no power to spend public money, was able to give a grant from a charitable fund for which it was responsible, e.g. by the L.C.C. to the Mental After-Care Association, from Queen Adelaide's Fund. Early in the 20th century a few local authorities were interpreting Public Health and Education Acts sufficiently widely to aid some of the new ventures in maternity and child welfare. But the amounts contributed to the income of voluntary organisations from statutory sources were relatively small. Some voluntary societies which had little public appeal, such as those working in the field of mental health, drew an increasing proportion of their income from 'payments for services' by beneficiaries.

The First World War marked the division between the old philanthropy and the new. Lloyd George's budget, 1914, made possible the first extension of payments to voluntary organisations providing certain services, but the new pattern emerged after the war.[2] The year 1919 was momentous in the history of voluntary societies, for a new financial relationship between public and private agencies was begun, which was to make a substantial difference to the balance of public responsibility in the provision of the social services. Private enterprise could no longer meet the increased demand for social services, and many of the societies were glad to accept subventions from statutory sources as they acted as agents for public bodies in carrying out new social legislation. Yet large sums were still drawn from charitable sources, and some voluntary societies continued to function without aid from statutory funds. Many of those which received grants were also ready to pioneer in other activities which did not qualify for aid. They were often helped to do so by Trust Foundations. After 1919, however, payments for services rendered on an agency basis formed an increasing proportion of the income of many voluntary organisations. A number of Exchequer grants to national organisations for special purposes were also available, but the development of the statutory–voluntary partnership depended largely on the extent to which individual local authorities chose to 'secure the provision of' a service. How far in fact, as well as in theory, voluntary organisations would continue to be 'an essential part of the

[1] Cf. p. 194, for example of blind child sent to a voluntary school, where payments were limited to the cost of maintenance in a workhouse. After the Act of 1893 grants were increased to two-thirds of cost of maintenance in the school.

[2] A Ministry of Reconstruction had been set up, and a variety of schemes prepared in readiness for new social legislation.

SOME ASPECTS OF THEORY AND PRACTICE

British social services' would rest largely on the application of social policy at the local level.

Motives for Social Action and their Effect on Voluntary Organisations and Social Policy

No outline of the theory and practice which prepared the way for the development of the social services in the 20th century would be complete without some reference to the motives which induced men and women to take part in organised voluntary action, whether for public or private bodies. We can learn from novels and biographies, as well as from occasional studies of particular organisations or of defined areas,[1] how varied these motives were. Few humanists threw themselves wholeheartedly into the task of demonstrating their ideals as did Robert Owen; not all philanthropists could aspire to the compassionate devotion of John Johns of the Liverpool Mission; nor were there many with the singleness of aim of Dr. Barnado, or with the scientific objectivity of Charles Booth. For the majority the motives were mixed.

There is little doubt that the attitude towards public service was much influenced by the prevailing social structure and the current assumptions on values. Dr. Peyser has argued that the starting point of assistance as a social function is inequality of men and conditions.[2] Early social policy was shaped, and many of the voluntary societies were founded, in a period of marked inequality. While the desire to break through class barriers had been the special concern of some organised groups, the acceptance of the existing social structure was an essential element in the attitude of others who, in the spirit of *noblesse oblige*, conceived it to be their duty to assist the needy. The easy assumption of the charitable well-to-do that they were at liberty to enter the homes of the poor at any time convenient to themselves[3] was an attitude which lingered on into the 20th century in the practices of some of the voluntary societies whose members went 'home visiting'.[4] Some took up voluntary work with a conscious superiority as they ministered to their inferiors in wealth or status.[5] A particular manifestation of class consciousness was the opportunity for the social climber to rub shoulders with the gentry in philanthropic ventures. Patronage and condescension were human weaknesses easily acquired in a class-conscious age: they were qualities bitterly resented by the recipients, forming barriers to the friendly relationship which others were working hard to establish. What remains

[1] e.g. M. B. Simey, *op. cit.*
[2] Dr. Peyser, *The Strong and the Weak*, p. 2.
[3] Such delightful studies as G. Raverat, *Period Piece*, and E. M. Forster, *Marianne Thornton*, throw incidental light on visiting the poor.
[4] 'Appointments' are an accepted practice by the more professional bodies, but unannounced visiting is still to be found in others.
[5] It was of this group that it could be truthfully said, 'You can't rely on voluntary workers'. They, unlike many others who gave regular and reliable service, e.g. as hon. secs., were a liability instead of an asset.

of hostility to voluntaryism in some quarters to-day owes much to the false values which attended the misuse of 'charity' in the past. Such hostility persisted even when changes in social structure following upon the First World War made the old attitude both intolerable and unfashionable.

We have seen the strength of the religious motive in initiating voluntary action and social reform. By the 1880's the nation was becoming sensitive to the more emotional revivalist appeals. While much renewed energy was generated for voluntary service of many kinds, charity tended to become increasingly eleemosynary, and indiscriminate alms-giving more widespread. By the 1890's 'slumming' had become fashionable. The impulse to love one's neighbour might be overlaid by sentimentality as an emotional response brought a warm glow of satisfaction or removed feelings of guilt. For some, a sense of religious obligation was associated with a desire to acquire merit. There is evidence, too, that an apparent humanitarianism was inextricably woven with the hope of receiving worldly honours, or with the sense of power which accrued from membership of public bodies and the prestige acquired in governing their fellows.

But it would be a mistake to emphasise such questionable conduct at the expense of the devoted service of the large numbers of men and women, whether religious or humanist, who were moved by profound sympathy, or who could not tolerate the conditions they found. Though some may have been narrow in their vision, failing to appreciate the larger issues, others gave intelligent and informed service. Some of the outstanding social reformers of the late 19th and early 20th centuries based their work on the intellectual acceptance of a political philosophy, whether that of the Idealist school or of the Fabians. A new approach to sociology was an inspiration to others. Beatrice Webb has told us that she went into the homes of the poor, not in the spirit of charity, but in the determination to investigate conditions. Many others, less famous, took part in the work of voluntary societies, or served on local councils, because they were keenly interested in their chosen field of activity. Many who served on advisory committees, whether voluntary or statutory, had a scientific or professional interest in the questions at issue. There can be no doubt, as we view the whole field of voluntary action in the 19th and early 20th centuries, that the spirit of enquiry, and charity in its true sense, produced remarkable results, whether in the work of individual pioneers for social reform or in the organisation of vigorous local and national voluntary societies.

The best results were achieved when accurate knowledge and a scientific approach were allied with the enthusiasm which comes from a genuine concern for social welfare. These qualities were to mark the work of some of the large-scale voluntary organisations and the progressive local authorities in the 20th century. Since it was the spirit of

SOME ASPECTS OF THEORY AND PRACTICE

enquiry which first led many 'men of sense and publick spirit'[1] to embark on social reform, it was not surprising that the investigations set on foot by some of the voluntary societies owed much to their vigour of mind. The practice of bodies like the Charity Organisation Society and the Central Association for Mental Welfare, of setting up expert committees before seeking by combined action to influence social policy, was an instance. The initiative of medical officers of health and their local authorities in co-operating with voluntary societies to discover various ways of reducing infant mortality, and of securing maternal and child welfare, was an outstanding example of intelligent, planned action, which bore rich fruit during the first half of the 20th century. In the sphere of blind welfare, the educational work and the research which helped blind men and women to play their part in the normal life of the community bore witness to the enlightened enterprise of such bodies as the National Institute for the Blind. How far these and other agencies were successful in working co-operatively with the statutory authorities in making the best use of resources, and in creating an informed public opinion, should appear in the course of the following three sections.

[1] See p. 270 below.

PART II

The Maternity and Child Welfare Movement[1]

[1] See p. xii, above, for reference to the scope of this section.

INTRODUCTION

The Position To-day: Some Unsolved Problems

In 1900, of every 1,000 children born, 154 died during the first year of life. By 1950 the infant mortality rate had fallen to 29·9. This spectacular reduction was founded upon a maternity and child welfare service which has proved to be one of the most successful of the preventive health services of the first half of the 20th century.

The service developed during a period of increasing awareness of social needs and a considerable rise in the standard of living. It was to be expected that mothers and children would share in the general improvement of social conditions. Nevertheless, experience had shown that such general progress was not necessarily accompanied by a reduction in the infant mortality rate[1] unless special care was taken. Much credit is due to the maternity and child welfare movement which, for fifty years, inspired the work of the centres, helping by sustained effort to improve the services offered and to educate the mothers, and sometimes the fathers, to take full advantage of the facilities.

Perhaps one of the most surprising features of an apparently successful movement is the discovery that we may still be faced with problems to which solutions were being sought in the pioneer stage, and that fundamentally the same remedies are being suggested to-day. For example, in 1950, in an area where the incidence of infant mortality was exceptionally high, the Medical Officer of Health called for measures many of which had been strongly advocated in the first decade of the century: ante-natal care, improved feeding (by now it included the vitamins supplied under the Government Welfare Foods Service), the importance of breast feeding and the need for cleanliness. The additional modern requirement was expert care in the rearing of premature babies.[2]

We find that there is still a call for vigilance and propaganda, even though standards as a whole have vastly improved. In a study made between 1939 and 1942 the Women's Group on Public Welfare[3] threw a searchlight on the condition of some of the evacuated mothers and children. Although the bitter complaints of some of the hostesses in the

---

[1] See p. 69, below.
[2] See the results of a special enquiry (Ministry of Health, *Annual Report for the Year ending December, 1952*, pp. 101–102).
[3] The Women's Group on Public Welfare, in association with the National Council of Social Service, published *Our Towns, A Close Up*, in 1943. See especially the Introduction, from which the quotations are taken.

reception areas related to a small proportion only of the evacuees, 'the intolerable and degrading burden to decent people' of those who were dirty and crude in their habits was sufficient to justify the outcry. The committee urged that 'a campaign for better education, academic, social and moral, must be waged side by side with the battle against poverty and bad material conditions'.

Thirdly, there is renewed interest in parentcraft, and the propaganda on this question recalls the appeals of the pioneers in the first decade of the century. To-day there is the additional advantage of encouragement and support from the Ministry of Health.

Finally, we note that the early stress on the desirability of a proper link between hospitals, voluntary organisations and local authorities is still relevant. The need for the co-ordination of all the services relating to the welfare of mothers and children is a matter of particular concern since the National Health Service Act, 1946, threw the question into prominence.

The interest of a review of the Maternity and Child Welfare Service is increased as we consider the example it offers of a close relationship, from its inception, between statutory and voluntary bodies. The early success of the movement was due in large measure to the co-operation between a group of medical officers of health and their local authorities on the one hand, and the voluntary organisations on the other. At a later stage the central authority was included in the partnership. The combined schemes put infant welfare on a sound footing, while the voluntary element helped to build up the essentially personal character of the service. The Maternity and Child Welfare Service became, especially in the urban areas, one of the most popular and generally acceptable of the social services.[1] How much the centres were missed, especially by mothers who were evacuated from large towns[2] to rural areas, was evident during the Second World War.

[1] An investigation made in 1946 brings out the progress made. In 1915, even in districts served by a total of some 650 infant welfare centres, only about a quarter of the babies whose birth had been notified attended. By 1933, with a total of 3,113 centres, the first attendances of children under one year were 60% of the notified live births. In 1944 the number of centres had risen to 3,932, and the percentage of attendance to 71. (*Maternity in Great Britain*, survey undertaken by a Joint Committee of the Royal College of Obstetricians and Gynaecologists and the Population Investigation Committee, pp. 93–94.)

[2] The wide difference between areas was noted by the authors of *Maternity in Great Britain*. While the percentage attending infant welfare centres among mothers of living babies interviewed, for all counties, was 47·6%, that for all urban areas was 62·2%. Of urban areas London was 77·4%, Wales 70·3%, South-East 67·7%, East 65·5%, South-west 64·7%, Midlands 61·1%, North 60·6%. (See p. 98, Table 28, *op. cit.*)

III

THE PIONEER PHASE

EARLY ATTITUDES TOWARDS INFANT WELFARE: THEIR EFFECT ON VOLUNTARY ACTION AND SOCIAL POLICY

IN the late 19th century infant welfare had to fight hard for public recognition. There had, indeed, been several early attempts to deal with the question, but they were sporadic, and failed to win general support. For example in the mid-18th century Dr. Cadogan had called attention to the seriousness of infant mortality,[1] supporting his warning by reference to his experience in the Foundling Hospital.[2] He was followed by Dr. Armstrong,[3] who set up the first dispensary 'for the relief of the infant poor', and by Dr. Davis, who was the first to advocate health visiting in association with the dispensary. But although the number of dispensaries increased, and more and more doctors called attention to the heavy infant mortality, the efforts to tackle the problem as a whole were ineffective, and the public could not be roused to any real sense of urgency.

Many influences gradually prepared the way for a new attitude towards infant welfare as the 19th century advanced. In the first place the community had become more health-conscious as Chadwick and Simon and the local sanitary authorities laid the foundations of a public health service. Secondly, public opinion had slowly come to accept the necessity for some legislative intervention on behalf of children. The factory children,[4] the chimney sweeps, children who were boarded out[5] and children who were cruelly treated[6] had all, in varying degrees, some

---

[1] 'Enquiry into Infant Mortality.'
[2] Dr. Cadogan was appointed physician to the Foundling Hospital in 1754. The Hospital had published *An Essay upon Nursing and the Management of Children from their Birth to Three Years of Age by a Physician*, which was acknowledged in a later edition to be his.
[3] 1769–81.
[4] Very slow progress from the limited Factories Acts of 1801 onwards.
[5] Infant Life Protection Act, 1872.
[6] Prevention of Cruelty to Children Act, 1889.

THE MATERNITY AND CHILD WELFARE MOVEMENT

measure of protection. The provision of elementary education was at last established as a public responsibility.[1] Thirdly, when the widening franchise made democratic government a reality, and when local government became vigorous and representative, there was greater readiness to appreciate the importance of a movement for the welfare of mothers and children. There is no doubt, too, that the more active part taken by women in public life, particularly as members of Boards of Guardians, helped towards a better understanding of the needs of mothers and children.[2] Above all, medicine had made considerable progress, and the doctors had secured a firm standing in the community. Some of the newly appointed medical officers of health[3] were to seize their opportunities and to play a vigorous part in the pioneer work for infant welfare.

By the end of the 19th century, however, the infant mortality rate had not reflected the progress made in other spheres. Although the general death rate had shown a marked decrease, infant mortality was as high as it had ever been since records were made. It required yet a further stimulus, the shock of the Boer War and the recruiting returns, followed by the revelations of the Departmental Committee on Physical Deterioration,[4] before there was any sense of urgency in dealing with the problem of 'the future of the race'. The population question was not, as in France, a foremost issue in the consideration of infant welfare.

Of the many forces which prepared the way for the movement for infant welfare, we cannot omit the influence of religion, and the strong moral fervour of the Victorian era, which inspired so many of the pioneers, whether doctors, social workers or local authority representatives. That this was still a force in the early 20th century is evident from the approval with which Sir George Newman, as late as 1910, quotes Dr. Newsholme, 'the prevention of infant mortality is largely a moral problem'.[5]

Once public interest was aroused societies were to spring up in all directions, reflecting the many facets of infant and maternal welfare. But the advance towards a co-ordinated movement was only possible when the voluntary organisations and the statutory authorities, with the active participation of the medical officers of health, worked together,

---

[1] Education Acts, 1870 and 1876, and also the recognition of the special needs of certain handicapped children, the blind and deaf and the mentally defective and epileptic in the 1890's.

[2] Many of them were women of outstanding quality, e.g. Louisa Twining. See p. 15, above.

[3] The 1st M.O.H. had been appointed in 1848. In 1871, power to appoint an M.O.H. was made general. It was made a duty in 1875. See W. M. Frazer, *A History of English Public Health*, for an account of their work.

[4] The Committee was set up in 1904.

[5] From the Special Report, 1910, to the Local Government Board on Infant and Child Mortality: Sir G. Newman, *The Health of the State*, 3rd edition, 1913, p. 133. Cf. 'Our Towns', quoted p. 29n., above.

THE PIONEER PHASE

first for the prevention of infant mortality, and later for the wider purpose of maternity and child welfare. Before we trace the various stages in the development of the partnership in the early 20th century, we should note the small part played by the central authority in the pioneer phase, and consider the legislative framework within which the movement grew.

It has been asserted that the Infant Welfare Movement in this country owed nothing in its early stage to the initiative of the central authority.[1] It is certainly true that the movement was well under way when the Local Government Board made a tardy entry. 19th-century efforts[2] to safeguard maternity by means of legislation for regulating the employment of midwives had met with consistent failure. The first Midwives Act did not reach the statute book until 1902.[3] Most of the pioneer work undertaken by a few enlightened medical officers for the prevention of infant mortality was done within the framework of the Public Health Act, 1875. The medical officers of health, backed by their enterprising local authorities, had a wonderful gift for interpreting the 'sanitary' measures allowed under the Act, cheerfully running the risk of a challenge by the auditors.

Two serious obstacles blocked the way to advance. One was the absence of statistics on the causes of death in early infancy.[4] The other was the lack of any obligation on parents to notify the medical officer of a birth.[5] As Sir George Newman pointed out, preventive action was effectively precluded when the first knowledge of a birth was a bill of mortality. It was due to the persistence of a few medical officers that the Board was convinced of the need for detailed official knowledge of the causes of infant mortality. It was the public-spirited action of a local authority[6] which led eventually to the passing of the first Notification of Births Act in 1907. This was a step forward, but it was an adoptive act of limited application. It was only intended to apply to those areas which were also arranging for instruction and advice to be given to mothers. The Local Government Board gave a decision that in other cases there 'was no occasion for imposing upon parents and others the obligation of notifying births'.

The public was now becoming more concerned about the excessive infant death rate, particularly as a series of diarrhoea epidemics in 1911 and 1913 took heavy toll.[7] But the response of the Board was to urge the

---

[1] See Dr. McCleary, *The Early History of the Infant Welfare Movement*, p. 112.
[2] Notably efforts by the London Obstetrical Society after its enquiry into midwifery, 1869, and by the Midwives Institute founded in 1881.
[3] It was amended by a series of Acts between 1902 and 1936.
[4] M.O.H.'s were first required to collect such information in 1905.
[5] The legal requirement of registration did not meet the need, as particulars might be given to the Registrar any time within six weeks.
[6] Huddersfield. See p. 36, below.
[7] The M.O.H.'s throughout the country were gravely concerned, as their reports repeatedly showed.

THE MATERNITY AND CHILD WELFARE MOVEMENT

sanitary authorities to make fuller use of the Public Health Act: 'to remove conditions in and about the home which facilitate the spread of infectious diseases'. It amounted, in fact, to a recommendation for better scavenging, and to a more general adoption of the Notification of Births Act, when home visiting could be arranged.

Although the Board initiated little in the early period,[1] they did accept a principle which was to influence future development in various parts of the country, that of co-operation between statutory and voluntary bodies. They went so far as to advise, in a circular on the notification of births, that where arrangements were made under the Act, they would usually best be carried out by 'local agencies' under the M.O.H.[2]

EXPERIMENTS IN CO-OPERATION BETWEEN VOLUNTARY ORGANISATIONS AND LOCAL AUTHORITIES

Although statutory activity at the centre was weak, local interest, both statutory and voluntary, had been gathering strength. The Maternity and Child Welfare Movement grew out of a number of distinct but closely related practical ventures such as the first tentative efforts to appoint health visitors; the various projects to secure the early notification of births; the establishment of milk depots, of classes on diet and child management, and of schools for mothers; the provision of nourishing dinners for nursing mothers; early work in ante-natal care, infant consultation centres and parentcraft and the foundation of local health societies. Sometimes one, sometimes another of these activities, or even a whole group of them, might be found in various centres in England and Scotland at the turn of the century.[3] They offer such excellent examples of combined effort and illustrate so well the many strands which went to the making of the service for mothers and infants that no apology is made for describing in some detail this early phase of development.[4]

The earliest example of effective co-operation may be seen in the Manchester and Salford experiment in health visiting. It was at the suggestion of a local doctor that the *Manchester and Salford Ladies Sanitary Reform Association* was formed in 1862.[5] After tentative visiting by a few volunteers who distributed pamphlets and soap,[6] it was decided to employ a visitor, 'a respectable working woman', to help and advise

[1] The Local Government Board had other interests, e.g. the administration of the Poor Law and local government. Public health seems to have been a poor third.
[2] See Local Government Board's circular on Maternity and Child Welfare on Notification of Births Act, 1907–08.
[3] Many of them were to be combined, later, in maternity and child welfare centres up and down the country.
[4] Dr. McCleary has written the standard works on the movement and I am indebted to those for much of my material.
[5] It was later renamed the Ladies Health Society of Manchester and Salford.
[6] Soap was both scarce and expensive at this time.

THE PIONEER PHASE

mothers in their own homes. This developed later into organised district visiting with a 'lady superintendent' and a 'working-class visitor' in each district. The venture had a strong religious basis, and in other ways had much in common with the charitable organisations of its time.[1] There were weekly mothers' meetings, social outings and the requirement of regular attendance at a place of worship. There was also considerable stress on thrift, self-reliance and other moral qualities. The distinctive features were the simple talks on health questions given at the meetings, the advisory child care service given in the homes, and the alertness of the visitors in reporting to the sanitary authorities any conditions in which intervention was possible, such as overcrowding, dilapidation and similar problems.

The real turning point came when Manchester Corporation, in 1890, officially recognised the venture and gave the medical officer of health the direction of the work of the health visitors, agreeing at the same time to pay the salaries of some of the workers.[2] A number of towns followed suit,[3] some of them employing women sanitary inspectors who were expected to specialise in the care of the health of mothers and infants. Many of the health visitors, or women sanitary inspectors as they were usually called, soon found themselves involved in social questions, which brought them into touch not only with the local authority but with such voluntary organisations as the *Society for the Prevention of Cruelty to Children*, the *Charity Organisation Society* and the *Invalid Children's Aid Association*.

Two points are worthy of note in this early experiment. The first is that from the start the visitors recognised that questions of hygiene could not be dealt with in isolation. Health talks and advisory pamphlets were insufficient by themselves, even when helped by gifts of soap, limewash and brushes or disinfecting powder. This was a personal service in which the interest and social needs of mothers and children must be remembered if the health service was to be effective. It was considerably later that a short course on the social services was included in the syllabus of training drawn up for health visitors.[4] The second point of

[1] The objects of the society are set out in typical Victorian form, namely 'to popularise sanitary knowledge, and to elevate the people physically, socially, morally and religiously'.
[2] Salford followed the example of Manchester a few years later.
[3] Dr. McCleary reported that by 1905 there were about 50 towns where women were employed in domiciliary educational work on behalf of local authorities.
[4] To-day the extent to which a health visitor can be a social worker as well as a health visitor raises difficult questions in view of the heavy case load and the emphasis on health which her training has given her. It is still a feature of the service, however, that the health visitor should be knowledgeable about the powers and duties of local authorities, and should keep in touch with voluntary agencies to whom she may refer any mother in need of help. This may be even more difficult now that the health visitor's role is extended to include the care of other sick persons as well as mothers and children under the National Health Service Act, 1946. See Report of An Inquiry into Health Visiting, Min. Health, Dept. of Health for Scotland and Min. Education, 1956.

interest in this first experiment in the appointment of health visitors is the early change of policy from the employment of working women to the employment of more educated women to visit mothers in their homes. At first the educated woman superintended, while the working woman did most of the house-to-house visiting, but before long we find local authorities and voluntary organisations appointing health visitors with recognised educational qualifications to do all the house-to-house visiting. It was reported that in 1905 several medical women and other university graduates held posts as health visitors.[1] As the century proceeded women doctors were appointed in increasing numbers to more responsible posts as medical officers in the maternity and child welfare service. In Huddersfield we find, by 1905, an organised scheme in operation, with two qualified medical women as assistants to the medical officer of health, devoting nearly all their time to infant welfare work. They had a band of some 80 voluntary helpers who worked in 9 wards, each with its lady superintendent.

But the distinctive contribution of Huddersfield lay in its efforts to secure early notification of births, first by a voluntary scheme and then by initiating legislation to make notification compulsory.[2] The voluntary scheme included the offer of two shillings for each birth notified to the M.O.H. within twenty-four hours. This was followed up immediately by a visit to the home by the assistant medical officers. Simple instruction on infant management was given on a card left with the mother, and arrangements were made with the lady superintendent to send one of her voluntary health visitors to follow up the doctor's visit and take an interest in the welfare of the mother and baby. She had a duty to report if the baby was not thriving, and to keep in touch with voluntary organisations who might help a family in need. Huddersfield thus made skilful use of both statutory and voluntary aid. The Corporation gave enthusiastic support to the pioneer work of its medical officer of health, Dr. Samson G. Moore, and his many voluntary helpers.

The authority was also keenly aware of the value of personal interest. How homely and simple some of these early ventures were is illustrated by the activities of the Mayor of Huddersfield, Alderman Broadbent, who was closely identified not only with the public health work of his Corporation but with the voluntary organisations in the area. He himself initiated a popular scheme to encourage mothers to bring up healthy infants. Recognising that the first year was the most vulnerable, he promised a gift of £1 on the first birthday of every child born during his mayoralty. The promise was accompanied by a card on infant welfare given to the mother personally by the assistant medical officer of health. Personal interest was also shown by the sending of a greetings card at

[1] McCleary, *op. cit.*, p. 90.
[2] Huddersfield Corporation Act, 1906.

Christmas and at Easter, and by a letter to the mother as the warmer weather, with its threat of diarrhoea, approached.

The early work in ante-natal care provides another instance of the value placed by the medical officers of health on the co-operation of statutory and voluntary agencies. Dr. Ballantyne,[1] working with the Edinburgh Royal Maternity Hospital, had placed great emphasis on the importance of ante-natal care, and a bed was specially endowed for the purpose in 1901. Another pioneer in ante-natal care was Dr. Sykes, medical officer of health, St. Pancras, who had already aroused public interest by his special report on infant mortality. He instituted a campaign for preventive work with stress on ante-natal care, and his first step was to call a conference of representatives of all the social workers in his area. Its immediate result was the issue of an advice card by the local authority on mothering and infant nurture, which was distributed with the co-operation of voluntary helpers. The distinctive feature of the scheme was the effort made to give the card to the mother before the arrival of her baby. General practitioners and the clergy were amongst those who helped to interest mothers in the scheme. The two women sanitary inspectors visited the mother not only after childbirth but, whenever possible, before. The voluntary health visitors followed up their work and, if the mothers needed treatment and could not afford a private doctor, they were put into touch with voluntary medical missions or dispensaries, or given an introduction to a hospital; or, if they needed food, they were referred to a suitable voluntary organisation.

Like so many of the progressive corporations,[2] St. Pancras was always ready to get ideas from home or abroad. When Mrs. Bertrand Russell brought back from Ghent the idea of a school for mothers, and when Mrs. Gordon described her 'dinner for mothers' scheme in Chelsea,[3] St. Pancras found its medical officer of health and its voluntary societies eager to co-operate in establishing such centres. Soon a comprehensive welfare scheme emerged, including meals centres, health visiting, antenatal work and a school for mothers. This school was many-sided, with provision of meals for nursing mothers, a department for non-nursing mothers and a consulting-room. The provision of dinners had a twofold aim—it offered a nourishing meal for the mother and baby, and at the same time gave a demonstration for the education of the mother.[4] The school's activities were noteworthy for the emphasis placed upon parentcraft: evidence of its progressive outlook was the inclusion of a bureau

---

[1] Author of the valuable *Manual of Ante-Natal Pathology and Hygiene*, 1902.

[2] The local authorities who were pioneers in infant and maternal welfare in this country had studied the earlier French experiments with considerable interest, sometimes sending a delegation to France for the purpose, e.g. Huddersfield.

[3] A voluntary worker who opened, in 1906, a kitchen for nursing mothers on the model of the French meals for mothers instituted in 1904.

[4] Later this was extended to the mother's own home, where a cookery demonstration might be given.

THE MATERNITY AND CHILD WELFARE MOVEMENT

for fathers. Thrift was encouraged by the institution of a provident club for parents. It was typical of the close link between these voluntary and statutory efforts that the medical officer of health for the borough was also one of the honorary secretaries both of the school for mothers and of the 'Babies Welcome'.

Many illustrations might be taken from other progressive areas where pioneer experiments were made in the first phase of the development of the maternity and child welfare movement. Perhaps two might be mentioned where the medical officers of health achieved distinction by their published work[1] and where the co-operation of statutory and voluntary agencies was highly valued. One was Battersea, where Dr. McCleary had been amongst the first to urge the setting up of a municipal milk depot on the model of St. Helens[2] and the first M.O.H. in London to institute an infant consultation centre[3]; the second instance comes from Finsbury, where the M.O.H., Dr. G. Newman, had encouraged the local association of social workers to start a milk depot in 1904. Both these medical officers did much to publicise the maternity and child welfare movement and to show how much depended on a good relationship between all helpers, whether in the service of voluntary or statutory agencies, who were working for the welfare of mothers and children.

Finally, an outstanding example is afforded by Glasgow of a comprehensive scheme supported by public and private agencies. Glasgow had, as early as 1903, come to an arrangement with the voluntary maternity hospital to have notification of all births within forty-eight hours. In the following year, the co-operation of the registrar was secured and weekly returns were made so that the women sanitary inspectors might visit the mothers and babies. The medical officer of health also prepared a leaflet on the management of children, which was distributed by the registrar, and was later followed up by visits from the health visitors. There were, by this time, a number of health visitors working for voluntary organisations, and when, in 1903, a Corporation milk depot was established, it was these health visitors who kept in touch with the mothers and visited them in their homes. The health visitors were an enterprising body who formed their own local association to co-ordinate their work. Glasgow followed up its milk depot by establishing 'infant consultations' in 1906, when babies were weighed, and classes were held on the health and diet of the mother. The statutory authorities and the voluntary societies were both concerned to stress the importance of the mother's health in

---

[1] G. F. McCleary, M.D., D.P.H., *The Early History of the Infant Welfare Movement*, 1933; *The Maternity and Child Welfare Movement*, 1935; *The Development of British Maternity Child Welfare Services*, 1945.

Dr. G. Newman, who later became Chief Medical Officer to the Minister of Health: *The Health of the State*, 1907, 1st ed.; *The Foundation of a Nation's Health*, 1939.

[2] St. Helens 1899, Liverpool 1901, Battersea 1902.

[3] In 1905.

THE PIONEER PHASE

any scheme for infant welfare. Not only did the Education Authority provide special classes in cooking, but a voluntary committee opened a special food depot where nursing mothers might get a cheap and nourishing dinner. Dr. McCleary aptly describes the work for mothers and children in Glasgow as one of the most interesting examples of a co-ordinated scheme of municipal and voluntary effort which had in it the germ of the modern maternity and child welfare service.

The establishment of local voluntary health societies such as those in York, the City of Westminster and in St. Marylebone showed the early recognition of the need for co-ordinated effort. One of the most interesting examples is to be found in the Borough of St. Marylebone Health Society. This society, founded in 1905, consisted of the Borough Public Health Department, the Local Health Society and the St. Marylebone General Dispensary. Its effective work in co-ordinating voluntary and statutory effort resulted in the enrolment and training of large numbers of voluntary health visitors. These in turn worked closely with the dispensary, where an infant consultation was held by the medical officer, to whom any babies might be referred for expert advice. The babies' future supervision was then arranged for, the dispensary, the M.O.H. and the health visitors working in full accord. London had indeed been amongst the pioneers, for not only had several of the Metropolitan Boroughs done valuable experimental work, but the County Council, too, had given a powerful stimulus to the service. The L.C.C. secured an early opportunity, through a General Powers Act in 1908, followed by a Health Visitors (London) Order in 1909, to appoint health visitors.

In assessing the influences which shaped the maternity and child welfare service in the early stages, some stress should be placed on the part played by individuals who devoted much of their energy and leisure-time to the welfare of mothers and children. Many of them, as we have seen, were active both in statutory and voluntary fields. Medical officers of health played a prominent part. There were, too, some notable women who took a large share in the campaign. Such were Gertrude Tuckwell and Mary MacArthur, whose work for the reduction of maternal mortality led eventually to the formation of the valuable Maternal Mortality Committee.[1] Others, like Mrs. Macdonald and Mary Middleton, have had their work commemorated in practical form by the foundation of a baby clinic which was a pioneer in the maternity and child welfare service.[2] In every instance they were men and women who

[1] Founded in 1927, changing its name later to the Maternal Health Committee. It closed down in 1950 'since other bodies are now continuing its work'. See *Maternity and Child Welfare Survey*, 2nd quarter 1950, published by the National Association for Maternity and Child Welfare (now, 1954, *Maternal and Child Welfare*).
[2] The Kensington Baby Clinic: in addition to its consultation and supervisory work, the clinic was the first to add the treatment of minor ailments in 1911. An in-patient department was added in 1919. Cf. the Violet Melchett Clinic, which retained its voluntary status after the introduction of the National Health Service.

THE MATERNITY AND CHILD WELFARE MOVEMENT

were closely associated with public work, and therefore in a position to see clearly the advantages of a partnership between voluntary and statutory organisations. We must return, however, from particular instances to consider the development of the movement.

IV

THE PIONEER PHASE

THE FOUNDATION OF A NATIONAL MOVEMENT

NO great advance could be made until the various local experiments were more broadly based. The pioneer medical officers of health had, indeed, early appreciated the need for wider consultation, and they had the backing of their progressive local authorities. They were prepared to examine experimental work wherever it could be found, whether at home or abroad. The initial inspiration for maternity and child welfare had come from France,[1] as early as 1899.[2] St. Helens had sent a deputation to study the Gouttes de Lait before setting up their model milk depot. It is characteristic of their enterprising spirit that three of the pioneer local authorities in this country, Battersea, Huddersfield and Glasgow, sent delegates to the First International Congress on Infant Welfare held in Paris in 1905.[3] The enthusiasm of the medical officers, who were greatly impressed by the work of Budin and Dufour in France, inspired them to plan a campaign for similar centres in this country. Their zeal is apparent in the great success of the First National Conference held at their instigation in the following year, at which public health authorities were represented in force.[4] Results followed immediately: from 1906 onwards the number of infant welfare centres set up both by local authorities and voluntary bodies, increased rapidly.[5] The pattern of municipal and voluntary co-operation established by Huddersfield, Glasgow, Battersea, St. Pancras and other pioneer authorities was closely followed wherever new services were started.

[1] Prof. Pierre Budin founded the first Consultation de Nourrissons in 1892, and had a great influence on the subsequent development of infant welfare. Dr. Léon Dufour set up the first Goutte de Lait in 1894 at Fécamp: provision was made for all classes: the poor had the service free, others paid half, while the well-to-do paid in full.
[2] The M.O.H., Dr. Drew Harris, published papers describing the work in France, and Dr. McCleary had reported on the work in America.
[3] Dr. McCleary was a vice-president of the First International Congress.
[4] There were 153 representatives of public health authorities present at the conference.
[5] By 1911 there were some 100 centres.

THE MATERNITY AND CHILD WELFARE MOVEMENT

The zeal of the medical officers of health was further illustrated by the fact that the successive national conferences on infant mortality were largely dependent upon their voluntary help: they were readily supported by enthusiastic laymen and backed by the interest of the municipalities concerned. No salaried officials were appointed until after the foundation of the *National Association for the Prevention of Infant Mortality and for the Welfare of Infancy* in 1912.[1] One of the outstanding features of the new association was the strength of its committee and the representative nature of its membership. It is worth noting its constitution in detail, since it shows clearly the inclusion of statutory and voluntary representatives, and the strong influence of the medical profession. The executive committee was presided over by the Rt. Hon. John Burns (President of the Board of Trade and ex-President of the Local Government Board); there were representatives of 11 county boroughs and 1 county council, 12 medical officers of health, 12 members of the medical profession engaged in clinical practice and 12 representatives of voluntary associations, etc.[2]

The success of this organisation[3] was largely due to the good relationship which existed between medical experts and lay members, and the backing it had from progressive public health authorities. Its first report calls attention to the fact that the National Association was appreciated 'as an auxiliary and a stimulus to Town Councils and other Boards'. From the start it set itself a high standard. Its propaganda was preceded by fact-finding enquiries, and its influence was the stronger when it was known that medical officers, experienced in infant and maternal welfare, were responsible for the investigations, results of which were circulated to public health authorities, medical schools and similar groups. Within the first year the association concerned itself with such questions as the teaching of infant hygiene to medical students, the provision and training of midwives, the registration of still-births, and the more complete certification of deaths. Post-graduate courses were also arranged on the feeding and care of infants. The association also took up the question of the fuller recognition by the Board of Education of the many infant welfare centres which were by now in existence. It had recognised from the start the importance of co-ordination,[4] and several agencies concerned with child welfare went to the making of the new association.

[1] This resulted from a public meeting at which the Rt. Hon. John Burns was in the Chair.
[2] First Annual Report for 1912–13, p. 1. In addition to the Chairman and two vice-Chairmen there were two Hon. Secretaries and an Hon. Treasurer.
[3] It was amalgamated with the Association of Maternity and Child Welfare Centres in 1937, and the new organisation, known as the National Association of Maternity and Child Welfare Centres and for the Prevention of Infant Mortality, was reconstituted in 1938. In 1948 it became the National Association for Maternity and Child Welfare. See below, pp. 72–73.
[4] 'That in the opinion of this meeting, it is desirable to co-ordinate the work of the various agencies at present concerned with Infant Mortality and the promotion of the welfare of children under school age, and it is accordingly agreed to form a National

THE PIONEER PHASE

In 1912 it federated with the *National League for Physical Education and Improvement*. The motive of economy in administration was emphasised when this step was taken, for propaganda expenses and the organisation of conferences had made heavy demands. In view of the prevailing methods of raising funds, it is interesting to find the association priding itself on the fact that, so far, it had had to make no financial appeal to the general public. It was dependent entirely upon conference fees and donations, not only from voluntary sources but from some generous local authorities; and upon the voluntary services received from its honorary officers. Later, the precarious financial position of the association led it to join forces with the *National League for Health, Maternity and Child Welfare*, and the *Association of Infant Welfare and Maternity Centres* (from 1917–28). It produced a joint report with these societies and seems to have been indebted financially to the National League.

The number of national associations concerned with the welfare of mothers and children is one of the astonishing features of the movement. Their ramifications are not always easy to follow. One of the oldest was the afore-mentioned National League for Health, Maternity and Child Welfare, originally the National League for Physical Education and Improvement, incorporated in 1905. The League had been formed as a direct outcome of the report of the Interdepartmental Committee on Physical Deterioration, and its scope included not only mothers and infants but the entire population. Its purpose was equally all-embracing and ambitious, for it was concerned with 'strengthening physically, mentally and morally' all those who came within its sphere. It seems to have given shelter to a number of struggling societies with kindred aims, and to have helped them over difficult periods of growth. It produced the annual reports of the autonomous societies which were associated with it, and later published the pamphlets prepared by some of its constituent bodies. These included reports on special investigations, such as on health visiting,[1] and others on school clinics and open-air schools. In these enquiries it enlisted the help of doctors of repute in the maternity service, and it seems to have had the backing of many local authorities.[2]

Another of its sales services was carried on on behalf of the *Association of Infant Welfare and Maternity Centres*, originally the *Association of Infant Consultations*,[3] whose specially invented feeding bottles had a wide distribution. The League's activities included the provision of

---

Association for this purpose.' Resolution passed at the public meeting, 4th June, 1912, held in Caxton Hall, Westminster.

[1] E.g. on the use of health visitors by local authorities in 1908. In 1911 it published a pamphlet, *Health Visiting in Rural Areas* containing letters from Florence Nightingale.

[2] It is interesting to note that the research medical officer of the L.C.C. had agreed to collate the material and preface the report for publication.

[3] Founded in 1911.

THE MATERNITY AND CHILD WELFARE MOVEMENT

holidays for tired mothers and children, and convalescent homes for babies and toddlers, and it ran an employment bureau for nursery and child nurses. Like so many of the kindred societies, it was a federating body, and it was itself represented on many voluntary organisations' committees. It arranged lectures, especially for youth groups, and it held conferences on selected subjects of concern to the movement.[1] Later it produced a film for 'health weeks'. Again, like its associates, it watched legislation and made representations to the relevant ministries.

When the League came to an end, in 1928, it wrote its own obituary notice in a final report and took pride in several pieces of pioneer work in the service. Amongst these it described six experimental ante-natal clinics, attached in 1915 to infant welfare centres in the London boroughs which used the Royal Free Hospital. The clinics had been set up by the League as the result of a special donation, and it was claimed that at the end of three years 'the example set was being copied by local authorities all over the kingdom'.[2] A second venture was the training in 1914–15 of four women to organise new infant welfare centres in co-operation with local health authorities, no matter 'whether a municipal or a voluntary centre was the ultimate outcome'.[3] It is of interest to note that it was a former President of the Board of Education, Sir Arthur Acland, who raised the sum needed for this scheme. All the national societies seem to have had a flair for securing the active support of public men.

Before we leave the account of the national voluntary societies in the first phase of development we should mention the inauguration of the National Baby Week which resulted in the foundation, in 1917, of the *National Baby Week Council*. The history of this active society belongs, however, to the second phase of development, and will be dealt with later.[4]

PROGRESS IN SOCIAL POLICY

The more active local authorities had often been frustrated by their lack of power to develop their services. Exceptional measures were costly, as when one authority went to the great expense and trouble of getting through a private bill, while another risked an adverse report from the local auditors for illegal spending. The Local Government Board was not yet ready for further legislation, however, and its hesitation was apparent in the extraordinarily roundabout way in which it took official note of the power to appoint health visitors. However, in view of the growing public restiveness in the second decade of the 20th

---

[1] E.g. on 'Schools for Mothers' in 1910. See Annual Report, 1928, pp. 5–6.
[2] In 1918 this movement received a fillip from a generous donation from the American Red Cross, and 26 new ante-natal clinics benefited.
[3] 154 new infant welfare centres in fourteen months were said to result from this effort.
[4] See p. 59. Later it changed its name to the National Baby Welfare Council.

THE PIONEER PHASE

century, it felt bound to encourage the more cautious authorities to follow the example of some of the progressive areas.

A circular issued in 1913 pointed out that, while local authorities were not specifically empowered to appoint officers for the execution of the Notification of Births Act, they had a duty to appoint them for the execution of the Public Health Act, 1875. The Board concluded that like powers could be properly used 'to employ and pay women to give advice with the object of preventing infectious diseases in infancy, including those arising in connection with improper feeding'. In the same circular, the Board called attention to the useful work of voluntary organisations, but noted that it lost much of its value if it was not co-ordinated with the work of the local sanitary authorities, and they urged the medical officers of health to try and secure such co-ordination. Although John Burns[1] had taken a lively personal interest in the first conferences to inaugurate the maternity and child welfare movement in this country, it was not until 1913 that the Government was sufficiently interested to send official representatives to the Third International Conference.

Meanwhile the Board of Education had been far more active and had shown its interest in tangible form. Under its powers to grant-aid educational work, it had recognised the schools for mothers,[2] and from the time of the first small grant to the St. Pancras School it gave increasing support to the movement, proving itself progressively generous to the associations which were arranging training courses of various kinds.

Lloyd George's famous budget of 1914 marked a distinct advance in governmental interest in maternity and child welfare, for the estimates included grants[3] to both local authorities and voluntary agencies, making provision for maternity and child welfare. The Local Government Board[4] took the opportunity of paying a handsome tribute to those who had already helped to secure improved conditions for children, and to reduce infant mortality; they pointed out, at the same time, that they hoped grant aid would help to extend and systematise the work for children from pre-natal life to school age. The voluntary agencies could claim a grant either through their local authority or direct from the Local Government Board. Both local authorities and voluntary agencies received for their guidance a memorandum which gave a detailed account of a complete scheme.[5] The two central departments were now working closely together; the Board of Education was to

[1] In 1905 he had become President of the Local Government Board.
[2] The Board of Education was responsible for grant-aiding schools for mothers until 1919, and for the training of health visitors until 1925.
[3] Grants up to 50% of expenses.
[4] The first indication of financial interest by the Local Government Board was announced in a circular to county councils and sanitary authorities in 1914, drawing attention to the estimates before Parliament.
[5] See Local Government Board circular and memorandum, Maternity and Child Welfare, 30.7.14, ref. 53/14.

THE MATERNITY AND CHILD WELFARE MOVEMENT

administer the grants available 'for those institutions the object of which was primarily education', . . . 'the provision of specific medical and surgical advice and treatment being only incidental', while the Local Government Board was concerned with those institutions which were primarily medical.

One important result was a measure of control from the central departments, since, with the application for grants, the authority or agency must send an account of their work and a detailed statement of expenditure incurred, while the Board's inspectors could now secure adequate standards.

Influence of the First World War

The country was now involved in a major war. With this new threat to survival, interest in the maternity and child welfare movement quickened. At the same time administration was tightened up and the quality of voluntary and statutory effort more closely scrutinised. A series of circulars to local authorities continued to urge greater efficiency[1] and co-ordination. Voluntary agencies were warned that they would earn a grant only if their work was 'co-ordinated as far as was practicable' with the public health and school medical services of the local authority. Similarly the Board of Education issued regulations on its grants for schools for mothers, pointing out that consideration would be given not only to the scope, character and efficiency of the work, but to the measure of co-ordination with similar institutions in the same district; it listed maternity centres, baby clinics or infant dispensaries and the school medical service amongst those to be considered. Both the Local Government Board and the Board of Education required that adequate records should be kept. The Board of Education also made it a condition that the Institution must be conducted by a responsible body of managers, nor must it be run for private profit. The circular[2] issued jointly by the two Boards, to maternity centres and schools for mothers provided by voluntary agencies, asked for full information of any assistance, whether in the form of service, use of premises or otherwise, from the County Council, the local sanitary authority or the local education authority.

In the same year, the Notification of Births Act, 1915, made notification generally compulsory,[3] and the Local Government Board proceeded to instruct local authorities in their new duties. Once more the importance of co-operation between all those in the public health service was emphasised. 'In the development of general schemes the Board desire that the services of hospitals and other efficient voluntary agencies

[1] See Circular 906, 1915, ref. 74/115, where the Local Government Board pointed out that they might at their discretion reduce or withhold the grant.
[2] Circular 906, 31.5.1915, ref. 75/15.
[3] So far 370 districts, mostly urban, covering 56% of the population, had adopted the Act of 1907.

THE PIONEER PHASE

should be fully utilised.'[1] They go on to specify the schemes they have in mind, noting that in London, where the work should be organised by the metropolitan borough councils, the chief need was to see that the services provided by the hospitals and the numerous voluntary agencies should be properly linked up with those of the local authority.[2] Outside London, it would be generally necessary to supplement the existing medical services.

By now the increasing expense of the war and the demands for manpower had led to the reduction of many of the social services. It is significant of the value at last placed on the 'importance of conserving infant life'[3] that, in spite of the general emphasis on the need for economy, the local authorities were still being urged to extend and improve the maternity and child welfare service. Between 1916 and 1918 there was a considerable increase in the number of infant welfare centres, both statutory and voluntary.[4] The Local Government Board pointed out that the manpower question would not arise since the health visitors and many of the doctors would be women. Women would also be largely represented on the committee. In view of the early history of the movement it is an interesting point that the central authority urged the appointment of working women to the committee, preferably representatives of a local women's organisation. In the following year this was emphasised and details were given of 'the four national organisations for women of the manual working class which have branches in many parts of the kingdom': at the same time, it was recommended that the committees should include representatives of the voluntary agencies working in connection with maternity and child welfare.[5]

In this first phase of the Local Government Board's activity in the field of maternity and child welfare, much stress was laid on the personal approach to the mother. In a memorandum issued in 1916 to maternity and child welfare centres on visiting,[6] the listed qualifications of a health visitor included tact, combined with knowledge, kindliness and humour. There is no doubt that the high esteem in which mothers in urban districts have since held the centres is in large measure due to the personality of the workers and the establishment of a friendly atmosphere.

[1] Local Government Board, Maternity and Child Welfare Circular, 29.7.1915, ref. 81/15.
[2] Unhappily, that link was never adequately forged and, after the passage of nearly forty years, the same issues are being debated, even though a comprehensive National Health Service is in being.
[3] See Local Government Board Maternity and Child Welfare Circular, 29.7.15, ref. 81/15.
[4] In these two years the statutory centres increased from 396 to 545, while voluntary centres increased from 446 to 588. 1918 was the last year in which the voluntary centres outnumbered those provided by local authorities.
[5] See Local Government Board Maternity and Child Welfare Circular, *ibid.*, 1916, ref. 101/16.
[6] Memorandum prepared by Dr. Newsholme, Chief Medical Officer to the Local Government Board, 23.9.16.

THE MATERNITY AND CHILD WELFARE MOVEMENT

The health visitors, doctors and voluntary helpers were working together as a team for the welfare of those under their care,[1] and social as well as health measures were valued. Specific reference is made in the memorandum to the valuable services of voluntary workers 'in arranging for any social work that may be desirable, and generally in making the centre as bright and attractive as possible'. They mention that tea is often provided, as well as advice on a number of practical questions, whether it concerned the infant or an older brother or sister.

Statutory Limitations: a Stimulus to Co-operation

The attention of local authorities was also drawn to the assistance which could be given by voluntary organisations in spheres where the statutory body had no power to help. For example, no grant was available in 1916 for expenditure on food, nor could material aid be given, except from voluntary sources, to meet exceptional needs. The motive of economy was a strong one at this time, and local authorities were urged to avoid waste of effort by co-operating closely with voluntary agencies, and by framing their schemes so that each one should have a definite sphere of work on satisfactory lines. Authorities were reminded of the various forms of co-operation open to them, by arranging for voluntary agencies to have the use of the services of their medical officer of health and health visitor, or of premises belonging to the authority. It was generally desirable, they argued, for local authorities to provide the health visiting staff. If the centre were provided by a voluntary agency, then the medical officer of health should supervise.

The central authority looked favourably upon voluntary efforts to experiment in various educational methods. One of these was the inauguration of the National Baby Week. It is pleasant to find the Local Government Board in 1917 responding to an appeal from the National Baby Week Council, of which the President of the Board was chairman, and urging local authorities to do all they could to further the movement in their district. The President gave high praise to the Council and reported in considerable detail on its function. Its scheme would 'materially assist in diffusing knowledge of the best methods to be adopted to safeguard the lives and health of mothers and children'. The personal interest of Ministers was shown also in the acceptance of the Presidency of the Council by Mr. Lloyd George. Expenditure on such schemes was by this time regarded as an essential service and an economical investment yielding good returns.[2] In February 1918, the Government took a further, though hesitant, step forward when it sanc-

---

[1] How great a sense of loss the mothers felt when they were evacuated from town to country and found no centre, in the Second World War, can readily be understood. It was not merely the distribution of orange juice and other foods which had made the centres popular, although such material advantages were a considerable attraction.

[2] See Local Government Board, Maternity and Child Welfare Circular, 1917, ref. 41/17.

tioned the expenditure of public money on the supply of food and milk 'in necessitous cases'.[1] The central authority was given discretionary powers in deciding what constituted 'necessity'.

As the war drew to a close more constructive measures were being prepared in several fields of social service.[2] Amongst them was the first Maternity and Child Welfare Bill. The Act, passed in 1918, inaugurated a new period in the development of the movement. Before we go on to consider this, however, we may refer briefly to the position in rural areas, and review the main features of central statutory intervention in the first phase of development.

In country districts more than half the health visitors were also district nurse-midwives, employed on behalf of the county councils by arrangement with the voluntary district nursing associations. The Local Government Board looked favourably on this scheme, since in sparsely-populated areas they were 'well-known and well received[3] by the women in a country parish, their advice was readily accepted, and the arrangement may obviate duplication of inspectors, and save time and money spent in travelling'.

Although the central authority had been a late entrant, once it accepted responsibility it did valuable service to the movement through its powers of grant-aid and inspection. In the towns considerable progress had been made. Central control and guidance helped in two important directions: in co-ordinating voluntary and statutory effort, and in securing efficient standards.

In conclusion it should be stressed that in spite of some progress in the first phase of the development of the maternity and child welfare services, central statutory intervention was largely restricted to advisory work and a minimum of grant aid for limited purposes. In spite of the pioneer work at the beginning of the century, it was not until 1918 that public money might be spent on the supply of food and milk, and then, as we have seen, only in necessitous cases. No positive preventive action was yet possible. It was left to the discretion of medical officers of health to supply food to the very poor, only when it could be shown that malnutrition had already occurred. It had been the task of the voluntary organisations to co-operate with local authorities in providing a more comprehensive service which would include preventive measures.

[1] The order applied to both voluntary and statutory centres.
[2] Including a new Education Bill, passed in 1918.
[3] Even in a crowded London borough this was an important factor, as was discovered by one local authority which appointed its own midwives and then found them unacceptable to the mothers, who preferred those working for a voluntary agency known to them. See Local Government Board Circular, *op. cit.*

V

DEVELOPMENTS BETWEEN THE TWO WORLD WARS

SOCIAL POLICY: INFANT WELFARE: MATERNAL MORTALITY AND MORBIDITY

THE Maternity and Child Welfare Act, 1918, was permissive,[1] but it was a popular Act and it made possible a considerable extension of the movement in the inter-war years. Grants were extended[2] to cover a number of services including hospital treatment for children up to five years of age, lying-in homes, and the cost of a home help service, mostly payable to local authorities. At last the provision of food for expectant and nursing mothers and for children under five was sanctioned and grant-aided. Creches and day nurseries, convalescent homes, homes for the children of widowed and deserted mothers and for illegitimate children (mostly provided by voluntary agencies) were all included in the scheme, while provision was made for grant-aid for experimental work, whether by local authority or voluntary agency, concerned with the health of expectant mothers, nursing mothers and infants and children under five. One of the conditions of grant-aid was the requirement that the work should be linked with that of the local authority. Co-ordination at the local level was thus greatly facilitated by government action, and, in the process, greater responsibility was being given to statutory authorities.

A change in administrative method marked the new relationship: all voluntary agencies applying to the central authority for grant-aid were required to do so through the local authority, or if not, to send the local authority a copy of the application at the same time as it was sent to the Board. The Board noted with satisfaction the increase in the number of

---

[1] The Maternity and Child Welfare Service was not made a duty until the passing of the National Health Service Act, 1946.
[2] In August 1918. See circular from Local Government Board, M. & C.W.4, ref. 128/18, to county councils (other than L.C.C.) and sanitary authorities.

DEVELOPMENTS BETWEEN THE WORLD WARS

centres, and generously gave credit to private enterprise for this advance.[1] The central authority was now ready to consult voluntary agencies on any plans for experimental work, and it is satisfactory to find it agreeing to consider for grant-aid a small research project: the provision of a small number of beds at a centre in order to study feeding problems and similar difficulties.[2]

More urgently now, the Local Government Board impressed upon all concerned in the movement the importance of training. Every centre, whether municipal or voluntary, should be supervised by a trained and salaried worker, 'although unpaid workers could give great assistance'. It was increasingly possible to insist on adequate qualifications for health visitors, although it was not yet practicable to prescribe a special course of training or a standard examination.[3] Meanwhile, a voluntary society, the *National Health Society*,[4] had taken the important step of providing training for infant welfare workers, and it secured recognition from both the Board of Education and, later, from the Ministry of Health, for approved courses for health visitors.

When, in 1919, the Ministry of Health replaced the Local Government Board it gave immediate attention to the question of the training and qualification of health visitors.[5] It at once asked the Board of Education to issue the required Draft Regulations and in an accompanying memorandum pointed out that health visiting should be placed firmly on a professional basis[6]: 'No doubt, as with other professions, personality and enthusiasm are essentials of success, but in themselves they do not suffice. There is at least an equal need for practice to be based upon a firm body of knowledge.'

The Ministry also hoped that, since it had not only replaced the Local Government Board but had taken over certain powers from the Home

---

[1] Local Government Board, Maternity and Child Welfare Circular, 19.8.18, ref. 128/18.

[2] This decision was taken after consultation with the representatives of a number of hospitals and voluntary agencies.

[3] Local Government Board, Maternity and Child Welfare Circular, 19.8.18, ref. 128/18. The Board reviewed the qualifications required under the L.C.C. Order, 1909, and added that the certificate of a sanitary inspector was also valuable.

[4] One of the constituent societies of the Central Council for Infant and Child Welfare. By 1923 we find the Society reporting on three recognised courses of training, one of two years' duration for full-time students, a shortened course of six to eight months for a fully-trained hospital nurse, and a course for a health visitor who had already spent at least three years in full-time employment in the service.

[5] It is interesting to note that although the Notification of Births Act of 1907 gave great impetus to the appointment of health visitors, the first draft regulations on Training (Board of Education) were not issued until 1919. See Ministry of Health Circular, 10th and 14th July, 1919.

[6] Ministry of Health, 4 M.C.W., 1919: Memorandum enclosing Draft Regulations of Board of Education. In 1925 the Ministry took over from the Board of Education responsibility for paying grants for the training of health visitors. 1928 was the last year in which a new appointment of an unqualified health visitor could be made, unless the Minister dispensed with any of the requirements of the Regulations (this proviso was inserted to cover exceptional circumstances).

THE MATERNITY AND CHILD WELFARE MOVEMENT

Office and the Board of Education concerning nursing and expectant mothers and children under five, that greater co-ordination both centrally and locally would follow, and that a more comprehensive service could be offered.

Unfortunately, the post-war economic difficulties forced the Government to cut down expenditure on the social services, including, this time, the maternity and child welfare service. But since there was considerable distress, the grant-aid for milk, earlier given free or at reduced cost, was continued, and local authorities were later asked to consider the provision of meals at the centres; the supply of meals and milk by voluntary agencies was to be financed and controlled by the local authorities. The restrictions lasted until 1924.

Meanwhile voluntary enterprise had eased the situation by establishing certain pilot centres. The Minister of Health, in his annual report for 1921–22, refers to the generous gift of £100,000 received from the Carnegie United Kingdom Trust, to provide model maternity and infant welfare centres in Liverpool and Birmingham County Boroughs, Shoreditch Metropolitan Borough and Rhondda Urban District. It was agreed that the local authorities should maintain the centres.

The Ministry had gradually been concentrating responsibility upon the local authorities, and, financially, the process was completed by the passage of the Local Government Act, 1929. The Exchequer grants to voluntary associations were to be replaced by an annual contribution from the appropriate local authorities who were to receive a block grant from the Treasury. This caused considerable heartburning amongst the voluntary organisations. They feared financial loss, and they feared lowering of standards with the withdrawal of central inspection. In fact there were safeguards, and the Ministry took precautions to see that the voluntary organisations should receive not less than the amount received in standard years.[1] Detailed returns were required from local authorities to show what contributions were proposed.[2] At the same time circulars from the Ministry stressed the importance of discussion between statutory and voluntary agencies in working out schemes.[3] It should be noted that although the local authority had a duty to see that certain defined conditions were fulfilled before grant-aid was given, they could not reduce the grant on the ground that any of the conditions were not ful-

---

[1] See Statutory Rules and Order made under Rule 6 of Part II of the 4th Schedule to the Local Government Act, 1929, and Memo. L.G.A. 5, Ministry of Health (M. & C.W.), ref. 145/29.

[2] The Ministry gave detailed lists of organisations and the amounts received in a standard year. See Circular 1043 enclosing Statutory Rules and Orders, 1929, to Metropolitan Borough Councils.

[3] In the second four-year period 1933–37 similar requirements were made, and any local authority wishing to modify the scheme of contributions to voluntary organisations had to make a full statement of the reasons for any omission or any variation in the existing scheme.

filled, without the consent of the Minister. The Minister himself would consider and decide in the event of dispute.

Considerable encouragement was given to extend the maternity and child welfare service. Reports for the last year before the outbreak of the Second World War show a total of 3,261 centres, of which 2,433 were provided by local authorities. Only in the provision of residential homes were the voluntary organisations in the lead, with over a hundred homes for mothers and babies, compared with less than ten provided by statutory bodies. The Minister of Health continued to call attention to the value of voluntary effort in providing a variety of services, including day nurseries and convalescent homes, in addition to homes for young children and homes for unmarried mothers and their infants. Many of the institutions were subsidised, since 'in recent years Welfare Authorities have displayed increased interest in these branches of maternity and child welfare work and have received the encouragement of the Minister in doing so'.[1]

Meanwhile the Departmental Committee's Report on Maternal Mortality and Morbidity[2] had aroused considerable public concern. Voluntary organisations had carried on widespread propaganda and the Ministry of Health was anxious. Their first reaction was to secure more effective use of existing services. The Ministry's efforts to link up the various local services were now intensified. In 1936 they urged the need to co-ordinate the work of local education authorities and maternity and child welfare authorities in the care of children between two and five. In the same year, the Ministry pressed for greater co-ordination in the midwifery service. He was particularly concerned with the difficulties to be overcome in rural areas.

The extension of ante-natal clinics was strongly recommended as another measure in the campaign to reduce maternal mortality and morbidity, and local authorities were reminded of their powers to establish and equip them. This was a sphere in which voluntary organisations had led the way, as they had in the educational and social work amongst mothers, but local authorities quickly took over the main responsibility for this branch of child care. In the twenty years following the Maternity and Child Welfare Act, ante-natal work expanded rapidly from 120 clinics in 1918 to 1,676 in 1938; by now the great majority, 1,389, were statutorily provided. At the same time local authorities in urban areas were tending to employ more of their own domiciliary midwives, whether whole-time or part-time, but by far the larger number were still working for voluntary organisations, while a substantial number were in private practice.[3] The Midwives Act, 1936, marked an important

[1] Ministry of Health *Annual Report for the Year ending 1939*.
[2] The Departmental Committee was set up in 1928: it issued an Interim Report in 1930 and a Final Report in 1932.
[3] By the end of the year 1939 there were still 5,630 practising domiciliary midwives employed by voluntary associations compared with 2,627 employed by local

THE MATERNITY AND CHILD WELFARE MOVEMENT

stage in the employment of qualified midwives. It now became the duty of local supervising authorities to ensure that the number of midwives employed by themselves and by voluntary organisations was adequate for the needs of the area.[1] In the same year the Ministry decided that sufficient safeguards for the co-operation of voluntary and statutory agencies in the midwifery service existed. Proposals still had to be submitted to the Minister but they no longer needed his sanction. Coordination was encouraged, since schemes had also to be sent to all voluntary organisations and welfare councils.[2]

CO-OPERATION BETWEEN STATUTORY BODIES AND VOLUNTARY ORGANISATIONS

The *District Nursing Associations* (D.N.As.) offer an excellent example of a cordial relationship between voluntary organisations and statutory bodies. The voluntary nursing associations had spread widely over[3] the rural areas and the Ministry recognised the value of their work. They drew the attention of local authorities to the various ways in which they were empowered to support district nursing associations. The county councils were encouraged to consult not only the district councils, which were welfare authorities, but the D.N.A. and, wherever possible, the county nursing associations, which were co-ordinating bodies. The Ministry saw that a skilled nurse-midwife could only be supported in sparsely populated areas with the aid of substantial grants from the county nursing associations, and county councils were advised to consider the provision of such facilities as a motor-car, a telephone and more leisure.

The central authority was also conscious of the saving in cost to the community when the D.N.As. could cover the whole of the rural parts of counties.[4] Local authorities were reminded that the D.N.As. would need more funds, since part of the time of the nurses would be devoted to ordinary nursing, and sometimes to health visiting or school nursing,

authorities, while as many as 4,070 were in private practice. Six years later the voluntary associations had lost slightly and the local authorities gained, the totals being 5,142 and 2,855 respectively, while a considerable number had left private practice (now only 2,020 in practice). This last reduction is noteworthy, since it was those in private practice who tended to accept a larger number of confinements annually, thus making it difficult for them to give the same standard of service to their patients. The latest figures show that at the end of 1954, of a total of 7,570 midwives employed in the domiciliary midwife service, 6,646 were employed directly by L.H.As. and 924 by voluntary organisations and hospital authorities.

[1] It was estimated that, by 1944, taking into account ante-natal care by private arrangement, nearly all expectant mothers had some form of supervision during pregnancy (*Maternity in Great Britain, op. cit.*, p. 22).

[2] They had the right to complain within two months to the Minister. The Minister could then alter the proposals as he thought fit.

[3] See C. Braithwaite, *The Voluntary Citizen*, Sec. III, for a study of district nursing as an example of an organised voluntary social service.

[4] See Ministry of Health Circular 1569 and Memo. 200/M.C.W., 1936.

DEVELOPMENTS BETWEEN THE WORLD WARS

by arrangement with the county council. The school work would, of course, attract contributions from the council, but ordinary nursing was ineligible for grants under the Midwives Act or the Maternity and Child Welfare Act. 'The local authority would do well to consider if it could not make a grant for such nursing... under Section 67 of the Poor Law Act, 1930.' Such support of voluntary nursing associations in rural areas is commended as 'by far the best arrangement', others entailing the use of the local authority's staff being pronounced 'second best'.

To sum up the policy of the Ministry, a paragraph in the circular and memorandum on the Midwives Act, 1936, might be quoted: 'As the local authorities are no doubt aware, where domiciliary midwifery services are provided on a properly organised basis by the salaried midwives of voluntary hospital and nursing associations, the maternal mortality rate is well below the national rate, and the establishment in all areas of a service of salaried midwives working under close and sympathetic supervision should do much to secure a reduction in that rate.'[1] After 1936 the number of municipal midwives rapidly increased and they became generally acceptable.[2]

The Ministry of Health continued to do all it could, through its inspectors, to see that local authorities used their powers and shouldered their responsibilities under the Maternity and Child Welfare Act, while at the same time proclaiming that the co-operation of voluntary associations was a valuable asset to the movement as a whole. It is indicative of the good relationship fostered by the central health authority, that a national voluntary association should regret the loss of inspection by the Ministry of Health.[3]

Wherever there was co-operation it was usually wholehearted. Another excellent example is found in the organisation of conferences and meetings, when both national societies and local federations worked closely with the local authorities. The meetings were often supplemented by visits of observation to clinics, maternity and child welfare centres, and other places of special interest, with the full co-operation of the local health authority. It was rare to find an annual meeting of a local federation of centres which did not have the mayor and the medical officer of health taking a prominent part, while the Chief Medical Officer of the Ministry of Health was generally associated with the national conferences. We have already seen how closely the local authorities worked with the voluntary associations in their educational work.[4]

[1] Ministry of Health Circular 1569 and Memo. 200, 18.9.36.
[2] See footnote, p. 49, above.
[3] With the passing of the Local Government Act, 1929, local authorities were made responsible. There was some misgiving lest, with no centralised inspection, standards might go down. The Ministry's reply was to promise Ministry inspection if it was desired.
[4] E.g. in the post-certificate course of the National Association for Prevention of Infant Mortality to infant welfare workers in Nottingham, Chesterfield and Derby, with the co-operation of the county and local health authorities.

THE MATERNITY AND CHILD WELFARE MOVEMENT

We also find the medical officers of health reporting time and again on the help they received during the year from voluntary agencies, sometimes associating their work with the reduction in infant mortality rates.[1]

Two examples of co-operation at a local level will illustrate the very good relationship which resulted in bringing to mothers and young children all the available resources of the area. The formation of the Herts Federation was undertaken by the Herts County Nursing Association[2] in 1923. The county nursing association had hitherto managed the massage clinic, which was attended by children referred from the child welfare centres (both voluntary and statutory) and from the local authorities' schools. The county council paid part of the fees, and the Herts Branch of the British Red Cross Society bore the cost of providing splints and surgical instruments for needy patients.[3] The Branch, at the request of the nursing association, took over the management of the massage clinic at the end of the year in order to co-ordinate the work. The local nursing associations were already responsible for the greater part of the service of midwives,[4] many of whom were also acting as health visitors and school nurses. The residential needs of the area were met in part by the county nursing association, which had a home containing a maternity ward,[5] and in part by the county council, which provided a convalescent home for mothers and infants at St. Leonards.[6]

The second example comes from Merseyside, where the Child Welfare Association had a history of co-operation with the local authorities from the time when it started infant clinics in 1911. In 1915 the medical officer of health worked in close co-operation with the association, and in 1942 it was reported that the local authorities were still referring mothers and babies to the various ante-natal, infant, sunlight and dental clinics. Visiting for children under five was carried out in co-operation with the local authorities' health visitors, and, at the request of the local authorities visiting of children over five was also undertaken, e.g. for the school medical officer or for the Corporation's orthopaedic clinics. Until the Government's scheme was launched the clinics had also supplied free milk. The local authority contributed in various ways: it paid the

[1] E.g. the Medical Officer of Health for Hertfordshire in the report for the year 1924–25.

[2] On the invitation of Dr. Barrie Lambert.

[3] In the year 1925–26 the Herts County Council agreed to make payment for in-patient treatment and the supply of surgical appliances for school children and infants recommended by the orthopaedic surgeon.

[4] 78 midwives in all associations were affiliated to the county nursing association.

[5] 16 pupils were at this time in training.

[6] A scheme for the rehabilitation of crippled children was also worked out under the auspices of the Central Council for the Care of Cripples between the Herts Massage and Orthopaedic Service and the Ministry of Labour, whereby the orthopaedic surgeon gave notification of special cases a year before the child was ready for training so that plans might be made and local interest secured.

doctors' fees, provided the record and weight cards and gave a substantial grant for the general work for children under five.

The pioneers who evolved the pattern of partnership within a local area made it possible, later, for the statutory bodies to take over smoothly much of the responsibility for the provision and maintenance of the service, and yet retain and value the help of the voluntary organisations. Local voluntary federations, fortunately, often recognised that it was a healthy development for local authorities to set up their own centres, just as they realised that their pioneer lecture courses were naturally devolving upon local authorities.[1]

We must not overlook the fact, however, that there were some local authorities who did not show similar enthusiasm. There are indications that the maternity and child welfare work was sometimes extensively 'farmed out', not so much from appreciation of the value of the voluntary associations' contribution, as from indifference and lack of interest by an M.O.H. who was more concerned with infectious diseases and other strictly sanitary aspects of public health. In other areas the local authority had accepted without question the work of well-established voluntary bodies and had contentedly turned its own energies to other spheres, leaving the burden to those already in the field.

The reverse of this attitude appeared when local authorities established their own maternity and child welfare centres and preferred to remain independent, seeing no need to co-operate either locally or nationally.[2] We find, indeed, a reference by the officers of the Association of Infant Welfare and Maternity Centres in 1928 to the fact that the total membership of 1,237 local institutions was less than half the total number of centres, and that those left outside were largely municipal. Failure to co-ordinate the work of an area was thought by the national voluntary organisations to be both short-sighted and unbusinesslike.[3] A more detailed study of the voluntary national organisations after the First World War will show more clearly their role in the development of the maternity and child welfare movement.

NATIONAL VOLUNTARY ORGANISATIONS FOR MATERNITY AND CHILD WELFARE: SCHEMES FOR CO-ORDINATION

The second phase in the development of the voluntary organisations was marked by an extension in range, and by an attempt to co-ordinate the work of the many national voluntary societies which had sprung up.

[1] See Annual Report, 1927, National Association for Prevention of Infant Mortality.
[2] They were, of course, glad to follow the general pattern in welcoming voluntary helpers within the centres.
[3] There were tangible benefits following upon affiliation, such as substantial discount on all publications, and prior claim on beds in Babies' Homes. In addition the Ministry of Health allowed affiliation fees to rank for grant aid.

THE MATERNITY AND CHILD WELFARE MOVEMENT

Co-ordination was secured mainly by federation, occasionally by amalgamation and, more rarely, by the decision of an association to leave the field to other agencies who were doing similar work. An example of the third process is seen in the winding up of the National League for Health, Maternity and Child Welfare. It was one of the organisations which had done valuable pioneer work but which found that its functions were being adequately carried out in the post-war years by two of its constituent associations. The issue was to a large extent brought to a head by the Carnegie Trust when, in 1928, it decided to grant-aid two of the daughter societies but not to assist the parent body. As the British Red Cross Society took the same view, the National League had to face the fact that its work was redundant, and to dissolve. Its aims had been wide and its interests, perhaps, too discursive, nor was there need for two federating associations within the same movement.[1] The range of work undertaken by the various agencies was great, covering many interests of concern to mothers. It is only by looking at the activities of a few of the oustanding organisations in some detail that we can appreciate the immense effort which had to be made to get any real measure of co-ordination.

One of the earliest and most successful efforts to secure co-ordination was made by the *Central Council for Infant and Child Welfare* (later the National Council for Maternity and Child Welfare).[2] It was a federating body whose affiliated groups included local federations of statutory and voluntary centres and national associations, some of which were specialised and others federal bodies. The Central Council also took direct action in standardising the training of social workers, and in helping to establish residential institutions for the care of mothers and children. Its educational work was organised on a practical basis and one of its more popular and successful ventures was its Travelling Exhibition which was much sought after, both at home and abroad. The Exhibition was so much in demand that it had to be extended, and sections were lent to a variety of groups including the British Red Cross and local education committees, particularly for the use of technical schools and infant welfare centres. There was also a loan of films to education authorities and maternity hospitals, and valuable propaganda was carried out by this means at many conferences. The Council secured support for its venture from numerous sources, and we find them expressing appreciation for 'the help and patience' of the Lancashire County Council and the London County Council, while its thanks were sent to the Dental Board of the United Kingdom which paid for exhibits in the dental section.[3] Recognition of the value of this effort was

---

[1] See the reference to its own obituary notice: p. 44, above.
[2] Incorporated in 1919 and renamed in 1928.
[3] It is interesting to note that local authorities who borrowed the Exhibition often added to it their own exhibition of related work. The cost was eligible for a 50% grant.

DEVELOPMENTS BETWEEN THE WORLD WARS

made during the Second World War, when it was difficult to get supplies. Both the Ministry of Health and the Board of Trade made special concessions so that its successful educational propaganda could go on. It was not until 1948 that the National Council for Maternity and Child Welfare, after doing valuable work for nearly thirty years, decided that its particular contribution had now been made, and it retired from the field leaving behind some of its flourishing constituent organisations.[1]

One of these, the *National Baby Welfare Council*,[2] had considerably extended its work, and it counted the great national societies, both statutory and voluntary, amongst its affiliated organisations. From the outset, this Council had secured wide publicity and enthusiastic press support. The organised competitions with their award of shields were not, as the popular press sometimes implied, merely lighthearted beauty competitions, but part of a planned effort to arouse sustained interest in infant welfare. It was often the means of focusing public attention on such vital matters as the provision of dental clinics, and the dental care of mothers and of children under five.[3] The public interest stimulated by the Council was such that many of the great national societies arranged to hold their annual meetings and conferences during the National Baby Week.[4]

One of the Council's chief aims had been to interest local authorities in the welfare of infants, and a typical entry from a later report notes the satisfaction felt by the Council that it was 'now the tendency of the local authorities to inaugurate their own continuous propaganda campaign'.[5]

The *National Association for the Prevention of Infant Mortality and for the Welfare of Infancy* was another of the early foundations which continued its successful policy of working harmoniously with other organisations. Its financial difficulties were greatly eased when, in 1928, it received support from the Carnegie United Kingdom Trust. The main concern of the National Association continued to be in keeping close watch on administrative and legislative action connected with the welfare of mothers and children, and in organising supplementary training

---

[1] The Council must not be confused with the National Association for Maternity and Child Welfare, footnote 1, p. 39.
[2] Initiated in 1917 as the National Baby Week Council.
[3] See Annual Report of National League for Health, Maternity and Child Welfare, 1927, pp. 22–23.
[4] See p. 48 for account of action of Local Government Board in advertising its work. By the turn of the half-century, the National Baby Welfare Council had 45 affiliated societies, representing a variety of voluntary bodies. Continuity with the past was kept, not only by the affiliation of such bodies as the National Association for Maternity and Child Welfare and the National Society of Children's Nurseries, but by the Association of County Medical Officers and the Society of Medical Officers of Health.
[5] Later, the journal *Mother and Child*, published by the National Baby Welfare Council, carried on the educational work in maternity and child welfare, including school children in its scope.

courses and national and regional conferences. The strong representation from medical officers of health, local authorities and voluntary organisations ensured close co-operation when any question concerning public health was at issue, or when a parliamentary bill came under scrutiny.[1] It was also in a strong position to make representation to a government department, particularly to the Ministry of Health.[2] Because its membership consisted mostly of those with knowledge and experience, both on the medical and administrative sides it could give valuable aid to any official committees of enquiry.[3]

We find its status recognised by the Board of Education, which from time to time asked the Association to co-operate in organising a course of lectures.[4] Lectures were given not only to workers in creches and day nurseries, to health visitor superintendents and others directly concerned with maternity and child welfare, but to elementary school teachers. This was the result of the importance attached to 'mothercraft', a question in which the Association had taken a keen interest, and it now extended its lectures and talks to more informal groups such as Women's Institutes. The usual financial arrangements in work of this kind resulted in the Association providing the lecturer and paying her fee, while the organisation concerned made itself responsible for travelling expenses. The Board of Education paid the travelling expenses of teachers, and the teachers themselves were responsible for their board and lodging.[5] The Association's difficulty in finding sufficient lecturers of the required standard for its educational work led it to institute training for lecturers, and a scheme was inaugurated with a grant from the *Pilgrim Trust*,[6] and the active participation of medical officers of health. Another source of aid for its educational work was the *Imperial Health Association Fund*.

We should note that the Association not only undertook educational work to interest the layman in maternity and child welfare. It also arranged courses for medical officers; for example, in 1934, on behalf of the maternity and child welfare group of the *Society of Medical Officers of Health*, a clinical course was organised for doctors attending the Association's conference. It was always ready to respond, too, to requests from individual medical officers of health, as well as from voluntary organisations, to give lectures in various towns.[7] Before leaving the

---

[1] E.g. it gave close attention to the Local Government Bill, 1929, and helped to secure some modifications.
[2] E.g. urging the Government in 1929 to ensure that all meat sold retail for human consumption should be of the required grade.
[3] E.g. the Ministry of Health into the Training of Midwives, and the enquiry into Maternal Mortality and Morbidity.
[4] See Annual Reports, Board of Education, e.g. 1928.
[5] In 1929 the course was residential, lasting a fortnight.
[6] 1931, £500 grant.
[7] See Annual Report, 1934, when the County M.O.H. for East Sussex asked for lectures (thirteen lectures were given covering four towns).

account of the valuable contribution made by this association to the movement, we might recognise the support it gave to similar organisations whenever concerted action was needed. For example, it supported the resolution sent by the *Midwives Institute* urging the Ministry of Health to require that all pregnant and parturient women in need of assistance should receive it through Maternity and Child Welfare Committees and not through Public Assistance Committees.[1] Another example of effective co-operation occurred when the National Association had a joint meeting with the Association of Maternity and Child Welfare Centres to discuss the supply of milk by the Milk Marketing Board to nursing and expectant mothers.[2] These two associations had so much in common that in 1937 it was decided to amalgamate.[3]

The National Association had always looked abroad, not only to learn from developments in other lands but to give of its own experience, particularly in the Dominions, and its conferences were increasingly attended by overseas representatives. Its own expert enquiries in the field of maternity and child welfare continued; we find Dr. McCleary, for example, reporting in 1934 on the enquiry into neonatal mortality. The Association's original concern with co-ordination was still strong, and it turned its attention to the need for better co-ordination between the work of infant welfare centres and school medical officers.[4]

The Association of Maternity and Child Welfare Centres[5] also had much in common with other national organisations, running lecture courses, producing pamphlets and holding conferences. But its chief functions were two: firstly, to co-ordinate the centres throughout the country and to encourage new centres to affiliate to the parent body, and, secondly, to stimulate the interest of parents and others in the movement by encouraging competitions, holding examinations, testing new inventions which purported to benefit mothers and babies, and by acting generally as an advisory body. It took over from the National League in 1928 its babies' homes department, the infant welfare workers employment bureau, the individual case department and the publications department. The Association also had some excellent practical suggestions to make towards greater co-ordination of services within an

[1] Section 5 of the Local Government Act, 1929, was permissive.
[2] See Annual Report, 1935.
[3] The new executive committee was modelled upon that of the National Association, so that the close partnership of statutory and voluntary agencies with strong medical support was preserved.
[4] It recommended a useful practical reform, namely, the automatic forwarding of medical records. See Annual Report, 1933.
[5] It is difficult to find one's way about the many titles and constitutions adopted, particularly in view of the constant federation and amalgamation. The Association was founded in 1911 and became *The Association of Infant Welfare and Maternity Centres*. Its forerunner had been the Association of Infant Welfare Consultations and Schools for Mothers, and in 1937 it was renamed the Association of Maternity and Child Welfare Centres.

area. For example, it pointed out the importance of notification to the medical officer of health of the precise nature of the illness of children discharged from municipal hospitals.[1]

The conditions of membership of the Association are of general interest since they included management by a representative committee, audited accounts and a requirement that the centre must have made approved efforts to secure the co-operation of the local health authority.[2] The step towards greater consolidation of the movement taken by the amalgamation of the two great national associations[3] during the year 1937 to 1938 gave fresh impetus at a time when municipalities were incorporating more and more voluntary centres in their schemes. The two Associations working together were also better prepared to take concerted action in face of the threat of war.[4]

SUMMARY OF WORK OF RELATED SOCIETIES. REVIEW OF TRENDS TOWARDS AMALGAMATION

The account so far given of the development of voluntary societies and their co-operation with statutory bodies for the welfare of mothers and children by no means exhausts the list of agencies involved.[5] There were other valuable fields of work, such as that provided in voluntary hospitals and convalescent homes; or by the *British Red Cross Society* and the *St. John Ambulance Brigade;* or the services given on behalf of deprived children, such as those organised by the *Church of England Moral Welfare Council*[6] in the various dioceses, providing for mothers and babies who were in special need of understanding and friendly aid; or by societies like the *National Council for the Unmarried Mother and Her Child*, which since 1918 had concerned itself, amongst other matters, with working for legislative reform; or the several other societies caring for deprived children, such as *Waifs and Strays Society*

---

[1] The L.C.C. promised as a result of these discussions to make every effort to see that records were sent to the M.O.H.

[2] Annual Report, Association of Infant Welfare and Maternity Centres, 1930.

[3] The National Association for the Prevention of Infant Mortality and the Association of Maternity and Child Welfare Centres now became the National Association of Maternity and Child Welfare Centres and for the Prevention of Infant Mortality. Dr. McCleary remained Chairman until 1939, when Dr. Jane Turnbull took over his office. Its change of name to the *National Association for Maternity and Child Welfare* came in 1945, and to that of *National Association for Maternal and Child Welfare* in 1953.

[4] See Annual Report, 1939, pp. 5–6, for discussion of evacuation schemes, the duties of maternity and child welfare centres in reception areas, the provision of midwifery, etc. The Association continued to keep in close touch with the Ministry of Health on questions affecting children under five, and evacuation problems (see Annual Reports, 1939–44).

[5] For a useful account of the part played by the Nursing Associations in health visiting and midwifery, as well as in general home nursing, see C. Braithwaite, *The Voluntary Citizen*.

[6] The Church of England had not only established moral welfare work in every diocese, but had developed a strong education section in its central organisation.

DEVELOPMENTS BETWEEN THE WORLD WARS

(later to be known as the *Church of England Children's Society*). *Dr. Barnardo's*, and the *National Children's Homes and Orphanages;* or the family case work of the *Invalid Children's Aid Association*, and the many other organisations concerned with handicapped children. Because such societies had combined personal service of a high order with sound practical schemes, it was natural that they should have been ready to co-operate with other agencies providing a variety of services whether voluntary or statutory. In many instances, they themselves made the necessary provision before it was available from public sources, and their educational work helped both to promote the welfare of the mother and her child and to create a responsible attitude within the community.

This study is, however, necessarily selective, and for the purpose of illustrating the development of a service based on co-operation between voluntary and statutory bodies, emphasis has been put on the maternity and child welfare service in the narrower sense of the term. It is significant that this branch has long been recognised as a social service available to all sections of the community; it has been welcomed by mothers of all classes, although it started as a service to encourage the poor.

Review of Trends towards Amalgamation

As we look back on the development of the maternity and child welfare movement we cannot but be amazed at the number of societies, national and local, which were thrown up. Many of them were federating bodies, and there was considerable cross-representation. It is not easy to find a way amongst these multitudinous societies which were so frequently given to changing their titles and extending their aims. It is indeed difficult to disentangle the distinctive purposes of some, and many members must have spent considerable time sitting on one another's committees, while the Minister of Health must sometimes have been hard pressed by resolutions and delegations from so many likeminded societies. Some of the agencies were themselves conscious of overlapping and, as we have seen, a number of attempts were made to amalgamate, not always with success.[1] Sometimes the impetus came from without, as when the Carnegie Trust made a constructive attempt to help bring together some of the still numerous societies by offering accommodation to nearly half the constituent bodies of the National Council for Maternity and Child Welfare, in Carnegie House, Piccadilly.[2] Sometimes dissatisfaction at the waste of effort involved in

[1] E.g. the National Council for Maternity and Child Welfare had constantly had this in mind in 1927 and 1937. See Annual Report, 1938, with foreword by Dr. McCleary. Efforts were still being made in 1947 by the National Association for Maternity and Child Welfare when it tried to induce the National Baby Week Council to amalgamate, but without success—the latter fearing to lose its identity.

[2] The movement was indebted to the Carnegie Trust in many ways, including the provision of funds for the setting up of model maternity and child welfare centres.

duplication of function came from a local area, as when the *London Federation of Infant Welfare Centres* decided in 1923–24 'to confine its operations to matters which will not involve overlapping with the work of the Association of Infant Welfare and Maternity Centres'.[1] After another year they expressed themselves more strongly still—'they felt they were no part of any systematic scheme', and they decided, accordingly, to dissolve.

One of the most difficult problems to be faced by an energetic voluntary society is to decide when its work is done, when it is time for it to retire altogether, or to sink its individuality and amalgamate with a kindred society. Within the Maternity and Child Welfare Movement the national societies seem to have been keenly aware of this issue and to have done much to secure co-ordination. Combined action was seen to be valuable, and it says much for the spirit of the movement that, in spite of the existence of so many societies working in allied spheres, there was considerable interchange of views, thus helping to reduce the conflict and waste which might otherwise have resulted. Sometimes there was joint discussion with public bodies; sometimes *ad hoc* committees were formed. More often the traditional pattern was followed, involving cross-representation on the council, executive or advisory committees of kindred societies.[2]

In spite of some acknowledged overlapping, on the whole the national societies seem to have reached a remarkable standard of harmony and efficiency. Public relations appear to have been excellent. Every conference, national and local, attracted speakers of repute from the statutory and voluntary services.[3] It is indeed characteristic of the movement that so much support came from men and women who were expert in their own field, whether in local or central government, or in medical work,[4] and that so many busy public servants were ready to give a great deal of time to the voluntary associations. The national associations seem, too, to have had a flair for publicity and to have had con-

[1] The London centres still apparently affiliated since fees were paid direct to the Association.

[2] An example will illustrate this tendency; e.g. the representation of the National Council for Maternity and Child Welfare both on the National Council of Social Service and on its active advisory committee 'The Women's Group on Public Welfare', and on the National Council of Women and the Women's Advisory Housing Council. (The widely read report *Our Towns: A Close-up* is one of several important studies made by the Women's Group on Public Welfare.)

[3] The societies were fortunate, too, in the co-operation of some of the schools of the University. One very useful exhibit was that shown by the London School of Hygiene and Tropical Medicine, when, in 1930, it had a maternity and child welfare section in its museum, and one of its charts showed how an infant welfare centre could co-operate with outside agencies (voluntary and statutory).

[4] E.g. Dr. McCleary and Dr. Turnbull as successive chairmen of the National Association for Maternity and Child Welfare (under its earlier names), and Dr. Menzies, the Chief Medical Officer to the L.C.C., actively associated with the Central Council for Infant and Child Welfare. (Later the chair was taken by Mr. George Mitchell, L.C.C.)

siderable press support.[1] They kept abreast of the times and were ready to interest themselves in any issues which affected mothers and children, whether it was smoke abatement or family and post-war planning.

[1] The popular press welcomed contributions, e.g. the *Woman's Pictorial* had a page devoted to 'Better Babies'; and letters and enquiries were answered by the Mothercraft Training Society. The placing of signed articles and the running of competitions in the press were a regular part of the propaganda campaigns during the National Baby Weeks.

VI

THE SECOND WORLD WAR AND THE POST-WAR TRANSITION PERIOD

Emergency Measures

DURING the first dislocation of the normal maternity and child welfare services at the outbreak of war many infant welfare and ante-natal centres were closed in the evacuation areas, and emergency services had to be organised in the reception areas. When, during the first year, many mothers with young children returned to the large towns, centres were re-opened, so that pressure was put upon both the reception and the evacuation areas to keep running as full a service as possible. The distribution of milk under the National Milk Scheme made new demands on the welfare authorities, and when the vitamin supplements were issued distribution was organised through the centres. At the same time arrangements had to be made for billeting in the reception areas, and when this sometimes proved too difficult, hostels were opened.[1] Improvised maternity homes had also to be established, and residential and day nurseries staffed. All these emergency arrangements put heavy pressure on the welfare authorities, and many of them welcomed the help of voluntary organisations. In addition to the organisations already in the field, the newly formed Women's Voluntary Services[2] took a responsible part in helping to secure the smooth working of the schemes in many areas. When, in 1942, the Minister of Health set up an Advisory Committee on Mothers and Young Children, he naturally included voluntary societies as well as representatives of local authorities and of various medical and other related professional

---

[1] These included ante-natal and post-natal hostels.
[2] The W.V.S. took an active part in many spheres of social service, including the organisation of Home Help Schemes, and a course of instruction for organisers. (See Ministry of Health Annual Report, 1949, and *Civilian Health and Medical Services*, Vol. 1.)

bodies.[1] A number of sub-committees were set up to which special questions were referred,[2] and it is interesting to note that several were matters in which voluntary societies had already been closely concerned.[3]

Education and Propaganda

One of the results of their efforts had been the teaching of mothercraft[4] in elementary schools[5] while from time to time attempts had been made to arouse keener interest in the secondary (i.e. grammar) schools, but with no great success. It must be remembered that the attitude of Victorian parents was still carried over into the early 20th century, and it often befogged the attempts to give informed teaching: the indirect approaches to the question of childbirth and motherhood failed to satisfy. It was difficult, for the same reason, to make much advance in public discussion. Nevertheless the National Association of Maternity and Child Welfare Centres and for the Prevention of Infant Mortality continued to make parenthood one of its chief themes, offering 'postgraduate' courses to health visitors, nurses and midwives, and arranging courses for teachers. The doctors had been pointing out for more than fifty years that preventive work for the care of infants was mainly a question of motherhood.[6] But it was not until the Second World War that the public in general began to show greater interest in the family and its welfare, and that the teaching of parentcraft came into its own. Subsequently the Ministry felt this question to be of such importance that they appointed a parentcraft adviser who had been closely identified with such work in connection with both voluntary and statutory agencies.[7] Meanwhile, the voluntary organisations had taken their teaching projects into the women's services. By 1944 organised courses for the W.R.N.S., A.T.S. and W.R.A.A.F. were generally accepted, and both the National Association and the local authorities in whose areas the camps were situated co-operated in the venture.

The National Association then went on to appoint teachers in

[1] The Committee included representatives of welfare authorities, the L.C.C., voluntary societies, Nursery Schools Association, and nursery training colleges, with members of Parliament, general practitioners, a director of education, an obstetrician and a paediatrician and officers of the Department with the Minister as chairman.
[2] See the variety of subjects listed on p. 102, Ministry of Health Report, *The State of the Public Health during Six Years of War*, 1946.
[3] E.g. existing arrangements for the teaching of parentcraft and how these might be extended and developed.
[4] We have seen that in the early days of the history of the movement much thought had been given to the teaching of mothercraft; the Mothercraft Training Society was affiliated to the Central Council for Infant and Child Welfare.
[5] The National Association of Maternity and Child Welfare Centres had prepared a syllabus for schools to suit both junior and senior groups, and it organised school competitions to try to rouse interest in a number of grammar schools.
[6] See Sir G. Newman, *The Health of the State*, p. 125.
[7] I.e. Dr. Housden, who was the Chairman of the Parentcraft Sub-committee of the National Association, and also a member of the Hants County Education Committee.

THE MATERNITY AND CHILD WELFARE MOVEMENT

mothercraft to interest the Girls Training Corps and other youth groups. The Ministry of Health and the Ministry of Education were closely concerned in this aspect of further education.[1] Some of the local authorities co-operating with the National Association were ready to inaugurate a special scheme for the teaching of mothercraft in girls' secondary schools. The teaching of parentcraft was also receiving special attention in some local authority areas. In 1947, for example, Hampshire County Council[2] received a promise of grant-aid from the Ministry of Health for this purpose. The voluntary agencies also called attention to the importance of teaching mothercraft in the home, and the use which might be made of day nurseries and nursery schools as an adjunct to such teaching. The National Association's advisory pamphlets aimed at a wide public, and some of them, e.g. *To Mothers and Fathers*, were ordered in very large numbers by both statutory and voluntary agencies for direct issue to parents.[3]

The National Association was ready to consider both detailed questions of practical use to mothers and children and wider issues of policy on a number of general questions affecting their welfare.[4] A glance at some of the questions considered by the executive committee during the year 1944–45 gives some idea of the range of interest.[5]

The Ministry of Health welcomed the publicity given to questions of maternity and child welfare in the various women's magazines and periodicals.[6] That education and propaganda were still needed after forty years of development in the maternity and child welfare field was abundantly demonstrated both during and after the war. The publication by the Women's Group on Public Welfare of *Our Towns: A Close-up*[7] focused attention upon conditions which cried aloud for

[1] See Circular 117, 1946. The Chief Medical Officer to the Ministry of Health and Ministry of Education, Sir W. Jamieson, took the chair at a session of the Conference on this subject.

[2] See footnote 7, p. 67.

[3] By 1953 the number distributed reached 1,640,000 copies. See Annual Report, National Association for Maternity and Child Welfare, 1953–54.

[4] The societies gave useful evidence to the Royal Commission on Population and to the Curtis Committee. They set up sub-committees on each issue. They recommended that a department within the Ministry of Health should be responsible for the care of deprived children and the Public Health Committee working with the Maternity and Child Welfare Committee at the local level. In the event it was the Home Office which was made centrally responsible, while a Children's Committee was appointed by each local authority.

[5] They included family endowment, the supply of day nurseries, a memorandum prepared by the Central Council for Health Education on the care of the feet, methods dealing with neglectful mothers (on which they had several constructive suggestions to make), and the fixtures and equipment required by a welfare centre in a rural area—this last at the request of the National Council for Social Service. See Annual Report of the National Association of Maternity and Child Welfare Centres and for the Prevention of Infant Mortality, 1945.

[6] See, for example, a reference to this in Ministry of Health Annual Report, 1949, p. 255.

[7] See p. 29n, and p. 64n above.

WORLD WAR II AND THE TRANSITION PERIOD

remedy. Later still the result of an enquiry by the M.O.H.[1] in an area where the infant mortality rate was more than 80 per 1,000 live births, at a time when the average for the country had fallen to 29·9, emphasised the urgency. When we examine the means advocated to reduce infant mortality in such an area we are struck by the similarity with those stressed at the beginning of the century by the pioneers of the movement.[2]

There is no doubt that the maternity and child welfare service played an important part in the spectacular decrease, over the country as a whole, in the infant mortality rate.[3] In 1900 the rate was 154 per 1,000 live births, dropping to 105 by 1914. Thereafter, with some slight fluctuations, it fell steadily to reach 51 by the outbreak of the Second World War. Save for a slight rise in the second and third year of the war, there was again a fall, until it dropped finally below 30 by 1950.[4] No such spectacular fall[5] had marked the maternal death rate, however. As the Working Party on Midwives[6] pointed out, the reduction which took place in the inter-war years was largely due to skilled midwifery in a co-ordinated service. When chemotherapy, penicillin and blood transfusion were available the rate was still further reduced.[7] The outstanding need was to see that every area had facilities such as those available in the most progressive districts, and that all mothers could take advantage of them. Improvements were called for, in particular in those areas where there was 'little sense of team work between health visitors and midwives'.[8]

EFFECT OF THE NATIONAL HEALTH SERVICE ACT, 1946

The National Health Service Act had an important effect on the work of voluntary organisations and their relation with statutory authorities. In the first place the Minister took over the control of most of the

[1] See Ministry of Health Annual Report (June 1952) for the year ending December 1950, p. 101.
[2] See Chapter 3, above.
[3] We must remember, too, that the physical condition of mothers was very much better with the improved standard of living.
[4] 29·9 in 1950 and a continued fall since then to date (25·4 for the year 1954; 24·9 in 1955—provisional figure).
[5] See the Report of the Ministry of Health, Part II, for the year 1950, of June 1952, pp. 98–100, for an account of 'The Trend of the Maternal Mortality Rate in the Past Fifty Years'.
See also the Survey of Social and Economic Aspects of Pregnancy and Childbirth: *Maternity in Great Britain*, undertaken by a Joint Committee of the Royal College of Obstetricians and Gynaecologists and the Population Investigation Committee, 1948.
[6] Report of the Working Party on Midwives, 1949, Ministry of Health, Department of Health for Scotland, Ministry of Labour and National Service.
Between 1934 and 1939 the rate dropped from 4·6 to 3·1.
[7] During the war years, with the exception of a slight rise in 1941 from 2·62 to 2·79, the rate dropped yearly. In 1948 it had reached the low level of 1·02. In 1953 it was 0·75, a slight increase over the figure for 1952, 0·72.
[8] See Ministry of Health Annual Report for year ending 1948.

THE MATERNITY AND CHILD WELFARE MOVEMENT

hospitals and some of the convalescent homes; Regional Hospital Boards, each covering a wide area, were made responsible, and voluntary bodies had to establish a new relationship. Medical practitioner services were organised at a local level, under Executive Councils, and every mother now had the choice of attendance by a doctor and, when required, a gynaecologist, in addition to the centre, clinic and midwifery services for which the medical officer of health was responsible to the local health authority. Thirdly, the local authority had extended powers and duties: all counties and county boroughs now had an obligation to provide maternity and child welfare services[1] and they became responsible for a number of ancillary services, particularly domiciliary nursing and home help, of direct concern to mothers and children. Provision was made, as in previous legislation, for co-operation between statutory bodies and voluntary organisations.

Voluntary associations gave a guarded welcome to the Act. They had no objection in principle to the assumption of control of many of the services by statutory bodies: they had always worked for a greater measure of statutory responsibility, and they had seen much of their pioneer work taken over. More than half of the remaining maternity and child welfare centres now passed to the local health authorities, and many of the nursing associations agreed to hand over their work.[2] In some cases the local authority itself decided not to continue subsidising a voluntary society, but to administer the service directly, on the grounds that as they were providing the bulk of the funds they should have control of the management.

The National Health Service was successful in the establishment of a comprehensive scheme, but co-ordination between the various statutory bodies responsible for different branches of the service was difficult to achieve. The voluntary organisations were specially critical of this problem as it affected maternity and child welfare. The Ministry was only too conscious of the structural weakness, and a series of circulars and reports[3] on the need for co-ordination, together with suggestions for co-operation between statutory and voluntary agencies, followed rapidly.

Voluntary organisations recognised that much of their early work was completed; the need for local centres and clinics was established.

[1] Since 1918 power had been given not only to all county councils and county borough councils but to some 243 county district councils. After the Public Health Act, 1936, came into force the authority for the administration of the Maternity and Child Welfare Act and the Notification of Births Act was no longer divided. The 1946 National Health Service Act took co-ordination a stage further.

[2] It was in line with the new trends that the Ministry of Labour and National Service reorganised its Nursing Appointments Service in 1950 so that many more employment officers would be available (125 instead of 33) for nurses, midwives or potential students in search of posts or advice on careers.

[3] E.g. the Reports of the Central Health Services Council, a statutory committee set up under the Act.

WORLD WAR II AND THE TRANSITION PERIOD

Statutory provision in the post-war years had steadily increased: those reported by the Ministry of Health numbered 3,932 in 1944, 4,721 in 1949 and 5,495 in 1954. Although there had been some disquiet at the falling off in attendance at ante-natal clinics in some areas,[1] the number provided by local authorities gradually increased after 1950 to reach 1,961 in 1954. It was still thought desirable to have voluntary workers in the centres,[2] although not all authorities made full use of their services. In view of the impending changes, the National Association of Maternity and Child Welfare Centres and for the Prevention of Infant Mortality[3] had undertaken, in 1947, a small investigation into the role of voluntary workers in maternity and child welfare centres.[4] The result indicated wide disparity in the use made of voluntary help: the majority were glad to have volunteers for the general ordering of the clinical and clerical work, and to a lesser extent in the weighing of babies. There was some difference, too, in the esteem in which voluntary help was held, but the National Association felt justified in deciding that the result was generally favourable and that the demand would continue.

How far co-operation with voluntary organisations in other branches of work for the welfare of mothers and children would extend depended to a considerable degree on the attitude of the local authority, particularly of the medical officer of health. In the care of mothers and illegitimate children the Minister had drawn the attention of local authorities to the useful experience of the voluntary agencies and to the valuable personal work which might supplement official help.[5] Some authorities welcomed their new powers and there was a close relationship, as, for example, in the provision of mothers' and babies' homes by the authority and their staffing and management by the voluntary agency. In some areas health visitors were encouraged to consult moral welfare workers when need arose. But there were also examples of indifference or self-complacency when the medical officer of health had no opinion of the work of voluntary organisations, or felt that health visitors could do all that was necessary. The hostility of a medical officer might prevent a recommendation to the local authority to grant-aid a voluntary organisation or to make use of its experience on an agency basis. It could not prevent the informal but active co-operation of social workers in the field, whether employed by statutory or voluntary

[1] See the reports of the Ministry of Health for 1949, p. 157 *et seq.*
[2] The Joint Committee of the Royal College of Obstetricians and Gynaecologists and the Population Investigation Committee, in 1948, agreed that in general 'voluntary workers render most valuable service'; they were more critical of the voluntary committees which ran welfare centres, considering that they suffered from serious faults. See *Maternity in Great Britain*, p. 105.
[3] The following year it was to simplify its title and become the National Association for Maternity and Child Welfare.
[4] A questionnaire was sent to 425 councils, to which 282 replied.
[5] See, for example, Ministry of Health Annual Report for year ending 1949, p. 176.

THE MATERNITY AND CHILD WELFARE MOVEMENT

agencies, where there was a longstanding tradition of consultation and mutual assistance.[1]

Many local authorities were glad to co-operate with voluntary organisations in carrying out their responsibilities under the National Health Service Act. A glance at the payments made to voluntary associations by the L.C.C. after the appointed day, 5th July, 1948 (see Table XIII), shows that substantial amounts continued to be paid under the general heading of 'Maternity and Child Welfare Services'. In addition, the L.C.C. used the services of voluntary associations for mother and baby homes and for recuperative holidays for children under five and nursing and expectant mothers. Increasing use was made of moral welfare associations, while two new items appear in the payments for family planning services and for mothercraft in-patients.

The chief need was to ensure that the various schemes for the welfare of mothers and children[2] worked smoothly. Divided responsibility, in fact, made the question of co-ordination urgent, and we find both statutory and voluntary agencies concerned with the means to this end.

Persistence and Change in the Work of Voluntary Organisations

It is significant that of the new aims of the National Association for Maternity and Child Welfare issued in 1952, the first was 'to bring into closer relationship all engaged or interested in the work of maternity and child welfare centres and similar institutions, and to co-operate with societies for infant welfare'. It still felt it to be necessary to carry on its work of publicity and education.[3] There was a call for change of emphasis in some of the work of voluntary organisations under the new conditions. The National Association had already decided in 1949 to broaden its administrative base and to extend its membership, not only to the local health committees, but to the authorities' children's committees and education committees. It also invited regional hospital boards and teaching hospital groups to affiliate. By 1953 this pattern was firmly

---

[1] An example was brought to the notice of the writer of the claim of a medical officer of health that his health visitors did all that was necessary, only to be met by proof from a voluntary organisation, a family case work agency, that it had dealt with large numbers of appeals made to them by these very health visitors on behalf of families who needed help.

[2] The L.C.C. by 1953 were grouping the services under the heading 'Services for Mothers and Children', which included maternity and child welfare clinics and day nurseries.

[3] The second and third 'aims' accepted in 1952 were:

(ii) The study and dissemination of information on infant mortality and health in all their relations, and the care and instruction of mothers.

(iii) Encouragement of prevention of maternal and infant mortality and ill-health; and of education in parentcraft; organisation of conferences and courses of lectures on infant care.

It no longer included 'assistance in the establishment and maintenance of residential institutions'. See Annual Reports of the National Association for Maternity and Child Welfare, 1950–53.

WORLD WAR II AND THE TRANSITION PERIOD

established,[1] except that hospital management committees instead of regional hospital boards were invited.[2] Practical co-operation was seen in the quick response of some of the statutory authorities to the suggestion that they should increase their subscription to a sum representing 6d. per 1,000 of the population. The Society also decided that the new emphasis in its work should be noted in a change of name. The title 'National Association for *Maternal* and Child Welfare' was selected 'in order to indicate more clearly its concern for the welfare of mothers and children of all ages and all stages'. The aspect of preventive care was to be stressed in the 'straight through' supervision of children, with the family as the unit.

At the same time the National Baby Welfare Council was continuing its work of popularising the service. It produced an illustrated journal *Mother and Child*, together with posters, advisory pamphlets and paper patterns. It proclaimed its function as that of educating public opinion: the competitions and the National Baby Week were intended to have a wide appeal, and the award of shields and trophies was still a feature,[3] while its permanent exhibition was now designed mainly to attract students.

The Central Council for Health Education was also concerned in maternal and child welfare in its broad aspects, while organisations like

---

[1] It is interesting to examine the representation on the Executive Committee for the year 1953–54. It includes representatives of health, education and children's committees of affiliated local health authorities, teaching hospitals and hospital management committees; representatives of a wide range of national organisations concerned with mothers and children; representatives of individual hospitals and maternity and child welfare clinics; unofficial representatives of the Ministry of Health, the Home Office and the L.C.C., together with a number of co-opted individuals, all but two of whom were doctors.

A list of the voluntary organisations represented gives some idea of the Association's interest in organisations concerned with mothers and children 'of all ages and stages':

The National Association for the Unmarried Mother and her Child
The National Adoption Society
The Central Council for Health Education
The Central Council for the Care of Cripples
The Save the Children Fund
The Association of Sick Children's Hospital Nurses
The Association of Nursery Matrons
The Royal College of Midwives
The Society of Medical Officers of Health
The Royal College of Nursing
The National Baby Welfare Council
The London Diocesan Council for Moral Welfare

[2] In that year local authority representation on the general council was 201, while teaching hospital groups, hospital management committees, national organisations and individual centres accounted for 40. Individual membership was 38. Any member was entitled to stand for election to the executive committee. See Annual General Report, National Association for Maternity and Child Welfare, 1953–54, p. 8.

[3] The awards were available to local authorities and organisations, including administrative territories of the Commonwealth.

THE MATERNITY AND CHILD WELFARE MOVEMENT

the National Association for Mental Health took a lively interest and were prepared to offer their own special knowledge. It is significant that a series of broadcasts by a woman medical psychologist on 'You and Your Children' were later published on behalf of the Ministry of Health, and that the doctor was an active member of the N.A.M.H.[1]

There was a growing concern with the question of preventive mental health in the maternity and child welfare service, both at home[2] and abroad.[3]

An element in the work of the voluntary associations which persisted throughout the development of the maternity and child welfare movement was the lively interest in child welfare overseas.[4] The National Association for Maternity and Child Welfare had become a member of the *International Association for the Protection of Child Welfare*, and it kept in close touch with the World Health Organisation and with U.N.I.C.E.F. It was increasingly used as an advisory and consultative centre by overseas visitors, especially by those who were about to develop their own services and wished to know 'how things began' in this country. It was in tune with this emphasis that it was decided to embark on a new quarterly, *Maternity and Child Welfare, Survey and Progress at Home and Abroad*.[5]

The Ministry of Health, too, had taken an increasing interest in international health: until the outbreak of the Second World War, the medical officers of the Ministry had been actively concerned in the various health organisations of the League of Nations. During the war, an inter-allied committee on medical supplies and services, including the requirements for maternity and child welfare, was organised. When U.N.R.R.A. was formed, one of its standing committees was on health questions. Finally, in June to July of 1946, an interim commission of the World Health Organisation of the United Nations was set up, and the World Health Organisation became the specialised agency of the United Nations in 1948. Of the seven main health interests, maternity and child health formed an important group.

It is relevant to our study to note that one of the items dealt with by

---

[1] Dr. Doris Odlum was a vice-president of the N.A.M.H., and the B.M.A. representative on the Council.

[2] E.g. the report by a study group from the Public Health Dept. of the L.C.C., and the Tavistock Clinic. See *The Medical Officer* (92, 303–307, 10th Dec., 1954).

[3] E.g. the interest of the World Health Organisation with its Expert Committee on Mental Health (quoted in the Report of the Central Health Services Council, 1952).

[4] See especially the first Congress in Paris in 1905 and the first International Congress, when Dr. McCleary was a vice-president. It is interesting to note that in 1925 the organisation of the English-speaking section was undertaken by the National Association for Prevention of Infant Mortality and the Save the Children Fund, while the Patronage Committee for Great Britain included the President of the Board of Education, the Minister of Health and the Duke of Atholl.

[5] See Annual Report of the National Association for Maternity and Child Welfare, 1950.

the first Health Assembly in 1948 was the establishment of working relations with inter-governmental and non-governmental organisations, and the procedure and criteria for consultation with them.[1] Amongst the sixteen non-governmental organisations admitted to relations with W.H.O. we find the International Union for Child Welfare.[2]

Governments still recognised that while they were responsible for seeing that maternity and child welfare services were available, voluntary organisations had a valuable part to play in making them widely acceptable.

In Great Britain public relations officers were glad to keep closely in touch with the national organisations both in supplying and receiving information. It is typical of the partnership that while the Ministry's pamphlets set out clearly what services were provided they looked to the voluntary bodies to persuade parents to use them. It was 'the personal note' which helped whenever new ideas needed to be made popular or well-tried methods reaffirmed.

The Ministry of Health or the British Council were always ready to refer overseas enquirers to the national voluntary organisations, which had wide experience of developments in the field of maternity and child welfare.

While such traditional forms of service were still valued, the statutory authorities were also glad to welcome new voluntary activities such as those offered by the W.V.S. and the Red Cross Society. The many amenities provided in hospitals and convalescent homes, such as canteens, trolley shops, flowers, the St. John and Red Cross Hospital Library Scheme, the circulation picture scheme and diversional therapy of many kinds, were valuable additions at a time when statutory authorities had neither the time nor the money for such 'extras'. They were services much appreciated by those mothers and children who needed, if only temporarily, some form of residential care. Voluntary action for maternal and child welfare, whether in institutions or in the community, far from being redundant with the extension of the National Health Service, is still in great demand: both the old and the new voluntary organisations seek all the support they can get, financial and personal, that they may the better fulfil their function as partners with the statutory bodies in carrying out social policy.

[1] See Ministry of Health Annual Report for year ending March, 1949, p. 199. The Assembly also recommended setting up an expert committee which met in 1949 with its own W.H.O. secretariat.
[2] See the publications under the auspices of W.H.O. dealing with maternity and child welfare, e.g. J. Bowlby, *Maternal Care and Mental Health*, published in 1951.

PART III

The Mental Health Services[1]

---

[1] See p. xii, above, for reference to the scope of this section.

INTRODUCTION

The Position To-day: Pressure from the Past

By the mid-20th century the Mental Health Services in Britain seemed to have come, at last, into their own. The new National Health Service Act integrated the services for the mentally ill, the mentally defective and the physically ill. The development of a social policy designed to secure the well-being of all classes within the community included a special concern for the rehabilitation of the handicapped. Increased recognition of the value of care within the community for the mentally ill and the defective, together with new opportunities for the treatment of voluntary patients in hospital, contrasted with the customary procedure at the beginning of the century when the only treatment available was dependent upon custody in asylums and institutions, with the inevitable preliminary of certification.

This change of attitude reflected advance in many fields of human endeavour: the pioneer work of doctors, philanthropists and voluntary societies; the experiments in treatment and care by local authorities; the encouragement of the central authority. We might add, the influence of the Universities as they sent out trained social workers, and the educative effect of the Mental Treatment Act itself; finally, the great advance in the medical field, as increased knowledge of psychiatry and neurology gave confidence comparable to that in general medicine and surgery.

Yet, while progress has been considerable, the mental health services are still struggling to free themselves from a legislative and social pattern worked out in the 19th century. The past lingers on, in spite of the National Health Service and the Mental Treatment Acts. So long as the Lunacy Act, 1890, is in force, with the requirement of certification for patients needing prolonged hospital treatment, so long will the old fear of custody continue to haunt mental patients and their relatives.[1] We may well ask, too, how fundamental has been the change in public attitude when we hear of town planning authorities who refuse application for permission to take over premises for a convalescent, or 'on trial' home, lest the neighbourhood should suffer from association with a 'mental establishment'.

Unfortunately, too, professional bodies, statutory authorities and

[1] Similarly certification under the Mental Deficiency Acts is frustrating to those who are concerned with training mental defectives.

voluntary organisations within the mental health field have, in the past, tended to concentrate on their own special interests. It has been one of the main weaknesses of the service that, not only have the provisions for the mentally ill and the mentally defective been sharply differentiated from the general medical services, but, within each branch, specialisms have developed, each with little or no relation to the others. It was the threat of the Second World War, and finally the pressure of war itself, which forced the issue and made a wider view imperative. The need for more effective co-ordination is still a live issue in the post-war years.

The new service has also to reckon with the fact, common to other social services, that while some local authorities have had a record of active interest and considerable experience in the mental health field, others have for so long been indifferent that they have little practical knowledge to guide them.

Another burden from the past which presses heavily to-day is the shortage of institutional accommodation, while unsuitable buildings and antiquated conditions have helped to make nursing in the mental health service relatively unattractive.

Perhaps equally urgent, though less generally recognised, is the shortage of trained and experienced social workers to work in mental hospitals, child guidance clinics, or in the field of community care. There is no doubt that the trend in the years between the two world wars was towards an increasing measure of community care.[1] This has been strengthened by the new duties placed on local health authorities by the National Health Service Act, 1946. Care within the community in the sphere of mental health obviously calls for workers with skill and experience, who can see the patient in relation to his family and his environment; yet it would seem that too little thought has been given to this problem. The proved urgency of institutional needs is something which the public can more readily appreciate. Facts concerning shortages of beds or nurses 'speak for themselves'. The more intangible needs of a preventive service in community care require greater imagination and insight to be fully appreciated.

The problem is not new, for we find similar regrets expressed by voluntary organisations in the late 19th century and the early 20th, as they pioneered in community care. The 19th century had already laid the foundations of lunacy reform, and the public conscience had been sufficiently roused to ensure that treatment of lunatics in asylums would be more humane, and that there were sufficient safeguards to guarantee that no one should be wrongfully held in custody, but care outside institutions had hardly been given a thought. It was the task of the pioneers working for community care to show that this form of treatment was both constructive and economical. The lesson has apparently not yet been fully learned. It is worth noting that, in attempting to solve

[1] See Table VIII.

INTRODUCTION

similar difficulties, the voluntary organisations sought every opportunity to work closely with those statutory bodies who were willing to co-operate. Since the general public were mostly indifferent to the whole question, social policy lagged behind voluntary action, and the voluntary societies, particularly in the sphere of mental deficiency, exerted considerable pressure on statutory authorities, and were vigorous in their campaigns to arouse public interest.

It is proposed, therefore, to examine afresh the methods and procedure of the voluntary organisations working in the field of community care for the mentally ill and the mentally defective, with special reference to their relations with statutory bodies, and their impact on social policy. Before doing so a fuller study of the historical background and the legislative framework is necessary since the past still presses heavily on the present in the sphere of mental health.

One of the greatest difficulties facing the reformers in the mental health field was the ignorance and suspicion which surrounded the whole question. For centuries the social attitude towards the insane and the mentally defective had been one of fear or shame. If the 'lunatic' or 'idiot' were from a well-to-do family the sooner the matter could be hushed up the better. Secrecy surrounded his condition. If he were a pauper lunatic he would most likely be found in a workhouse, or, if he had been violent, in a gaol or house of correction. He might be unfortunate enough to be an object of entertainment and ridicule in the Bethlem hospital. Compassion played little part in the attitude to these unfortunate people in the 18th century, while any effective advance in scientific knowledge of causes and treatment had to wait till the 20th century.

The 19th century saw the development of a measure of public responsibility in several fields of social welfare: factory reform, education, public health, lunacy reform, were all part of the same urge to remedy newly discovered abuses, or to remove newly recognised dangers to public safety, motives which were inextricably linked with a stirring of the public conscience on behalf of the unfortunate and the helpless. It is significant that the same reformers often took an active part in more than one sphere. Lord Shaftesbury is an outstanding example.[1] Only a minority of the public had any concern with such matters as lunacy reform, but the ardour of the pioneers kept the issues alive. Select Committees might make inconclusive reports, legislation might be ineffective when it eventually reached the statute book, but the cumulative effect of successive attempts was such that the public was eventually made aware of the issues. The publicity given to a few scandalous cases no doubt helped. A more lasting and effective method was the practice of forming small groups of interested people who might in time form a local or national society. They would keep in touch with Members of Parliament,

[1] See Part I, pp. 9–10.

and be ready to supply information on practical issues: they might also, if need be, act as a pressure group.[1] The result of these many influences in the 19th century was the establishment of Lunacy Law which is still the foundation of procedure in the mid-20th century.

It is possible to look upon the 18th and 19th centuries in England as a period of considerable progress in the care and treatment of the insane.[2] It may be true in relation to the barren years which went before. Looking back, however, from the mid-20th century, lunacy reform seems rather to have proceeded by slow and laborious stages, and to have achieved success in a strictly limited field. Legislation had gone little beyond safeguarding members of the public from wrongful custody in a lunatic asylum, protecting them from the more dangerous patient and improving the organisation and administration of the asylums. Some measure of progress had been made in the care of those certified and detained for institutional treatment, but medical psychology and clinical practice had made little advance in this country by the end of the 19th century.

The greatest obstacle to the development of social policy on mental health in the 20th century was the state of the law relating to the insane—that is, those who were mentally ill—and the mentally defective—that is, those who had never reached full mental development. Three aspects of legislation inherited from a past which had little knowledge of causes and little understanding of treatment, made progress difficult: these were the legal confusion between lunacy and idiocy, the unfortunate association with the Poor Law and the emphasis placed on certification and custody.[3]

---

[1] Many administrative reforms of the 19th and 20th centuries owed their origin to such methods.

[2] This is the theme of K. Jones' *Lunacy, Law and Conscience*.

[3] The first two were gradually broken down in the first half of the 20th century. The question of certification is still a problem, although the Mental Treatment Act, 1930, has allowed for the reception of voluntary and temporary patients. There were no clear powers and duties on behalf of the mentally defective until 1913. As late as 1929, the Wood Committee was reporting that many mental defectives were still being certified under the Lunacy Acts, and never transferred to the care of the Mental Deficiency Authorities. The Poor Law Guardians, meanwhile, had the power, but not a duty, to report defectives in their care to the M.D. Authorities. (See Joint Committee of the Board of Education and the Board of Control, *Report*, 1929.)

VII

FIRST PHASE IN THE DEVELOPMENT OF SOCIAL POLICY

TREATMENT OF 'LUNATICS' AND 'IDIOTS': OUTLINE OF STATUTORY INTERVENTION

IN spite of a series of Select Committees, the 18th century had achieved little more than the closing of Bedlam as a place of entertainment in 1770, and an ineffective measure for the inspection of madhouses, in 1774. 'Pauper lunatics' could be sent to the workhouse under the Poor Law, others might be sent to the gaols or houses of correction under the Vagrancy Acts,[1] while 'single lunatics', perhaps in the worst case, were often lost sight of altogether, since secrecy was the essence of their confinement. Custody and restraint were the time-honoured methods of dealing with the insane, whether in private asylum or public institution.[2] Those in charge of these unfortunate people had legal sanction for the practice of chaining their victims if they were considered to be 'dangerous lunatics'.[3] No special arrangements were made for the mentally defective. If they were harmless they might be left alone. If they became paupers they, like pauper lunatics, might be sent to the workhouse, there to do whatever tasks the Master could set them to.[4]

---

[1] Amendment of the Vagrancy Law did little more than secure for the insane the safeguard of requiring apprehension by two J.P.'s instead of the one required for rogues and vagabonds. The main purpose of the Act was to protect the public from all who were dangerous to the community whether by 'disorder of the senses' or otherwise.

[2] That there was some distinction, however, is suggested by the evidence of Dr. Monro before the Select Committee. When asked about the use of chains and fetters for his private patients, he replied 'they are fit only for pauper lunatics; if a gentleman were put in irons he would not like it'. (The horror of this statement lies, of course, in its implications concerning the nature of 'a pauper' as something less than human.)

[3] By an Act of 1743, they might be 'safely locked up and put into chains'. See Webb, *English Local Government*.

[4] This practice continued throughout the 19th century and into the 20th. See Report of the Royal Commission on the Poor Laws, 1909, for instances of the continued mixing of defectives and others, including children.

THE MENTAL HEALTH SERVICES

It is no wonder that the *Committee of Enquiry* which reported in 1815[1] found much suffering and many abuses. For example, at Bethlem, a man was found to have been chained continuously for nine years, and those in charge justified this on the ground that he was violently homicidal. Yet, by the time he was discovered, in 1814, he was in the last stages of tuberculosis, 'so physically weak that he would have been unable to escape or harm others even had he so desired'. A workhouse at Liskeard was cited where two women were confined in low damp buildings, one of which had neither light nor air. Each woman was chained to the stone floor. Upon enquiry it was revealed that one was in custody because she was 'troublesome' . . . and 'continually roved about the country'. The Select Committee heard evidence, not only of inhuman treatment, but of financial peculations, and falsification of records. One of the most notorious examples was that at York, where it was noted that 11 deaths had been recorded at York Asylum, but other sources of information revealed that there had been 24 funerals. What had happened to the 13 unaccounted for was left to the imagination. Dr. Thurnam, writing later,[2] described some horrifying conditions: he asserted that not only were patients filthy and verminous, and herded together in cells, but that flogging and cudgelling were systematically resorted to.

The urgent need to safeguard the interests of patients largely accounts for the fact that 19th-century legislation was almost exclusively concerned with the removal of flagrant abuses, and with the improvement of administration and organisation of institutions, whether madhouses run for profit, asylums supported by public subscription or workhouses under the Poor Law. The emphasis on custody made it imperative, too, that procedure for the detention and protection of patients should be carefully regulated.

By a series of statutes from 1808 to 1845,[3] a measure of public responsibility was accepted. The period was chiefly remarkable for the fact that provision was made, for the first time from public funds, for the establishment of lunatic asylums: some nine counties provided asylums between 1808 and 1828. Nevertheless, pauper lunatics continued to stay in the workhouses in large numbers. Nearly fifty years later, in 1874, an attempt was made to induce Boards of Guardians to send them to certified asylums by an offer of 4*s*. towards the cost of

---

[1] 'Report from the Select Committee Appointed to Consider of Provision being made for the Better Regulation of Madhouses in England, 1814–15.' This committee was set up largely as a result of William Tuke's and his son's investigation of alleged facts about the York asylum and the new treatment at 'The Retreat'. See p. 91 below.
[2] Dr. Thurnam, *Statistics of Insanity*, 1845.
[3] In 1808 the first Act was passed giving power for the erection of County Asylums. In 1828 two Acts were passed: (i) An Act to amend the laws for the Erection and Regulation of County Lunatic Asylums, and more effectively to provide for the Care and Maintenance of Pauper and Criminal Lunatics in England; (ii) An Act 'to regulate the Care and Treatment of Insane Persons in England'.

THE DEVELOPMENT OF SOCIAL POLICY

each patient transferred. The new Acts were also important for the appointment of Commissioners in Lunacy. They at first moved cautiously, looking with some alarm at the new-fangled notions which would remove the customary restraints and perhaps jeopardise the safety of the community.[1] Amelioration of these conditions owes much to Lord Shaftesbury who took an active part in securing the passage of the famous acts of 1845.[2] Some further interest in the question was evinced when a Royal Commission was set up in 1855 to investigate conditions in the asylums of Scotland,[3] but it had little practical effect in England. Indeed, no further important statutory action was taken in the field of mental health in this country until the Idiots Act of 1886 and the Lunacy Act of 1890. The public was still dominated by anxiety for protection. Concern for the treatment of the insane and of the defective had not appreciably affected legislation, except from the medico-legal angle.

The purpose of the Idiots Act is set out in the preamble as 'Giving Facilities for the Care, Education and Training of Idiots and Imbeciles'.[4] One of its chief contributions was greater administrative simplicity whereby it was possible for the mentally defective to be separately dealt with. Local authorities might build special institutions for mental defectives, and a capitation grant might be given, as for pauper lunatics. However, the Act was permissive, and little was achieved. The Lunacy Act, 1890,[5] was a consolidating measure reflecting 19th-century developments in the prevention of ill-treatment and of illegal detention. Its provisions emphasised the legal aspect of insanity, a principle which was to prove something of a difficulty to those who were concerned with the medical aspects of mental ill-health in the 20th century. Unfortunately, the section[6] concerned with the mentally defective was largely inoperative, in spite of repeated pressure from the Commissioners in Lunacy. As late as 1907 we find Dr. Shuttleworth calling attention to the inadequacy of the statutory provision for idiots and imbeciles whether by County or Poor Law Authorities.[7] However, in spite of shortcomings,

[1] The subsequent history of the Commissioners who were succeeded by the Board of Control is a story of enlightened support and encouragement.
[2] Two Acts of 1845 provided for 'the Regulation of the Care and Treatment of Lunatics' and amended the laws for 'the Provision and Regulation of Lunatic Asylums for Counties and Boroughs and for the Maintenance and Care of Pauper Lunatics in England'. They provided, for the first time, a permanent Lunacy Commission.
[3] As a result, Scottish law enabled voluntary patients to be admitted from 1866 onwards. See p. 92 for reference to the influence of Dorothea Lynde Dix.
[4] See pp. 88, 99 and 100, below, for account of pioneer work by Duncan, and propaganda by the C.O.S., which led up to this legislation.
[5] The Lunacy Act, 1890, with certain amendments is still, in the mid-20th century, the principal Act, together with the Mental Treatment Act, 1930, and the National Health Service Act, 1946.
[6] Lunacy Act, 1890, Sec. 241.
[7] See C.O.S. Annual Register & Digest, 1907, p. ccxxix. He reported that the Metropolitan District Asylums numbered five with 6,591 patients who were imbeciles and harmless lunatics. Outside this area scarcely more than 600 were provided for by the Poor Law.

a century of effort had resulted in considerable advance in the institutional care of the insane. Provision was also made for the protection of single lunatics received for profit since they, too, were to be certified and visited. Above all, the 19th century had achieved its main goal, that of safeguarding the liberty of the subject.

Educable Feeble-minded Children

One further step in statutory intervention on behalf of the mentally defective in the 19th century should be noted. The Royal Commission on the Blind, the Deaf and the Dumb drew attention in the last decade to the needs of feeble-minded children.[1] There followed in 1899 the Elementary Education (Defective and Epileptic Children) Act, which for the first time gave power to school authorities to provide education either in special schools or special classes certified by the Education Department. There was also power to board children out or to provide guides or conveyance where necessary to enable defective children to attend school. Since these were permissive sections it is not surprising to find that few local authorities had made such provision by the end of the 19th century.

Early in the 20th century the new Local Education Authorities[2] were concentrating upon the great educational reforms on behalf of the abler children[3] or were 'attending in the first instance to the ordinary children',[4] although there was no conscious planning of priorities. Little consideration was given to the feeble-minded. Such few special schools as had been established were generally to be found in certain areas where there was 'a large industrial population and a high assessable value'.

Public disquiet was, however, sufficiently strong to warrant setting up a Royal Commission on the Care and Control of the Feeble Minded, in 1904. Their report four years later was a document of great social importance, and the conditions they found were widely reported. 'Of the gravity of the present state of things there is no doubt. The mass of facts that we have collected, the statements of our witnesses and our own personal visits and investigations compel the conclusion that there are numbers of mentally defective persons whose training is neglected, over whom no sufficient control is exercised and whose wayward and

---

[1] The terms of reference of the R.C. were widened to include other handicapped groups. The R.C. also suggested special provision for 'educable imbeciles' but this had to wait longer for fulfilment, see p. 125, below.

[2] These replaced the old School Boards under the 1902 Education Act.

[3] Secondary Education was established under permissive sections of the Education Act, 1902.

[4] *Report of the Royal Commission on the Care and Control of the Feeble Minded*, 1908, Part III, p. 88. The Royal Commission reported that less than half of the County Boroughs (31 out of 69) between 1899 and 1902 had adopted the Act of 1899, and scarcely any County Authorities. They were waiting 'to see how things develop'.

irresponsible lives are productive of crime and misery, of much injury and mischief to themselves and to others, and of much continuous expenditure wasteful to the community and to individual families.'[1]

The Commissioners enunciated several important principles: one, 'that persons who cannot take part in the struggle of life owing to mental defect ... should be afforded by the State such special protection as may be suited to their needs'; two, that 'the mental condition of these persons, and neither their poverty nor their crime, is the real ground of their claim for help from the State'; three, that 'the protection of the mentally defective person, whatever form it takes, should be continued so long as it is necessary for his good'; and four, that 'it is necessary to ascertain who they are and where they are, and to bring them into relation with the local authority'.

There is no doubt that the real obstacle to advance was the lack of knowledge of the incidence of mental defect. The Royal Commission estimated that some 4·6 per thousand of the population was defective, but there was no local machinery for collecting statistics. The Report shocked the public and gave valuable evidence to those who were agitating for statutory intervention.[2] In particular, the Commissioners had emphasised the social consequences, drawing attention to the relationship between mental defect and illegitimacy, and to the number of those committed to prison for drunkenness who were defective.[3]

The Commissioners also drew attention to the needs of higher grade, educable feeble-minded children. Comparatively few Education Authorities had adopted the Education Act, 1899, yet the Royal Commission showed conclusively that 'where special schools or classes have been established a distinct advance had been made, both in the study of the question and in a knowledge of the conditions and limitations under which education of any effectual kind is in their case possible'.[4] Worse still, there was no system for providing for the permanent needs of mentally defective children. Little could be done until statutory responsibility was accepted for all groups of the mentally defective who were in need of care, and the first step had to be the ascertainment of the extent of the need. The Royal Commission made valuable recommendations on these questions, many of which were later embodied in legislation.

[1] *Ibid.*, 1908, Vol. XI, p. 9 of Introduction.
[2] See p. 100, below.
[3] Their enquiries revealed that 'many mentally defective persons pass through prisons. Thus at Holloway Prison, out of 803 women there on 29th November, 1904, 83 were of that type, 41 of them chronic inebriates, 39 feeble-minded and 3 insane; and of 1,297 convicted prisoners received during that month, 56 were feeble-minded, suggesting that there is a constant procession of these feeble-minded persons, men and women, ... each in turn receiving a short or comparatively short sentence and then disappearing, sometimes only to return again'. (*Ibid.*, pp. 60–61.)
[4] *Ibid.*, p. 115.

THE MENTAL HEALTH SERVICES
Social Implications of Mental Deficiency

It was not until 1913, however, that the first Mental Deficiency Act was passed. The influence of the Royal Commission was evident in the official recognition of the social implications of mental deficiency. The Act made provision for the care of defectives who were found abandoned or cruelly treated, or guilty of a criminal offence, or who were habitual drunkards, or who were unmarried mothers in receipt of poor relief: that is, they were to be dealt with primarily as defectives, not as offenders, drunkards or paupers.[1] Provision was also made for defectives who were 'ineducable', either idiots or imbeciles at the instance of their parents or guardians, or children found by the local education authority to be incapable of benefiting from education in special schools. Finally, the L.E.A. had a duty to notify the mental deficiency authority if it was of the opinion that a child about to leave a special school would benefit from institutional treatment or guardianship.

Under the Act new administrative provisions were designed to make effective the statutory responsibilities of local authorities. The new machinery included the substitution of the Board of Control for the Commissioners in Lunacy, and the establishment of local committees, i.e. the mental deficiency committees of local authorities. The accent throughout, both in the role assigned to the statutory authorities and in the definition of defectives, was upon supervision, protection and control.

The general powers and duties of local authorities included ascertainment, supervision, the provision of institutional accommodation and guardianship. The definition of defectiveness followed to some extent that suggested by Dr. Duncan some fifty years earlier,[2] with a classification based on the extent of mental defect and the need for supervision and control. But in addition to the three grades, idiots, imbeciles and feebleminded persons, a fourth category was added, that of moral imbeciles, which was to raise more questions than it solved. The Act also required proof that mental defect had existed 'from birth or an early age', a requirement which was to cause serious difficulty until an amending Act was passed fourteen years later.[3]

The relationship between mental deficiency authorities and education authorities was far from satisfactory.[4] The recommendation of the Royal

[1] See Mental Deficiency Act, 1913, Section 21.
[2] See p. 99, below.
[3] The Mental Deficiency Act, 1927, substituted 'before the age of eighteen years' for 'from birth or an early age'.
[4] The Royal Commission had recommended in 1908 that the Mental Deficiency Authority should be made responsible for all mentally defective children, including those in special schools. The 1913 Mental Deficiency Act, however, continued the arrangement begun under the 1899 Education Act, whereby school authorities (now Local Education Authorities) were responsible for feeble-minded children in special schools. The plight of children for whom no special education was available, particularly the failure of after-care, was a problem to which voluntary organisations drew continual attention.

Commission that all mental defectives should be the responsibility of one authority was not accepted. The Local Education Authority was made responsible for ascertaining which children between seven and sixteen were defective, while the Poor Law Authority retained their powers and duties in respect of those defectives who were in receipt of poor relief. Subsequent history was to show that divided responsibility left a gap through which many children who needed after-care were to fall. Before we leave this brief summary it should be noted that the Act not only defined circumstances rendering defectives 'subject to be dealt with'[1] but gave powers to local authorities on behalf of those defectives who were outside this category. This was important since it gave opportunities to evoke statutory aid before disaster had overtaken the defective, and it was in this sphere that voluntary co-operation was to prove valuable.[2]

The first Mental Deficiency Act fell short of what many would have desired,[3] but it imposed important duties, and gave new powers to mental deficiency authorities which might have made possible considerable progress both by statutory and voluntary effort. Unhappily it came into operation in the year of the outbreak of the First World War when no central authority had the time or the inclination to urge hard-pressed local authorities to initiate new schemes.

Meanwhile, the Lunacy Act, 1890, remained the principal Act regulating the statutory procedure for the insane, and no legislation of importance dealing with the treatment of the mentally ill was passed until 1930.[4] But this belongs to the second phase of development and will be considered later.

---

[1] These were mainly those where disaster had already occurred: such as defectives who were abandoned, or cruelly treated, etc.
[2] Local Mental Deficiency Authorities may 'if they think fit' maintain, etc., Section 30 (e). See also Section 48 for Treasury Contributions towards expenses of societies assisting defectives.
[3] Dr. Rayner called attention to the failure to deal adequately with the first five years of life, 'the most important period in the life of a defective'... the young defective was often given narcotics, etc., to keep him quiet, see C. R. & D., 1914.
[4] The Mental Treatment Act, 1930. See p. 113, below.

VIII

PRIVATE ENTERPRISE: PIONEER WORK FOR THE INSANE

RESIDENTIAL CARE: THE BETHLEM HOSPITAL AND THE RETREAT

UNTIL the 20th century English doctors seem to have taken little interest in the development of medico-psychological theories, and few were concerned with the nature of mental illness.[1] Changes in attitude towards mental disorder, and consequent changes in the treatment of mental patients, came slowly and intermittently in this country in the 18th and 19th centuries. Although, as we have seen, publicity given to the findings of select committees, and the notoriety caused by certain scandals, roused sufficient interest from time to time to secure safeguards against gross ill-treatment, or unlawful custody, the main advance was dependent upon a few exceptionally enlightened medical officers and charitable laymen who attacked the abuses which they found in the institutional care of the insane. They proved by experiment that humane care was both practicable and beneficial: reform at this stage depended largely upon individual enterprise. The development of voluntary organisations was a feature of the late 19th and early 20th centuries. Their special contribution was to be community care, that is to say, care within the community as distinct from residential care in asylums and other institutions. This will be considered later.

The Bethlem Hospital, which had earned notoriety as 'Bedlam', had, in 1769, taken the first step to end some outstanding abuses by appointing 'an apothecary' as the first resident medical officer. He, together with the visiting physician who had been most critical of the old regime, was said to have 'introduced or inspired reforms which gave patients more tranquillity, privacy and medical attention'. How far short of modern methods such medical attention was, can be gathered from the publication by Dr. Crowther, surgeon of Bethlem and of Bridewell, of his

[1] See Zilboorg and Henry, *A History of Medical Psychology*.

PIONEER WORK FOR THE INSANE

Treatise: *Practical Remarks on Insanity*.[1] The use of mechanical restraints, and the reliance on purges, vomits and blood-letting to reduce violence, were upheld as time-honoured and effective methods. Dr. Crowther also believed in the cold bath and the 'circular swing', the latter a device in which the patient was rapidly rotated until he lost consciousness. Meanwhile John Howard[2] reported on treatment in France, where he had found the insane locked up with prisoners, both undergoing the same brutal regime. In England lunatics were hardly better off in some of the madhouses where custody under ill-paid attendants, selected largely for their physical strength, was the general practice. Nor was the life of those of the insane who were admitted to workhouses as paupers necessarily less horrible.

The attack on abuses in the treatment of lunatics was made on several fronts. Philanthropists, for the most part inspired by religious conviction, and doctors, seeking an enlightened approach to the question of treatment, both contributed to the new methods. Several pioneer ventures made in the late 18th century have persisted to this day. One of the most renowned in this country was that of William Tuke,[3] a merchant of York, and one of an influential group of Friends. Tuke, when attempting to enquire into the death of a Quaker woman in York asylum, discovered that visitors were not allowed at this subscription institution.[4] Allegations by ex-patients of ill-treatment could not be substantiated since they were ridiculed and vehemently denied by the officers in charge. The Friends decided that in order to see for themselves, a body of them would become substantial subscribers. As Governors they would have the right of entry, a right hitherto not exercised by the notable citizens who met on the governing body to receive the reports of their complacent medical officers. In systematic visitations individual Friends uncovered some terrible practices, but less than three weeks after the meeting at which they demanded a thorough investigation, a mysterious fire, started under most suspicious circumstances, destroyed part of the building and all incriminating records, and resulted in the death of some of the patients, the exact number remaining unknown. In spite of this setback the efforts of the Friends were eventually successful in focusing public attention on conditions in madhouses.[5]

Meanwhile, William Tuke and other Quakers founded 'The Retreat'

[1] Published later, in 1811. As K. Jones comments, 'Dr. Crowther seemed to be solely concerned with gaining ascendancy over his patients'. *Lunacy, Law and Conscience*, p. 93.

[2] In 1780 when he reported on his visits to European prisons.

[3] William Tuke, a Quaker of insight, sympathy and drive, was deeply concerned about the treatment of lunatics, and carried out several enquiries on their behalf. His son and grandson continued his work.

[4] It is a sad commentary that the York Asylum had been started as a charity for poor lunatics in 1772, with the support of a number of generous citizens, and the patronage of notable public men. The governors seem to have relied entirely on the reports of the officers in charge and never to have visited the patients.

[5] See p. 84n, above.

between 1792 and 1797.[1] Its unique contribution was the treatment of the inmates as patients, by medical officers and carefully selected attendants, in pleasant surroundings, and in an atmosphere of goodwill and understanding. This break with tradition proved an undoubted success and 'The Retreat' attracted visitors from home and abroad. It was long, however, before such methods became generally acceptable in this country. Considering the strong forces and the vested interests opposed to interference with the practices common in the treatment of lunatics and idiots, it is remarkable that the early reformers achieved so much. They persisted in spite of numerous setbacks: their ingenuity in discovering means of entrance, their perseverance and patience in collecting reliable evidence, their flouting of threats of prosecution for libel, their practical experiments in alternative methods of treatment, their willingness to spend both time and money in the pursuit of all these objects, command great respect. Though progress was slow, they had thrown out a challenge which could not be ignored: 'The Retreat' remained a permanent example of enlightened treatment, and its work played an important part in the gradual change of attitude as the 19th century advanced.

Pioneer work abroad also helped to break down traditional attitudes in this country. The association of religion and philanthropy was seen in the work of Dorothea Lynde Dix,[2] in America. While working in a Sunday School for female prisoners, she became convinced that public policy towards the insane poor must be revolutionised 'out of respect to Christianity and advancing civilisation'.[3] Not only did she found institutions, and revolutionise the treatment of the insane in America, but she studied conditions abroad, and had a direct influence upon reform in Great Britain. She was credited with being responsible for the appointment of a Royal Commission to enquire into the conditions of lunatic asylums in Scotland: in the words of Mr. Ellice, M.P., 'She came to London and put herself into communication with the Secretary of State for the Home Department ... and at her instance, and without any public movement on the subject, a Royal Commission was accepted'.[4] There is no doubt that the practical results of her untiring zeal had considerable interest for reformers, and gave an added stimulus to those who were seeking an enlightened policy in Great Britain.

[1] See the description of 'The Retreat' written by his grandson, S. Tuke, in 1813. His great-grandson, Daniel Hack Tuke, was a medical psychologist of some repute and the author of many contributions to mental science.
[2] A retired school teacher who began her work in 1841, achieved an outstanding success in America and acquired an international reputation. She stayed with the Tuke family in York while she was in this country.
[3] Zilboorg and Henry, *op. cit.*, p. 583.
[4] Quoted by Francis Tiffany, 'Life of Dorothea Lynde Dix', p. 239, from Parliamentary Debates, Vol. cxiv, p. 1025. See also the quotation from a debate in which Sir George Grey gave his approval but regretted that it was left to the initiative of 'a foreigner, and that foreigner a woman, and that woman a dissenter'.

PIONEER WORK FOR THE INSANE

Meanwhile, increasing attention was given to the question by doctors since Pinel in France had established an international reputation for his reforms in the treatment of mental patients. Although Pinel roused much opposition in his own country,[1] he was an inspiration to those doctors in England who were anxious to give further study to the question of mental alienation.[2] In the 1830's enlightened resident physicians in two of the largest county asylums were experimenting in the removal of mechanical restraints, emphasising the treatment rather than the custody of their patients.[3] Their practical experiments[4] were followed with cautious interest, further stimulated by Connolly's *Enquiry Concerning the Indications of Insanity, with Suggestions for the Better Protection and Care of the Insane*. The next few decades saw the gradual spread of knowledge of remedial measures, and the slow improvement of conditions in the asylums.[5] The Commissioners in Lunacy were watching the new method with increasing interest, now that their first fears for public safety had proved groundless.

COMMUNITY CARE OF THE INSANE: THE MENTAL AFTER-CARE ASSOCIATION (M.A.C.A.)

So far interest was concentrated upon treatment within the asylums, and little thought had been given to the needs of those who were discharged. It was the chaplain of Colney Hatch Asylum[6] who first called attention to this question in two papers published in the *Journal of Mental Science* in the 1870's. His two articles, 'A Plea for Convalescent Homes in connection with Asylums for the Insane Poor',[7] and 'After Care', roused widespread interest. One immediate result was the foundation in 1877 of a voluntary association, later to become the *Mental After-Care*

[1] In 1793 he worked on lines suggested by Daquin and others. On one occasion he was rescued by a patient from an infuriated mob who tried to hang him.
[2] A society, later to be known as *The Medico-Psychological Association* was founded to bring together doctors interested in mental alienation.
[3] Dr. Hill at Lincoln and Dr. Connolly at Hanwell.
[4] By 1839 all restraints were removed, and in 1844 Dr. Connolly was relating that five years' experience had convinced him of the universal efficiency of these methods.
[5] As Zilboorg and Henry have pointed out, the question of non-restraint continued to be a controversial issue for almost half a century, e.g. the publication of *The Theory and Practice of Non-Restraint in the Treatment of the Insane*, as late as 1878, by W. L. Lindsay, *op. cit.*, p. 415.
[6] The Rev. H. Hawkins. This asylum was later to become well-known as The Friern Hospital. The common sense and humanity of his suggestions, especially his enlightened approach to the problem of social adjustment, have a modern ring, far in advance of public opinion of his time, or of generations to follow. At one point he reminds his readers, 'Even apart from motives of Christian benevolence, considerations of economy might prevail with some'. In line with ideas of his own day he thought it right that his 'halfway houses' should be staffed entirely by unpaid workers including an honorary superintendent.
[7] This article was reprinted in 1885, to commemorate the anniversary of the establishment of After Care, as a special report of the Ladies' Committee. It is interesting to find Louisa Twining listed as a member (cf. p. 15n, above).

Association,[1] the first organisation to make provision for the community care of the mentally disordered. The origins and development of this society are of interest in throwing light on the methods by which a voluntary organisation felt its way towards an ever widening conception of its function, and as an illustration of an early attempt to form a statutory–voluntary partnership in a specific field of social welfare.

In spite of distinguished patronage[2] the Association began in a very small way. It undertook no large-scale publicity but depended entirely upon voluntary helpers and voluntary donations. Even at the turn of the century its total income had only just passed the £500 mark. But although the number of patients helped was necessarily small[3] the contribution made by this society towards a new understanding of the needs of the insane was valuable. It was the policy of the Association from its foundation to co-operate with any agency, whether statutory or voluntary, which could advance the cause of those who were mentally disordered. At first it was naturally concerned with the poor,[4] and its reports were couched in terms familiar to Victorian readers who might be moved, by compassionate appeals, to send gifts. But though the form of its appeals was conditioned by the age, its outlook was enlightened, and its creative enthusiasm led to a continual extension of its boundaries.

The first purpose of the Association was to offer help to the patient by forming a bridge between the asylum and active life in the community. For this reason the foundation of convalescent homes was an essential part of its work. It was particularly important for those who had no relatives willing to look after them. The only alternative, in most cases, was the workhouse. The Association found it necessary in 1886 to appoint a paid secretary, but it depended on its unpaid 'working associates' for its personal work such as the boarding-out of patients, placing them in employment or helping them to readjust themselves to their families. We find them getting into touch with various societies, e.g. that for *the Welfare of Women and Girls in England and Wales*, inviting them to appoint an Associate so that immediate help could be given. It was also in close touch with some of the Boards of Guardians. By 1890, several Boards had become subscribers or donors,

---

[1] Its first title, typically Victorian, was 'The After-Care Association for the Female and Friendless Convalescent on leaving Asylums for the Insane'. In 1891 'friendless' was dropped, in 1892 'female' disappeared, and 1894 saw a new title altogether which became in 1914 'The Mental After-Care Association for Poor Persons convalescent or recovered'. Finally, in 1940 the first four words were retained without the descriptive embellishment—M.A.C.A.

[2] Lord Shaftesbury was closely concerned in the new venture and became the Association's president from 1880–86, while the Archbishop of Canterbury and Cardinal Manning became vice-presidents.

[3] The number of patients helped annually rose from 41 in 1887 to 195 in 1900. See Table I.

[4] The attitude of this voluntary agency can be summed up in its own words: 'Members of the Association believe that much mutual good may be arrived at by co-operation between public and private bodies whose work is to benefit the poor.'

e.g. Wandsworth, St. Pancras and Chelsea. In return, the Association looked after patients who had recovered but were chargeable, and needed help until work could be found for them. The increase in its work of placement led in 1895 to the appointment of another paid worker, the first to give special help in this field.

By this time several County Asylums were seeking the Association's help, and Asylum 'Visitors' now appear on the subscribers' lists. But the Association was not satisfied that it was reaching 'all those who were likely to be benefited'. It made the novel suggestion that Poor Law Guardians and Medical Superintendents should give 'advance information' on those who were due for discharge from asylums. By 1909 the Association was reporting that it regarded finding suitable employment as one of its most important functions. It was the germ of the modern conception of rehabilitation although the importance of paid employment as part of the total cure of the patient was not yet fully appreciated. Certainly, most Poor Law Guardians and Medical Superintendents of Asylums were not yet ready to advance so far.[1] When official support was given, the main emphasis at the end of the 19th century, and early in the 20th, was on the need to prevent transference to the workhouse, and on the economic advantages of turning out self-supporting citizens, whereas the Association was concerned with a convalescent patient who needed help in the difficult transition period between the regime of an institution, and life in the community.

The propaganda of this small society was very gentle, and its work in community care proceeded patiently and slowly in the early years of the 20th century.[2] Its annual income was only gradually climbing towards the £1,000 mark. By this time the Commissioners in Lunacy were taking an active interest in the Association's experimental work.[3] It was, in fact, on the suggestion of one of them, Dr. Hubert Bond, that the Association decided on a new venture. In 1913 it offered assistance to patients 'on trial', so that a probationary period would give an opportunity of testing whether or not they were fit to be recommended for discharge.

1913, the end of the pre-war era, is a good point at which to review the special contribution of this voluntary society. It had shown the possibilities of community care: the essence of its work was personal help to meet the needs of individual patients within the community. It recognised that one of the greatest difficulties for a discharged patient was his adjustment to the outside world. His relation to his family was of special importance and must be prepared for. Lack of understanding and fear on the part of the patient's family and neighbours made for a friendless or even hostile reception. Preliminary visiting of relatives of the patient

---

[1] The Society was reporting in 1905 that the importance of finding work for patients on discharge was not always appreciated by the asylums.
[2] See Table I, pp. 96–97.
[3] An Honorary Commissioner in Lunacy became one of their vice-presidents.

became a normal part of procedure. The Association thus pointed the way to a change in social attitude towards mental illness; it aimed at the conversion of fear of a returned lunatic to the acceptance of a convalescent patient. The boarding-out of patients in convalescent homes, or in cottage homes in the country, was a practical first step towards rehabilitation. Finding suitable work followed quickly after. Another characteristic of the Association was its eagerness to co-operate with any private or public body willing to help. At the same time it sought to work closely with medical officers,[1] persevering in spite of occasional rebuffs from the unconvinced. Its small financial resources and its dependence for the most part on voluntary help limited its scope,[2] but it was ever on the watch for opportunities to try out new ways of helping the mentally disordered. The First World War made some further demands upon its resources, and by 1916 the number assisted began to show an appreciable increase, though no great expansion could be attempted. The following table brings out the small but steady advance up to 1915, and the rise in the war years. It also shows the gradual increase in the number of men helped, though women patients always predominated.

TABLE I

Number of Cases (Mental Illness) who 'were dealt with' by M.A.C.A., 1887–1918*

Year	Male	Female	Total
1887		41	41
1888		50	50
1889		56	56
1890		65	65
1891		73	73
1892 ⎫	'several'	?	138
1893 ⎭			(2 years)
1894	18	100	118
1895	22	99	121
1896	29	106	135
1897	42	105	147
1898	55	131	186
1899	77	145	222
1900	63	132	195
1901	75	139	214
1902	72	149	221
1903	95	155	250
1904	87	168	255
1905	112	176	288
1906	124	184	308
1907	140	208	348

[1] It was 1921 before we have the first reference to the use of the Mental After-Care Association in getting home histories *before* the discharge of a patient.
[2] Although a Birmingham branch was founded in 1912, and various local secretaries acted for the central association elsewhere, visiting was difficult to organise except in London.

TABLE I—*contd.*

Year	Male	Female	Total
1908	140	248	388
1909	109	239	348
1910	147	232	379
1911	178	221	339
1912	141	250	391
1913	149	228	377
1914	148	225	373
1915	109	270	379
1916	131	377	508
1917	196	424	620
1918	218	452	670

* Tables compiled mainly from information in the annual reports of the M.A.C.A.

Psychological Medicine and Preventive Treatment

Medical interest had been centred mainly on institutional treatment and after care so that patients might be helped towards convalescence and full recovery. A new approach was made when attention was focused on the need for preventive measures. This was dependent upon professional skill and the advance of psychological medicine.[1]

Clinical studies of early mental disorders had been carried out in Germany in the last quarter of the 19th century, In this country pioneer work in early treatment and prevention was done in several of the large voluntary hospitals, such as St. Thomas', in 1889, and some further development took place in the first decade of the 20th century. But the real impetus came from experience gained during the First World War in the treatment of civilians and 'shell-shocked' service men. Studies in the psycho-neuroses led to the establishment of special departments of psychiatry or psychological medicine, and a number of out-patient departments were established by voluntary general hospitals. These developments were to have an important influence on public opinion in the inter-war years.[2] Patients were more ready to accept a service provided as part of general medicine. There was no stigma attached to treatment for 'nerves'.

The same could not be said for those sent to public asylums, reserved for those suffering from the more serious forms of mental disorder. Certification, a necessary preliminary to treatment in an asylum, added to the dread which patients and their relatives had of these institutions. As a result the services for psychotics and those for neurotics developed as separate branches of medicine, to the detriment of the mental health

---

[1] See Zilboorg and Henry, *op. cit.*, for a full account of the history of Medical Psychology.
[2] The foundation of the *Tavistock Clinic* in 1926 gave further opportunities for study and special treatment. It played an important part in various training schemes and in research.

THE MENTAL HEALTH SERVICES

service as a whole.[1] There was, however, an important exception, an exception which illustrates a venture in co-operation where scientific interest, philanthropy, and the initiative of an enlightened statutory authority were combined. This experiment in the development of preventive measures was made possible by Dr. Maudsley when in 1907[2] he made a donation of £30,000, increased later by a bequest of £10,000, towards the foundation of a special hospital for early treatment of recoverable mental disorder. The hospital was also to be a centre for teaching and research. The L.C.C. welcomed the opportunity to co-operate, but it had to secure a local Act, in 1915, before it could have the necessary powers to make provision for voluntary patients.

Although the outbreak of war meant the postponement of the comprehensive purpose of the Maudsley Hospital,[3] the L.C.C. had laid the foundations upon which an experiment of great value could later be carried out. Nor were the years of war wasted, for the reception of service patients for the treatment of nervous diseases gave valuable opportunity for further study and experience. Meanwhile, the enlightened attitude of the L.C.C. was illustrated by its recognition of the preventive aspects of community care. It showed its appreciation of the personal work of M.A.C.A. in the re-establishment of the ex-patient, and, although it had, as yet, no power to give financial aid, it was ready to co-operate in the administration of a small charity for which it was responsible.[4] M.A.C.A. had its first conference with the L.C.C. Asylums Board in 1915, and was asked in the same year to visit individual patients who might be in need of a grant from Queen Adelaide's Fund. Thus began a fruitful partnership which was to last for some forty years, a bond which was considerably strengthened in the inter-war years when public money became available for grant-aid to voluntary organisations.

[1] See C. P. Blacker, *Neurosis and the Mental Health Services* for a discussion of this question.
[2] See 10th Annual Report of Board of Control, Appendix B for an interesting account of Maudsley Hospital.
[3] The hospital was lent immediately to the War Office and then to the Ministry of Pensions for the treatment of nervous diseases arising from the war. It was opened by the Minister of Health in 1923 to fulfil the function for which it was originally intended.
[4] Queen Adelaide's Fund administered by the L.C.C.

IX

PRIVATE ENTERPRISE (Continued): PIONEER WORK FOR THE MENTALLY DEFECTIVE

WE now recognise that the term 'mental defect' is so wide as to include idiots and imbeciles at one end of the scale, and higher-grade feeble-minded persons at the other who shade off into the 'backward' amongst the normal grouping. Yet mental defectives have this in common: that they need some measure of supervision and control both for their own wellbeing and for the welfare of the community. From the point of view of society it is their social inefficiency which creates the problem of care.

For many years, in this country, there was little or no recognition of the various needs of different grades of defectives, and they were commonly referred to, indiscriminately, as idiots. It followed that, in spite of the work of Itard and his pupil Séguin, in France, and of other pioneers in Germany and Switzerland,[1] little interest was shown, in England, in these early experiments in training. When the need for care was eventually realised, the first response was the provision of institutional accommodation. One of the earliest private ventures was the opening, in 1841, of a small establishment for imbecile children, by two sisters, the Misses White of Bath.

A more widely famed experiment was made in Essex when Andrew Read founded a general institution for the care of idiots. With the help of charitable funds, centres[2] were established which later had permanent homes in Earlswood House, Highgate, and the Eastern Counties Asylum,[3] Colchester. These became renowned as pioneer establishments in the study of mental deficiency in this country. It was here that Dr. Duncan noted the wide range of defect, and the consequent differences in the possibilities of training. The first report of the Eastern Counties

[1] Séguin working in Paris in 1842, Saegert in Berlin and Guggenbuhl in Switzerland.
[2] E.g. at Park House, Highgate.
[3] Founded at Colchester in 1859.

Asylum, in 1860, had the distinction of suggesting a classification of defectives which has hardly been improved upon since.[1] In the second half of the 19th century further institutions were founded in the Western Counties, the Midlands and the Northern Counties.[2] They were charitable foundations, but all were willing to co-operate with the Poor Law Guardians in accepting paupers.[3] By the mid-19th century there was a growing interest in the question of mental defect, and we find a eugenist reporting to the *National Association for the Promotion of Social Science* on the deplorable lack of institutions for the care of idiots.[4] Few practical results followed, however, and many more years were to pass before the relation between mental deficiency and social inefficiency was brought forcibly to public notice.[5]

Voluntary Organisations and Propaganda: Influence on Social Policy

Some progress in voluntary action was made when, in 1875, the *Charity Organisation Society* took up the question and gave it publicity. This organisation was in a vigorous stage of its development, and it was to prove adept in its technique of propaganda in several fields of social service. It now set up a Committee to consider the special needs of idiots and lunatics, and, after carrying out an investigation and publishing its results, it organised a deputation to the central authorities concerned. Its report on the enquiry into 'The Education and Care of Idiots, Imbeciles and Harmless Lunatics' received considerable attention[6] and paved the way for the legislation which followed a few years later. Doctors were also taking an increasing interest in the question, and in 1890 the British Medical Association appointed its own committee of enquiry. In 1895 a further step in voluntary effort was taken when *The National Association for the Care of the Feeble-Minded*[7] was formed 'to collect and diffuse information, to suggest and initiate the formation of homes for the feeble-minded, and to make grants in aid of such homes'.[8]

[1] Dr. F. M. Duncan suggested the threefold categories: idiots, imbeciles and simpletons. The Mental Deficiency Act of 1913, slightly amended by that of 1927, in force to-day, substitutes the term feeble-minded for simpleton, and adds the somewhat doubtful category of moral defective.
[2] Starcross, Devon; Knowle, Birmingham; The Royal Albert, Lancaster.
[3] The Western Counties Asylum was in fact largely used by the Guardians who paid for the maintenance of the paupers. The other two accepted only a limited number. See *C. R. & D.*, 1906, article by Dr. Shuttleworth.
[4] Dr. Brodie's paper in 1860. See reference E. Cohen, *English Social Services*, p. 63.
[5] See Report of the Royal Commission on the Care and Control of the Feeble-Minded, 1908, and of the Mental Deficiency (Wood) Committee, 1929.
[6] The C.O.S. continued to report regularly on the question in its *Annual Charities Register and Digest*.
[7] The National Association for the Care of the Feeble-Minded later became the National Association for the Promotion of the Welfare of the Feeble-Minded.
[8] See the Objects of the National Association for the Care of the Feeble-Minded. *C. R. & D.*, 1895.

PIONEER WORK FOR THE MENTALLY DEFECTIVE

During the second half of the 19th century several local associations were also established. So far their main concern was to find a place in an institution for those who might otherwise drift into the workhouse or to prison. Nineteenth-century interest was mainly concentrated upon institutional accommodation, as it had been in the case of the insane.

But although physicians, eugenists and charitable agencies were making their various contributions to a better appreciation of the problems of mental deficiency, the public as a whole remained unresponsive. Such care and treatment as were given were still largely the concern of voluntary organisations, many of which had valuable assistance from honorary medical staff. It was the effort to arouse wider interest and to bring the whole matter forward as a question of social policy which led the *National Association for the Promotion of the Welfare of the Feeble-Minded* to combine with others to collect signatures for a petition which resulted in the appointment of a Royal Commission early in the 20th century. The National Association, meanwhile, worked effectively to keep up public interest by organising conferences, and by making a direct approach to members of Parliament. Its special function in the field was that of co-ordinator. In this role it was responsible for the formation of a Union of Homes.[1] It also tried to co-ordinate the various attempts being made to carry out the after-care of mentally defective children who were leaving school.[2]

In Lancashire and Cheshire a *Society for the Permanent Care of the Feeble-Minded* was working 'in cordial relationship with School Associations'.[3] The majority of the homes and of the branch societies affiliated to the National Association were giving training, and from some of them the children attended the local authorities' special schools, few though they were. Co-operation with the Boards of Guardians usually took the form of acceptance by the voluntary home of children paid for by the Guardians.[4] The special merit of the homes was their smallness, so that children could be given individual attention. Meanwhile the Poor Law Schools Committee was drawing attention to the needs of mentally defective children in the metropolitan poor law schools,[5] and charitable organisations were emphasising the need to extend provision to children who left special schools and needed continued care. 'In this, as in other ways, private charity must point the way for State action to follow.'[6] But State action was very slow to follow.

[1] By 1905 there were some 23 Homes in the whole country with a total number of 355 inmates; 14 Homes were affiliated to the National Association.
[2] I.e. the higher-grade feeble-minded children.
[3] E.g. in Manchester. See *C. R. & D.*, 1906, article by Miss P. D. Townsend.
[4] The Local Government Board sanctioned payment up to 12s. weekly for children sent to Homes of the National Association.
[5] See *C. R. & D.*, 1906, *op. cit.*
[6] Dr. Shuttleworth argued that charitable organisations had as much as they could do to maintain existing training institutions; when permanent institutional care was needed, its provision should be a public responsibility.

THE MENTAL HEALTH SERVICES

Although both the Royal Commission on the Feeble-Minded and the Royal Commission on the Poor Laws had emphasised the social evils resulting from failure to deal with the mentally defective,[1] and urged the need to give protection 'so long as it was necessary for his good', there were no immediate results. In 1910 the situation was summed up in the following words: 'Unfortunately ... reforms of this class, on which everyone is agreed, but which cost money and are not likely to affect votes, are extremely difficult to bring about.... A large proportion of the public still regard it as of quite minor importance.'[2] Two comments may be made on the lack of a social policy on the treatment of mental defectives; one, that the Government had been much engaged in the previous decade in developments in other fields of social service[3]; secondly, that there was in fact some considerable opposition to legislation, if only from a minority, for fear lest it might be used as a means of oppression; this became manifest when a Bill introduced in 1912 to deal with the mentally defective had to be withdrawn.[4] Interference with the liberty of the subject was still a strong plank in the political platform.

Meanwhile, those working in the community on behalf of the mentally defective were struggling to meet the many problems arising from the failure to provide after-care or from the lack of preventive measures. They pointed out that some 800 children were leaving special schools in London alone, yet it was no one's duty to follow-up and provide continued care. They pleaded too for some legal powers to detain children receiving institutional care who were found to need permanent care. The only colony for such defectives was that established by the Lancashire and Cheshire Society, and they had no legal powers to detain. They quoted from their experience to prove that children partly trained might be withdrawn and exploited by relatives.

COMMUNITY CARE OF THE MENTALLY DEFECTIVE

The 19th-century aim of the *National Association for the Care of the Feeble-Minded* had by now been extended: 'To promote the permanent

---

[1] 'We find, also, at large in the population, many mentally defective persons, adults, young persons and children, who are, some in one way, some in another, incapable of self-control and who are, therefore, exposed to constant moral danger to themselves, and become the source of lasting injury to the community.' (*Op. cit.*, Vol. XI, Introduction.)

[2] *C. R. & D.*, 1910, cccxxvi.

[3] Including the Education Act, 1902, legislation to provide meals for necessitous children and medical inspection of all elementary school children, the Old Age Pensions Act, Labour Exchanges Act, the Trade Boards Act, etc., and it was about to embark on a great new social service in the inauguration of health and unemployment insurance schemes.

[4] The C.O.S. pleaded with the opponents of the Bill to visit prisons, hospitals and workhouses to see the problem for themselves. *C. R. & D.*, 1913, 'Review of the Year'. The writer also added that opposition may also have been due to the widespread feeling that 'the whole community is in danger of rapidly becoming the slaves of the medical profession, and that it will soon be impossible to live or move or work or play without a medical certificate'.

PIONEER WORK FOR THE MENTALLY DEFECTIVE

care and control of the feeble-minded through After-Care Committees and Industrial Homes and Colonies; to strengthen local centres and unify the work by the creation of branches throughout the country and to collect statistics showing local needs; to further the movement by legislation and educational measures', etc.[1] After much propaganda, including letters to the press, deputations, and joint efforts by various groups interested in the feeble-minded,[2] Parliament at last showed itself ready to accept a Bill. The Mental Deficiency Act was passed in 1913.[3] In the same year a number of voluntary associations were founded to promote community care for the mentally defective. These included two which were particularly active, namely *the Brighton Guardianship Society* and the *Central Association for the Care of Mental Defectives*.[4] It is proposed to examine the development of the latter as an example of a 20th-century foundation which sought close co-operation with statutory and voluntary agencies, together with the promotion of a vigorous policy of experiment in community care. Its origins, aims and methods will be considered in some detail, as they throw light on the function of a voluntary society during a period when statutory intervention was officially accepted, but when public opinion was not sufficiently strong to press for action; a period when war and post-war difficulties absorbed much of the attention of administrators in the public services; yet a time of opportunity for voluntary organisations who were ready to devote their energy to a cause to which in their view, calamitous times gave urgency. Before doing so we may refer briefly to the work of some of the local associations with whom the Central Association was most eager to co-operate.

We have seen that the practice of forming local associations had already been established in the 19th century but that these voluntary agencies were mainly concerned with finding vacancies in institutions for those with anti-social tendencies, a logical outcome of the still prevailing emphasis on custody and protection. When training in special homes was available for some of the more educable, the agencies were ready to assist in the selection of candidates. Strong local associations with representatives of voluntary and statutory bodies were formed in certain areas such as Cambridge, Yorkshire and the West of England where new ideas were finding acceptance. Two interesting local experiments made in 1909 were the establishment of occupation centres[5] to

[1] By the year 1911–12 the income of the Society had reached £5,000 of which about half was from payments for patients in the various homes, the other half being mainly charitable contributions; a small proportion, £357, was accounted for as 'earnings'.
[2] They formed themselves into 'The Joint Committee for the Passing of the Mental Deficiency Bill'.
[3] For the provisions of this Act, see pp. 88–89, above.
[4] Later, 1921, to become the Central Association for Mental Welfare; (referred to as the C.A.M.W.). A number of local associations were also formed, e.g. in Oxford City—see the *Mental Health Services, Oxford, etc.* by Dame E. F. Pinsent, 1937.
[5] One in London and one in Brighton.

which low-grade but educable feeble-minded children might come daily from their own homes. They were valuable contributions towards the training of defective children who were too low-grade to receive education in special schools: children who needed almost constant supervision and control. Training was given through simple activities where habits of cleanliness and obedience could be learned. The mid-day meal was to be included as an important part of social training; co-ordination and control were learned through handwork, while singing and simple games helped the defective child to share activities with others. The encouragement of co-operation from the parents was not the least of the aims of the occupation centres. Yet the great value of the centres, both in helping the defective child to enjoy such activities as he was capable of, and in easing the strain on the mother, were recognised only by the few. Nevertheless, the pioneer venture of 1909 gave valuable experience for the future development of occupation centres in a number of large towns.

Reference has been made earlier to a few of the larger towns which had after-care committees. These brought together members of school authorities who had special schools or classes, and the voluntary workers who were prepared to visit school leavers' homes and give continued care. It should be remembered that no system of ascertainment was yet in existence. The incidence of mental defect was still a matter of estimates[1] and guesswork. The collection of statistics came to be an accepted responsibility of the voluntary societies concerned with the welfare of defectives. The formation of local Health Societies in some of the larger towns was also a useful means of ascertainment since they were extending their general supervision of children beyond the first year of life, sometimes even up to five years of age. They could enable more cases of mental defect to be discovered and reported[2] and could form an important link with the Maternity and Child Welfare Movement.

Beginnings of a Three-fold Partnership: Work of the Central Association for the Care of the Mentally Defective (later the C.A.M.W.[3])

The Board of Control which replaced the old Commissioners in Lunacy[4] showed a close interest in the work of voluntary organisations. The Board, indeed, included amongst its permanent members men who had practical experience with voluntary societies,[5] and it is not

[1] See the Report of the Royal Commission, p. 87, above.
[2] See *C.R. & D.*, 1916.
[3] The initials C.A.M.W. will be used for the sake of simplicity although the name of the Association was not in fact changed to that of Central Association for Mental Welfare until 1921.
[4] Under the Mental Deficiency Act, 1913.
[5] Of the paid commissioners originally appointed, one was the originator and Hon. Secretary of the Lancashire and Cheshire Society for the Permanent Care of the Feeble-Minded, and another was the founder and manager of the Sandlebridge Schools and Colony.

PIONEER WORK FOR THE MENTALLY DEFECTIVE

surprising to find that the foundation of the new national voluntary organisation was the direct result of a suggestion by the Chairman of the Board—that representatives of all the societies, organisations, homes and institutions, whether voluntary or statutory, concerned with mental defectives should be called in conference. The National Association for the Care of the Feeble-Minded responded with enthusiasm, and in 1913, the *Central Association for the Care of the Mentally Defective* was formed, representing both statutory and voluntary agencies from its very foundation. This venture in co-operation between the central and local authorities and the voluntary agencies is of general interest in the light of the development of the voluntary–statutory partnership in the social services of the 20th century, and is worthy of some detailed study.

Before we go on, however, to consider questions of administration special mention should be made of the influence of social pioneers in a relatively unknown field. By great good fortune the new association had not only Mr. Leslie Scott, K.C., as chairman, but Miss Evelyn Fox as Honorary Secretary. Mr. Scott, later a Lord Justice of Appeal, combined a distinguished professional life with active work for voluntary societies.[1] The C.A.M.W. owed much to his chairmanship from the foundation of the association in 1914 to its amalgamation in 1946: Miss Fox, later Dame Evelyn, devoted much of her long and vigorous life to the cause of the mentally handicapped, and she served the C.A.M.W. with energy and wisdom.[2] There is no doubt that the resilience of the association and the good relations with statutory bodies owed much to her outstanding qualities. Her training, first as an Oxford graduate, then as a student of social work, led her to demand high standards from her colleagues, and to insist on the value of the accurate marshalling of facts and careful preparation of arguments. Her humanity and insight, combined with initiative and drive, led to valuable experiments in community care at a time when philanthropists were mainly concerned with institutional treatment. Like pioneers in other fields, she looked to see what advance had been made abroad, and travelled extensively to study experiments in mental health in America and Europe. Those who came into contact with her were convinced that it was largely through her inspiring work and breadth of vision that the C.A.M.W. was able to continue and extend its work in the face of repeated setbacks.

The first executive council of the C.A.M.W. included members of Local Authority Associations, of Poor Law Unions, of Asylum Boards, of Institutions and of a number of individual Corporations and

---

[1] Lord Justice Scott devoted much of his later life to the interest of the countryside.
[2] Dame Evelyn was also connected with other voluntary societies concerned with mental health, and served as a co-opted member of the mental deficiency and health committees of the L.C.C.

An appreciation of Dame Evelyn is to be found in an article in *Social Service*, Spring, 1955, and offprints of this article have been prepared by the N.A.M.H. who have opened a memorial fund.

THE MENTAL HEALTH SERVICES

After-Care Committees of large towns,[1] while voluntary societies were also strongly represented. It is interesting to note that local education committees were given separate representation, since education was to be a valuable feature of the new association's work. In fact, one of the Central Association's first acts was to set up an education committee which was representative of local authorities and voluntary societies working for the education of the mentally defective.[2]

The Association drew up a wide programme in its original constitution,[3] and this was faithfully followed in the subsequent development of its work. Some comment on its avowed objects is called for if we are to appreciate the range of its work. The general aim of the Association was 'to forward the efficiency of voluntary work for mental defectives in England and Wales', and 'to render assistance directly or indirectly to public authorities'. Its usual method was to work through local associations whenever possible, but, where necessary, to make direct provision through its own central organisation. In either case, the immediate co-operation of the local statutory mental deficiency authority was sought, and the resources of the Association were offered.

Efficient administration was another of the objects of the Society, and we find the Central Association building up a valuable system of recording. In the first year of its work, some twenty-three local associations sent in returns to the parent body showing in detail their co-operation with the mental deficiency authorities, local education authorities, Boards of Guardians, societies and homes and private individuals, in the care of the mentally defective. They also reported upon the purpose of the applications, and the method of dealing with requests for help. In all, over 5,000 cases were dealt with by local associations in the year 1915. The Central Association itself was asked to help directly with some 300. These were often requests for help in particularly difficult cases where private individuals, institutions or statutory bodies had been unable to find a solution. Not only did the Central Association keep records of the work of local associations, but it also recorded the names of mental defectives moving from one area to another, and of institutions, etc. who were dealing with them.

The Association next set itself the task of developing the work for the community care of the mentally defective in poorly-served areas. Propaganda was an important part of its policy, and it tried to stimulate

[1] Including the after-care committees of Birmingham, Bradford, Leicester, London, Liverpool and Bristol. The Council regretted that the Association of Municipal Corporations had not responded to the invitation to send five members, though individual Corporations were welcomed.

[2] It included members of education committees from Worcester, Lancashire and Northants, Bristol and Liverpool; a superintendent of L.C.C. special schools, the President and the Hon. Secretary of the National Special Schools Union and a representative of Furzedown Training College.

[3] See the ten objects set out in the first annual report of the Central Association, 1914–15.

interest by the organisation of conferences, by press reports of its work, and by the issue of various publications. But an even stronger and more lasting method was the formation of new local associations. These were required to follow the practice of the existing associations in making partnership with the statutory authorities the keystone of their policy; they must also aim at co-ordinating the work for the mental defectives in their area if they were to be accepted as members of the Central Association.

One of the most successful methods of the Central Association was the appointment of a travelling organiser as an adviser. Her special function was to help form local associations. The service was well advertised and requests for help generally brought the organiser for a two months' stay. If the local association was started with the recognition of the local mental deficiency authority, the Central Association paid all expenses of the organiser's work. That such voluntary action was appreciated in official quarters is instanced by the fact that in many cases the statutory committees took the initiative in forming local associations, sometimes with the help of the Central Association's organiser.[1] Whatever the method, the voluntary societies were encouraged to work closely with the statutory mental deficiency authority.

In addition to the Central Association's organising and propaganda activities, it was prepared to provide, or help others to provide, necessary places of safety or of observation, and to promote occupational opportunities. We shall see, when we examine its later work, that it made several important contributions in these spheres.

One of the most valuable services which voluntary organisations can perform is that of keeping watch upon legislation as it affects their particular interests. The C.A.M.W. was active in this field. The circumstances which influenced the passing of the first Mental Deficiency Act were also responsible for the foundation of the Society. It was natural, therefore, that C.A.M.W. should keep close observation on the working of the Act and that it should be ready, later, to suggest amendments based on its experience. In this role it sent a memorandum to the Ministry of Reconstruction on 'The Care of the Mentally Deficient after the War', and negotiated with the relevant central departments for the joint provision by local education authorities and mental deficiency authorities of institutions for all grades of mental defectives. Unfortunately, the times were unpropitious and the shortage in the provision of institutional accommodation, and the legal and other obstacles to co-ordinated effort by the two responsible committees of the local authority, held up adequate development of this service for more than a generation. The Association was also in close touch with the Board of Education during the passage of the 1918 Education Bill when it

[1] An increase in grant-aid from the Board of Control for the services of an organiser was first reported in 1915–16.

submitted a memorandum on the effect of the Bill on feeble-minded children. It also took an active part in negotiations for the improved status of teachers and other officers in certified institutions, which resulted in their eligibility for superannuation. It took up the question of the care of discharged soldiers who were mentally defective, with both the Ministry of Pensions and the Board of Control.

From this summary of the activities of the C.A.M.W. it will be seen that its programme was ambitious. Yet, in the first phase of its existence, its resources were few,[1] and it found itself in the midst of severe crises almost at the outset of its work. It was the quantity rather than the quality of the work of the C.A.M.W. that was most affected by such serious emergencies as the outbreak of the First World War, and a succession of severe economic depressions. The Association had need of all the driving force and resilience at its command to struggle through the first few years of its existence. The outbreak of war in 1914 was followed by the postponement of many of the statutory services which should have been set up under the new Mental Deficiency Act. When the nation's resources were involved in a world war, it was not an opportune moment to arouse public interest in the welfare of the mentally defective. As subsequent history showed, few times were opportune. The Association had persistently to overcome the indifference of the general public. However, it was helped in its task by the strong support of the Board of Control, the Board of Education, and of a few progressive local authorities, and the foundations of a threefold partnership were well established in the first phase of development. A few examples[2] of the relationship of the Board of Control and the Board of Education with the national associations will show what motives helped to establish the statutory-voluntary partnership.

Examples of Co-operation between the Central Statutory and Voluntary Bodies: Influence of the First World War

The Board of Control watched the progress of the society it had sponsored with considerable pride. The Chairman of the Board, kept fully informed of the Association's work, wrote a warmly appreciative introduction to the first report[3], congratulating it in particular upon the representative character of its executive committee. The Board had weighty reasons for noting with gratification[4] the work of the voluntary associations for mental health, and for encouraging the extension of their schemes. The first of these was undoubtedly the limitations of

[1] Of the total income of £320 in the months 22.7.1914 to 31.3.1915, £300 appears as grants from the Board of Control of which £16 10s. was earmarked for local associations.
[2] Further examples will be found on p. 142, below.
[3] First Annual Report of the Central Association for the Care of Mental Defectives, 1914–15.
[4] See Second Annual Report, 1915, p. 42.

PIONEER WORK FOR THE MENTALLY DEFECTIVE

statutory action. As it was itself to point out in a later report,[1] the Board's statutory duties were largely concerned with institutional care, which was admittedly a very costly part of the service. Yet the Board took the view that 'this was one part only of a health service which included all aspects of mental hygiene'. There were special medical, social and educational problems associated with mental health, and the Board emphasised the point that community care both for the mentally defective and for mental patients was a valuable contribution for which the voluntary organisations deserved every encouragement.

No one reading the annual reports of the Board of Control can fail to be impressed by its thorough appreciation of the work of both the M.A.C.A. and the C.A.M.W.[2] It had special reason to welcome the work for the community care of defectives for, as we have seen, the Mental Deficiency Act came into force when a large-scale war broke on the country, resulting in the preoccupation of the local authorities with pressing emergency problems. They had little time to spare for the study of a new Act and the preparation of schemes for its implementation. Public interest in the welfare of the mentally defective, which had been temporarily aroused during the passage of the Bill, quickly subsided. At the same time, the heavy cost of the war entailed strict economy and the mental deficiency service was one of the first of the social services to be affected by Treasury restriction. In 1915 the Board of Control was reporting that local authorities had been advised that 'in present circumstances, it is not open to them to provide institutional accommodation for defectives'.[3] Such accommodation was to be reserved for cases of urgent need. For this reason, it was important that the most should be made of any voluntary efforts for community care which would relieve the pressure on institutional accommodation.[4] At this time the Board seemed to imply that guardianship was a necessary but less satisfactory alternative. Later it was to come out strongly in favour of guardianship as an additional form of care valuable in itself, so long as there was careful selection.

In community care, too, the Board welcomed voluntary aid to hard-pressed local authorities faced with new duties in war-time. The close relationship between the Board and the Central Association made for ready exchange of views, and each partner was prepared to consider suggestions for improvement of the service. It was at the suggestion of the C.A.M.W., in April 1916, that the Board sent a circular to all local authorities reminding them of their duty to ascertain who were 'defec-

[1] See Twenty-second Annual Report, 1935.
[2] At that time still known as the Central Association for the Care of Mental Defectives.
[3] This was given as the reason for the increasing use of guardianship by local authorities. See Fifth Annual Report, 1918, pp. 44 ff.
[4] There were, of course, one or two minor exceptions when arrangements could be made with existing institutions. Second Annual Report, 1915, p. 43.

THE MENTAL HEALTH SERVICES

tives subject to be dealt with', and to provide for their suitable supervision. The Board took the opportunity of pointing out that local authorities had power to delegate the work of supervision to voluntary associations.[1] In their annual report for that year, they called attention to the valuable assistance which was already being given by voluntary associations in the working of the Act, particularly in the supervision of defectives and the provision of suitable guardianship. In this connection, the Brighton Guardianship Society was cited, and a detailed account of their work in boarding-out the mentally and physically defective was included. The Board's active concern in this matter led them to discuss with the Society some reorganisation of procedure which would bring a more efficient working of their scheme.[2] The Board noted with gratification that the local authorities of Brighton and East Sussex had recognised the Society.

Another illustration is afforded by the Board's interest in training. After collecting information about various proposals for the establishment by local education authorities of training courses for teachers and attendants, the Board decided to ask the C.A.M.W. to prepare 'a simple and economical scheme'. This was done and the scheme was subsequently discussed, approved and recommended. The Board of Control also supported the voluntary associations in taking up the question of feeble-minded children who left ordinary elementary schools. They were concerned that these children entirely escaped notification. Even many of those leaving special schools failed to have any after-care, since notification was limited to those who were thought to need either institutional care or guardianship. It was the Board which suggested the need for amendment of the Act so that children who needed only supervision might be included in schemes of notification.[3]

The immediate post-war difficulties, however, postponed legislative action, and the Board looked to the voluntary associations to supplement the work of local mental deficiency authorities through the lean years to follow. It also relied largely upon voluntary associations to promote ascertainment. Complete ascertainment was still not within the powers of the local authorities since the mentally defective within poor law institutions were not the responsibility of the mental deficiency authority.[4] But the limitations imposed by legislation and by economic stress upon local authorities were not the only obstacles recognised by the Board of Control. The fault lay in the indifference of many authorities to their responsibilities under the Mental Deficiency Act. The Board noted that some of them by 1917 were not even proceeding with

[1] Third Annual Report, p. 33.
[2] It is interesting to note the practical suggestions for careful selection of suitable homes and of suitable cases for boarding-out, etc.
[3] See Fourth Annual Report, Board of Control, 1917, pp. 4–5.
[4] This was not remedied until the passing of the Local Government Act of 1929 when local authorities were given power of 'appropriation'.

PIONEER WORK FOR THE MENTALLY DEFECTIVE

preparatory measures such as ascertainment and registration 'which do not', the Board adds, 'entail large expenditure', and they did all they could to invigorate the mental deficiency authorities. It was largely for this reason that they welcomed the pioneer work of voluntary organisations in backward areas.

Meanwhile, the Board of Education had been quick to appreciate the opportunities for training teachers who had charge of feeble-minded children. The short courses offered by a national association which was in touch with experienced workers in local areas were the only means then available. It was ready to give official support to the short course organised by the C.A.M.W.[1] Several local education authorities participated by paying either the expenses or the fees of their students, while individual institutions and an Asylums Board also sent a few students. His Majesty's Inspectors reported very favourably on the courses and recommended their continuance. So began a very fruitful field of co-operation in a venture which continued throughout the first half of the century.[2]

These few examples of active co-operation between statutory and voluntary bodies illustrate the mutual benefit derived from so close a partnership. The Board of Control, which was directly responsible to Parliament for the mental deficiency service, was working under statutory limitations, and had little power to give tangible aid in the first phase of development. But much was done by encouragement and interest. The Board was able to make suggestions, to help raise standards, and to commend the work of the voluntary organisations to the local mental deficiency authorities. When further grant-aid became possible it was ready to support the voluntary organisations and to strengthen the partnership already built up in the first stage of development.

Meanwhile it was left largely to the few and widely-scattered local mental welfare societies to do what they could to help in the supervision and after-care of boys and girls in their area. The full extent of the problem, and the social cost involved, remained unknown, although the findings of the Royal Commission had left no doubt of their reality.

[1] The first course was held in Birmingham in 1915.
[2] After the first successful effort, the courses inevitably suffered from wartime curtailment, but a few local authorities sent teachers who were responsible for mentally defective children, while some officers of mental deficiency authorities were amongst the students. Before the end of the 1914–18 war, the C.A.M.W. had prepared a new scheme of training suitable for teachers of all classes of defectives.

X

EXPANSION BETWEEN THE TWO WORLD WARS

I. OUTLINE OF SOCIAL POLICY

Reforms in the Treatment of Mental Patients

THE war had to some extent quickened public interest in the service for those suffering from mental illness,[1] as experience was gained in the treatment of 'shell-shocked' and other service patients. But statutory action was still limited in this field. The Lunacy Act, 1890, remained the principal legislation for more than a generation after the First World War.

The mental hospitals provided by local authorities were still precluded from developing out-patients' departments where early diagnosis and treatment could have prevented more serious disorders.[2] Nor could public money be used to collaborate in research.[3] There was still no legal sanction for after-care, and hospitals were often dependent upon small charitable funds for any assistance they might give. Voluntary hospitals sometimes offered out-patient service in co-operation with a public mental hospital, but no other public hospital yet had the facilities granted to the L.C.C. Maudsley Hospital.[4]

Two reports in the post-war decade drew attention to the need for reform in the treatment of mental patients. Both the Committee on the Administration of Public Mental Hospitals,[5] which reported in 1922,

[1] By this time mental illness was a term more acceptable than lunacy.
[2] The complexity of the Lunacy Act, 1890, in fact hindered effectual early treatment; see description of this in the Report of the Feversham Committee, *The Voluntary Mental Health Services*, 1939.
[3] See Ninth Annual Report, Board of Control, 1922, deploring this fact.
[4] In the inter-war years the Maudsley was able to develop hospital in-treatment for voluntary patients, an out-patients' department for the encouragement of early consultation and treatment, and a strong teaching and research team. Developments included postgraduate courses in psychological medicine, and the acceptance of trainees for psychiatric social work.
[5] The Committee was appointed on 8.12.1921 to investigate and report on charges made by Dr. Lomax in his book *The Experiences of an Asylum Doctor* and to make recommendations as to any medical or administrative improvements which might be necessary or practicable.

EXPANSION BETWEEN THE WORLD WARS

and the Royal Commission on Lunacy and Mental Disorder, 1926, were largely concerned with in-patient treatment, the legal aspects of certification,[1] and questions of administration. The Royal Commission drew special attention to the new conception of mental illness and the emphasis on treatment, and paid tribute to the medical profession in labouring to change the attitude of the public towards the insane. They also drew attention to the question of after-care, and the reports of both the Committee and of the Royal Commission acknowledged the value of the work of M.A.C.A. in the sphere of community care. At the same time they noted the restricted scope of the work of voluntary organisations in relation to the need.[2] They recommended that after-care should be strengthened, particularly in the provinces. In spite of the acknowledgment of the need, however, the Commission did not recommend that after-care should be an integral part of the official machinery. It was a service which, in their view, had better be performed by voluntary agencies working closely with the statutory authorities. They recognised, however, that charitable funds would be insufficient to meet the need, and they approved the proposal embodied in the new Mental Treatment Bill that local authorities should be empowered to provide for the after-care of patients 'through voluntary organisations or otherwise'.

The Mental Treatment Act, 1930, marked a considerable advance in the mental health services. Public mental hospitals could now receive voluntary patients and temporary patients without certification; they could develop out-patient departments and do preventive work, the value of which was already demonstrated by the Maudsley Hospital; they could undertake research in relation to mental illness and its treatment, and could make contributions towards the expenses of any body or person engaged in such research.

These were considerable advances. Further co-operation with other agencies was now possible in the field of community care, for local authorities were empowered to make provision for after-care and to contribute to the funds of voluntary associations formed for that purpose. More generally, they had power to contribute to the funds of voluntary organisations concerned with the prevention and treatment of mental illness. Moreover, the complexity of the Lunacy Act was in part removed. There was no longer the sharp division between paupers and private patients, and the move which had been made the year before, under the Local Government Act, to take 'rate-aided patients of unsound mind' out of the hands of the Poor Law Guardians was now taken further, with the admission of any patient, rate-aided or otherwise, for

[1] The Royal Commission urged that 'certification should be a last resort and not a necessary preliminary to treatment'.
[2] In 1924, 1,167 cases were dealt with by the Association when the total number of discharges from mental hospitals exceeded 10,000. See the Report of the Royal Commission on Lunacy and Mental Disorder, Qu. 7695 ff.

treatment in a public mental hospital. When 'pauper lunatics' became 'rate-aided patients' under the new Act, the English language may not have been enriched, but a new humanity in administering the service was given official recognition. Since all charitable intent had departed from the term 'asylum', 'mental hospital' took its place, another step in the education of the public towards an enlightened attitude to mental illness.

Progress in Statutory Provision for the Mentally Defective

On the whole the mental deficiency service suffered more than the lunacy service as a result of four years of war. The new Mental Deficiency Act was largely inoperative and the immediate post-war economic difficulties still further postponed advances which involved the spending of public money. Some progress had, however, been made in the legislative provisions for the care of mental defectives. In 1923 the Board of Control reminded local authorities[1] that Regulations now provided for a 50% grant towards occupation centres, whether set up by local authorities or voluntary organisations. By May 1924 only one out of a total of 58 grant-aided centres had been set up directly by local authorities.[2] Experience showed that the principal Act needed amending before further progress could be made. Two short Acts had been passed in 1919 and 1925 respectively, but more far-reaching changes had to wait for the *Mental Deficiency Act, 1927*. This made several important amendments. One of the most valuable was the recognition that defectives need not only supervision, protection, and control, but also occupation and training.[3] In widening the categories of those 'subject to be dealt with', public responsibility was no longer limited to those defectives who had already met with disaster. The importance of prevention was acknowledged in the power given to parents to make representation to the local authority 'that he is in need of care or training which cannot be given at home'.[4] It also amended the definition of defective in order to include those who, by injury or disease or through any other cause arising before the age of eighteen, were in need of care, supervision or control by reason of mental defect.[5]

But little was yet known of the extent and incidence of mental defect although a generation had passed since the Royal Commission had recommended a system of ascertainment. It was therefore decided to ask the Board of Control and the Board of Education to set up a Joint Com-

[1] Circular 619, 14th June, 1923.
[2] See pp. 125–126, Table III, below.
[3] Cf. Section 21 and Section 30 of the Mental Deficiency Act, 1913, with Section 7 (1) and (2) where the functions of the Central and Local Authorities are defined. There is no doubt that the experience gained in the voluntary occupation centres influenced social policy.
[4] Mental Deficiency Act, 1927, Section 2. Amending Section 2 of the principal Act.
[5] The 1913 Act had a limited classification to include only those showing defect from 'birth or an early age'.

mittee to investigate.[1] The Report of the Mental Deficiency Committee (The Wood Committee) was published in 1929 after a special enquiry had been made in six sample areas. They reported in detail on the provision so far made, and the many gaps which remained to be filled. One of the most outstanding of these was the need for special education and after-care for feeble-minded children: no less than 77% of children between seven and sixteen ascertained to be feeble-minded were attending ordinary elementary schools, in spite of the fact that an Act of 1914 had made it obligatory for local education authorities to provide suitable education for such children. Another disturbing feature was the apparent increase in the incidence of mental defect since the report of the Royal Commission in the first decade of the century. It was now estimated that some 8 per 1,000 of the population were defective, if those who were educationally defective (i.e. within the meaning of the Education Acts) were included. At first sight this result seemed to indicate that there were twice as many defective persons in England and Wales as formerly.[2] The Board of Control made a renewed effort to ensure that local authorities carried out their duties and used their powers under the Mental Deficiency Acts, 1913 and 1927. There was no further legislation in the inter-war years directly concerned with mental deficiency. Subsequent changes in the legislative framework for the care of mental defectives were consequent upon other legislation such as the Local Government Act, 1929, which gave power of appropriation to local authorities whereby defectives might be removed from the jurisdiction of the Poor Law and placed under the mental deficiency authority.[3]

II. PRIVATE ENTERPRISE IN MENTAL AFTER-CARE

The years following the First World War were both difficult and stimulating for the voluntary organisations working for mental health. They were difficult in that economic depressions and the scarcity of money limited the response which might be expected from appeals to private generosity, while public interest was more readily evoked for reconstruction in fields of recognisable urgency. Mental health had to take second place when the need for housing, education and employment was pressing. The post-war years were at the same time stimulating since ideas were in a state of ferment, and psychological medicine and educational psychology were receiving influences of a far-reaching nature. Freud's work in the field of psycho-analysis was late in penetrating this

[1] It is interesting to note that the work of the C.A.M.W. was recognised by the appointment of the secretary of the Association on to the Committee. Four other members of the Committee were also drawn from the Executive Council of C.A.M.W.
[2] In fact much of this increase is thought to be due to more exact methods of ascertainment, but no direct comparison is possible between the two investigations.
[3] Local Government Act, 1929, Section 5.

country, but recognition came in the 1920's.[1] Interest in behaviour problems of children was quickened by an investigation by Cyril Burt into delinquency[2], carried out with the aid of L.C.C. Care Committee workers.[3] Magistrates, social workers and psychiatrists were looking with interest at the work being done in the U.S.A. in psychological clinics and in juvenile courts.[4]

Meanwhile, practical experiments in the field of community care for the mentally ill and for the mentally defective were pursued with energy and persistence by the voluntary organisations which had secured a recognised place in the mental health services before the war.

Co-operation between the Mental After-care Association and Statutory Bodies

M.A.C.A.'s concentration on community care for the mentally ill who lived in and around London made it a ready agency for co-operation with the L.C.C. The advantage was mutual since the Council was glad to avail itself of the experience of the voluntary agency, while M.A.C.A. was considerably strengthened by the partnership. There is no doubt that the progressive improvement in its financial position depended largely upon L.C.C. support.[5] The first step was taken when, in 1919, the L.C.C. resolved to make payments from public funds for patients 'on trial' who were in the care of M.A.C.A.[6] They authorised payments up to the full amount of the weekly cost of maintenance. At the same time they made grants from Queen Adelaide's Fund which would approximate to the expenses incurred by the Association for voluntary patients discharged recovered, but placed in the care of M.A.C.A. The payments for patients needing after-care, as distinct from those 'on trial', were thus dependent upon a small charitable fund and the services of a voluntary agency.

The Board of Control watched these small ventures with considerable interest. It continued to deplore the fact that so small a proportion of the patients discharged from mental hospitals had any after-care (some

---

[1] *The International Journal of Psycho-Analysis* was first published in England in 1920 under the leadership of Ernest Jones. See Zilboorg and Henry, *op. cit.*, p. 506.

[2] The results were published in 1925 in *The Young Delinquent*.

[3] Voluntary workers organised by salaried social workers employed by the L.C.C. in connection with its children's care work within the school medical service. See p. 22, above.

[4] See *Social Service and Mental Health*, M. Ashdown and S. Clement Brown, Chapter II.

[5] In the five-year period 1915–19 the Association's annual income averaged £1,851 of which some £45 was derived from grants and payments for services rendered. In the period 1934–39 the corresponding figures were £20,625 and £16,977 respectively, the bulk of which was payments for services. See Table VI.

[6] This was done by virtue of powers under the Lunacy Act, 1890, Section 283. Payments to patients on trial from mental hospitals were, and still are, authorised by Section 55 (2).

939 patients out of a total of 9,368 in 1924) and of these almost the whole was carried out through M.A.C.A. Only three hospitals had their own after-care arrangements. The system of arranging for a period 'on trial' before discharge was by this time more common though by no means general,[1] and the Board regretted the lack of power of visiting committees to subsidise after-care effectively from public funds.[2] It has been noted that the Committee on the Administration of Public Mental Hospitals had made similar references to the need for extending the practice of after-care done 'by a small but valuable organisation in London' (i.e. M.A.C.A.) and had urged the provision of such facilities, especially convalescence, cottage homes,[3] and boarding-out in the provinces. Throughout the 1920's we find praise of the after-care work of M.A.C.A. running like a refrain through the Board of Control Reports.

In 1930 there was a slight change of emphasis. The new powers of local authorities under the Local Government Act, 1929, and the Mental Treatment Act, 1930, included, as we have seen, legal sanction to provide contributions to voluntary associations, and the Board continued to urge authorities to use this power. But it also stressed the wisdom of direct appointment of trained social workers, especially by the larger local authorities. The ideal policy, the Board suggested, was to have a nucleus of trained professional workers with voluntary assistants. The volunteers should be encouraged to attend training courses arranged by the voluntary organisations experienced in the field. The Board had already recommended the use in the larger mental hospitals of a trained almoner who would work closely with the voluntary after-care association.[4] They considered that the after-care work for discharged patients was still 'in some respects more appropriately done by voluntary effort'.

In 1930 the Board of Control had occasion to regret that certain local authorities refused the help offered by a voluntary association; in fact the interest taken in mental health, and the extent to which the new powers were used by local authorities varied considerably, and there was great unevenness throughout England and Wales in the provision made for the mentally ill. It was unfortunate that the country was in the midst of an economic depression when the Mental Treatment Act of 1930 came into force, but even so, in the progressive areas the opportunity to set up psychiatric out-patient centres in mental hospitals was eagerly seized in spite of financial stringency.

[1] Twenty-four hospitals allowed preliminary leave before discharge to nearly all their patients, while 23 hospitals used the system very little.
[2] It is worth noting that the Mental Treatment Bill which failed to pass in 1922 had made provision for this necessary part of after-care.
[3] By 1930 M.A.C.A. had 15 cottage homes by the sea and 5 in the London area.
[4] The Board in its Annual Report for 1928 quotes the success of the Rotterdam experiment where a medical officer for after-care was appointed.

THE MENTAL HEALTH SERVICES

1930 was a memorable year for M.A.C.A.; we find the Association welcoming the decision of the L.C.C. Public Assistance Committee to recommend payment for assistance given to patients in their care. The Mental Treatment Act gave further opportunities for co-operation. Local authorities at last had power to treat voluntary patients,[1] and to subscribe to the funds of voluntary associations for mental welfare.[2] As a result, M.A.C.A. was able to extend its help to include patients from several hospitals, in addition to the Maudsley, and within a year or two its work for the L.C.C was given a broader basis. Hitherto it had been concerned mainly with arrangements for convalescence or for the allocation of grants from private funds. After 1933 the L.C.C. accepted the policy of boarding-out men and women[3] who needed some care and supervision, and M.A.C.A. was asked to find homes and supervise selected patients from three L.C.C. Mental Hospitals.

The close relationship with the L.C.C. was marked in 1934 by the selection of the Chairman of the L.C.C. Mental Hospital Department as a new vice-president of the Association. When the L.C.C.[4] appointed its own psychiatric social workers to the mental hospitals, it still asked the Association to visit some of the relatives of patients in hospitals, especially when long journeys were involved. It also asked the Association to co-operate in supplying 'locums' during the absence of a psychiatric social worker on holiday or in sickness. The Association's Homes were also freely used for those who could not be sent to relatives but were sufficiently recovered to become the responsibility of the matron. In some instances patients were able to work outside while continuing to live in the Home. As the Association pointed out, the Homes gave valuable help to the statutory authorities since they relieved the pressure on hospital beds and were more economical for the authority. Table II, below, shows the increase in the number of cases dealt with in the years between the wars.

When we leave London and view the position of the service over the country as a whole, we find that institutional accommodation was still far short of the need, and community care totally inadequate, even non-existent in some areas. Voluntary aid was also on a relatively small scale. Although M.A.C.A. had in its quiet, persevering way done valuable work, its scope was limited. It is a matter for some wonder that so many new ventures were started, and so many patients assisted, with so small a paid staff. It was doing excellent personal work in close co-operation with a powerful county council, and it continued to receive the strong support of the central authority, but its influence had not

[1] I.e. patients received without certification.
[2] Section 6 of the Mental Treatment Act, 1930.
[3] Sections 55 and 57, Lunacy Act, 1890.
[4] In 1933, the L.C.C. appointed a part-time psychiatric social worker as a result of a loan service from the Child Guidance Council. This was followed by the appointment of trained workers serving four hospitals.

EXPANSION BETWEEN THE WORLD WARS
TABLE II
Number of Cases (Mental Illness)
who 'were dealt with' by M.A.C.A., 1919–39

Year	Male	Female	Total
1919	224	512	736
1920	258	556	814
1921	286	588	874
1922	320	624	944
1923	390	652	1,042
1924	438	738	1,176
1925	451	980	1,431
1926	509	1,151	1,660
1927*			1,936
1928			'over 2,000'
1929			2,324
1930			no data
1931			2,412
1932			2,776
1933			2,865
1934			3,190
1935			3,307
1936			3,515
1937			3,381
1938			4,269†
1939			4,222

* After 1926 the Association no longer recorded the sex of the patients.

† Many patients were now being sent on holiday from mental hospitals: the number in 1938 was 1,174.

reached much beyond London.[1] Nor had it thrown its energy into the formation of local societies,[2] although a number had in fact been started through local interest.

It preferred to concentrate its effort in its chosen field and to demonstrate the value of community care in the schemes for mental health. M.A.C.A. still retained characteristics derived from its Victorian ancestry, one of which was a strong desire to maintain its independence. Though it had always been anxious to co-operate with voluntary and statutory agencies in particular ventures, it was not ready to carry co-ordination so far as to agree to amalgamation at a national level. During the Second World War it refused the invitation to become a constituent member of the National Association for Mental Health, since it feared to lose its identity in the larger organisation.[3]

[1] Its homes were, however, used by other local authorities who appreciated the therapeutic value of a transition period in one of these small, homely establishments.

[2] The Association had, however, since its foundation, kept in touch with various societies in England and Wales working for the welfare of women and girls, suggesting that they nominate members as 'Associates'. They hoped that such associate members would refer any cases they came across to the After-Care Association. It seems to have been more active in seeking patients from Boards of Guardians and Medical Superintendents in the first phase of its development.

[3] See p. 149, below.

THE MENTAL HEALTH SERVICES
Education in Mental Health and Progress in Medical Psychology

The need for voluntary work of wider scope had to some extent been appreciated by two other organisations working in the field of mental health. A short account of the activities of the *National Council for Mental Hygiene* and of the *Child Guidance Council* will illustrate some of the early efforts towards integration.[1] These two voluntary organisations owed their existence to the development of psychological medicine in the inter-war years, and to the realisation of the importance of education in questions of mental health. There could be no final advance towards linking up general medicine and psychological medicine until the public was better prepared to understand and co-operate. When the National Council for Mental Hygiene was founded, in 1923, it was particularly concerned with the causes of mental ill-health and the development of preventive measures, with a view to the creation of a more enlightened public opinion. One of its earliest ventures was to agitate for a larger place for psychiatry in medical schools. It worked closely with local authorities, and was ready to provide speakers when local authorities held their Health Campaigns. One of its chief methods in the formation of an intelligent lay public was the organisation of conferences and lectures. It secured public confidence by enlisting the support of experts in various fields of mental health. Its interests were wide,[2] and it kept in close touch with kindred organisations overseas. Such preventive educational work was carried on with few financial resources, and was necessarily limited.[3] Much of its lecturing was, in fact, done by eminent doctors without fee.

Meanwhile, medical psychology was making considerable progress. An increasing number of doctors interested in mental health were qualifying as psychiatrists, by adding clinical experience and the study of psychological medicine to their basic medical qualification. At the same time the Universities were offering degrees and diplomas in psychology, and educational psychologists were giving attention to mental testing and the behaviour difficulties of children. But, so far, no social workers were receiving any specific training for work in the field of mental health. It was the Child Guidance Council which tried to bring together the psychiatrist, the psychologist and the social worker to form a team based on the clinic.

The Child Guidance Movement affords an interesting example of pioneer work under voluntary auspices which became acceptable to statutory authorities after a period of experimentation. The stimulus

---

[1] They, together with the C.A.M.W., co-operated in the Second World War to form the National Association for Mental Health.

[2] We find it, for example, concerned not only with research into the mental health of children, but with a study of crime and prostitution in their relation to mental health.

[3] See the Feversham Committee's Report on the inadequacy of Mental Health propaganda. *Op. cit.*, p. 181 ff.

came, in the first instance, from America, where considerable advance had been made in the psychiatric study of children and in the training of psychiatric social workers. Amongst the first studies of children's behaviour problems in this country were those made in the Children's Department of the *Tavistock Clinic*[1] and at the clinic set up in East London by the *Jewish Health Organisation*.[2] In the same year, a representative of the Commonwealth Fund of America came over to help found the Child Guidance Council and to offer generous support to the new movement. A team of British social workers took a year's course in America and, in 1929, the Council co-operated with the London School of Economics where the first mental health course was instituted in this country.[3] The training of psychiatric social workers (P.S.W.'s), though numbers were relatively small, was a valuable step in the progress of treatment both in mental hospitals and child guidance clinics. The 'social history' was to become a recognised requirement in diagnosis, while the contribution of the P.S.W. as a caseworker was increasingly welcomed. What part she might play in schemes of community care outside the work of the hospital and clinic had yet to be discovered. Meanwhile, a demonstration clinic, set up in Islington with the financial backing of the Commonwealth Fund, supplied part of the necessary opportunity for practical training, and helped to popularise the new idea of Child Guidance.[4] Publicity by the Child Guidance Council brought the treatment of behaviour difficulties in children to the notice of teachers and parents.

Some clinics were established in connection with voluntary hospitals, especially those which had a department of paediatrics, but the majority were linked with education rather than with medicine. Birmingham was one of the first authorities to get the sanction of the Board of Education to set up a clinic as part of its school medical service. Other local authorities followed suit, but many chose rather to make a grant to a voluntary clinic for services rendered to children referred by the school medical officer. The Child Guidance Council was also to make a contribution to the practical training of psychiatrists and psychologists. For some eighteen years it administered a scheme for the selection of trainees and the approval of training centres, awarding Fellowships in both psychiatry and psychology.[5]

[1] Opened in 1926.
[2] The Jewish Health Organisation of Great Britain established the East London Child Guidance Clinic, 1926–27.
[3] For a full account of the training of psychiatric social workers, see Ashdown and Brown, *Social Service and Mental Health*, 1953.
[4] The London Child Guidance Clinic gave a valuable demonstration of the importance of co-operation between psychiatrists, psychologists and social workers. The Maudsley Hospital soon became the second centre of practical training for the Mental Health Course.
[5] The scheme was carried on by the N.A.M.H. after amalgamation during the Second World War. In 1948, 10 Fellowships in child psychiatry and 16 in psychology were awarded—see N.A.M.H. Annual Report, 1948–49, p. 16.

THE MENTAL HEALTH SERVICES

For a long time there was little connection between psychiatrists working in mental hospitals (asylums) and the workers in clinics connected with the education service[1] or with voluntary hospitals. Nevertheless, though child guidance developed as a separate movement, it made an important contribution to preventive treatment in the field of psychiatry. Its propaganda amongst local education authorities was most effective and was often followed up by a loan service of an experienced psychiatric social worker. This, at a time of scarce supply, was a welcome form of co-operation. The scheme was later extended to include psychiatric departments of mental hospitals.[2] By 1935, the first stage of development was complete. Interest was now sufficiently wide to enable the Council to divert its resources to other constructive schemes.[3] It continued to act as an advisory body, and its services were used by both local authorities and voluntary agencies.

The Child Guidance Council co-operated with a number of organisations in its own sphere of work, and it formed an inter-clinic committee on which both voluntary and statutory bodies were represented. But it was conscious of the lack of co-ordination in the wider field of mental health. From the early 1930's, various attempts were made, in co-operation with other organisations, to co-ordinate the work of the voluntary associations. One of the results of these efforts was the formation of the Feversham Committee which issued a valuable report in 1939 on *The Voluntary Mental Health Services*.[4] The Committee had the goodwill and support, not only of the national voluntary organisations, but of the local authorities and the Board of Control. Those concerned with mental health were now generally agreed that one of the main lines of advance was by united action by all the voluntary mental health organisations throughout the country. The immediate necessities of an emergency war service led to the final stages. Before we consider the impact of the Second World War, however, we should follow the second phase of the development of one of the most vigorous and highly organised voluntary organisations in the inter-war years, namely the Central Association for Mental Welfare which, together with the Child Guidance Council and the National Council of Mental Hygiene, saw the advantages to the mental health service of co-ordination of all branches at a national level.

[1] See Dr. Blacker, *Neurosis and the Mental Health Services*, for an interesting discussion of this problem. He points out that, as late as 1944, of 95 Child Guidance Clinics, only 22 were served by psychiatrists attached to mental hospitals.
[2] Cf. the L.C.C. Maudsley Hospital.
[3] Its loan service, however, continued to function and we find it reporting, in 1940, that such a service sometimes led to a permanent appointment, either by a local education authority or the Ministry of Health.
[4] The Feversham Report was unfortunately unobtainable after the war since the whole stock had been destroyed by bombing.

XI

EXPANSION BETWEEN THE TWO WORLD WARS (Continued)

VOLUNTARY ORGANISATIONS FOR THE MENTALLY DEFECTIVE: THE C.A.M.W. AND THE VOLUNTARY-STATUTORY RELATIONSHIP

THE second phase in the development of the mental deficiency service offers a striking example of good relations between some of the voluntary and statutory bodies, particularly in the sphere of community care. It demonstrates, on the other hand, that more apathy existed amongst a number of local authorities and a large section of the general public on the question of the care of mental defectives than in most spheres of social welfare. It is not surprising to find, therefore, a very wide range in the quality and extent of the services available in different parts of the country.

We have seen from our study of the first phase of development that the obstacles to advance in the mental deficiency services were particularly heavy. Perhaps for this very reason voluntary associations, when they established a footing, pressed on with a persistence and vigour which has been a characteristic feature of so much of their work. The C.A.M.W., in particular, met the challenge with a crusading zeal. It is worth studying in some detail the development of the various activities of this society, for it is an outstanding example of a national voluntary agency which continued to represent both statutory and voluntary interests. It also gives an excellent illustration of the qualities which informed many of the voluntary agencies which were struggling to win public support. Its intense interest in its function as a pioneer kept it working persistently through wars, economic depressions and other crises. Its enthusiasm was upheld in spite of widespread indifference, and it aimed to keep up its standards in the face of severe financial stress.

We have seen that the policy of the Association had been laid down in 1913, and the pattern was set by the end of the First World War. The second phase was one of development and expansion, making cooperation with statutory authorities and the encouragement of local participation the basis of its work. The formation of local associations and the affiliation of those already in existence were cardinal features.[1] In the post-war depression of the early 1920's the work of stimulating co-operation between voluntary and statutory agencies was particularly difficult. There were some exceptions, as in Chesterfield, where a subcommittee of the Borough Welfare Committee formed itself into a voluntary committee for Mental Welfare.[2] But in many other areas the C.A.M.W. had to work hard for several months before a successful local association emerged. Over and over again in the Association's Reports we find a reference to the difficulty of forming an association in any locality where little statutory work for the mentally defective was done.[3]

One of the most successful methods pursued by the Central Association was the appointment of organisers who were 'loaned' for a period to work in a particular locality at the request either of a statutory or of a voluntary body. It was rewarding when, after strenuous efforts, the organiser could report the formation of a local association with the promise of a local authority grant in addition to a grant from the Board of Control.[4] Occasionally the local authority expressed sympathy, but refused any tangible help.[5] Sometimes economic and industrial circumstances held up the work, as in Sunderland, where the organiser spent some five months, only to be baulked by the coal stoppage which prevented the local authority from incurring the expense.[6] But the most persistent efforts had to be made in the weaker areas, and we find the Board of Control encouraging the C.A.M.W. to send an organiser to stimulate interest in those areas 'where the Mental Deficiency Act had not previously been operated in its entirety'. The Association received a special additional grant of £400 for this purpose.[7] Occasionally the request came from the local authority itself, as when Wolverhampton asked the C.A.M.W. to send an organiser to make suggestions for reorganising a local association of some years' standing.[8] It was more usual, however, for a local voluntary agency or a group of agencies, or

[1] For a description of the variety of work undertaken by a long-standing and active local association, the reader is referred to p. 147, below.
[2] See Report of the C.A.M.W. for 1920–21.
[3] See, for example, the Report of the C.A.M.W. for 1923–24.
[4] As in 1925–26 in the Isle of Ely.
[5] This was sometimes due to their uncertainty as to their own financial position, e.g. two local authorities refused grant-aid owing to their uncertainty over the Local Government Act.
[6] In this instance a return visit was paid by the organiser and a local association was formed with a permanent secretary. See Report for 1928–29, *ibid.*, *N.B.*: reference to the co-operation of the local social service organisation.
[7] See C.A.M.W. Report for 1926–27.
[8] *Ibid.*, 1928–29.

for the Central Association itself, to take the initiative. The Association's reaction to difficulties is reflected in its response to restrictions imposed by the Treasury in the immediate post-war years; all the more need, decided its council, for voluntary associations to keep their work going on behalf of the mentally defective. In this instance, the immediate result was a resolution to keep up at all costs their 'free loan service' of organisers.[1]

Occupation Centres and other Pioneer Work

It was not long before the C.A.M.W. began to appoint specialist organisers in various fields. It had, as we have seen, already been closely interested in the formation of occupation centres[2] for low-grade defectives who might respond to training, and it had already appointed occupational organisers to work in various parts of the country.[3] The value of occupation centres for imbecile children who needed close supervision, yet who were able to respond to simple training, was still not generally appreciated. The Board of Control reported regularly and in detail on their methods: 'These centres provide simple manual and physical training and aim in the first place at the cultivation of cleanly and orderly habits . . . it is then possible to proceed to manual work and occupations and in some instances saleable articles have been produced.'[4] Parents who were fortunate enough to secure one of the rare places in a centre, had good cause to be thankful. Too few mental deficiency authorities made such provision, however, and in 1923 the C.A.M.W. decided to appoint a travelling occupational organiser, to encourage local authorities and local associations to use their powers, and to help them start occupation centres. Her services were also available for Boards of Guardians, responsible for institutions.

In the same year the *Agnes Weston Training Centre* was opened in London in response to the emphasis placed by the Board of Control on the need for the training of supervisors of occupation centres.[5] The part played by occupation centres in helping local authorities in the supervision of the mentally defective was only gradually being realised. Although the first occupation centre had been started as early as 1909, the rate of increase was slow until after the First World War. The impetus came from the Central Association in the early 1920's when many new centres were added.[6] So far all existing centres had been provided by voluntary agencies. The following table illustrates the changing

---

[1] C.A.M.W. Report, 1919–20.
[2] See p. 114, above. The parents were encouraged to visit the centre and learn how to make the best use of the child's capacities. Some centres catered for older defectives as well.
[3] C.A.M.W. Report, 1922–23.
[4] Ninth Report of the Board of Control, 1922, p. 46.
[5] The centre was welcomed by the L.C.C. and several other local authorities.
[6] In the years 1921–23, alone, some 30 new centres were added.

THE MENTAL HEALTH SERVICES
TABLE III
Occupation Centres, Industrial Centres and Clubs for the Mentally Defective under Statutory and Voluntary Control, 1921–50

[Information extracted from Annual Reports of the Board of Control and of the Central Association for Mental Welfare, with checks, where available, from the Feversham Report]*

Date	Occupation centres		Industrial centres		Clubs		Total	Numbers on register*
	I Stat.	II Vol.	III Stat.	IV Vol.	V Stat.	VI Vol.	VII Total	VIII Total
1921		17					17	
1922		20 or 16†					20 or 16†	
1923		CAMW 30					48	
May 1924	1	57					58	
Mar. 1925	1	69					70	920
Mar. 1926	3	80					83	1,157
1927	3	96					99	1,266
Apr. 1928	5	104					109	1,452
1.1.1929	5	106					111	1,536
1.1.1930	12	149					161	2,180
1.1.1931	10	161					171	2,708
1.1.1932	41	115	4	13	—	9	182	2,924
1.1.1933	41	112	5	14	—	8	180	3,494
1.1.1934	52	102	6	16	—	10	186	3,563
1.1.1935	56	98	9	18	—	10	191	3,711
1.1.1936	57	96	9	19	—	11	192	4,008
1.1.1937	57	97	9	16	—	10	189	4,021
1.1.1938	60	95	10	16	—	10	191	4,143
1.1.1939	59	95	9	15	1	12	191	4,244
1.1.1940	32	56			1	3	92	3,137
1.1.1941	33	61			—	4	98	2,335
1.1.1942	30	60			—	2	92	2,164
1.1.1943	38	53			1	1	93	1,909
1.1.1944	37	51			1	1	90	2,298
1.1.1945	36	52			1	1	90	2,258
1.1.1946	40	47			1	—	88	2,431
1.1.1947	46	52			1	2	101	2,784
1.1.1948	51	49			1	3	104	3,474
1.1.1949	129				5		134	4,009
1950	159				7		166	no data

* At 1st January in each year.

† Sometimes this information is of a general character, as when the Board of Control speaks of 'some 20 centres' in 1922. The Feversham Report quotes 16 for 1922. There is also some variation in the month in which the assessment is made (varying from March, April, May between 1924 and 1928; thereafter the figures are those established in January). After 1940 separate centres or classes in one building are counted as one centre, whereas they were listed separately before 1940.

1918–21 Reports of the Board of Control contain no mention of occupation centres. After 1948 totals only were recorded, for occupation centres were now part of the community care provided under the National Health Service Act.

EXPANSION BETWEEN THE WORLD WARS

relation between voluntary and statutory provision in the subsequent years.[1]

The remarkable increase from 17 to 161 centres in the ten years 1921–31 in the provision by voluntary agencies reflects the intensity of the drive, which was made by the C.A.M.W. and its affiliated associations in this form of community care. It will be seen from Table III that between 1924, when the first statutory centre was set up, and 1931, only 10 were established by local authorities. From 1932, however, until the outbreak of the Second World War, the number of statutory centres rose to 59. Meanwhile, the provision made by voluntary organisations having risen to the peak of 161 in 1931, declined to a total of 95 by 1939.

During the years 1932–39 industrial centres were listed separately for the first time, although they had received favourable notice in the reports of the Board of Control as early as 1920. These centres were intended for the higher-grade mentally defective, some of whom may have been to special schools. 'The object of the training in industrial centres ... is to provide suitable, and as far as possible, remunerative work for those who are unable to compete in the open market and for whom unemployment is the direct road to disaster.'[2] In the early 1930's the voluntary organisations were in the lead in the provision of such centres in the proportion of 13–4. By the outbreak of war the ratio was 15–9.[3]

Clubs, which had also been separately reported upon since 1932, were nearly all run under voluntary auspices. They were established to provide leisure-time facilities in a neighbourhood where a number of young defectives of sufficient intelligence to derive pleasure from informal education or training could meet together at a centre. Members might be living at home, or be boarded out, or under guardianship, or living in hostels. Many would be doing some sort of work, e.g. residential domestic work, when the companionship of the club would be particularly welcome. For the first seven years there were no clubs provided under statutory auspices, and after 1939 only one is recorded. The total number of defectives registered in the centres and clubs exceeded 4,000 in the four years preceding the Second World War. The decline during and immediately after the war was arrested in 1946, and by 1949 the figures approximated to those of the pre-war years. By 1948 the provision of occupation centres and clubs was equally divided between voluntary and statutory agencies, the statutory authorities having 51 centres and 1 club and the voluntary organisations 49 centres and 3 clubs.

In addition to its general organisers and its occupation centre organisers, the Central Association later added travelling teachers who

[1] In order to see the series as a whole the period is extended beyond 1939, although the later figures belong properly to the next section.
[2] See the Tenth Report of the Board of Control, 1923.
[3] Industrial centres were not listed separately after 1939.

specialised in speech therapy.[1] Few, so far, had realised that many mentally defective children could be helped to speak more clearly, and so be brought a little nearer to the enjoyment of normal human intercourse. The experiment was fully justified, and the C.A.M.W. was glad to respond to requests from local authorities for the services of their speech therapist. The following year, 1932, a travelling handicraft teacher was added to the staff, and we find Middlesex local authority reporting on the successful work done by the older girls. In all these experiments the Association was not only demonstrating to the supervising authorities the possibilities of training within the community, but making a valuable contribution to family life, by easing the burden on the parents or guardians responsible for a defective child.

About the same time the C.A.M.W. had under consideration the appointment of a travelling educational psychologist. The policy of keeping in close touch with statutory authorities and of consulting them on any new proposals under consideration was followed when the Association approached the local education authorities to see whether they would welcome such an appointment. Unfortunately, at this time the severe economic depression made support financially impossible, and the decision was postponed. By the beginning of 1935, however, we find the Association's first educational psychologist at work making preliminary surveys of educational experiments in various parts of the British Isles. By the end of the year bookings for her services were so heavy that a second appointment had to be made. The L.C.C. cooperated in the venture by seconding their own educational psychologist for the purpose. By 1937 two more were appointed by the C.A.M.W. for specific work.

One of the most interesting features of the 'loan service' of these general and specialist organisers was the response made by a gradually increasing number of local authorities. In several instances a visit resulted in a permanent appointment by the local authority; sometimes by the retention of the visiting organiser's services. In every instance we find the C.A.M.W. rejoicing that the local authority had decided to make itself responsible for the work.[2] The only regretful note came when a statutory authority cut itself off entirely from the voluntary organisations. This happened occasionally when the authority appointed the secretary of the local association and then took over its work in its entirety. The C.A.M.W. pleaded that more effective work could be done

[1] The first appointment was made in 1931. In 1932 it was reported that she had already worked in Birmingham, Stoke-on-Trent, Coventry, Cambridge, Rotherham, Kent and the Rhondda Valley.
[2] In the late 1930's Southend retained the services of the Association's visiting psychologist, while temporary employment of the C.A.M.W. psychologist led Swansea, Somerset and Rotherham Education Committees to make their own appointments. See Reports of the C.A.M.W. 1936–37 and 1937–38. In 1938–39 a speech therapist was appointed jointly by three Welsh authorities and then a permanent appointment was made.

when voluntary and statutory agencies maintained their identity, with close co-operation, each appreciating the other's function. It was most fruitful when the statutory authority was fully represented on the voluntary agency's executive committee.

The organisers' work for local authorities continued to increase until the outbreak of the Second World War and much of it was carried on throughout the war.[1] The special emergency service, however, will be discussed later. Meanwhile, we should examine in more detail the sphere of work in which the C.A.M.W. probably made its most valuable contribution, namely its supplementary education and training schemes.

Supplementary Education and Training Schemes

During the First World War the C.A.M.W. had kept some skeleton training courses going. Immediately after the war it determined to increase the range of facilities offered. By the early 1920's, a postgraduate course was added, while some health visitors were included amongst the students attending the short courses. A special course for doctors, primarily for school medical officers, was the next venture, but after a good start it met with a setback when local authorities refused to pay expenses.[2] It was the need for training supervisors of occupation centres which had led to the opening of the Agnes Weston Occupation Centre, mainly as a demonstration and practice centre. Courses for magistrates were added in 1924, followed by two courses for social workers. Meanwhile the C.A.M.W. had approached local authorities to discuss the possibility of providing facilities for training teachers for special school work in the authorities' training colleges. As a result, courses were established in training colleges in London, Manchester and Liverpool. One or two local authorities started their own training schemes, but the difficulty of getting qualified lecturers led to several appeals to the C.A.M.W. for special courses in the authorities' areas. By the mid-1920's the time had come for refresher courses to be offered to teachers who had taken the earlier course. The other training courses were meanwhile continued and extended, and we find them regularly attended by medical officers, social workers and some enquiry officers. By 1929 a rather longer course for teachers of retarded children was organised in London with the support of the L.C.C. who paid the teachers' fees for a period of ten weeks. In the same year, an evening course for supervisors of occupation centres was arranged in London.

The C.A.M.W. welcomed the opportunity to co-operate with the University by giving facilities for practical work in community care for defectives. It offered to give experience to students of the London School

---

[1] An account of the close co-operation with Middlesex illustrates the representative nature of its organisation. See, p. 144, below.
[2] Owing to post-war economy cuts. This was an interesting experiment, run in co-operation with the University of London (Extension and Tutorial Classes).

of Economics when the Mental Health Course was inaugurated, and it undertook to arrange the practical work required by the London School of Hygiene and Tropical Medicine as part of the course for the Diploma in Public Health. It also co-operated with the College of Nursing in providing a short course for nurses who were training to be health visitors. The Association was not entirely satisfied with some of its courses and it conducted a 'follow-up' to see how useful they had been.[1] It was concerned, too, at the lack of any sustained training in mental deficiency work amongst health visitors and school nurses. It noted that only a small minority of the associations or local authorities who employed health visitors arranged any training at all, and even when the training was given it was often superficial.

One of the new courses started in the inter-war period was that on mental testing. It proved very successful, but had to be curtailed at the outbreak of the Second World War. Apart from this new venture, the 1930's had seen extensions and refinements of the general pattern worked out in the '20s. Elementary and advanced courses for various groups of workers and refresher courses for teachers and medical officers were now generally accepted as the function of the C.A.M.W. Not all the courses were grant-aided by the Board of Education, but they were recognised and approved. There was no doubt that such supplementary training was a valuable part of the Association's work, resulting in the raising of standards and in the improvement of status of those working for the mentally defective.

Advisory Service and Special Projects

The C.A.M.W. had, as we have seen, a wide range of activities to its credit. Others should be noted if we are to appreciate the full scope of its work; they include a number of schemes, relatively small considering the total need, but valuable as indicating possible lines of development. Its headquarters' advisory service was at the disposal of local authorities, voluntary associations or private individuals. We find the Association readily responding to appeals for help in particularly difficult problems. Where a local authority or other agency had been unsuccessful, the C.A.M.W. often succeeded by means of personal work carried out in close co-operation with all those concerned. In its report on its casework for the year 1920–21, the Association gave instances of co-operation with mental deficiency authorities, local education authorities, Boards of Guardians, the Minister of Pensions, the National Institute for the Blind, the Public Trustee and the medical superintendents of Holloway and Brixton.[2]

The early 1920's were particularly active years. After concentrating on the foundation of occupation centres, the Association turned its

[1] In 1937–38 it carried out such a survey in connection with its teachers' courses.
[2] See Table VII for development of Case Work.

attention in 1924–25 to a scheme for guardianship. This form of community care had already been successfully carried out by the Brighton Guardianship Society, which had received the recognition of the local authorities of Brighton and East Sussex with whom there was good co-operation. The C.A.M.W. was now prepared to help local authorities and Boards of Guardians in other parts of the country. After three years' working, the scheme was reported to be satisfactory, with some 118 placements. This was never to be a widespread form of community care,[1] but it demonstrated a useful method of placing certain high-grade defectives who could not be adequately cared for in their own homes, in families prepared to look after them for a moderate payment.[2] In the early 1930's we find C.A.M.W. urging the extension of guardianship, particularly in rural areas where so little had been done so far for the mentally defective.[3] They accordingly set about exploring the possibilities of finding guardians in Northamptonshire and Bedfordshire. Middlesex, meanwhile, asked the Association to undertake guardianship on behalf of its various local authorities.[4] A few years later a scheme was successfully established in the North[5] when C.A.M.W. co-operated with the North-Eastern Council for Mental Welfare, and some seven local authorities participated. This was part of a constructive plan to find suitable employment for high-grade defectives on licence or under guardianship. Negotiation with the Agricultural Wages Committee led to an agreement whereby those who showed sufficient improvement might be given a small wage for their farm work.

Another valuable activity was the provision of holiday camps and holiday homes. These were welcomed by a number of local authorities. The homes and camps not only provided a holiday for the mentally defective children, but also a much needed respite for those who were looking after them. Girls in domestic service for whom local authorities were responsible could go to the holiday camp opened at Seaford.[6] A second home, opened at Littlehampton, was available for girls under guardianship. A hostel was reserved for mentally defective girls who

[1] See Table VIII.
[2] Later it was found possible to make the payment to the parents of the mentally defective child who, with the extra help made possible by this means, could care for him at home. The parent or guardian would have the help of the home teacher or supervisor in methods of training.
[3] It was noted by the Royal Commission early in the century that the incidence of mental defect was relatively greater in rural than in urban areas.
[4] The agreement was made from January 1932. See p. 144, below, for further account of co-operation.
[5] The scheme was first suggested by the Joint Conference of Northern Local Authorities in 1932, but consideration was postponed for a few years. An agreed scheme was accepted in 1935 for an experimental period of one year. Two workers were appointed by the C.A.M.W., one of whom was also the psychiatric social worker in Newcastle mental hospital.
[6] Local authorities agreed to pay £3 per head, while the girls contributed 2s. 6d.

could not be accommodated in ordinary holiday homes. Local authorities could, if they wished, send their own staff, or the C.A.M.W. would provide supervision for a small extra charge. The demand was so great that two other homes were opened.[1] The range of those who could use the homes was now extended to include parties from certified institutions and occupation centres. In 1938-39 patients from mental hospitals were also accepted, and an appeal for a new home to be opened in 1939 at Weston-super-Mare brought in donations from some mental hospitals using the homes. Thus by the outbreak of the Second World War five homes were established as holiday centres in various parts of the country and a great part of the cost was met by *per capita* fees from local authorities. The value of this work cannot be measured simply in terms of the number of homes. Five homes to cover the whole country was not excessive, but it was an experiment which showed the benefits to be derived by the mentally defective from a short break in new surroundings, and the immense relief to parents and others of such a temporary easing of the burden of responsibility. Men and women suffering from mental defect were found to have been in public assistance institutions for from twenty to thirty years with not a single holiday.[2] It was part of the more enlightened policy of several local authorities that they were ready to welcome the opportunity offered by the voluntary associations to provide such holidays.

Extension of Care of Epileptics and Mental Patients

Another project of the C.A.M.W. which received the support of some of the more progressive local authorities was the result of an enquiry the Association made into the Care, Training and Employment of Epileptics.[3] A preparatory enquiry amongst local education authorities and local associations was followed by a special enquiry in selected areas in Essex. A trained worker secured the co-operation of various hospitals and local authorities in investigating the home conditions of 565 epileptics. In this effort to discover the needs of epileptics for community care the Association received support from public assistance committees, local education authorities, public health authorities, the Royal Eastern Counties Institution and from private persons. A further investigation in North London was made in co-operation with the *Council for the Promotion of Occupational Industries amongst the Physically Handicapped*. The results of these enquiries were then discussed by the C.A.M.W. at the Congress on Public Health, and a committee was set up in 1937 to give further study to the question.

Meanwhile, co-operation with other voluntary agencies resulted in

---

[1] At Rhyl and Bognor Regis.
[2] This was, of course, still true of many ordinary families where income was insufficient to allow for the expense of a holiday.
[3] Enquiry initiated 1935-36.

certain practical schemes, such as sending a few epileptics to craft centres,[1] and giving holidays to epileptic children.[2] The Committee realised that the first requirement was to discover the incidence of epilepsy, since little information was available on the numbers who needed help. The immediate practical step indicated by the pilot survey was a detailed scheme of after-care. This was worked out in co-operation with the *National Society for Epileptics* and a doctor with experience in a colony for epileptics. The Association planned to help young epileptics discharged from residential schools and colonies, but unfortunately the scheme had to be curtailed, since the Council for the Provision of Occupational Industries amongst the Physically Handicapped was very short of funds by 1938. It had to discontinue its employment scheme, and its training centres were closed down at the outbreak of war.[3]

The C.A.M.W. therefore decided to concentrate on an experimental schemes of after-care and work-seeking for those between fourteen and eighteen, discharged from Lingfield and Chalfont colonies. This scheme was in the nature of a research project to see what was likely to be successful, and by the end of 1938 some 75 patients were helped. The colonies themselves gave close co-operation and some substantial grants. A supplementary enquiry was also carried out amongst selected epileptics between twenty and twenty-five years of age. The C.A.M.W. continued its after-care work in co-operation with two colonies after the outbreak of war, and it was able to include both younger and older patients in its schemes. By 1941, it could report that the demand for their work was greater than the supply, and that it had been able to help some 276 epileptics. The C.A.M.W. now began to look to the future and to consider the possibility of opening a workshop to replace the centres closed by the C.P.O.I.P.H.

Finally, we should note the extension of the Association's work to include some mental patients. This was done as early as 1921, and was one of the reasons for the change of name. This branch of the work was not so extensive as that for the mentally defective, but the statutory authorities were often glad to avail themselves of the Association's help in areas outside London. C.A.M.W. was already in touch with many of the local associations which were experienced in community care both for the mentally ill and the mentally defective.[4] In 1933, the C.A.M.W., after consultation with the Board of Control, agreed to experiment in boarding-out harmless patients from mental hospitals.[5]

---

[1] Centres run by the Council for the Provision of Occupational Industries amongst the Physically Handicapped.
[2] The Relief Committee of St. Martin's co-operated.
[3] Nine of the fourteen epileptics who had been attending were included in the Home Teaching scheme.
[4] Local Mental Welfare Associations in various parts of the country were often concerned with both branches of mental health.
[5] Suffolk was chosen for this experiment.

THE MENTAL HEALTH SERVICES

The following year a scheme was prepared for boarding-out in Wales, and the Board of Control called a conference of Welsh local authorities to discuss the question. Once the scheme had been started in South Wales, it was extended first to Monmouthshire and mid-Wales[1] and later, at the request of the local authorities, to North Wales. Similarly, in 1935, the local authorities of the North East accepted a scheme for an experimental period of one year. In each case the local authorities made contributions, and in some cases the experimental period was extended with the offer of increased contributions.[2] The C.A.M.W. usually had to meet from special funds any costs in excess of the contributions, and it usually started off the experiment by sending one of its own trained workers to the area. On the whole, the C.A.M.W. felt that boarding-out was a method more successful for the mentally defective than for those who were mentally ill. In the last report before the outbreak of the Second World War, it was noted that the boarding-out of mental patients was 'full of difficulties' whereas there were increasing possibilities in the boarding-out of the mentally defective.[3]

The C.A.M.W. did useful experimental work in several other spheres. For example, a joint register of foster homes for nervous, difficult or retarded children had been drawn up in co-operation with the Child Guidance Council. Social workers had always found that very careful and patient selection was necessary in these cases, and it was even more urgent in time of war.[4] Although the numbers which could be dealt with directly by the Association were small, the register gave a useful pointer to the most effective way of tackling the problem.

The Association had a close relationship with several of the central statutory authorities and it was ready to co-operate and to criticise as occasion arose. One very interesting contact was that with the Broadmoor State Mental Hospital: a scheme, which was in an experimental stage in this country,[5] was carried through between 1935 and 1936 with the co-operation of the Broadmoor authorities. Selected patients referred to the C.A.M.W. by the hospital were given conditional discharge and placed under the Association's supervision. The patients had all been interviewed in the hospital by the Association's trained worker, who had co-operated with the medical officer. The work done for the after-care of other discharged prisoners was already established,[6] and the C.A.M.W. worked closely with the *Royal Society for the Assistance*

---

[1] See the examples given p. 148, below.
[2] See C.A.M.W. Report 1936–37 for example of S. Wales.
[3] Patients of lower grade were now being referred for placing within the community.
[4] The lack of such careful selection in the early stages of evacuation led to much re-billeting and frustration.
[5] It was well established in Belgium.
[6] E.g. from Wormwood Scrubs psychopathic prisoners had been so referred. The number decreased while experimental work by the prison authorities was carried out over a period of four years.

EXPANSION BETWEEN THE WORLD WARS

of Discharged Prisoners. This experiment in community care showed the importance of rehabilitation for those who had spent a long period in institutions. It also indicated that much-needed accommodation could safely be released if patients were carefully selected and supervised within the community.

XII

THE RELATION BETWEEN VOLUNTARY ACTION AND SOCIAL POLICY

Methods and Practice of the C.A.M.W.

THE contribution of voluntary societies to social policy is one of special importance. From their accumulated practical experience they are able to gauge the effect of legislation upon individuals or to appreciate the need for further public action. Owing to their specialised knowledge, national societies are often in a position to give evidence to official committees, to suggest clauses for insertion in new legislation, to propose amendments, and above all to scrutinise the working of existing legislation and to bring any criticisms to the notice of the appropriate ministries. If necessary they may organise public opinion to secure support on any question which they consider is not receiving sufficient attention. The C.A.M.W. took an active part in all these spheres and a few examples will illustrate their methods. They were sometimes, but not always, successful.

In some instances they joined forces with kindred organisations, as when a joint memorandum was presented by the C.A.M.W. and the B.M.A. to the Lord Chancellor's Committee on Criminal Responsibility; or when they co-operated with other organisations to suggest amendments to the Mental Treatment Bill, 1930. When they were invited to give evidence their usual method was to set up a special committee, consisting of medical and lay members, to prepare a memorandum, e.g. in their evidence to the Royal Commission on Lunacy and Mental Disorder, and to the Departmental Committee on Sexual Offences against Young Persons.[1] They submitted draft amendments on the Mental Deficiency Act, and were invited into consultation with the Board of Control in the preparation of a new Mental Deficiency Bill.

[1] Both reports, issued in 1926.

Their active campaign through their local associations, Members of Parliament and the Press helped to win support for the Bill which became law in 1927. Similar tactics secured amendments to the Local Government Bill, 1929.

The C.A.M.W. had been examining the Joint Report of the Board of Education and the Board of Control on Mental Deficiency (the Wood Committee Report, 1929)[1] and they resolved to give active support to a number of the recommendations. The need for a study of the causation of mental deficiency, its relationship to other abnormal mental conditions and social problems, and the part to be played by segregation and sterilisation was urgent and, in the view of the Association, merited a Royal Commission. They were concerned about the suggestion, canvassed in some quarters, that there should be compulsory sterilisation of the mentally defective. They immediately sought an assurance from the Minister of Health that local authorities should not be pressed to adopt the policy of sterilisation until more scientific data were available; the urgent need, they argued, was for more institutional accommodation.[2] In 1932 the C.A.M.W. joined with other organisations in supporting the setting up of a joint committee for voluntary sterilisation. The publication of the Brock Report[3] was followed up by a committee to help educate public opinion on the question, and to promote legislation. The following year the C.A.M.W., supported by a number of local authority organisations and by the *Mental Hospitals Association*, took part in a deputation to the Minister of Health. They went armed with a draft bill, but the Minister, while receiving them sympathetically, urged that the time was not ripe for legislation: more intensive education of public opinion was needed. The Committee therefore organised meetings and lectures under the auspices of the newly formed *Voluntary Sterilisation League*.[4] They made another attempt later to introduce a private member's bill, but failed to secure a place in the ballot.[5]

The C.A.M.W. failed in their long negotiations with the Board of Education and the Board of Control for legislation which would secure the notification of feeble-minded children who were leaving ordinary elementary schools. In view of the inadequacy of the provision of special

[1] It will be remembered that the C.A.M.W. had five members serving on the Committee.
[2] The Minister of Health wrote a reassuring reply, 27.1.30.
[3] A committee on sterilisation under the chairmanship of Sir Laurence Brock which reported in 1934.
[4] A number of branches were formed in the first year of its existence.
[5] The thoroughness of their methods is indicated in the exploration of some 200 constituencies to get an idea of the probable support and opposition. See Annual Report of the C.A.M.W. 1937–38.
In 1955 this question was still under discussion and we find the N.A.M.H. sending a questionnaire to medical superintendents of Mental Deficiency Institutions in the United States, inviting their views on the desirability of sterilisation of Mental Defectives. See *Mental Health*, Vol. XIV, No. 3, pp. 102–104.

schools, this matter was of grave concern in some areas. The Association were more successful in their direct negotiations with local education authorities responsible for the notification of feeble-minded children leaving special schools. The C.A.M.W. had sent a special memorandum to all local education authorities urging a greater measure of after-care, and they were able to report increased interest and closer co-operation with local assocations.

When an after-care scheme was in operation in connection with a special school, their successful placement of boys and girls in occupations within their capacity proved the value of the sustained and patient work involved. Not only was the individual happily engaged, but he was contributing to the well-being of the community instead of adding to the cost. It was a tragedy that for so long, so many young people amongst the higher-grade feeble-minded were denied this help, and the community suffered needless loss.[1]

The persistence of the C.A.M.W. in the face of set-backs was characteristic. They rarely gave up when there was apparent failure in any part of their work, but awaited a more favourable opportunity.[2] For example, their efforts to include children attending occupation centres in the milk scheme was for long unavailing, but they were eventually successful by direct negotiation with the Milk Marketing Board.[3] Reference has several times been made to one of the most intractable questions on which the C.A.M.W. worked for many years, namely, that of the education and notification of defective children. They were still negotiating with the Board of Education and the Board of Control in 1941, when they submitted a report for consideration in any proposal for reconstruction after the war. They had already taken up the question of the issue of new regulations for the boarding-out of children in areas of day special schools.[4] The Association were also in touch with the Ministry of Agriculture on the question of the exemption from the minimum wage claim of defectives working on farms, and they were able to conclude successful negotiations which made such employment practicable.

Meanwhile, C.A.M.W. were keeping a close watch on statutory intervention, particularly on the circulars issued by the various Ministries. A few examples of the action taken will illustrate the influence they exerted. In 1921 when the Board of Control issued a circular in regard to Treasury cuts, the C.A.M.W. made a vigorous protest. They pointed out that local authorities would, if effect were given to the ruling, be

---

[1] This situation was not finally remedied until the passing of the Education Act, 1944. See p. 160, below.

[2] A special committee was often set up to examine possibilities after an apparent failure.

[3] Children in occupation centres were included in the milk scheme in October 1936.

[4] These regulations were in fact issued in July 1939, but were not operated as evacuation had begun.

prevented from undertaking any fresh cases, however urgent. They twice made representations to Members of Parliament, while their president saw the Minister of Health, the Chancellor of the Exchequer and the Home Secretary. They secured the support of the B.M.A., the County Councils Association and other organisations. This combined pressure resulted in the withdrawal of the circular six months after its issue.[1]

A final example of successful intervention may be given, namely, when they secured the withdrawal of a Board of Control circular which would have excluded high-grade defectives from the National Health Insurance Scheme.[2] A number of other questions on which their various committees were watching the interests of defectives had to be held in abeyance owing to the outbreak of war,[3] but the C.A.M.W. by 1941 was looking to the future, and a small committee was appointed to consider proposals for post-war legislation on mental health problems. True to their practice of co-operating whenever possible with kindred societies, they sent an invitation to the Child Guidance Council and the National Council for Mental Hygiene to serve on the committee.

It will be seen that in all these activities, the C.A.M.W. was at pains to secure the backing, not only of their own local associations, but of a number of interested organisations. Their method of appointing a committee of professional and lay members to study special questions gave weight to their findings, and the Association's president seems to have been in direct consultation with the Ministers on a number of issues concerning the welfare of the mentally defective. The function of the voluntary association as 'watchdog' was consistent with very friendly relations with the Ministries concerned. Though on occasions they may have acted as pressure groups to the embarrassment of the Central Authority, on the whole there was close and cordial co-operation. The C.A.M.W. welcomed the strong support of the Board of Control and the Board of Education. The Boards, in turn, were glad to avail themselves of a specialised agency such as the C.A.M.W. The services of the Association on behalf of local authorities was especially valued. There was no question, in the sphere of mental health, of the voluntary organisations having to rouse the interest of the Central Authority. On the contrary, a partnership of statutory and voluntary agencies had been explicit since 1913, and this partnership was strengthened in the inter-war years.[4] A few examples of co-operation between the Board

---

[1] Issued 9.8.21 and withdrawn 28.2.22.
[2] Board of Control Circular, October 1937. The C.A.M.W. case was strengthened when it could show that it had co-operated with local authorities in pressing for the reversal of the decision.
[3] A recommendation that certification by the medical officer for attendance at special schools should only be resorted to when necessary to apply compulsory powers was not submitted in 1939 for this reason.
[4] See p. 148, below, for further examples of statutory–voluntary relationship.

of Control and the C.A.M.W. in stimulating local authorities to undertake their statutory duties and exercise their powers, will further illustrate the closeness of the tie, and some of the reasons for the Central Authority's welcome to voluntary effort.

The Relation between the Board of Control, Local Authorities and Voluntary Organisations

The Board of Control, directly responsible to Parliament[1] for the administration of both the Lunacy and Mental Deficiency Acts, did much to encourage the local authorities to carry out their responsibilities in the difficult inter-war years. There is no shadow of doubt that it was the official policy, as represented by the Board of Control, to welcome co-operation with voluntary organisations. In the sphere of mental deficiency in particular, the Board was anxious to bring to the notice of local authorities the assistance which might be available from voluntary sources. It is worth looking a little more closely at the methods adopted by the Board, and the reasons given for encouraging the voluntary-statutory partnership. In its detailed and stimulating annual reports it was the Board's practice to call attention to the contrast between those local authorities which undertook their duties with energy and thoroughness, and those who neglected them or gave them but a perfunctory performance. It was specially concerned to arouse interest in the mental deficiency service, since it was in this field that public interest was particularly faint. With this in view, the Board gave whole-hearted support to the voluntary organisations, for they were ready to go into the backward areas, to stimulate interest and to show by practical demonstration that it was to the advantage of the local authority to exercise their powers and duties for the welfare of the mentally defective.

Table IV, following, shows the contrast between progressive and backward local authorities and the improvement recorded during the 1920's and early 30's.

In nearly every case, the Board comments that the high rates of ascertainment were to be found in areas where there was close co-operation between the statutory and voluntary agencies, the low rates where this was lacking. An example brings out clearly the great variation in local authority practice. In 1923, the Board compared an active local authority in the Midlands with an inactive urban local authority. In the former city, there was efficient ascertainment and supervision of mentally defective children in the local authority's schools; it had special school accommodation which, although not yet sufficient, was increasing; excellent relations existed between the various statutory authorities concerned, i.e. the mental deficiency committee, local education committee, the Court, the Poor Law Guardians, etc.; the local authority made arrangements for the medical examination of prison and remand cases;

[1] The Minister of Health was the Board's spokesman in the House of Commons.

TABLE IV

Mental Deficiency Service: Improvement in Backward Areas

Number of local authorities with poor supervision, guardianship and ascertainment rates. [Extracted from Annual Reports of the Board of Control, 1922–36.]

Date	Supervision (M.D.)		Guardianship (M.D.)		L.A.s with rate of M.D. ascertainment under 1 per 1,000 of population
	L.A.s with none under supervision	L.A.s with few under supervision	L.A.s with none under guardianship	L.A.s with few under guardianship	
1922					(No full returns available)
1923	33		54	33	
1924	19		57	27	64
1925	19		54	29	56
1926	18		40	34	30
1927	20	4	41	29	36
1928	12	5	31	30	27
1929	6	7	28	30	23
1930	9	4	17	33	9
1931	8	3	15	29	8
1932	7	3	16	22	4
1933	8	3	16	23	3
1934	6	2	16	19	2
1935	'a number'	not given	17	19	1
1936	not given	not given	not given	not given	0

the authority's staff 'showed zeal and efficiency'; finally, there was most valuable work by the after-care committee in co-operation with other social and philanthropic agencies. In the backward area there was as yet no special school, although there was a population of 116,667; there was a very low ascertainment rate; there was no mentally defective person under guardianship or supervision. In fact, there was no organised enquiry, nor had the authority deputed such work to a voluntary society.

The Board of Control did all in its power to bring to the notice of local authorities the new ideas and experiments offered by the voluntary associations; travelling organisers would help form a local association; a speech therapist[1] was available to local authorities who had their own institutions; training courses were open to superintendents of occupation centres, etc. The Board was always ready to remind local authorities of their various powers to grant-aid voluntary associations. It declared its disappointment on more than one occasion when a local authority

---

[1] The L.E.A.'s and M.D. authorities had been circularised to see whether they would welcome such an appointment by the C.A.M.W., and to indicate the possibility of employment by the local authority of such a specialist.

recognised the value of the voluntary association's work, but failed to give any financial support.[1]

Reasons for the Board's Encouragement of Co-operation

The relation between the Board of Control and the C.A.M.W. illustrates the Board's reasons for advocating co-operation as a matter of public policy. The advantage of securing voluntary effort in war-time has already been noted, when the Board referred to the 'arduous effort' made on behalf of the mentally handicapped during the First World War. Post-war difficulties and recurrent economic depressions in which certain public social services were immediately curtailed called for increased effort by voluntary agencies. The Board was the first to call attention to the economy which might be effected in public resources when voluntary organisations were willing to undertake responsibility. The Board's annual reports during the inter-war years contain many such references. One or two examples will serve as illustrations. In 1925 the Board issued a circular asking local authorities to let them know what steps had been taken to secure effective ascertainment of mental deficiency in their area. They considered the merits of alternative methods; either the local authority should itself appoint trained officers or it should ask a voluntary association to undertake the work of ascertainment; 'if sufficient trained officers are employed' states the Board, 'this plan may prove quite as efficacious as seeking the help of a voluntary association; but it is likely to be more expensive, for one officer cannot cover a whole county or a large county borough, whereas the voluntary association has generally a body of voluntary workers who can report cases from the village, town or suburb in which they live'.[2] A few years later they were calling attention to the use by out-county authorities[3] in Devon of the steadily developing work of the voluntary county association 'the yearly grant of £100 made by the local authority has been repaid several times over in the amount of fees saved in respect of defectives who would otherwise have remained in institutions'.[4] They had pointed out earlier that there was no doubt that voluntary supervision by local associations had prevented many defectives from becoming 'subject to be dealt with'.

This brings us to one of the chief reasons why the central authority welcomed the co-operation of the voluntary associations. Local authorities could only act within their powers: they were limited by legislation. The voluntary associations, however, were at liberty to extend

[1] See Board of Control Sixteenth Annual Report, 1929, when Oxfordshire County Council approved the request of the rural community council for help from the C.A.M.W.'s organisation, but 'in spite of much hard work', there was no agreed payment (*op. cit.*, p. 85).
[2] Twelfth Annual Report, Board of Control, 1925, pp. 69–71.
[3] Fifteenth Annual Report, Board of Control, 1928, p. 86. £95 was received in fees from out-county authorities.
[4] Tenth Annual Report, Board of Control, 1923, pp. 46–47.

VOLUNTARY ACTION AND SOCIAL POLICY

their work in any promising direction, so long as they could attract sufficient financial support for their schemes. The Board took every opportunity to remind local authorities that there were voluntary associations 'which could supply voluntary supervision for cases which do not come within the purview of the Mental Deficiency Act'.[1] Another example further illustrates the limitations upon the activities of mental deficiency authorities. We have seen that no occupation centre was established by a local authority until 1924,[2] although there were a number of local authorities using centres set up by voluntary associations. It was 1923 before the Board sent a circular to local authorities informing them that the power to provide supervision would extend to the provision of occupation centres for suitable cases. By the end of the year, the Board could report one centre established by a local authority and some 57 centres under the auspices of voluntary associations.[3] It took the opportunity to report very favourably upon the Agnes Weston Training Centre run by the C.A.M.W. for the training of occupation centre supervisors.[4]

The Board drew attention some nine years later to another severe limitation, when it was considering the fact that only about one in seven feeble-minded children received education in special schools. The remaining six-sevenths, therefore, might escape notification since they would be leaving elementary schools at the age of fourteen: 'It is clear that in the present state of the law ... the powers of the authorities to take statutory action are limited.'[5] The Board went on to suggest that it was only by 'close and informal co-operation' with the various statutory committees concerned and the voluntary associations that the gap could be 'in any way bridged, and the danger resulting from a break in the continuity of care and training at the age of fourteen averted'.

The Board took special interests in any attempt to co-ordinate the various branches of Mental Health in local areas and it reported favourably on such efforts, e.g. on the successful negotiation of a scheme by the C.A.M.W. with the local authority in Derby where, after some months' preparatory work, 'a scheme was presented to the Borough Mental Hospital Committee and the Education Committee suggesting the formation of a mental welfare association, the Association to

---

[1] See Thirteenth Annual Report, Board of Control, 1926, p. 80, with reference to the work of the London Association on behalf of the L.C.C. This Association also undertook after-care for the local education authority and for the Medical Officer of Health.
[2] See p. 126, above.
[3] May 1924, see Tenth Annual Report, 1923, pp. 47-49.
[4] Grants from the L.C.C. were not sufficient to cover the cost, even though the employment class was run by voluntary help, and in 1930 the London Association took over the centre (*ibid.*, Sixteenth Annual Report, 1929).
[5] See Twenty-first Annual Report, Board of Control, 1934, p. 42. This particular limitation of the 1913 Mental Deficiency Act was not removed until the passing of the Education Act in 1944. In this Act children of two to sixteen years may be reported, and must be if they are ineducable in the local authority's schools.

undertake work for the Borough Authorities, both under the Mental Deficiency and the Mental Treatment Acts'.[1] This was typical of the arrangements made in the formation of local associations in many parts of the country. The Board was also most ready to encourage 'unofficial help', in rural areas. If the area had a good supervision officer he could secure the help of 'charitably-minded individuals' who would undertake to train and employ defectives, thus doing what the 'Industrial Day Centres' could do in urban areas.

Another very strong reason for the support given to voluntary organisations was the belief of the Board of Control that publicity was the function of the voluntary agencies. It was their part to rouse public interest and influence public opinion. 'There are limits', it believed, 'to the extent to which central departments can influence, or indeed, ought to attempt to influence, public opinion'.[2] Nor, it felt, could local authorities be criticised for failing to do more than their constituents wanted them to do. The Board was always ready, however, to call the attention of local authorities to the educational and propaganda activities of the voluntary societies. It was ready, too, to give strong support to the conferences of the C.A.M.W. Indeed, many of the conferences were opened by the Minister of Health, and the papers and discussions received much publicity.

The Board of Control had more than once shown its true appreciation of the spirit which infused the work of voluntary societies by itself offering suggestions for improvement or for new enterprise.[3] There had obviously been times when they were less certain of the relationship, as we see in a report issued immediately after the First World War,[4] but they came to the conclusion that 'any misgivings that may once have existed as to the possible overlapping or friction with the statutory authorities or their officers have been dispelled by experience'.

This section may suitably close with an example of partnership at the local level: of combined action strongly supported by the Board of Control between a voluntary organisation and a local authority.

A Scheme of Partnership at the local level: Middlesex and the C.A.M.W.

Middlesex set an example of long-standing co-operation which had the full support of the central authority. Many of the reports of the Board of Control bear witness to the 'vitality and progressive spirit'[5] of this authority, which had entered into a close partnership with the C.A.M.W. in 1928. The Board showed its appreciation when the original

[1] *Op. cit.*, Seventeenth Annual Report, p. 92.
[2] Twenty-Second Annual Report, Board of Control, 1935.
[3] Twenty-Fifth Annual Report, Board of Control, p. 9. As late as 1938 we find the Board pleading with the voluntary organisations to give more attention to physical training, and suggesting that C.A.M.W. add a P.T. instructor to its visiting staff. (This was to benefit mental patients as well as defectives.)
[4] Sixth Annual Report, 1919, pp. 3 and 4.
[5] See Seventeenth Annual Report, 1930, p. 60.

agreement, whereby the C.A.M.W. undertook the organisation of occupation centres and home training in return for a substantial grant, was extended for a further period with a greatly increased grant. From the inception of the scheme until the outbreak of the Second World War, there was a continuous history of development, and the Board gave special credit to the C.A.M.W. for working out a co-ordinated scheme which gave strength to local interest, yet used the experience and resources of the national agency. The representative statutory–voluntary nature of the committees laid the foundations for its success. Some details of this scheme are worth noting as an example of the method by which co-operation was achieved. In 1927, the C.A.M.W. undertook responsibility for organising and supervising occupation centres[1] on behalf of the authority. This was followed by the appointment of two home teachers[2] by the association to work especially in Middlesex. The C.A.M.W. now set up a special committee which was fully representative of statutory and voluntary agencies to be responsible for the work in Middlesex. At the same time, local committees were formed in each area representing the county council, the public assistance committee, and the local education authority, together with voluntary agencies such as the Invalid Children's Aid Association, local rescue work, and the Central Aid Society. Each committee had a responsible part to play both in the creation of local interest and in the organisation of many of the activities associated with the occupation centres.[3] From January 1932 the C.A.M.W. agreed to be responsible for the Authority's guardianship scheme, while a travelling handicraft teacher was added to the staff. Thereafter we find steady development in the work for the mentally defective in Middlesex, and they were amongst the first of the authorities to avail themselves of the services of the Association's educational psychologist. Middlesex was, in fact, using the C.A.M.W. as its agent for much of its work for the community care of the mentally defective, as the L.C.C. had used M.A.C.A. for much of the community care of its mental patients.

While the C.A.M.W. and their local associations had considerable success in combining voluntary and statutory help in particular areas, there were parts of the country where local authorities found co-operation difficult because there were too many competing voluntary societies. At the national level, too, the public was bewildered by the multiplicity of organisations. The crux of the matter was that no one agency covered or attempted to cover the whole field. Each had its own limited objective, and if on the whole there was no serious overlapping, there was also little effort towards a complete scheme of co-ordination.[4]

[1] Ultimately 8 centres.
[2] The number was later increased to six.
[3] Such as outings, discussion of centre difficulties, training facilities, etc.
[4] Twenty-sixth Annual Report, Board of Control, 1939, unpublished abridged copy, pp. 7 and 8.

THE MENTAL HEALTH SERVICES

The Board had called attention in 1935 to the want of unified direction and the lack of a comprehensive central body able to view the problem of mental health as a whole.[1] It believed that 'the development of any health service depends upon close co-operation between voluntary effort and governmental or municipal activities'. The statutory authorities had to wait for further legislation,[2] but the voluntary agencies were free to put their house in order. That they were endeavouring to do this is evident in the setting up of the Feversham Committee which reported in 1939. Co-ordination was the outstanding need, when a Second World War threatened to test the resources of the community to the uttermost.

Finally, some examples will be given, in summary form, to illustrate in greater detail the variety in the 'services rendered' by voluntary bodies in the years just preceding the Second World War, both on an agency basis for local authorities, when payment was received, and in a voluntary capacity.

[1] Twenty-Second Annual Report, *op. cit.*
[2] This was accomplished in the National Health Service Act, 1946.

Notes on Co-operation between Voluntary Organisations and Local Authorities in the Mental Health Service in the years preceding the Second World War

I. CAMBRIDGE: SHOWING DETAILED AGENCY WORK

Activities undertaken on behalf of statutory authorities by the *Cambridgeshire Voluntary Association for Mental Welfare, 1937–38*: Income from statutory and other sources. [From Annual Report for year 1938.]

1. ON AN AGENCY BASIS (i.e. work paid for)

(A) *Work for Cambridgeshire County Council*

(i) Ascertainment of all alleged defectives in the County by means of supervision direct or indirect of all cases reported to the local authority.

(ii) Notification to M.D.Com. of cases which appear subject to be dealt with under 52 (1) *b* of Mental Deficiency Act.

(iii) Statutory supervision of defectives liable to be dealt with under the Act in whose cases circumstances do not at the time exist which make it urgent for them to be sent to institutions.

(iv) Provision of escort, when desired, for cases being sent to certified institutions or elsewhere.

(v) Provision of occupation and training centre for ineducable and defective children living at home in Cambridgeshire (borough and county cases) with classes for defective boys and girls of sixteen plus.

(B) *For County Education Committee*

(i) Supervision in own homes of M.D. children leaving ordinary elementary schools at the age fourteen to sixteen.

(ii) Enquiry into history, home conditions and circumstances of children referred by school medical staff for special report.

(C) *For Borough Education Committee*

(i) As in B (i) above.

(ii) Supervision in own homes of all children attending the special school section of the open-air school.

(iii) Reports to School Medical Officers on cases referred to them for investigation only.

(D) *For Public Assistance Committee*

(i) Investigations into cases referred by individual guardians or relieving officers.

(ii) After-care of alleged defectives leaving P.A. Institutions or receiving outdoor relief.

(E) *For Fulbourne Mental Hospital*

(i) Enquiry into and report upon home circumstances, etc., of patients on admission and of those about to be allowed out on trial.

(ii) Visiting and after-care of patients.

THE MENTAL HEALTH SERVICES

2. VOLUNTARY WORK (not paid for)

(i) Supervision in own homes of M.D. children under seven and care of M.D., persons either under or over sixteen who are not subject to be dealt with under Mental Deficiency Act, 1913.

(ii) Cases of mental instability or disorder who are not certifiable under Lunacy Act, 1890, and after-care of patients discharged from institutions under the same Act.

Total Income for year ended 31.3.39 = £1,131 17s. 0d. which includes Grants as follows:

		£	s.	d.
Cambs. C.C.		270	0	0
„ County Ed. Com.		25	0	0
„ Borough „	„	40	0	0
„ P.A.C.		15	15	0

£350 15s. 0d.

II. OTHER AREAS: SHOWING VARIETY IN TYPES OF CO-OPERATION

(1) The travelling speech therapist of the C.A.M.W. was employed jointly by the local education authorities of *Pontypridd, Aberdare* and *Mountain Ash* for the whole of 1938. At the end of this period it was decided by the authorities to make a permanent appointment (welcomed by the C.A.M.W. who had worked to this end).

(2) *The Mid-Wales and Monmouthshire Mental Hospitals* financed the boarding-out scheme, the C.A.M.W. receiving and distributing grants from the two hospitals, and seconding one of their own social workers to the hospitals. The C.A.M.W. received £5 p.a. *per capita* grant from the Monmouthshire mental deficiency committee for the supervision of mental defectives boarded-out.

(3) The *C.A.M.W.* had for some years supervised patients on licence from *Cell Barnes Colony* with the hope that statutory authority would eventually take over the work. In 1938 Hertfordshire County Council appointed a petitioning officer and the C.A.M.W. handed over this work although the council continued to use the C.A.M.W. for supervision on licence of those placed outside the county.

(4) The C.A.M.W. successfully co-operated with the *U.A.B.* and with some P.A.C.s (especially in London) in the placement of applicants who were 'very difficult to place' by reason of mental inferiority not amounting to mental deficiency. The C.A.M.W. gave general supervision and often succeeded in helping them to become self-supporting. If they were unemployed or in need, and within the scope of the U.A.B., then arrangements were made for assistance without delay, since they were known as C.A.M.W. cases.

(5) In 1939, the *North Eastern Council for Mental Welfare* was able to become independent of support by the C.A.M.W. 'having satisfactorily stabilised its position and obtained the support of 7 local authorities'.

(6) *The Joint Register of Foster Homes* for Nervous, Retarded and Difficult Children established in co-operation with the Child Guidance Council in 1937, was used throughout 1938 by statutory and voluntary agencies. These included 24 L.E.A.s, 2 P.A.C.s, 12 voluntary societies, 10 child guidance centres, and 33 individual social workers, doctors, etc. Of 321 cases referred, 100 were placed in foster homes.

(7) *The C.A.M.W. Holiday Homes* were used in 1938 by statutory and voluntary agencies, including 27 parties from certified institutions, 24 parties from mental hospitals, 1 from an occupation centre (3 homes were in existence in 1938, 2 more were opened in 1939).

XIII

THE RESPONSE TO THE EMERGENCY: THE WAR AND POST-WAR DEVELOPMENTS

Co-ordination: The National Association for Mental Health (N.A.M.H.) War Casualties and New Projects

THE process of co-ordination went on rapidly after the publication of the report of the Feversham Committee, and the call by the Minister of Health for a Mental Health Emergency Committee. The immediate practical result was the establishment of regional offices and the selection of key workers for each of the Civil Defence Regions.[1] Further co-ordination of the national voluntary organisations who were co-operating with the Minister of Health proceeded by stages to a Provisional National Council for Mental Health,[2] and finally to the formation of the *National Association for Mental Health (N.A.M.H.)*[3] when amalgamation was effected. (The Mental After-care Association, as we have seen, remained independent.)

The contribution of N.A.M.H. and its immediate predecessors during the emergency, and in the difficult transition years which followed, is a striking illustration of elasticity and resilience. Much of their existing work had to be curtailed, some was discontinued for a time in the immediate dislocation which followed evacuation. But the tradition of experimental work was maintained and the role of the voluntary organisation as a pioneer was justified in the new ventures which were set on foot. The rapidly changing conditions called for considerable powers of

[1] By the end of 1939 Regional psychiatric social workers were established. In 1942 the Minister of Health inaugurated his official scheme to meet the needs of evacuees, and trained social workers were appointed as welfare officers, many of them coming in fact from the field of mental health. Several were trained psychiatric social workers.

[2] The Provisional National Council was formed, after long negotiation, at the end of 1942, and it took over the work of its constituent bodies on 1.1.43.

[3] The amalgamation of the C.A.M.W., the Child Guidance Council and the National Council for Mental Hygiene proceeded by stages and was finally completed in 1946.

adjustment. There is no doubt that psychiatrists expected far greater casualties in the field of mental health, just as military experts forecast heavier casualties to life and limb, than were justified by the event. The mental health organisations were determined not to be caught unawares. So energetic was their response that they were said at times to be a source of embarrassment to the Ministry.[1] Fortunately, the organisations also possessed powers of self-criticism and could learn from experience. Later, it was a psychiatrist, the main speaker at an Interclinic Child Guidance Conference, who was to warn the members that there was danger in trying to oversell their speciality.[2]

However, the amalgamation of three of the main societies in the field of mental health brought together valuable experience which was welcomed by the Minister of Health. The N.A.M.H. made regular reports to the Minister on its After-care Scheme. In 1943 he invited the N.A.M.H.[3] to be responsible for the Ex-Services After-Care Scheme, extended three years later to include civilians. This was the beginning of a unique experiment in community care.[4] The psychiatric social workers appointed by the N.A.M.H. had, in common with other P.S.W.'s, been trained to work in a team based on a clinic or a hospital. They now found themselves being called upon to advise, often as the only workers in their area trained in mental heath, on the after-care of 'psychiatric casualties'. The response of the N.A.M.H., with the support and financial backing of the Ministry, was to build up a new team: senior regional officers, all qualified and experienced P.S.W.'s, supervised a group of social workers, most of whom had relevant experience and many of whom had a social science certificate. Each region had a regular case conference, and after 1946 the team was supervised by the Association's Medical Director. Wherever possible they co-operated with other workers in the area, but sometimes, especially in rural districts, they had to work largely in isolation.[5] Seen as a whole this was a new pattern of community team work, evolved to meet special needs at a time of acute shortage of mental health workers. The N.A.M.H. hoped that it would afford valuable experience for the extension of the health services after the war.[6]

---

[1] See R. M. Titmuss, *Problems of Social Policy*, p. 381. The pressure for the extension of psychological work to many branches of the social services was instanced as a particular source of embarrassment.

[2] Dr. Alan Maberly in 1949, reported in *Supplement to Mental Health*, Vol. IX, No. 3, p. xi.

[3] N.A.M.H. in turn invited M.A.C.A. to take over one area (parts of London and Essex).

[4] See 'Mental Health Community Care', by Dr. Soddy, in the *British Medical Bulletin*, Vol. 6, No. 3, 1949.

[5] See Ashdown and Brown, *opus cit.*, for discussion of the difficulties met by psychiatric social workers under these conditions. The N.A.M.H. approached the problem as a challenge, and did not themselves emphasise the difficulties.

[6] See the useful pamphlet by Dr. Soddy, Medical Director of the N.A.M.H., 'Some Lessons of War-Time Psychiatry', published by the N.A.M.H.

THE RESPONSE TO THE EMERGENCY

The study of the development of the national voluntary organisations for mental health during the Second World War and the immediate post-war period throws light on some of the characteristic features of the more active voluntary organisations.

At first they had many disappointments and frustrations. For the C.A.M.W. the first casualties were the fine holiday homes which had been increasingly used by statutory and voluntary agencies; they had to be diverted immediately to other uses.[1] A number of occupation centres were also closed as soon as evacuation started. The C.A.M.W. met this situation by a scheme of group teaching.[2] Another long-standing scheme received a setback at the outbreak of war when the Board of Education withdrew its grant towards the Teachers' Training Course. The C.A.M.W. responded by offering another course on similar lines, without the Board's financial support, but with its official approval. Its courses for medical officers were continued in a less vulnerable area than London.[3] It was an illustration of the traditional good relationship with local authorities that a new course for teachers was run in 1942 directed by the educational psychologist of the C.A.M.W. with the assistance of lecturers from the local authority service.[4]

Another early war casualty was the guardianship scheme and the licensing of defectives from institutions, with the result that high-grade defectives were again being retained in institutions. The response of the N.A.M.H. to this challenge was a decision to set up agricultural hostels. This served a double purpose: defectives on licence could make a contribution to the community's need for increased food production, and at the same time release much-needed beds in institutions. These hostels had the backing of the Ministry of Agriculture, and of the County Agricultural Executive Committees who were responsible for maintenance and for employment. The voluntary organisation supplied the staff (wardens, etc.) and administered the hostels. Farmers found this scheme so successful that the first hostel was quickly followed by a second, until by 1947 there were eleven hostels employing 360 land workers and 30 housemen. Through its residential services[5] the N.A.M.H. showed particular enterprise in meeting new needs.

Sometimes experiments were undertaken in the early years of the war

[1] One was requisitioned by the military authorities, two were used as reception centres for defectives.
[2] Four out of seven Home Teachers in London added some 64 children to their registers to be given social training in small groups of 3–5. The Organisation heard with great regret the decision of Middlesex in 1941 to discontinue the Home Teaching Service. 160–170 children had been visited regularly, some 70 of whom were taught in small groups.
[3] The courses were organised in Oxford. By 1942 part of the course was again given in London with the co-operation of the L.C.C. and Middlesex in the arrangements for visits of observation.
[4] The course was held in University College, Nottingham.
[5] The N.A.M.H. changed its descriptive title from 'Homes and Hostels' to 'Residential Services' in 1948 to mark the new approach to this branch of its work.

THE MENTAL HEALTH SERVICES

on the suggestion of one of the Ministries. In 1941 the Board of Education asked the Council to open a Home School for boys sent by local authorities,[1] while it was at the request of the Minister of Health, and in co-operation with the Waifs and Strays Society that the C.A.M.W., in 1942, took responsibility for the staffing and administration of the special residential nursery for children under five.[2] The N.A.M.H. hoped to keep this going after the war as a boarding home for young maladjusted children, but it had, unfortunately, to be closed after five years of successful working,[3] when the Board of Education ruled that local education authorities had no power to pay for handicapped children unless they attended school. As the majority of the children at the home were under five, this was a severe blow to finance.

Holiday homes were also gradually re-opened as the premises were released. Once more parties of patients from mental hospitals, colonies for defectives, patients under licence and under guardianship were received for two weeks' holiday. In 1947 the N.A.M.H. was actually seeking new premises for another home, so great was the demand. Another welcome new venture was the provision of a convalescent home[4] for epileptics recovering from other illnesses. Social workers were constantly being met by refusals to take anyone with epilepsy in the ordinary convalescent homes. In 1950 the N.A.M.H. was encouraged by the demand to establish a second home.

The Association also took part in various discussions on the possibility of setting up special hostels for dull and backward children, and it opened a small observation hostel for boys under twelve found to be in need of prolonged treatment at a child guidance centre.[5] Later projects of considerable interest were undertaken in co-operation with the Home Office. Such was the opening of Duncroft Approved School for adolescent girls in need of psychological treatment, in 1949, while a similar school for boys aged eleven to fifteen was projected for the following year. The N.A.M.H. nominated the board of managers, which was approved by the Home Office, and the girls were received through the Home Office classifying schools. A full team, including psychiatrists, an educational psychologist and a psychiatric social worker were appointed in addition to a headmistress and other staff.

---

[1] Either under Section 80 of the Education Act, 1921, or under the Children and Young Persons Act, 1933 (when the local authority was a 'fit person').

[2] These were children transferred from the ordinary residential nurseries by reason of pronounced behaviour problems. The whole cost was met by the Minister's evacuation account.

[3] The organisation hoped that other means would be found to re-open at a future date; meanwhile they had regretfully to let it for other purposes.

[4] The first home was established in 1948 when a suitable house was bequeathed for the purpose and grants were made from King Edward's Hospital Fund for the equipment.

[5] This was in connection with referrals to the Joint Register of Foster Homes undertaken by the C.A.M.W. and the Child Guidance Council.

THE RESPONSE TO THE EMERGENCY

By 1950 two experimental homes of another kind were opened, one to receive emotionally disturbed children sent through the London juvenile courts,[1] the other a home for senile old people not sufficiently ill to require care in a mental hospital. The establishment of these two homes illustrates a fruitful field of co-operation when charitable trusts supported the scheme by generous grants, and other voluntary organisations co-operated. The home for maladjusted children was made possible by a gift from the Henderson Trust of £19,000, the Home Office asked the N.A.M.H. to act as agents for the Governors; the establishment of the home for senile patients was undertaken in co-operation with organisations for old people and a City Company, grants being received from the *National Corporation for the Care of Old People*, the *National Old People's Welfare Committee* and the *Clothworkers' Company*. A further project resulted from a recommendation by some regional hospital boards and medical officers of health: a short-term home established for mentally defective and sub-normal children met the urgent needs of mothers who needed a rest from their charges, or who were going into hospital for their confinement or for treatment.[2] This was in addition to the home for mentally defective children in Sussex which had been a long-standing commitment.[3]

A recent development of special interest was the opening of a short-stay home, Orchard Dene, bought and equipped by the *National Association of the Parents of Backward Children*,[4] to provide for the temporary care of children while the families had a much needed rest, or during a period of emergency. The N.A.M.H. was asked to administer the home, and it was anticipated that local authorities would welcome this opportunity to use some of the vacancies.[5]

Recovery and Extension of Traditional Work

Meanwhile, the advisory service of the N.A.M.H. had grown steadily during the war years. It was found that case work made increasing demands on its resources since 'war problems were super-imposed on peace-time ones'. One of the early problems had been the unsettling of defectives by evacuation or bombing.[6] It is interesting to note that a

---

[1] 'Ponds', opened in November 1950, taking children between the ages of seven and twelve, intended to co-operate closely with the parents during the year's absence from home. The psychiatric social worker visited the children's homes and the pscyhiatrist held meetings either singly or as group discussions. Unfortunately, Ponds had to be closed in 1954 'owing to insurmountable financial and staffing difficulties'. See *Mental Health News Letter*, Spring, 1954.

[2] Under Section 28, National Health Service Act, 1946.

[3] Approved under Section 50, Mental Deficiency Act, 1913.

[4] This association was soon to change its name, 'backward' being replaced by 'mentally handicapped'.

[5] See MIN/Health circular 5/52. In the summer of 1952, of the 52 children received, 33 were maintained by their local health authorities, a few were helped through voluntary funds, and the parents paid fees for the remainder.

[6] See Twenty-Seventh Annual Report, C.A.M.W., 1941.

THE MENTAL HEALTH SERVICES

number of the difficult cases were referred to the voluntary organisations by local authorities, government departments and medical practitioners.[1] By the year 1947–48 the case load of N.A.M.H. had reached 12,707, of which 5,127 were new. Many of those now seeking help were neurotics and psychotics.[2] The value of the voluntary organisation as an early advice centre, when clinic services were quite inadequate to meet the demands, was increasingly recognised.[3]

Another of the cherished projects of the N.A.M.H. which was extended after the war, was its supplementary training schemes and lecture courses, and the various loan services undertaken by its training and education department. In addition to its short courses varying from one to three weeks for teachers[4] and doctors, it had an eight weeks' course for local authority officials, and a four weeks' course for staffs of children's homes on behalf of the Home Office. It also organised a year's diploma training course[5] for staffs of occupation centres and children's departments of institutions for defectives.[6] Refresher courses were also a recognised feature of the schemes. In addition, series of lectures were organised on behalf of several local authorities[7] and for various professional groups.[8] Its loan service met the needs of various groups who needed help in investigating new problems, or in training; or N.A.M.H. staff were loaned to child guidance clinics and other organisations, attending usually for several sessions weekly for a term.

In addition to sustained help of this nature, speakers were provided to give public lecture courses and individual talks in a number of areas throughout the country.[9] In many instances such talks were given in co-operation with the Workers Educational Association or a Settlement or a University College. The increasing interest taken in these subjects

[1] In 1941, out of 1,170 cases, 126 came from statutory authorities and 111 from medical practitioners, while schools, hospitals and voluntary associations accounted for 343. Individual social workers sent the largest single number, 369. The rest were mostly from parents and relatives, 212. (Individual patients applying were 9.)

[2] Of the adults about 40% were neurotic and 30% psychotics. See Annual Report of N.A.M.H., 1947–48.

[3] The N.A.M.H. keeps a useful 'Register of Facilities' including schools for maladjusted children, homes for defectives, homes taking senile patients, etc.

[4] On behalf of the Ministry of Education.

[5] This course was the only recognised course under the Mental Deficiency Act.

[6] This was the result of a scheme which received the warm approval of the Board of Control in 1945. It was the only recognised systematic training for workers in occupation centres and training departments of institutions. Some students were helped by Further Education grants; others were seconded by their local authorities. In 1955 the N.A.M.H. announced a change of name for this course, to be known in future as the Diploma Course for Teachers of the Mentally Handicapped (in occupation centres, Mental Deficiency Hospitals, or in their own homes).

[7] In 1948–49 the L.C.C. and Kent both asked for such lectures, Kent having nine series of 8–10 lectures each.

[8] Including lectures for Fellows in Educational Psychology.

[9] Dealing with such subjects as 'the psychology of normal children' and 'frustration and fulfilment in adult life'.

THE RESPONSE TO THE EMERGENCY

was evidenced by requests for speakers from a variety of organisations such as Parent Groups, Teachers' Groups, Women's Institutes, Toc H., etc. Although the N.A.M.H. preferred, as a matter of principle, to concentrate on its lecture courses placing little reliance on the single talk or lecture, it had to recognise that the public was now keenly interested in psychological questions. When the press, the film and the radio took up the subject as one which had interest value, it was important that those concerned with mental health should do what they could to get the right balance. For this reason the N.A.M.H. was ready to respond not only to calls for courses for professional workers who wished to supplement their knowledge, or from statutory authorities who wished their staff to be better qualified, but from community groups such as Young Wives Fellowships and Rotary Clubs who wanted an interesting speaker on a topical subject.

One war-time venture which the N.A.M.H. gave up with considerable regret was its Regional Advisory Service. Although the N.A.M.H. was encouraged in 1948 by an experimental grant for one year from the British Legion for the appointment of psychiatrists, the Minister of Health was not disposed to grant-aid the scheme when the British Legion withdrew. The N.A.M.H. felt strongly that this regional work had served a valuable purpose by demonstrating a successful scheme of community care.[1] They argued that the withdrawal of experienced key workers at a time of scarcity when there would be undirected competition for the services of trained personnel was short-sighted. They pleaded that for the transition period, at least, until local authorities' 'duly authorised officers', mental health officers and welfare officers[2] could become familiar with their responsibilities and, if possible, receive some training, it would be wise to retain the regional scheme. It was in vain, however. The National Health Service Act placed community care in the hands of local authorities and the N.A.M.H. must negotiate with them if it wished to offer its services. Each local health authority must decide to what extent it would use a voluntary association on an agency basis. With the cessation of the substantial Ministry grants, the Association's regional offices had gradually to be closed.[3]

A few years later the N.A.M.H. secured the support of a charitable trust and a national voluntary association,[4] in opening a Northern Branch and it welcomed close association with the University of Leeds in its educational work.

[1] In a memorandum to the Mackintosh Committee the Association pointed out that nearly 18,000 cases were dealt with by November 1948.
[2] Officers responsible for duties under the Lunacy and Mental Treatment Acts, the Mental Deficiency Act, the National Health Service Act and the National Assistance Act.
[3] Seven were closed in 1949 and three more in 1950.
[4] The Carnegie Trust gave a generous grant and the regional branch of the National Council of Social Service offered accommodation. See N.A.M.H., *Mental Health News Letter*, Spring, 1953. The Northern Branch was established in Leeds.

THE MENTAL HEALTH SERVICES

M.A.C.A.: Its Independent Status

M.A.C.A., meanwhile, continued to maintain its independent status and its essentially metropolitan character, working in close association with the L.C.C. throughout the Second World War in the community care of the mentally ill, and in the provision of convalescent homes, etc. After the war, with the passing of the National Health Service Act and the National Assistance Act, M.A.C.A. had some moments of disquiet. There was some uncertainty about responsibility for payments for the maintenance of patients in homes, and since M.A.C.A. depended so largely upon income from payments for services rendered, it was naturally somewhat anxious. However, it found the L.C.C. most helpful[1] during the period of transfer. In spite of its regrets that certain sources of income had dried up (e.g. Queen Adelaide's Fund on which the Association had been able to draw to the extent of £600 per annum), M.A.C.A. was still strongly supported by public funds. The change in its financial position since the early part of the century illustrates the great development which had taken place in the voluntary–statutory partnership. In 1910, when M.A.C.A.'s total income was approximately £1,200, only £66 had come from statutory sources. In 1949 the total income had passed £45,000, over £31,000 of which was income from payments for services rendered, by far the greater part of which was received from public authorities. While income from charitable sources had been preponderant in the years before the First World War, it was a very small proportion of the total before the half-century was reached.[2] It was perhaps surprising that the L.C.C. should continue to use M.A.C.A. to assist in 'community care' instead of administering the service directly,[3] as the majority of local authorities had chosen to do since the National Health Service Act had come into operation.[4] It was indicative of the very good relationship which had existed for so long a time that the L.C.C. continued to carry through much of its care of the mentally ill in close association with M.A.C.A.

Yet the work of the Mental After-Care Association had inevitably changed, as local authorities were given greater powers and duties under the new social legislation. Even earlier, when the L.C.C. had begun appointing its own psychiatric social workers, it had had progressively less need to use a voluntary association for its community care. Nor since the appointment of almoners in most of the hospitals was

[1] See Annual Reports of M.A.C.A. for the years 1948 and 1949.
[2] See Table VI, p. 166.
[3] As indeed the L.C.C. had done in the 1930's in the field of mental deficiency.
[4] By 1952 all except the L.C.C. and Middlesex were making direct provision; a few were appointing trained psychiatric social workers, as the L.C.C. had itself done some years before. The L.C.C. did in fact terminate some of their arrangements with the Voluntary Bodies in April 1953. This affected both M.A.C.A. and N.A.M.H.

THE RESPONSE TO THE EMERGENCY

M.A.C.A. asked to visit patients returning to their own relatives.[1] Most of the visiting by the Association's officers was now done in response to requests from out-patients themselves, for those who were not expected to need immediate hospital treatment: in fact, pre-care rather than after-care. Its small residential homes still made a valuable contribution, but the emphasis had changed. The majority of patients were no longer convalescents, having a period of adjustment before plunging into life in the community, but those having a short change from the hospital to which they would return, or the chronic sick who would return to the local authorities in whose care they were. The homes still had room for patients on 'prolonged trial', or for patients whose own homes were far distant, and for whom special arrangements must be made. But the original work of after-care, for which M.A.C.A. was founded, had largely disappeared. The Association had taken part in the after-care of ex-service patients in Essex and Surrey when the scheme was started in 1943, but in 1946 this part of its work was handed over to the National Association for Mental Health with the agreement of the Board of Control.

Such changes, together with the loss of some of its homes through bombing, meant that M.A.C.A. was no longer in a position to help as many patients as before the War. The following table shows the immediate drop in numbers after 1939, and the partial recovery in 1941; by 1950, however, the total was still less than 3,000, compared with 4,222 in 1939.

TABLE V

Number of Cases (Mental Illness) 'dealt with' by M.A.C.A., 1939–50

Year	Total
1939	4,222
1940	1,602
1941	2,764
1942	2,509
1943	2,736
1944	2,657
1945	2,834
1946	2,955
1947	2,767
1948	2,838
1949	3,007
1950	2,980

It is of interest to note the various ways in which the Association was helping patients halfway through the century. A breakdown of the total,

[1] M.A.C.A. was always prepared to act as 'locum' when the psychiatric social worker was on holiday or to do any special visits when asked, but this was now exceptional.

THE MENTAL HEALTH SERVICES

2,980, shows that the great majority, 1,734, were sent for convalescence and holiday, 330 were patients 'boarded out'[1] from hospital or from private sources, 313 were first visits paid to the homes of patients 'on trial' from hospitals, while 603 were patients coming directly to the office or privately referred.

[1] The term 'boarded out' is not used in its technical sense (Lunacy Act, 1890, Sec. 27) but to describe the chronic sick, not in need of mental hospital care, who are boarded in special homes run by approved matrons.

XIV

CHANGES IN SOCIAL POLICY: THE EFFECT ON VOLUNTARY ORGANISATIONS

New Social Legislation affecting the Mental Health Services

THE first measures to affect mental health were contained in legislation mainly concerned with other services, i.e. the Education Act, 1944, and the Disabled Persons (Employment) Act, 1944. They will be referred to later. The most important measure of direct concern to the mental health services was the National Health Service Act, 1946.

The National Health Service Bill had been closely watched by all the voluntary organisations, for it would have wide repercussions on the mental health services. The Act made important administrative changes, bringing together the mental health services and the general health services under the single control of the Minister of Health. At first it looked as though the influence of the Board of Control was to be confined to its quasi-judicial functions,[1] but in practice it was found impossible to separate the legal, administrative and medical aspects of mental treatment. Accordingly, the Minister appointed the members of the Board as the Mental Health Division of the Ministry of Health,[2] so that they were responsible to the Minister for the co-ordination of all the functions assigned under the Act to the Central Authority.[3] Mental hospitals, institutions for defectives, certain convalescent homes

---

[1] 'The administrative functions of the Board of Control, as distinct from their quasi-judicial duties, will be transferred to the Minister...the Board...as an independent body...will continue to be responsible to the Minister for the matters affecting the liberty of individuals' (Ministry of Health circular 33/481).

[2] *Civilian Health and Medical Services*, Vol. I, p. 192.

[3] The Board's full and encouraging annual reports, so helpful in the growth of the movement, were perforce discontinued. Reports on the Mental Health Service now took their place in the general reports on *The Nation's Health* issued annually by the Minister.

and some child guidance clinics[1] were under the control of the Minister acting through his regional hospital boards. Local health authorities were now fully responsible for community care, and the association with the Poor Law and its relieving officers was finally broken.[2]

Powers to co-operate with voluntary organisations were embodied in the new legislation, and circulars, memoranda and public speeches again emphasised the value which the Minister placed on the partnership of statutory and voluntary agencies. The voluntary organisations in their turn welcomed the new community responsibility and the promised integration of the health services. They were, however, critical of the administrative dichotomy consequent upon the division of responsibility for hospital and community care services.[3] It was in an endeavour to watch the interests of the patient while this complex machinery was put into operation that the voluntary organisations felt that they still had a vital part to play. They were confident that the time had not yet come for self-immolation.

Meanwhile, the Education Act, 1944, had removed the necessity for certification of feeble-minded children educable in special schools,[4] and provision was made for special educational treatment for maladjusted children. At last the vexed question of the responsibility for reporting *any child* with a disability of mind of such a nature or to such an extent that, either he is 'incapable of receiving education at school', or that he will 'require supervision after leaving school', was now placed firmly upon the education authority.[5]

The Disabled Persons (Employment) Act, 1944, provided a comprehensive definition of disablement which included the mentally defective and the mentally disordered; they were therefore entitled to the facilities offered by the disablement resettlement officers of the employment exchanges,[6] by rehabilitation centres, remploy factories, etc. Finally, the National Assistance Act, 1948, placed wide responsibilities on local authorities for the welfare and assistance of the handicapped, including the mentally handicapped.

---

[1] Some clinics remained under the control of the Local Education Authority.

[2] In practice a number of relieving officers were transferred from the Poor Law Services to the new Health Service and became 'duly authorised officers', as others had become 'welfare officers'.

[3] The Medical Director of the N.A.M.H., in putting the case for a strong community service, argued that under the National Health Service 'there is some danger that in the interests of organisation, opportunities may be missed of creating the most effective instrument possible for the furtherance of Mental Health, by regarding social work as merely an adjunct to clinical treatment'.

[4] These schools were now to be known as schools for the educationally sub-normal —another change of name indicating a new attitude.

[5] See Education Act, 1944, Section 57. See also Section 34 for the duty of ascertainment.

[6] The new Disablement Resettlement Officers had much to learn of the difficulties in placing the mentally handicapped.

EFFECT OF CHANGES ON VOLUNTARY ORGANISATIONS

The Effect of Social Policy on the Function of the Voluntary Organisations

The function of voluntary bodies in scrutinising Bills and bringing their experience to the task of suggesting amendments had in the past been jealously guarded, and the N.A.M.H. felt that insufficient scope had been given them in the rush of important bills into the committee stage in the 1940's. They regretted that their traditional methods of 'examination by a representative and democratically constituted body' could not be used, and they were grieved that the Government thus deprived itself of independent professional and expert help.[1] Moreover, in the sphere of community care, the N.A.M.H. found itself constrained to examine the separate proposals of local health authorities,[2] and the vast correspondence involved put considerable strain on their resources. In 1948 the N.A.M.H. decided to form a special mental deficiency group to watch the results of legislation on the welfare of mental defectives. True to tradition it was a co-operative effort including representatives of voluntary and statutory interests. Useful information was collected from all over the country and memoranda were sent to the Ministry of Health, the National Assistance Board and the Ministry of National Insurance. In its first enquiries general attention was given to questions of training and employment.

The N.A.M.H. was particularly anxious to get some enlightenment on the relationship between regional hospital boards and local authorities. In the field of child guidance it sought for some elucidation of the position of child guidance centres administered under the Education Act[3] and child guidance clinics administered under the National Health Service Act. The former were the responsibility of the local education authority, the latter of the regional hospital boards, and it seemed to the N.A.M.H. that the Ministry was drawing an unwarranted distinction between ascertainment and diagnosis and treatment.[4] It was urged that 'all workers must be based on the clinic team', and the dichotomy in administration must not affect the treatment of the patient under a unified scheme. This drew an assurance from the Ministries concerned that no rigid distinction between clinics and centres should be drawn, but each should co-operate with the other when collaboration was in the best interests of the child.

Another practical difficulty to which the N.A.M.H. drew attention arose from the operation of the National Assistance Act. It was pointed out that some local authorities were transferring financial obligations for the maintenance of defectives under guardianship to the N.A.B.

[1] See N.A.M.H. Annual Report, 1947–48, Social Services Department, p. 10.
[2] Under Sections 28 and 51 of the National Health Service Act, 1946.
[3] Education Act, 1944, Section 34, *re* Ascertainment of Maladjusted pupils.
[4] See Ministry of Education Circular 179, 1948, on the School Health Service and Handicapped Pupils, and the Report of the Eighth Inter-Clinic Child Guidance Conference, 1949.

This had the effect, in their view, of making it even more difficult to find householders who would accept the responsibilities of guardianship. It was becoming increasingly difficult to place defectives on licence from institutions and to give them community care, yet beds in institutions were urgently needed. The N.A.M.H. was soon to decide[1] that its own guardianship work must come to an end, for by 1950 most local authorities and regional hospital boards were making their own arrangements.[2] It felt some regret at closing down the service of placement and supervision for defectives under guardianship and on licence, for it had been one of its earliest pioneer ventures. The winter of 1950–51 also saw the process of transference of its agricultural hostels to regional hospital boards. The Minister of Agriculture's responsibility ceased with the end of the employment of pool labour. The scheme was now to be run in connection with the mental deficiency institutions, and the N.A.M.H. was asked to make arrangements for men admitted uncertified or placed under guardianship but not on licence. Again the N.A.M.H. expressed some regret, largely due to the fact that each hostel was now to be administered as part of particular mental deficiency institution, and might become 'institutionalised'. It was hoped that the wardens of the hostels[3] would transfer to the employment of hospital management committees. There was considerable uncertainty about the future, and the N.A.M.H. watched the change-over with apprehension.

The N.A.M.H. accepted some of the changes with good heart, for it had long advocated increased statutory responsibility and an integrated health service. It welcomed the appointment of many of its workers as members of regional hospital boards, and noted with approval the appointment of regional psychiatrists by most of the Boards. Its main criticism was the haste with which some of the changes were made, and the fundamental division of responsibility in the administrative structure which was 'at variance with sound medico-social principles'.[4]

The curtailment of much of its work following the new legislation reduced its income and put some strain upon its finances, but the N.A.M.H. was determined to press on with its enquiries. The sub-committee on mental deficiency embarked on two investigations, one on the social adaptation of educationally sub-normal boys and girls during the first two years after leaving school, and the other on the problem of the defective mother in relation both to her own welfare and that of her children. These were fact-finding enquiries in which local education authorities and local health authorities were invited to give information, and the co-operation of various organisations concerned with mothers

---

[1] The decision was made in 1950.
[2] A club for girls under guardianship was, it was hoped, still to be run under voluntary auspices.
[3] There were twelve in existence by 1950.
[4] See N.A.M.H. Annual Report, 1947–48, p. 11.

and children was sought.[1] It was in line with this emphasis on investigation that its conference in 1953 was upon 'The Practical Application of Research and Experiment to the Mental Health Field'. Expansion also took place in the Association's training schemes. Not only was a second centre established for the one-year diploma course, but an 'In-Service' course was projected for members of occupation centre staffs,[2] and a course of seminars for social case workers was begun as an experiment to serve social workers already in the field.[3] The Association was also seeking a wider public for its literature. In addition to the continued publication of its journal, *Mental Health*,[4] advisory pamphlets were produced on a number of questions of interest to parents, teachers and others,[5] and parent guidance posters suitable for maternity and child welfare centres, child guidance clinics, etc., were prepared.

The close interest of the N.A.M.H. in the activities of its local associations was maintained. In spite of the fact that the local voluntary agencies were relieved of many of their responsibilities when local authorities took over services under the National Health Service Act, many of them decided to carry on. Cambridgeshire Mental Welfare Association,[6] for example, in appealing for local subscribers, reported that not only was much of its old voluntary work continuing but it was hoping to initiate new enterprises. It had already taken part in many pioneer experiments, and had recently handed over to the local authority's children's committee its valuable register of foster homes.[7] By the summer of 1953 some 23 local associations were reporting vigorous growth.

It was evident from applications for urgent help still being received by the associations, and by the headquarters of the N.A.M.H. that there was a continued need for central advisory service and for case work. Often the appeal came from a parent, worried about his defective child, or a husband who was fearful lest the doctors should want to 'put away' his wife who was mentally ill, or a young married woman who sought advice because she feared she was heading for a breakdown. Sometimes the request for help came from a doctor who had been unable to obtain a vacancy for an idiot child in a hospital for defectives in his own area, or from a hospital almoner who asked for suggestions about placing a mongol baby whose mother was mentally ill and about to go into hospital.[8]

[1] E.g. the *Association of Children's Officers* and the *National Council for the Unmarried Mother*.
[2] See *Mental Health News Letter*, Summer, 1953.
[3] This scheme was tutored by an American psychiatric social worker.
[4] Edited by Dr. Tredgold.
[5] E.g. *Children's Jealousies, Habit Training*, etc., by Miss Ruth Thomas.
[6] One of the first to be formed after the passing of the Mental Deficiency Act, 1913.
[7] In 1948. This local association also had a Samaritan Fund to help assist a mentally ill person in the community when help was not available elsewhere.
[8] See the N.A.M.H., *Mental Health News Letter*, Autumn, 1950, and Spring, 1951.

THE MENTAL HEALTH SERVICES

Perhaps one of the most rewarding projects was the international contacts made through the N.A.M.H. When the *World Federation for Mental Health* was established in 1948, replacing the *International Committee for Mental Hygiene* the N.A.M.H. was one of the founder members, and the first president was a member of the N.A.M.H. council.[1] It had a close link with the United Nations,[2] and the Federation was granted consultative status as a non-Governmental International Organisation by both U.N.E.S.C.O. and W.H.O. A British standing committee was set up which would act as a medium for collecting information for the Federation and for W.H.O. It was hoped that the Federation would act as a clearing-house for the experience and viewpoints of the several professions engaged in the development of mental health.[3] The bulletin, *World Mental Health*, gave news of the Federation's activities throughout the world. Meanwhile, the N.A.M.H. was the advisory centre for enquirers from overseas, and the British Council's 'advisor' for United Nations Fellows. Close touch with the Colonial Office and with U.S.A. Fulbright Fellows widened the sphere of international contacts and added further to the responsibilities of the Association.

One of the greatest difficulties to be faced by a national voluntary organisation which means to keep its vigour is the need to maintain a staff which can meet new demands. Unfortunately, the N.A.M.H. found difficulty in offering the salaries and the security open to civil servants, and in the field of mental health there was now competition by statutory authorities for the scarce supply of skilled workers. It had, therefore, to scrutinise its work carefully to see where its resources, already stretched to the uttermost, could best be used, and to limit its undertakings to those which could be adequately dealt with. Internal re-organisation led to closer co-ordination of its various branches.[4] Certain committees were disbanded[5] and the essential work taken over by existing groups. We have seen that some of its long-standing community care work was given up in the light of statutory developments.[6] It was part of the same process which had led to amalgamation at the national level: 'The organisation of mental health work cannot be merely departmental'.[7] Looked at from another angle, the changes may be seen as part of the fluidity of the N.A.M.H. as it responded to new needs. It avoided a

[1] Dr. J. R. Rees.
[2] Membership was open to any voluntary society in any country eligible to join the United Nations or any of its specialised agencies whose purpose in whole or in part was the promotion of mental health and good human relations.
[3] Thus supplementing the work of the Mental Health Advisory Group of W.H.O.
[4] See particularly the several changes made in the year 1948–49 to co-ordinate all its educational work.
[5] E.g. the Public Relations Committee. The work was carried on by the Executive and the Finance and General Purposes Committee. It was later decided to restore its special public relations work.
[6] E.g. the placement and supervision of defectives under guardianship and on licence in 1950.
[7] Quoted, Annual Report, N.A.M.H., 1947–48, p. 7.

EFFECT OF CHANGES ON VOLUNTARY ORGANISATIONS

departmentalism linked to traditional methods of organisation and structure, and related its committee procedure to changing demands. Although it had to give up with some regret certain of its long-standing work for local authorities, e.g. Middlesex, it welcomed other contacts such as that with Kent,[1] which involved close co-operation in the educational field. It was still prepared to do special case work[2] when difficult problems were submitted by local authorities or other agencies, and it placed particular emphasis on its regular training courses which were officially recognised and largely used by statutory bodies.[3] It felt that much educational propaganda was still needed to convince many local authorities that mental ill-health was 'something more than lunacy or idiocy', and that preventive measures were of vital importance. It knew, too, that its long experience qualified it to make an informed contribution to a number of outstanding problems. It was able to prepare useful memoranda for the several statutory enquiries conducted in the mid-1950's, such as that on Maladjusted Children, on the Rehabilitation of Disabled Persons, on Marriage and Divorce, and on the question of special concern to the association, that of the Law relating to Mental Illness and Mental Deficiency.

In sum the N.A.M.H. was convinced that it had a part to play in the future. It was particularly well-equipped, it felt, to keep medical and non-medical elements in balance, both in education and training, and in practical service.

It had certainly maintained this policy in its constitution where professional and lay elements were well represented, and in its local associations where statutory administrators and lay voluntary workers were co-operating in a number of areas. Whether its enthusiasm for mental health led it to over-stress the psychological needs of the community is a matter for future judgment. Claims by the participants in the several fields of social welfare must be viewed in the light of further experience of the community's needs in relation to the total supply of skilled and experienced officers. A nice balance has to be held by all voluntary organisations between the enthusiasm which is vital to their existence, and the danger of 'trying to over-sell a speciality'. After the passage of the National Health Service Act in 1946, the N.A.M.H. had still to convince many local authorities that co-operation with voluntary agencies was desirable and that such a partnership had a valuable contribution to make to a comprehensive mental health scheme. They no longer had the long-standing support of the Board of Control as a separate entity concerned with the various aspects of mental health. It remained to be seen how far the Minister of Health, with his wider interests, would infuse

[1] Kent local education authority asked for several series of lectures, and about 100 lectures were given. Other local authorities, including London, also made use of this service.
[2] See Table VII.
[3] Local authorities and regional hospital boards sent students.

local authorities with the desire for a statutory–voluntary partnership in the provision of community care in the mental health service,[1] and how far the National Health Service would in fact provide a truly integrated scheme.

It may be useful to review some of the significant developments during the whole period, as revealed by a group of statistics. Table VI, below,

TABLE VI

Mental After-Care Association Average Income, 1890–1954*
(Showing statutory and voluntary sources)

	Average annual income for 5 yr. period	Rate of increase, %	Public authority grants† and payments for services rendered	All other incomes: i.e. donations, legacies and investments	Grants† and payments for services (% of total income)
	£		£	£	
1890–94	325	—	—	325	Nil
1895–99	587	80	—	587	,,
1900–04	670	14	—	670	,,
1905–09	1,172	75	21	1,151	2
1910–14	1,641	30	41	1,600	2
1915–19	1,851	14	45	1,806	2
1920–24	4,560	146	607	3,953	13
1925–29	8,263	82	1,630	6,663	20
1930–34	11,616	40	7,322	4,294	63
1935–39	20,625	78	16,977	3,648	82
1940–44	28,475	37	24,466	4,009	86
1945–49	34,685	21	29,521	5,164	85
1950–54	51,855	49	48,263	3,593	93

* Statistics extracted and analysed from accounts published in annual reports of the association.

† Grants formed a very small proportion of the total in later years. At different periods the sources were Queen Adelaide's Fund, and Sunday Cinema contributions.

shows the changing financial relationship between the Mental After-Care Association and the statutory bodies. With a total income of less than £2,000 at the end of the First World War, only 2% was received from grants and payments for services. By the end of the Second World War income had risen to more than £28,000, and the proportion from grants and payments to 86% (the greater part of the payments for services rendered came from public funds). This trend continued after the War, the proportion reaching 93% by 1954.

[1] That local authorities with a tradition of co-operation with voluntary associations continued to avail themselves of their help as they exercised their powers for the care and after-care of the mentally ill and the mentally defective is illustrated by the practice of the London County Council during the first years of the operation of the National Health Service Act, see Table XIV, p. 294.

EFFECT OF CHANGES ON VOLUNTARY ORGANISATIONS

Since 1949 separate figures are given in the Association's reports for payments from public and private sources for services rendered. The following table brings out clearly the large proportion of such payments contributed by public authorities.

TABLE VIb

Year	Total payments for services	Payment for services by public authorities	Payment for services by private contributors	Sundry payments (rent of furniture)
	£	£	£	£
1949	42,371	31,445	10,831	105
1950	43,497	32,426	11,001	70
1951	41,765	32,068	9,627	70
1952	49,577	39,243	10,264	70
1953	48,542	37,365	11,107	70
1954	57,935	44,490	13,375	70

Table VII shows the development in community care recorded by the Central Association for Mental Welfare (later by the National Association for Mental Health). The increase in the total number helped reflects,

TABLE VII
Developments in Community Care by the C.A.M.W. (later by N.A.M.H.)
[Statistics extracted from Annual Reports of the Central Association for Mental Welfare and the National Association for Mental Health], 1915–54

Year ending March	I Case work* Total number of cases recorded (i.e. received from local or regional associations and direct applications at H.Q. by C.A.M.W.	II Applications received direct at H.Q. of C.A.M.W. [and N.A.M.H.]	III Number of affiliated local associations†
1915	5,243	296	24
1916	no data	no data	34
1917	no data	no data	37
1918	11,000	484	41
1919	18,448	618	47
1920	22,856	603	45
1921	25,303	600	48
1922	25,903	600	49
1923	32,800	617	no data
1924	34,800	658	48

* These figures do not include cases sent to holiday homes or emergency homes. They do include those under guardianship or on the foster-home register, and those who were epileptic, as well as the ordinary social case work.

† Local associations might cover the area of a number of local authorities, e.g. in 1935, of 51 local associations the areas covered include 25 county councils, 43 county borough councils and 166 local education authorities (see Feversham Report).

THE MENTAL HEALTH SERVICES

TABLE VII—continued.

Year ending March	I Case work* Total number of cases recorded (i.e. received from local or regional associations and direct applications at H.Q. by C.A.M.W.	II Applications received direct at H.Q. of C.A.M.W. [and N.A.M.H.]	III Number of affiliated local associations†
1925	35,940	700	51
1926	38,161	650	53
1927	no data	no data	53
1928	no data	843	53
1929	no data	1,041	54
1930	41,270	805	53
1931	no data	704	52
1932	no data	743	51
1933	no data	713	50
1934	no data	686	40
1935	no data	777	51
1936	over 44,000	785	no data
1937	no data	764	no data
1938	no data	758	no data
1939	no data	709	no data
1940	no data	777	no data
1941	no data	1,871	46
1942	Provisional National Council for Mental Health	1,978	46
‡1943		3,099§	46
1944		2,076‖	(regional offices only recorded)
1945		2,011‖	
¶1946	National Association for Mental Health	1,329‖	
1947	total 12,707	5,127 new	
1948	4,490	792 ,,	
1949	2,027	991 ,,	24
1950	1,493	1,181 ,,	25
1951	no data	1,527 ,,	24
1952	1,773	1,650 ,,	23† Northern
1953	no data	1,800 ,,	22 Office
1954	no data	1,663 ,,	22 ,,

* These figures do not include cases sent to holiday homes or emergency homes. They do include those under guardianship or on the foster-home register, and those who were epileptic, as well as the ordinary social case work.

† Local associations might cover the area of a number of local authorities, e.g. in 1935, of 51 local associations the areas covered include 25 county councils, 43 county borough councils and 166 local education authorities (see Feversham Report).

‡ Ex-services After-Care scheme begun.

§ Includes 526 Community Service After-Care cases.

‖ Excludes Community Service After-Care cases which numbered in two years, 1944–46, 7,274 cases, and in 1946–47, 3,239 of which 439 were new.

¶ Ex-services After-Care scheme extended to civilians.

EFFECT OF CHANGES ON VOLUNTARY ORGANISATIONS

in particular, the growth and vitality of the affiliated local associations. This was noticeable in the years between the wars when the totals rose from 11,000 applications in 1918 to over 44,000 in the late 30's. The Second World War and the immediate post-war period made greater calls upon the resources of the national headquarters, which administered the After-Care Scheme, while many of the local associations found that much of their work would be taken over by the statutory bodies after the introduction of the National Health Service.

Table VIII brings out clearly the development in the statutory care of the mentally defective, particularly in the inter-war years, the most significant feature of which was the relative increase in community care.

TABLE VIII

The Number of Defectives Reported to Local Authorities and How they were Dealt with*

(Extracted and aggregated from Annual Reports of Board of Control and Annual Report of Ministry of Health, 1954)

At five-yearly intervals	I Total No. reported and ascertained	II Total in community care (including statutory supervision, voluntary supervision, under statutory guardianship, and on licence)	III Total received in institutions† (under the M.D. Acts and outside the M.D. Acts)	Total in care addition of II and III
1924	36,413	17,964	17,104	35,067
1929	66,458	41,729	24,207	65,936
1934	106,439	59,173	35,794	94,967
1939	129,395	72,653	46,054	118,707
1944	127,411	72,321	51,214	123,535
1949	129,700	73,640	54,887	128,527
1954	137,456	81,880	55,984‡	137,864

* Complete figures for each column were not available before 1924. Statutory supervision was first noted in 1922, voluntary supervision in 1924, those on licence in 1929. Those under statutory guardianship were given in 1917 but not again until 1923.

† Institutions included Certified Institutions, State Institutions, Approved Institutions certified under Section 37, Certified Homes, and Approved Homes. A number of defectives were received in Poor Law Accommodation, some of which was in ordinary Poor Law Institutions, some in Approved Poor Law Institutions (Sec. 37). The total number of defectives in all Poor Law Institutions was as follows:

Five-year Intervals
1924	5,064
1929	7,844
1934	9,262§
1939	16,120‖
1945	10,125‖
[1949	New Act in operation]

‡ This excludes patients under guardianship or notified and those on licence.
§ This includes Approved Poor Law Institutions.
‖ This includes Public Health General Hospitals.

PART IV

The Welfare of the Blind

(See Introduction, p. xii, for reference to the scope of this section.)

INTRODUCTION

The Position To-day: Outstanding Problems

Services for the welfare of the blind in this country have reached a standard above that for any other handicapped group. The system of registration has been built on a sound foundation, and the incidence of blindness is well recorded. Research has been progressing into the causes of blindness, and a continued reduction in the numbers of the blind in the lower age groups has testified to the success of early preventive measures.[1] The importance of special education and training has been recognised, and greater care is being given to placement in employment. Welfare services have become increasingly widespread, and assistance is given on a relatively generous scale.

There are, however, weaknesses in the system, many of which arise from the traditional pattern of development of services for the handicapped. The dependence upon charitable enterprise, with its local variations and unevenness of operation, has been characteristic. The development of the movement for the welfare of the blind in the 20th century has not been founded, as in the maternity and child welfare and the mental health services, upon a national effort to co-ordinate voluntary and statutory enterprise.[2] Voluntary services for the blind have been built up for the most part on local interest, the national organisations concentrating largely on special activities such as the production of books, magazines and apparatus, or acting as consultants on questions of education, training and employment.

As statutory responsibility became more acceptable, local authorities were given increasing powers: once more the extent to which action was taken depended on local interest. The quality and range of the services provided by local authorities have, in fact, shown very wide variations. Measured in terms of the expenditure per head on the blind, the unevenness has been startling.[3] Diversity of service, both voluntary and

[1] An exception was the recent report of the increased incidence of retro-lental fibroplasia amongst premature babies of low weight. The Medical Research Council suggested that the incidence and severity of this condition could be controlled by reducing the use of oxygen to a minimum concentration, and for the minimum time necessary to relieve respiratory embarrassment. See Ministry of Health Annual Reports for the years 1953 and 1954, Part II. Signs of reduction are already apparent (1955).

[2] See, however, the early regional efforts to secure co-ordination, p. 186, below.

[3] See p. 210n., below.

statutory, throughout the country is still a characteristic feature of blind welfare.

Not only has there been considerable difference in the quality of service, but also variation in the method of assessment of blindness[1] for the purpose of registration.[2] Even when it became a requirement for certification that there should be an examination by a qualified ophthalmic surgeon,[3] a measure of discretion had to be given, taking into account such factors as the age of onset of blindness, or whether the defect of vision was recent or long-standing. Added to this cause of lack of uniformity, there was an additional problem set by official definitions of blindness, that of the Ministry of Health: 'too blind to be able to perform any work for which eyesight is essential', and that of the Board of Education: 'too blind to be able to read the school books ordinarily used by children'. Some, trained under the definition contained in the Education Acts, found when they reached the stage of finding work, that they did not come within the Minister of Health's definition.

An even greater problem was the prevailing attitude towards the blind. Since the days when the Elizabethan Poor Law gave specific mention to the blind, and philanthropists found them specially worthy of charitable action, the public has been long accustomed to regarding the blind as a dependent section of the community. The 20th century was well advanced before public recognition was given to the principle, already proclaimed by blind men and women themselves, that the blind were not to be set apart as though they were different in kind: that they were, indeed, to be given every opportunity of sharing in normal social and economic activities: that many blind men and women had, in fact, a contribution to make to the community.

It was more difficult to induce the public to accept this idea in view of the large proportion of the blind population who were unemployable. Of necessity, much of the social action on behalf of the blind partook of the nature of welfare service, while the large-scale appeals made by

[1] Such variation arose originally from lack of special knowledge of what constituted useful vision for day to day living, and from lack of precise apparatus for measuring it. A simple definition at that stage was better than an attempt, without expert knowledge, to express blindness in rigid terms.

[2] It should be noted that only a small proportion of blind persons are totally blind, having no perception of light. Some can see hand movements, etc., but in every case the field of vision is markedly contracted. A recent analysis of blind certificates made from those registered in 1948–50 showed some 5·9% totally blind, and 17·1% with perception of light only. About 36% had vision enabling them to see hand movements, and 18% had vision up to and including 3/60 Snellen. Some 22·6% of those registered as blind had vision of more than 3/60. Professor Sorsby pointed out that the percentage of borderline cases registered previously was considerably less. 'There is apparently a greater readiness for examining surgeons to certify such patients as blind'. *Op. cit.*, p. 24. Arnold Sorsby, *The Causes of Blindness in England, 1948–50*, p. 3.

[3] See p. 219, below. The Minister of Health did not make this a requirement until after 1930. Not until 1955 were local authorities recommended to appoint ophthalmic surgeons of consultant status.

INTRODUCTION

voluntary organisations were associated with the traditional attitude towards charity for the needy.

One of the outstanding problems, to-day, is to give reality to the principle that blind men and women should be given every chance to take part in normal activities: if they are of working age, they should have the opportunity of placement in ordinary industrial or professional life, in so far as their capacity allows: or if their disability prevents this, they, like other handicapped persons, should be offered special facilities in sheltered occupation. For the majority, who, by reason of age or the severity of their disability are unfit for work, welfare services should be so offered that, instead of passive acceptance of charity or assistance, the blind may be encouraged to enjoy so far as possible the normal amenities available to the whole community.

To achieve this aim all resources must be used, whether statutory or voluntary. The State to-day accepts a heavy financial responsibility. The voluntary organisations have long experience and special knowledge, with opportunities for personal work not always possible for official bodies. Neither group can cover the field alone. In some areas, until recently, little had been done beyond the statutorily required minimum. In others, separate action had been taken, and public and private agencies had scarcely met. Some voluntary societies have cherished a tradition of independence, and some local authorities have determined to use their powers of control to the full, without reference to existing organisations.

Co-ordination has been a late development in the service as a whole, and to-day the extent of local co-operation varies considerably. Where relations between voluntary and statutory bodies have been cordial, some excellent results have been achieved. Recent legislation has given new powers and duties to local authorities, while leaving ample room for combined action with voluntary organisations, whether local, regional or national. A closer study of the achievements of the past, and of recent developments in social policy, may help to give a clearer picture of the alternatives available for the future.

XV

VOLUNTARY ACTION IN THE PIONEER PHASE

ALTHOUGH the Elizabethan Poor Law had established relief for the necessitous blind as a statutory duty, no comprehensive legislation for their welfare was passed until more than three hundred years later.[1] Charitable effort had meanwhile proved more active: 18th-century philanthropists were specially concerned with helping the old and infirm by establishing almshouses and pensions schemes for the blind. Much of the voluntary enterprise in blind welfare was the result of local charitable effort to meet the personal needs of the friendless or the destitute. Many local societies which sprang up in the 19th century had a religious basis, and men and women set out with missionary zeal to read the Bible in every home in their neighbourhood where a blind person could be traced. They soon found that spiritual aid was not the only call upon their devotion. Voluntary societies were constantly adding to their commitments as they discovered new needs.

The objects of one of the first *Indigent Blind Visiting Societies*[2] in London give some idea of the nature of their service: 'to assist and ameliorate the condition of the aged and destitute blind poor in London and its vicinity, by providing them with daily reading of the Scriptures at their habitations, with conductors to Church, and with temporal relief in necessitous cases'.[3] When embossed literature became available, the visitors, many themselves blind, added the teaching of Braille or Moon type[4] to their ever widening activities. By the 1880's there were nearly 80 *Home Teaching Societies*, some employing paid teachers.[5]

[1] The Elizabethan Poor Law Act was passed in 1601, and the first Blind Persons Act in 1920.
[2] Lord Shaftesbury and Lord Ebury founded this society in 1834.
[3] Quoted in N.I.B. Bulletin, No. 7 (1934 ed.), p. 8.
[4] See p. 178, below, for an account of experiments in the production of different types of embossed literature.
[5] A guide to the Institutions and Charities for the Blind published in 1884 mentions 79 Home Teaching Societies.

VOLUNTARY ACTION IN THE PIONEER PHASE

Many of the local voluntary societies did their best work in providing pastime occupations and other amenities for the unemployable blind, and in offering facilities for friendly social contacts. Most of the voluntary organisations were dependent upon unpaid, sometimes irregular, help,[1] but many had active executive committees which worked closely with other charities for the blind. They could select and recommend from personal knowledge any who needed to be cared for in a home for the blind, or whose meagre savings could be supplemented by a pension from charitable sources.

Not all philanthropic effort was conducted on the assumption that blind persons were 'poor and unable to work'.[2] At the end of the 18th century, the *Liverpool School for the Indigent Blind* had established a training institution where trades such as the making of baskets, rugs and mats were taught, so that blind persons might carry on such saleable work in their own homes. By the mid-19th century a few societies were experimenting in the provision of workshops in which those who had already learnt a trade might work under sheltered conditions. It was necessary, in most cases, to supplement the weekly earnings, to bring them up to normal. Few could compete with the sighted, under workshop conditions. Throughout the century various experiments were made to improve facilities for training and to widen the range of employment. Printing centres gave opportunity to some, piano tuning to others, until gradually an increasing number of blind persons were to be found among the skilled workers, the black-coated workers and in the professions.

There is no doubt that interest in the welfare of the blind had been stimulated during the 19th century, though the claim that there was 'a network of voluntary societies and institutions over the country'[3] was a little optimistic. Some idea of the progress of voluntary effort may be gained from an article in the Annual Register of the *Charity Organisation Society* (C.O.S.), for 1899. The writer claimed that whereas there had been only four known institutions for the blind in the United Kingdom at the end of the 18th century, there were in the records of the C.O.S. 154 societies and institutions, a hundred years later. They were classified by the secretary of Gardner's Trust under four headings: those administering pensions, generally to the aged past work; homes receiving adult and aged blind, and industrial and convalescent homes;

---

[1] Sometimes a society was kept going only by the vitality and enterprise of its secretary. This had serious consequences if a successor could not be found, occasionally leading to the foundering of the voluntary association. This happened in the case of *The Society for the Prevention of Blindness and the Improvement of the Physique of the Blind* upon the death of Dr. Roth. See *Charities Register and Digest*, 1897 (*C.R. & D.*). Fortunately, *Gardner's Trust* took over some of its work, such as the issue of advisory leaflets.
[2] The official description of those entitled to statutory assistance under the Poor Law since 1601.
[3] See *C.R. & D.*, 1899, Article by H. J. Wilson.

THE WELFARE OF THE BLIND

those concerned with education, maintenance and employment, largely in schools, etc.; and those concerned with the education and employment of non-residents, e.g. workshops and printing centres, home teaching societies and classes. By this time, he added, in addition to preparation for trades, there was opportunity for education for the professions such as music, or entrance to the university to read for Holy Orders or the legal profession.

Blind Pioneers and the Foundation of National Organisations

No summary of the development of blind welfare would be complete without special reference to the part played by blind men and women themselves. The foundation of the training institution in Liverpool, already mentioned, was inspired by two blind men, Rushton and Christie.[1] Important contributions in several other fields were the direct result of the vigour and initiative of blind persons. For example, among the many experimenters in the 19th century working upon a raised type, were Louis Braille, a blind Frenchman who perfected a type invented in 1829, and Dr. Moon, one of several English experimenters, whose first book in embossed type was printed in 1847.[2] A blind woman who contributed to the new spirit of independence was Elizabeth Gilbert who, in 1853, demonstrated the value of giving employment to blind persons in their own homes.[3] Francis Campbell, the first blind principal of the *Royal Normal College*, was another of the pioneers who founded a tradition of self-reliance, and participation in normal activities, of which the school has been justly proud.[4] It was a group of blind men, led by Dr. Armitage, who, in 1865, founded the *British and Foreign Blind Association*, later to achieve fame as the *National Institute for the Blind* (N.I.B.) under its energetic blind president, Sir Arthur Pearson. Sir Ian Fraser of *St. Dunstan's* was to be well known at a later date for his work on behalf of blinded ex-service men. Meanwhile, a blind woman had begun the formation of the first *National Library for the Blind*, in 1882.[5] Finally we should note the organisation of some of the blind industrial

[1] They were much indebted to the suggestions and active help of a local curate named Dannett.
[2] Moon type was found to be specially suitable for those blinded in adult life since it was based on the alphabet already familiar to the sighted, and it did not need such sensitive touch as Braille.
[3] The Society formed to carry on her work became later *The Incorporated Association for Promoting the General Welfare of the Blind*.
[4] To a visitor unfamiliar with the activities which blind children can be helped to enjoy it is most inspiring to watch them taking part in such interests as gardening, country dancing and even high jumping.
[5] It is interesting to note that both she, and the principal of the Royal Normal College, in evidence before the Departmental Committee of 1914–17, pleaded for a greater measure of public responsibility for the education of the blind. The latter strongly deprecated having to make constant appeals to charity to make good the deficit (the college was not endowed) in work which should properly be maintained, he urged, as an obligation upon the local authority. (It was, at that time, only permissive.)

VOLUNTARY ACTION IN THE PIONEER PHASE

workers under the National League of the Blind,[1] whose slogan, 'We desire work rather than beggary', was emphasised in their journal, *The Blind Advocate*, in 1898.

The foundation of national organisations helped gradually to change the prevailing attitude which had for so long accepted the dependence of the blind. An undiscriminating public had seen only the blind beggars in the streets, while philanthropists had generally sought out the indigent for their ministrations. That there were some exceptionally talented blind individuals could not be denied, but it was only by slow degrees that the community recognised that the blind were as diverse as the sighted, with interests and aptitudes which needed a variety of opportunities for expression.

Two developments, in particular, deserve closer attention since they did much to meet such needs and to influence public opinion. The first was the work of the British and Foreign Blind Association,[2] and the second the experiments in Higher Education.

The N.I.B., unlike many other national societies, did not set out to establish local associations or branches, nor did it intend to act as a federating body. It found institutions and local associations already in being, and sought to offer them specific services which could more effectively and economically be carried on at a national level. Some of the Association's first 'objects' are worthy of notice, especially its intention 'to diffuse knowledge of those means of education which appeared to be best suited to the wants of the blind'. It set itself a high standard by maintaining that careful investigation must always precede an advisory service: 'the general diffusion of information after preliminary investigation' was to remain in the forefront of its aims. As a centre to which inventions were reported, it was of special value in the pioneer stage when new methods of learning and of teaching were constantly being sought. It was also acknowledged as the headquarters for the production of books, magazines, music and various appliances for the blind. The early recognition of the diversity of aims and the spirit of independence within the movement was expressed in the Association's further object: 'to produce harmony among institutions for the blind.., by persuading them to accept those methods of education and modes of employment which experience has proved to be the best'. This object was to be amongst the most difficult of achievement. With such a comprehensive programme it is surprising to find the total income of the British and Foreign Blind Association in 1880

[1] Founded in 1893.
[2] It was this society which finally succeeded in establishing the superiority of Braille and Moon type amongst the several being tried out in the 19th century. Its secretary, Dr. Armitage, was largely responsible for this, and for the improvement in school appliances. It later became the National Institute for the Blind and, after the Second World War, the R.N.I.B. For the sake of simplicity it will be referred to as the N.I.B.

amounting to no more than £453 13s. 1d.[1] In the same year the management of the Association was still in the hands of the blind.[2]

Education and Co-operation with Statutory Bodies

It was in the provision of educational opportunities that some of the most constructive voluntary work was achieved and a good relationship with statutory bodies established. Reference has already been made to one of the first ventures at the end of the 18th century, when two blind men, Rushton and Christie, together with a local curate named Dannett, set up an institution in Liverpool to offer training to the young and able-bodied.[3] In the 19th century a further step forward was taken by the establishment of residential special schools for blind children. Amongst the most famous were Worcester College for boys, founded in 1866, and the Royal Normal College for boys and girls, opened in 1871. The pioneer educationists, Dr. Armitage and Mr. Campbell, set out to equip blind boys and girls to take their place as active and responsible members of the community, a revolutionary step in the history of blind welfare. It was long before it became the underlying principle of 'rehabilitation' in the twentieth century.[4]

The objects of the Royal Normal College and Academy of Music, to give it its full title, are worth quoting as an illustration of this new spirit: 'The moral, physical, social, mental and musical training of the blind with a view of sending them into the world active, useful and self-supporting men and women.'[5] The college only accepted girls and boys 'of suitable ability', and, to make sure that standards were high, pupils were received first as probationers. By 1880 the income of the school was £6,393, of which fees accounted for £3,462. Provision was made for scholarships for poor children.

It is of interest to note the eagerness with which London and a few other authorities used their powers to maintain blind children at this residential school,[6] and the competition from the authorities' day schools for the Queen's scholarships.[7] London was glad, too, to be able to use the services of the Headmaster of the College who acted as expert adviser on the work of the London School Board's centres.[8] In addition, an important development in the activities of the College aroused the

---

[1] See *C.R. & D.*, 1st edition, 1882, p. 129.
[2] Management by Executive Council consisting of 'gentlemen either blind, or so nearly blind that they have to use the fingers instead of the eyes for the purpose of reading' (*ibid.*, p. 129).
[3] In the last decade of the 18th century four such institutions were founded: in addition to the one in Liverpool, in 1791, there was one in Bristol and Edinburgh respectively in 1793 and in London in 1799.
[4] See p. 234, below.
[5] See *C.R. & D.*, 1882.
[6] See p. 183n., below.
[7] The Queen's Scholarship, later the King's Scholarship, examination was first held at the Royal Normal College, 1897–98. See *C.R. & D.* 1898.
[8] *C.R. & D.*, 1884, p. lxxvii.

VOLUNTARY ACTION IN THE PIONEER PHASE

interest of the central statutory authority: a training department for blind teachers had been started in 1895, and it secured recognition by the Board of Education the following year.[1]

The gradual increase in the number of special schools for blind children[2] drew attention to the need for more trained teachers. By 1907 the time was thought to be ripe for the establishment of a specialised organisation concerned with the training of teachers of the blind: *the College of Teachers of the Blind* was founded under voluntary auspices 'to promote the education of the blind, to encourage the training of teachers of the blind and to raise their status, to hold examinations and grant diplomas, to foster comradeship, and to facilitate united action in matters affecting their professional welfare'.[3] It worked very closely with the British and Foreign Blind Association, the secretary of the Association acting as the College registrar. In 1909 it was recognised by the Board of Education, when some 26 teachers received a diploma. The College has enjoyed statutory recognition and encouragement ever since.[4]

Meanwhile relations had not always been as happy in the provision of elementary education[5] as in that of higher education. The promise of the Education Act of 1893[6] had not been fulfilled, and the statutory contribution was pitifully small.[7] Managers of voluntary schools were complaining that inadequate use was made of powers to aid special schools, or that local authorities were acting without consultation with the managers. They disapproved of the impersonal attitude of those authorities who determined the capacity of schools 'solely in terms of size of rooms without reference to staffing and other relevant matters'.

However, in spite of many difficulties, some progress was made in the

[1] Under the title 'The Smith Training College.' An interesting experiment in the transfer of responsibility took place shortly after. In 1897, the London School Board decided to take over the Royal Normal College, with the exception of one or two departments, but after two years they determined to re-transfer the College. In 1899, it was again under full voluntary management, with its own council and voluntary management committee.

[2] By 1907 the L.C.C. had several day schools and three residential schools. Nine other local education authorities had day schools, while Leeds and Stoke-on-Trent each had a residential school. The majority of special schools were still provided by voluntary agencies and were used by L.E.A.'s. As early as 1884 a Directory of Institutions for the Blind listed some 26 voluntary residential schools for boys and girls.

[3] See 'A History of Blind Welfare', *N.I.B. Bulletin*, No. 7, 1934 ed., p. 24. The College held its first examination in 1908.

[4] It is still a requirement for appointment of a Home Teacher that the candidate should hold, or obtain within two years of appointment, the Certificate of the College of Teachers of the Blind.

[5] See the report of the Senior Inspector of Schools to the Committee of the Council on Education in Schools for the Deaf and Blind in 1899. Cf. the repeated efforts of the voluntary societies to secure legislation for technical training for the blind between the ages of sixteen and twenty-one.

[6] See p. 194 below for an outline of statutory provision.

[7] Over the country as a whole there were by the end of the 19th century 23 certified residential schools with accommodation for 1,702 blind children.

quality of education available for blind children. By the end of the 19th century the syllabus had expanded a little: for example, general attention was focused on the possibility of gymnastics; by 1900, most schools had added typewriting[1] to the curriculum. Where institutions for the blind included both a school and a training department, in the next few years shorthand was added to the vocational training, and the use of a knitting machine became general; training in music in all its branches, and in piano-tuning gave further opportunities for employment. The variety of trades taught was increasing year by year. In 1906, massage[2] was added to the professional training, while telephony[3] was just beginning to prepare blind students to take their place in an expanding market.

The whole question of vocational training and entry to employment was fraught with difficulty. It had been one of the unresolved problems of the 19th century. The voluntary organisations had found no statutory support for the recommendation of the Royal Commission for the provision of after-care on the lines of the Saxon System. This system, strongly advocated by Dr. Armitage in 1883 after he had seen its successful working abroad, would have been particularly valuable in helping blind trainees to sell work done at home.[4] More than a generation was to pass before a satisfactory scheme was evolved, in which statutory and voluntary agencies could combine.[5]

Once the 1902 Education Act was on the Statute Book several enterprising local authorities sought to tackle this vexed question and to use the experience of voluntary agencies. A vital issue on technical training was being raised by some of the voluntary educational establishments, notably in Birmingham and Nottingham, where some doubt had been expressed by the Board of Education as to whether certain instruction of a technical character to older blind pupils could rank for a grant. The practical results of the activities of voluntary agencies in securing a generous interpretation of the Act are evident from the successful negotiations on this issue, for recognition was finally given 'in view of the representations contained in your letters and the favourable report of H.M. Inspectors'.[6]

With technical education in mind, propaganda was now undertaken

---

[1] It has been taught at the Royal Normal College since 1887; shorthand was added in 1898.

[2] It had been given first in Manchester in 1895.

[3] A Birmingham firm employed the first blind telephone operator in 1906.

[4] Cf. Elizabeth Gilbert's advocacy in 1853, p. 178, above.

[5] See Ministry of Health Circular 1086, 1930, referring to the Home Workers' scheme.

[6] The enterprising superintendent and secretary of the Midland Institution for the Blind, Nottingham, received a grant for the previous session, as well as assurance to cover his future venture. Nottingham Institution provided workshops, a thorough course of technical training and music, singing, piano tuning, shorthand and typing, etc.; see *The Blind*, No. 28, 1904, and No. 35, 1906, July and October issues.

VOLUNTARY ACTION IN THE PIONEER PHASE

by the voluntary societies, both local and national, to urge local education authorities to make full use of their powers for higher education. Local voluntary societies were reporting some success in this direction, as when the Staffordshire education authority offered two scholarships for further training, in response, it was claimed, to representations made to the committee by the chairman of the North Staffordshire Workshops for the Blind. At the same time a determined effort was being made to interest local education authorities in the general work of voluntary associations, and a number of societies were inviting members of the Authority to their meetings.[1]

Sometimes the initiative was taken by local authorities. For example, the London County Council was vigorous and enterprising in the educational field, and took an active part in the progress of technical education. In considering what could be done for blind children in this sphere it decided to set up a special committee, the 'London Blind and Deaf Children's Scholarship and Apprenticeship Committee', on which it invited voluntary organisations to serve. The composition of this committee is worth noting as an example of combined voluntary and statutory representation. It included five members from the London School Board, one from the L.C.C. Technical Education Board, one from the Metropolitan Asylums Board, one from the Charity Organisation Society, one from Gardner's Trust for the Blind, one from the Royal Association for the Deaf and Dumb and three representatives of special schools.[2] In the same year, 1903, the L.C.C. granted two scholarships to blind boys and girls tenable at schools provided by voluntary organisations at Leatherhead as well as at the Royal Normal College.

Some further advance in the voluntary contribution to vocational training was made possible through *Gardner's Trust*. This charity, founded in 1882, upon a bequest of £300,000, was an educational trust for 'the instruction of poor blind persons in suitable trades, handicrafts and professions, and for instruction especially in music'. A useful clause gave power to the trustees to administer the fund 'generally in such other manner as the committee shall from time to time think best'. Gardner's Trust was to be a powerful influence in the development of blind welfare, particularly in the field of education, while the publication of its magazine, *The Blind*, was an event of importance to the movement. The foundation of the Trust marked a new phase in charitable giving. Hitherto bequests had been made for specific institutions, or for use in particular localities. Gardner's Trust was instituted for the benefit of blind persons in any part of England and Wales, while the flexibility of its general purpose of furthering education and training made advance possible in many fields, to keep pace with changing social and

---

[1] E.g. the Yorkshire School for the Blind in 1904.
[2] See report in *The Blind*, No. 22, published by Gardner's Trust, 1903, and reference to *The Education of the Blind under the London School Board*, by Rose F. Petty.

economic needs. It helped to foster co-operation between voluntary and statutory agencies and, through its journal, *The Blind*, to publicise educational developments in both private and public provision.[1]

Although close and friendly relations between voluntary and statutory bodies continued in a few areas, there were many setbacks before full co-operation was to be achieved. The fault lay sometimes with the voluntary organisation which preferred to play a lone hand, sometimes with the local authority which was parsimonious,[2] while the failure of the Poor Law authority to support the initial efforts towards blind welfare presented one of the greatest obstacles to advance in the 19th century.

In the early 20th century several further attempts were made by voluntary societies. Some interest was taken in the opening of an employment agency by the British and Foreign Blind Association in 1902,[3] the year in which the Labour Bureaux (London) Act gave power to the local authority to spend public money on an employment advisory service.[4]

Voluntary agencies were still thought to be the proper bodies to provide and maintain workshops. Indeed, although the Royal Commission had recommended that central workshops should be set up in all large towns, it made it clear that no public funds should be used. The workshops in existence at the beginning of the 20th century were giving employment to some hundreds of blind persons. This was a valuable illustration of what might be done for those who had failed to find work in competition with sighted workers, but it must have been a lamentably small proportion, no one knew how small, of the total number of adult blind who might have profited from such provision.[5]

In 1904 the voluntary societies noted with approval that the L.C.C. was approaching the London School Board about the possibility of establishing municipal workshops for the blind. In the next few years

---

[1] Its imposing list of Local Education Authorities who submitted proposals, under the Education Act, for Higher Education was intended to be an encouragement to others to do likewise.

[2] As late as 1899, we find Gardner's Trust complaining that the Guardians shirked their duty, making the child of secondary consideration to that of chargeability. See *The Blind*, 20.4.1898 and 20.1.1899. The year before, the Guardians' motives had been questioned when certain Boards subscribed to a Home Teaching Society which provided books and teachers for the inmates of workhouses: 'mainly because the poor blind people under their charge are much less irritable and discontented if they can amuse themselves with books'.

[3] See Annual Report of the Association for the year 1902.

[4] The Labour Exchanges Act, 1909, made the Central Authority responsible for employment exchanges throughout the country while local education authorities had the option in 1910 (under the Choice of Employment Act) of maintaining juvenile employment bureaux.

[5] It was estimated that some 800 were employed in workshops in 1874, compared with approximately 2,000 in 1914. See *Working Party Report on the Employment of Blind Persons*, 1951, p. 10.

VOLUNTARY ACTION IN THE PIONEER PHASE

a national voluntary committee[1] was considering problems concerning the better and more general employment of the blind. In 1906 a deputation went to the several government departments concerned, hoping, in particular, to persuade the central authority to give part of the contract work of the departments to blind workers.

Meanwhile, opportunities for co-operation were offered when several municipal free libraries, and a few local authorities, used their powers to subscribe to voluntary agencies who were ready to assist their blind readers.[2] Nottingham, Bradford, Brighton and Leeds had a cordial, if informal, relationship with the *Braille Book Society*,[3] which was very ready to supply books to the municipal libraries. The British and Foreign Blind Association carried on a similar partnership. Although its usual method became that of selling, at less than cost price, the books it produced, it was always ready to consider an application for free grants of books, either to lending libraries or to necessitous blind readers.[4] Encouragement had been given to these efforts when the Postmaster General was able to reduce postage rates on embossed literature,[5] and the opportunities for the blind to exchange letters, parcels and books, and to receive special apparatus at reduced postage rates were improved.

The next few years were mainly years of consolidation in the general field of voluntary blind welfare, but there were several extensions worth noting. By 1904 we find that some twelve magazines were being printed in raised type and a quarterly magazine on the blind was available in ordinary type. A committee which had been concerned with blind children who were also mentally defective published its report this year, and the voluntary societies were considering what action could be taken for these specially afflicted children.[6] A new venture was also announced: the foundation stone of the first kindergarten school for blind children was laid in 1904[7] in Birmingham, and a Home of Rest was established in 1905.[8]

The next two years were active preparatory years for the first effective attempt to co-ordinate the work of voluntary organisations embracing a variety of institutions, societies and agencies for the blind.

---

[1] See p. 200n., below.
[2] It is interesting to note that amongst the subscribers to the British and Foreign Blind Association in 1901, and for some years after, is to be found the Nottingham Corporation Free Library.
[3] This Society had been formed in order to produce books and present them to free libraries and to schools. It also let libraries have manuscript books at a cheap rate.
[4] See Annual Report of the Association, 1911. In this year some 1,200 free volumes were distributed to the lending libraries.
[5] Since the Association had been successful in arousing the interest of the Postmaster General, who became one of their vice-presidents, the concessions had gradually increased.
[6] A special home was opened for them considerably later. See p. 217, below.
[7] Opened in 1905.
[8] See *C.R. & D*, 1907, article by H. J. Wilson.

THE WELFARE OF THE BLIND
The Problem of Co-ordination, and the Extension of Community Care

One of the chief weaknesses of voluntary organisations so far had been their failure to co-ordinate their work. The British and Foreign Blind Association had concentrated mainly on the unification of effort in the sphere of the production of embossed literature. The 'promotion of harmony between institutions', which had been one of their early avowed aims, was scarcely attempted, except in so far as they were able to persuade existing institutions to adopt proved methods of education and employment. The broader issue of co-operation in community care was not at first a welcome subject of discussion, and attempts to set up machinery for this purpose were resisted, both by local and national societies.[1] It was, therefore, something of an achievement when the *North of England Union of Institutions and Societies and Agencies for the Blind* was announced in 1907, with the following object: 'to promote such intercourse among existing agencies and individuals in the six northern counties interested in the welfare of the outdoor blind as may lead to the organisation, unification and extension of work, and the formation of societies in districts where there are none existing'.[2] Two years later an attempt was made to cover the whole of England and Wales by the formation of seven Unions,[3] which combined to found a *Union of Unions*. This was later[4] to become better known as the *Union of Counties Associations for the Blind*. Its objects show clearly that it had in mind the promotion of co-operation not only amongst the voluntary associations but between voluntary and statutory agencies. Research was to be one of its aims, and it was destined to contribute valuable work in this field, particularly on the causes and prevention of blindness. The circulation of information of national import, another of its objects, helped to give breadth of vision to its constituent members, and did much to facilitate the smooth working of subsequent legislation for the welfare of the blind.[5] It has to be recognised, however, that the Union was mainly an advisory body: it had neither the machinery nor the workers[6] to secure effective co-ordinating machinery in all the branches of blind welfare. It is, therefore, surprising to find how active the Union was in view of its entire dependence upon voluntary helpers.

This attempt to break down the parochialism which had been characteristic of 19th-century blind welfare was watched with considerable sympathy by the statutory authorities. It is worth noting that the first conference of the North of England Union, held in York in 1907, was

[1] See J. F. Wilson in *Voluntary Social Services*, ed. A. F. P. Bourdillon, p. 67.
[2] See H. J. Wilson in *C.R. & D.*, 1908, p. cclxii.
[3] The Union included the Metropolis and Adjacent Counties Union, North of England, Midland Counties, Eastern Counties, North West Union, South Wales and Monmouthshire and Western Counties.
[4] The name was changed in 1919.
[5] The 1920 and 1938 Blind Persons Acts.
[6] It had no paid secretary and no central office until 1929.

attended by representatives of the statutory health authorities as well as the local education authorities.[1] The Secretary of Gardner's Trust, writing in 1911, looked upon the establishment of the seven unions not only as an opportunity to form new societies in areas where none so far existed, but to carry on the important work of compiling a register of all the blind. 'In this way only could the wants of each individual be known and attended to.'[2]

Another small advance was also made in 1910 when the seven workshops for the blind decided to form a federation with a representative board. Workshops had been among the most sturdily independent of institutions, and the later history of the attempts at a closer relationship with other organisations for blind welfare reflected the difficulties of co-ordination in this sphere. Workshops were not alone in resisting attempts at federation. Regional Associations were not successful in bringing all local associations within their fold. Neither were relations between regional and national associations entirely happy.[3] There was not yet a single federating national society sufficiently representative to speak for voluntary organisations as a whole. There was still a tendency for national societies to concentrate on particular efforts, while in local areas independent action in specific spheres of blind welfare was common. In the first phase of the development of voluntary organisations co-ordination was mainly regional and sectional. The impetus for more effective co-operation was to come from the experience gained in the war years 1914–18. Some of the voluntary agencies had, meanwhile, been discovering the value of wider contacts, and many of them were in a position better to understand the difficulties facing statutory authorities, both local and central, who could not advance beyond the powers given by legislation, nor go far ahead of public opinion.

The voluntary organisations had begun to extend their vision not only beyond their own locality, but beyond the United Kingdom. The first of a series of international conferences was held in Edinburgh in 1905.[4] Thereafter international conferences were held at two- or three-yearly intervals. The one in Manchester in 1909 was organised for action: its three committees are significant: to consider employment, prevention of blindness, and pensions for the blind respectively. The prevention of blindness was a problem which was of concern to the

---

[1] The interest of the central authority was shown in the address given by Dr. Eichholz, an inspector of the Board of Education, where he welcomed the contribution made by the voluntary organisations and encouraged them to work for a closer relationship between statutory and voluntary agencies. Dr. Eichholz was to take an increasingly important part in the work for the blind and the deaf blind, and his contribution to the later Advisory Committees was outstanding.

[2] See C.R. & D., 1911, p. cclxix, H. J. Wilson.

[3] Cf. the difficulties inherent in public appeals. See p. 226n., below.

[4] It was at this Conference that the initiative was taken to set up a National Committee to study the problem and take action. The Committee continued to meet over a number of years.

statutory authorities as well as to the voluntary societies, and Gardner's Trust[1] and other interested organisations were watching with sympathy the efforts of local health authorities to use what powers they had to make ophthalmia neonatorum[2] compulsorily notifiable in their area. They noted with approval the announcement by John Burns at the International Medical Congress of his intention to introduce compulsory notification of the disease throughout the kingdom.[3]

Developments during the First World War

The war years, 1914–18, were years of rapid expansion for voluntary organisations concerned with the welfare of the blind, and even the Local Government Board was stimulated to action by the awakening of public interest. The National Institute for the Blind[4] found its new president, Mr. Arthur Pearson, bringing remarkable vitality and organising ability to its service. Not only was the production of Braille literature and general apparatus vastly expanded,[5] but many new projects were launched. Technical improvements had led to a new process of printing books so that the new demands could be met by a much accelerated service.[6] Many more magazines were also available in raised type.[7] Above all, the intention of the Institute's founders was achieved by the establishment of an After-Care system.

The work of other national societies, and of many local societies, also expanded[8] considerably. *The National Library for the Blind*, for example, had a fine record. When the Departmental Committee reported, the Library had just made the loan of books, some 21,000, free of cost. There were also about 4,000 pieces of music, and, since postal concessions were increasingly generous, the circulation reached a high level. The Library's 500 voluntary Braille writers received special training. By 1938, it not only had some 600 voluntary writers but employed 115 blind copyists.[9] It had been considerably helped during the

[1] See *C.R. & D.*, 1913, p. cclxxvii, H. J. Wilson.
[2] This disease was responsible for a large proportion of the blindness in the lower age groups, see p. 203, below.
[3] This was done in 1914.
[4] The N.I.B. had been renamed in 1914 (formerly the British and Foreign Blind Association).
[5] The output of Braille and apparatus was trebled, that of Braille music quadrupled. See *Voluntary Social Services*, ed. Bourdillon, p. 66.
[6] *C.R. & D.*, 1914; article by H. J. Wilson.
[7] Even by 1913 the number had reached 20. *C.R. & D.*, 1913.
[8] No attempt is made to give a complete list. A few only of the national and local societies are mentioned, as illustrating the general trend. The total receipts of charities for the blind who sent accounts to the Charity Organisation Society increased from an average of approximately £329,000 in the first decade of the 20th century to £497,000 in the second, and £1,159,000 in the third. The actual number of charities in fact decreased from an average of 101 in the first decade, to 74 in the second, and 64 in the third. (See *C.R. & D.*—yearly reports of charities between 1904 and 1927.)
[9] It had its headquarters in London with a branch in Manchester to serve the north, and its circulation in 1937–38 was 345,868 volumes.

VOLUNTARY ACTION IN THE PIONEER PHASE

First World War by the Carnegie United Kingdom Trust which housed it in a fine new buildings.

The work of *St. Dunstan's*[1] is of special interest for its modern approach to 'rehabilitation' although the term was not current until some thirty years later. It began as a hostel set up by a committee of the N.I.B., the *Blinded Soldiers and Sailors Care Committee*, which had been formed in 1914. By February 1915 St. Dunstan's began work in the hostel and some adjoining houses in Regent's Park, London, for a small number of officers and men recently blinded in the war. With imaginative insight they also arranged to accommodate relatives, free of charge, for a week at a time.[2]

St. Dunstan's first object was to help the men to readjust themselves to the new conditions. They felt, therefore, that it was important to begin their work in the hospitals and this was done by special permission. In this, as in so much else, they were anticipating the recommendation of the Tomlinson Committee[3] in the Second World War. When the men were well enough to come to St. Dunstan's, they were surrounded by every comfort, and the six months or longer in pleasant open surroundings were considered to be an important part of the process of readjustment.

Re-education and training were divided between the classroom, the workshop and social contacts, according to the wishes and aptitudes of each individual. The mental strain of learning to read embossed literature, to write in Braille and to practise an unfamiliar occupation was fully appreciated, and the day was planned accordingly. The organisers found by experience that a short working day was necessary: the men 'therefore acquired knowledge and training with speed'. Typewriting was taught mainly to enable the blind man to communicate with others, and every man was given his own typewriter, once he had passed the test.

Whenever possible a man was encouraged to return to his former occupation.[4] Failing that, he had a choice of training, graded according

---

[1] St. Dunstan's was fortunate in having two outstanding directors, firstly, Sir Arthur Pearson who worked for St. Dunstan's till his death in 1921, followed by Sir Ian Fraser, C.B.E., M.P. Its interests included blind men and women at home and overseas.

[2] Relatives also had their fares paid to and from the hostel.

[3] See the Report of the *Interdepartmental Committee on the Rehabilitation and Resettlement of Disabled Persons* (Tomlinson Report), 1943: 'Rehabilitation in its widest sense is a continuous process, partly in the medical sphere and partly in the social or industrial sphere' (*op. cit.*, p. 42).

[4] *The Departmental Committee on the Welfare of the Blind, 1914–17*, reported with considerable interest on the work of St. Dunstan's and gave several case histories of men who had successfully returned to the same or similar work. The following extract is taken from the Report and much of the material for the description above is also from the same source:

'An English private soldier, who was employed in a large firm of hot water engineers, was, much against his own inclination, persuaded to continue in that business. It was impossible for him to go on with his original occupation of planning

to ability and interest. The highest intelligence group could begin their training in massage, and then go on to the N.I.B.'s massage school, with opportunity, at a more advanced stage, of practice in three of the large voluntary hospitals. Others might be trained on the poultry farm which was established on up-to-date lines. A feature of this training, typical of the practical foresight of St. Dunstan's work, was the opportunity given to their wives, mothers or other relatives to acquire similar knowledge on a farm in the Midlands. Their training, too, was given free of charge. For the majority there was training in cobbling, where earnings were said to be good, with mat-making as a second string for slack times. Basket-making and joinery were taught with a view to making saleable articles.

Great care was taken to see that the blind man was properly equipped with an outfit and raw materials, and that he had a good start on completion of his training. The N.I.B. had a special after-care department, and regular visits were paid, and assistance was given in marketing. The National Library offered free membership, for it had by now established an excellent circulating system.

St. Dunstan's had a number of paid trade teachers, most of whom were blind, but they depended mainly on a large staff of voluntary workers. They were supported by voluntary subscriptions, with contributions from the N.I.B., the *Red Cross Societies*, and the *National Relief Fund*. During and after the war their work steadily developed and they decided, in 1923, to establish a separate organisation and hold their own funds, although they continued to work closely with the N.I.B.[1]

Meanwhile the N.I.B. continued its less spectacular work on behalf of the unemployable blind. Its concern for those living in their own homes, trying to manage on the miserable outdoor relief customary at that time, led it to make representation to the boards of guardians to make a more generous allowance. The success of their efforts was 'beyond all anticipation'. The reasons suggested for this result by the N.I.B., in 1916, throw some light on the relationship between statutory and voluntary agencies at this period: 'Mainly because its staff have always been able to demonstrate to the satisfaction of Boards of Guardians that such aid was not invited to relieve the Institute of *its obligations*[2] but to improve the status of the persons for whom the appeals were made, for in every case the Institute has supplemented the

---

out heating systems in large buildings, but he returned to the business in a general office capacity. In a very short time he was responsible for the whole of the ordinary correspondence of his firm, and a little later was entrusted with making out specifications and ordering materials to carry out the rough plans prepared by the men doing the work in which he was formerly occupied. His remuneration is now twice as high as it was before he was blinded, and he has given perfect satisfaction to his employers and himself.' (*Op. cit.*, Vol. VII, p. 45.)

[1] E.g. in the production of 'Talking Books', see below.
[2] Italics mine.

help derived from Boards of Guardians.'[1] The Institute also continued its charitable work of alleviating the miserable tedium felt by blind inmates of workhouses. We find the Local Government Board officially recognising the gifts of pastimes to some ninety-two unions in London and the provinces.[2] In sundry other small ways the Institute was invited to use its experience on behalf of the blind, as when in 1918 it organised the payment of extra profits for blind tea agents allowed by the Ministry of Food.[3]

The work of the N.I.B. had expanded so rapidly that new money had to be found on a large scale. Public appeals were organized with the same thoroughness as had marked all the Institute's recent work. Collecting branches were founded to cover not only large areas in this country, but in the Empire.[4] In the year preceding the war, its annual income was under £15,000. By 1918, it had reached over £250,000.[5] This vast expansion had its reverse side in the loss of local support for some of the smaller charities. The N.I.B. in its post-war efforts to achieve a representative character as a co-ordinating body was to meet some resentment and suspicion on the part of regional and local associations who feared that their traditional standing and achievements were threatened by this great national agency. The N.I.B. maintained, however, that the interests of the blind as a whole demanded that certain services should be nationally provided, and if local loyalties prevented efficiency, then they must give way. They had already proved conclusively the advantage of working nationally in securing uniform embossed literature and in providing special schools. They were ready for further national ventures.

In spite of some friction, local societies were beginning to show an inclination to look to the powerful National Institute for support. The N.I.B., for its part, was becoming more conscious of its function to act as a representative national society in any relations with the central authority. This attitude was considerably strengthened when the Government set up its first Advisory Committee on the Welfare of the Blind in 1917, and several of the chief officers of the N.I.B. were invited to become members.

The opportunity for statutory–voluntary co-operation at a national level was assured. The extent to which the representatives of the voluntary organisations made use of this opportunity would depend largely upon their ability to co-ordinate their own scattered forces, particularly upon their success in gaining the confidence of the many local societies and of the independent regional and national organisations. Many of the local associations had also to learn to co-operate

[1] Annual Report, N.I.B., 1916, pp. 8–9.
[2] Annual Report, N.I.B., 1918, p. 12.
[3] This service was undertaken at the request of the Local Government Board.
[4] In fact Empire collections were not very lucrative, and were soon dropped.
[5] See J. F. Wilson, *op. cit.*, p. 66.

with the local authorities, but this was a later venture for the great majority.[1]

Failures and Achievements in the Pioneer Phase

The contribution of private enterprise on behalf of the blind must be considered in relation to the temper of the times, and to the extent of the need, so far as it was known. In fact, few statistics were available[2] of the incidence of blindness, neither was there adequate knowledge of the causes of blindness. In spite of the vigour of many voluntary societies and local associations, and of one or two enterprising local authorities, there were regions where little or nothing was done. Moreover, those who organised charitable aid were in the minority: the public as a whole were largely ignorant of, or indifferent to, the real needs of the blind.

In the late 19th and early 20th centuries the dislike of statutory 'interference' was still strong, while the fear of encouraging improvidence played a large part in the resistance to Collectivism. Little approval was found for the propaganda of the *National League of the Blind*, nor for the suggestion of the Royal Commission on the Blind, that to deal liberally with this handicapped group, the majority of whom were not impoverished by their own fault, could hardly offer a reward to folly: the latter had pointed out, in vain, that even if State aid were given there would still be ample room for private benevolence. On the contrary, so highly esteemed was the voluntary principle that anything which appeared to jeopardise it in the introduction of measures for public welfare were immediately suspect. The signatories of the majority report of the *Royal Commission on the Poor Laws* had a proper appreciation of this point of view when they recommended a dominant role for the voluntary organisations in the administration of public assistance.[3]

In the second decade other stronger influences were to play a part in changing public opinion: firstly, the new political temper which helped to focus attention on the needs of blind workers, and, secondly, the First World War, which prepared the way for an entirely new outlook on

---

[1] It belongs especially to the years following the Local Government Act, 1929.

[2] The Census scheduled some statistics on the blind: from 1851 the proportion of blind to sighted persons was estimated to be 1/1,979 in 1851, 1/1,037 in 1861, 1/1,052 in 1871, 1/1,138 in 1881. But, as the Departmental Committee pointed out in 1917, census figures were not reliable, partly because there was no agreed definition of blindness.

[3] The C.O.S. under its able secretary, C. S. Loch, was one of the chief exponents of this point of view. It also took an active part in many pioneer social services: in the sphere of blind welfare there is no doubt that its enquiry into the needs of the blind in 1874, and the publicity given to its findings, helped to stimulate the Government to set up the Royal Commission in 1885, to be followed by the first Education Act concerned specifically with blind and deaf children. One of the valuable contributions of the C.O.S. was its publication of regular information on statutory and voluntary progress through its *Annual Charities Register and Digest*.

VOLUNTARY ACTION IN THE PIONEER PHASE

social questions, and gave special prominence to the demand for a comprehensive scheme of blind welfare. Yet it was the experience gained through long years of voluntary action which showed how social policy could effectively be carried out.

The time has now arrived to consider the legislative framework within which blind welfare developed.

XVI

SOCIAL POLICY IN THE PIONEER PHASE[1]

REFERENCE has been made to the Poor Law, under which, for more than three hundred years [2] the community had accepted some responsibility for the necessitous blind. Yet few or no constructive measures had been taken for their welfare, and those who were destitute found themselves in a miserable plight. In the 19th century many blind paupers were to be found in the mixed workhouses, or else eking out a living on a meagre pittance of out-door relief supplemented, in many cases, by begging. Some inroads into Poor Law procedure had been made, however, on behalf of the blind,[3] and a few groups were excluded from the customary treatment accorded to paupers. For example, the parents of a blind child who was educated and maintained in a school acceptable to the Guardians were not subject to the usual disqualifications for citizenship; neither was the husband of a blind woman who was granted relief.[4] If the Guardians chose to use their powers they might send a poor blind child to any school fitted for its reception, even although uncertified by the Local Government Board. This was important at a period when fees were charged for elementary education. If the child was sent, as it might be, to a voluntary certified school (supported wholly or partly by voluntary contributions) the payment made by the Guardians was limited to the same amount as the cost of maintenance in a workhouse.

The Guardians also had power to provide for the maintenance and instruction of any adult pauper who was blind, in any hospital or institution established for their reception. The Guardians were thus

---

[1] There is some slight repetition in this chapter. On balance it seemed better to risk this, in order to give an all-round view of social policy.
[2] The Elizabethan Poor Law Act was passed in 1601.
[3] A small concession to provide for the needs of a limited number of blind persons was made in 1878 through the Customs and Inland Revenue Act. Blind Persons were thereby permitted to have a guide dog without licence.
[4] See three Poor Law Acts of 1862, 1867 and 1879.

empowered to pay contributions both towards the schooling and maintenance of blind children, whether living at home or in residential schools, and towards the maintenance and instruction of blind adults. But the permissive nature of the enactments resulted in failure to provide adequately for the blind. Gardner's Trust, at the end of the century, declared that many Guardians thought it their first duty to avoid chargeability. However that may be, the principle of differential treatment for the blind in need of assistance was established.[1]

After the passing of the 1870 and 1876 Education Acts, School Boards had a duty to see that all children had the opportunity to attend school, but the Acts included no separate provision for blind children.[2] In some of the largest towns efforts were made to meet their special needs. In London, for example, centres were established to give instruction to blind children who attended part-time from the ordinary day schools. That the child was expected to share the education provided for sighted children is indicated by the provision that he could learn Moon type, in addition to Braille, 'as enabling the child to be sooner prepared to read with the class of sighted children to which it belongs'.[3]

The difficulties under which teachers laboured, and the limited education available for blind children is illustrated by a quotation from the report of Dr. Campbell, Principal of the Royal Normal College for the Blind, who visited the London Schools in 1883–84. After noting that the work was elementary but good, and making special reference to the inspiration and affection shown by certain teachers who concentrated on the teaching of blind children, he drew attention to the fact that their efforts were necessarily limited by the other demands made upon them: for example, the majority of classes had not taken up geography 'owing to the necessity of the teachers devoting their energy to preparing the pupils for passing the standards'.[4] He added 'if the seeing teachers can be induced to take a little interest in the blind children when the ordinary classes are having gymnastics, great benefit will be conferred on the blind children'.

It is no wonder that parents were not always willing to send their blind children to school, even if there were special centres for their occasional attendance. Wherever possible, persuasion was used. It was difficult, in any case, to compel.[5] Voluntary organisations were doing their best to co-operate, and we find a comment in the first *Annual*

[1] See *The Blind*, 20th April, 1898, and 20th January, 1899.
[2] This was later made possible by the Act of 1893. See p. 196 below.
[3] By 1882 the London School Board had established 29 centres at which 103 blind children attended on certain mornings or afternoons. They came from 49 schools, board schools and others, and they were charged no extra fee. The school fee ranged from 1*d.* to 6*d.*
[4] Quoted *C.R. & D.*, 1884, p. lxxvii.
[5] See *C.R. & D.*, 1882, p. 76. We learn that 'when a blind child is found by a visitor the parents are desired to send it to the nearest Board School'. If there were reluctance or objection 'no pains are spared to meet and remove it'.

Charities Register and Digest, 1882, which sums up the position: 'Every opportunity should be taken for turning to account the permissive powers of the Guardians and the machinery of the School Boards. In this way by degrees, a distribution of work between these bodies and the charities may be effected.'[1]

Royal Commission on the Blind and the new Education Act. Statutory-Voluntary Co-operation

By this time public interest was sufficiently aroused[2] to warrant setting up a Royal Commission on the Blind.[3] One of the most valuable results of the recommendations of the Royal Commission was the Elementary Education (Blind and Deaf Children) Act, 1893. The important changes effected by this Act, which came into force in 1894, were three. Firstly, the duty of providing for the education of blind children of poor parents was transferred from the poor law authority to the education authority,[4] i.e. the School Boards, except where the children were in workhouses: until now the Guardians were the only authority with statutory powers to pay for the maintenance of a blind child in school, whether the parents were in receipt of relief or not.[5] Secondly, parents now had a duty to see that their blind children received education between the ages of five and sixteen. Thirdly, special schools for blind children were eligible for grants.

The making of efficient and suitable provision under the Act included sending blind children to boarding schools, all of which were in fact provided by voluntary organisations, or making arrangements for the boarding out of a blind child near a special school. The Education Department had already taken a lively interest in the reports of H.M. Inspectors on the education of the blind.[6] The new powers of grant-aid gave opportunities for a closer relationship between the statutory and voluntary agencies, for grants might be made to a voluntary school to the extent of two-thirds[7] of the cost of maintenance, and the Department

---

[1] *Op. cit.*, p. 75.

[2] See footnote 3, p. 192, above, for influence of the C.O.S. in stimulating public interest.

[3] The Commission sat from 1885–89. Its terms of reference included 'the investigation of the condition of the blind, the various systems of education existing at home and abroad, the employments open to them, and the means by which education might be extended and the number of persons qualified for suitable employment be increased'. Its full title extended in 1886, was the Royal Commission on the Blind, Deaf and Dumb, etc., of the United Kingdom (C. 5781).

[4] By 1897 ten School Boards had started classes for blind day scholars.

[5] It should be remembered that fees for children at board schools were not abolished until 1891, and voluntary schools still normally charged a fee. Residential schools were largely dependent on fees as well as on charitable contributions.

[6] H.M. Inspectors were making special reports to the Education Department. See Reports on Education of the Blind by Messrs. Oakley, Sharpe and Fitch (C. 4747 ... xxv, 553 of Printed Bills, Reports and Estimates, Accounts and Papers of Sessions 1 and 11, 1886).

[7] In 1907 this was amended so that voluntary schools no longer had to find at least one-third of the expenses before they were eligible for grant-aid.

SOCIAL POLICY IN THE PIONEER PHASE

of Education might require the governing body of the school to be representative of both voluntary and statutory interests. A constructive partnership was now possible in the field of elementary education.

By 1898 the majority of blind children were still attending half-time at the special centres, the other half of their education being shared with sighted children in ordinary schools.[1] A minority were sent to special residential schools run by voluntary societies, in London, Brighton, Southsea and Liverpool, the last providing for Roman Catholic children.

The growth of special schools for the blind provided by the local authorities was slow. The majority of the residential schools remained in the hands of the voluntary agencies, who were very ready to receive children from council schools on payment of the appropriate fee.[2] One or two large towns were, however, beginning to provide not only full-time day special schools but residential schools. By 1907 London had three residential schools, Leeds and Stoke-on-Trent each had one, while nine day council schools were established in various parts of England.[3] Little further advance in elementary school education for the blind took place over the next few years,[4] with the exception that London was now beginning to classify special schools: two of the eight day special schools were, by 1914, reserved for partially-sighted children, and that number was increased to seven in 1915. Two other towns, Bolton and Gorleston-on-Sea, now had residential schools, and Leeds added a second school in 1915. In eight years the total number of day special schools had increased by four.[5]

Full development of co-operation in higher education had to wait for the passing of the Education Act of 1902. Meanwhile, as we have seen, the more progressive school boards had welcomed the offer of vacancies in the Royal Normal College. The London school board[6] was particularly interested since its teachers in the centres for the elementary education of blind children had been trained at the college.

In the 20th century general progress in higher education for the blind went side by side with that for sighted children. The Education Act,

[1] In 1898, 139 children were attending day schools and going to the centres for part-time special instruction, 73 were sent to certified board schools, and 8 were boarded out in private families. (See *C.R. & D.*) By 1900 the figures were 195 on roll, 47 in boarding schools.
[2] Board schools were renamed council schools when local education authorities replaced school boards in 1902. In 1906 the income of the Royal Normal College included payment of fees by local authorities for pupils under sixteen at the rate of £35 per annum for pupils under thirteen, and £45 for those thirteen to sixteen years of age. See *C.R. & D.*, 1908.
[3] The total accommodated in these schools was still far short of the need.
[4] The number reported in 1911 was the same as that in 1907. London, in fact, reduced the number of residential schools from three to two, and its day schools by one.
[5] By 1915 only thirteen such schools were established outside London.
[6] When in 1882 a vacancy occurred at the Royal Normal College, 25 children were sent in by the London school board (ages ten to fourteen) for the entrance examination.

1902, was the responsibility of the new and active Board of Education, and of the newly constituted local education authorities which replaced the *ad hoc* school boards. One of its most valuable provisions was the power to supply or aid the supply of education other than elementary. It gave renewed opportunity for a partnership of voluntary and statutory effort.

It was fortunate that the new Board of Education took a broad view of its responsibilities in various fields of social service.[1] It was prepared to do all in its power to support educationists working specially on behalf of the blind. It recognised the role of voluntary organisations 'to leaven public opinion by stimulating local authorites to exercise their powers for higher education'.[2] At the same time the Board made it clear that it expected a high standard of work; grants would only be given for 'progressive' teaching and withheld if the pupils were engaged on merely routine employments. The Board of Education was keeping a special watch on the schemes for technical training and 'they hoped that in addition to making things, the cultural activities, including literature and music would be thought of'. The Board, indeed, showed increasing interest in the efforts to give technical training to blind students, and, after some discussion with voluntary agencies,[3] it was announced that it would do all it could to support institutions and authorities (i.e. voluntary and statutory agencies) who were training pupils beyond the age of sixteen. It was even prepared to offer a substantial grant for classes conducted in workshops.

Social Policy in other Spheres of Blind Welfare

Ancillary developments helped the blind to profit from the new opportunities for education, particularly the wider distribution of books. After repeated attempts to secure legislation for the reduction of the heavy postage involved in distributing embossed literature, a concession was at length secured in 1906. This was gradually followed by others until in 1915 reduced rates were extended to include the U.S.A. and the British Empire. But progress was slow: however sympathetic the Postmaster General was personally, he could not move ahead of public opinion, nor would he trespass in fields which properly belonged to the Local Government Board.[4]

Meanwhile, the record of the Local Government Board had indeed been poor, whether in the sphere of assistance, or of preventive health

[1] It had already supported schools for mothers in the Infant Welfare Movement. See part II, p. 45.
[2] The address by Dr. Eichholz, H.M.I. Board of Education, at the first Conference of the North of England Union of Institutions in 1907.
[3] See p. 182, above.
[4] He had refused to accept the suggestion of the Royal Commission that the G.P.O. should distribute free leaflets on the after effects of infant ophthalmia, arguing that this was a health matter and the responsibility of the Local Government Board.

measures. As the responsible central authority it did little or nothing to encourage Boards of Guardians to use their power or perform their duty to relieve the poor. There was some reason for its hesitation since public policy was still uncertain on this issue. As we have seen, two fears had for long dominated those who were actively concerned with assisting the needy. The first was that recipients might be made improvident; the second, that increase in State aid might react unfavourably upon voluntary effort. The Royal Commission on the Blind, etc. had given effective replies. They maintained that it could not be said that the great majority of the blind were impoverished through any fault of their own. Therefore to deal with them liberally could not be viewed as 'offering any reward to vice, folly or improvidence'.[1] Moreover, they argued that 'when it is remembered how much remains to be done for them, it is obvious that, even if such aid (i.e. State aid) be given, there will still be room for the action of private benevolence, which experience shows to be often stimulated rather than discouraged by State aid'. They were careful to add 'when judiciously given'.

The Royal Commission had also drawn attention to the need for action for the prevention of blindness. In spite of powers under the Public Health Act, 1875, little had so far been done towards the prevention of blindness in newborn infants. Yet it was known that simple methods of cleansing the eyes at birth had proved effective, and that much preventable blindness occurred through lack of proper precautions. The Local Government Board, however, for some time yet, remained indifferent to the efforts of voluntary organisations and of local authorities to secure notification of ophthalmia neonatorum as a first step towards prevention. It was the local authorities in the Potteries who made history by making this disease notifiable: a few other authorities followed suit, but it was not extended to the whole country until, in 1915, notification was made compulsory.

By the end of the 19th century we have a few signs of a changing attitude towards assistance to the blind, when both statutory and voluntary agencies were beginning to view the possibility of more generous State aid as beneficial to the blind without harming the cherished principles still held to be applicable to the 'indigent' as a class. A few local authorities were actively pioneering at the turn of the century in the field of education and health.[2] The general improvement due to advances in ophthalmic surgery did much to reduce the incidence of blindness in the population. But the Local Government Board still remained indifferent, nor did the public show much interest in the activities of the National League of the Blind which had been agitating for statutory intervention

---

[1] Quoted with evident approval in the introduction to the first edition of the *C.R. & D.* by C. S. Loch, secretary of the Charity Organisation Society, p. cxxviii.

[2] The new movement for infant welfare is closely linked with the welfare of blind children. 'After-Care' of blind boys and girls was also an important addition. See London's Committee, 1903. See p. 183, above.

since the early 1890's.[1] The propaganda of the National League was conducted with some bitterness towards philanthropy, and this, together with its known left-wing political bias, accounted to some extent for its failure to secure sufficient support in the House of Commons. From 1909 onwards[2] a number of Bills were prepared, but to no purpose. When a deputation saw the Home Secretary in 1912 it was advised to come back again after an understanding had been reached between the charitable organisations and the National League.

The 1914 Resolution and the Departmental Committee, 1914–17

At length, in March 1914, Mr. Wardle, backed by the National League and supported by the Labour Party, was able to get a sympathetic hearing for the resolution that 'the present system of voluntary effort in aid of the blind people of this country does not adequately meet their necessities, and that the State should make provision whereby capable blind people might be made industrially self-supporting, and the incapable and infirm maintained in a proper and humane manner'.[3] Both sides were now ready to accept some statutory intervention. The debate revealed that the condition of voluntary finance and the unsatisfactory nature of some blind charities had persuaded most of the voluntary agencies that the time to seek aid from public funds had arrived. The representatives of trade unions and of the Labour Party stressed, firstly, the failure of philanthropic effort to meet the total needs, secondly, the unsatisfactory wages and employment conditions, and lastly, the duty of the State to see that the employable blind were self-supporting.

In spite of an attentive House, the Government was still not ready to admit the need for special legislation. In a typical Parliamentary reply setting out the benefits already enjoyed by the blind under the existing schemes, such as old-age pensions, Poor Law assistance and education schemes 'which were increasingly generous', the parliamentary secretary to the Local Government Board wound up by promising a Departmental Committee of enquiry if the resolution before the House was carried. There was general support, and the committee[4] was set up in the same year. It collected evidence over the next three years on the

[1] The National League later forced public attention on the need for further statutory action when, after the First World War, it organised a march of some 200 blind workers from the North who demonstrated in Trafalgar Square (1920). The first Bill had been introduced in 1909 as a result of 'a strong National Committee' set up after the International Conference of 1905 (*Hansard*, 11.3.1914, Mr. Burgoyne).

[2] It was then that the Labour Party sponsored a Bill introduced on behalf of the National League of the Blind. As the two Bills 'ran parallel', the National Committee refused to consider them again, so Mr. Burgoyne introduced another in 1913; this new Bill was an agreed measure between the two groups.

[3] *Hansard*, Vol. LIX, Cols. 1313–55, 11th March, 1914.

[4] It is interesting to note that Mr. C. Arthur Pearson, the new President of the N.I.B., was asked to assist the Departmental Committee. See N.I.B. Report, 1914, p. 29.

condition of the blind, the means available for their industrial and professional training, and the provision made for assistance.

The Committee's work was hindered by the outbreak of war, but it was able to get some comparative material, as an International Conference on the Blind happened to be held in London during the early part of its investigations. Evidence was taken from witnesses from America, Australia and Sweden, and the Committee several times made recommendations based on experience abroad: e.g., that establishments producing books should be assisted by grant, as in Sweden. This was urgently needed in this country in view of the poor equipment in schools for the blind, where books and apparatus were in short supply. The Committee also deplored the fact that several important recommendations of the Royal Commission of 1889 had not been carried out. Aftercare was still one of the weakest links. Only a few institutions and local education authorities attempted any form of care in helping to place their trainees, or in keeping in touch with children who had passed through special schools.[1] Although favourable reference was made to the Saxon System, which had already been strongly recommended to institutions by Dr. Armitage,[2] the Committee was not in favour of State aid for such a system: they believed such work to be the proper sphere of the voluntary bodies. In the same spirit they hoped that workshops would be started in every large centre, 'but not to be directly subsidised by the State'. In order to achieve these aims 'there should be greater solidarity among the institutions so that they would work harmoniously together'.

The Committee suggested that 'the State might be fairly called upon to assist a secondary school', and that 'school authorities should have the duty of assisting able pupils to maintain themselves while learning a trade'. There was a case, too, for similar help for those between twenty-one and fifty. The Committee commented that charitable funds would thereby be released to be applied to the enlargement of workshops or the assistance of old pupils.

Voluntary effort in several spheres was warmly commended, and the developments reported by Gardner's Trust were quoted: in 1915 there were provided under voluntary auspices, 56 workshops for the blind, many of which also provided industrial training for those over sixteen; there were 23 homes, 71 pensions societies, 62 home teaching societies, and a considerable number of libraries and miscellaneous societies. The income of the chief organisations totalled over £100,000 in subscriptions and donations, and another £100,000 derived from investments and stocks.

But voluntary action was not adequate to the need. For example,

---

[1] The L.C.C., Leeds, and North Stafford Joint Authority were cited. The Committee noted too, that a child could not be dealt with directly under the Elementary Education Act, 1893, if it was in a workhouse or boarded out: it was the concern of the Poor Law Authority.

[2] See p. 182, above.

voluntary effort was no longer sufficient to keep up the registers, nor could there always be effective 'follow up'. There was need for more paid workers, e.g. in London. Even more difficult was the problem of finding work for those who were trained,[1] and for increasing the number of workshops for some 3,000 who, it was estimated, were capable of training and employment but who were unemployed. The institutions were not financially in a position to extend so as to meet the deficiencies of accommodation. The workshops in existence were, indeed, meeting special difficulties: the first was the market value of the goods produced, the second, the need to supplement the wages of the blind worker to bring them up to trade union rates in force in the district. There was an 'almost unanimous opinion' that 'goods made by the blind can rarely, if ever, be put on the market at such a price as will secure a profitable sale under ordinary conditions of business competition'. Although goods might be equal in quality, production costs were higher. The Committee suggested that possibly Government contracts might give preference to certain articles, such as brooms. On the question of wages, the Committee quoted from the evidence of the *National Committee for the Employment of the Blind*, giving examples of wages in fact paid, as distinct from those actually earned,[2] and pointed to the practice of other countries, e.g. Sweden, where State aid was given for augmentation of wages.

It seemed to the Committee that the suitability of certain occupations for the blind was established, for example, basket, brush, mat and mattress making, boot repairing, chair caning, upholstering and cork fender making, carpentry and cabinet making for men; for women the range was small: knitting, sewing, chair caning and light basket work.[3] But it had been suggested that some of the blind who worked in industry felt frustrated, and would have found one of the professions more congenial. Those who sought a commercial opening were often disappointed, since employers were reluctant to engage a blind typist: insurance travelling, tea agencies, poultry farming and market gardening, and more recently, massage, had been made possible by the training given by voluntary bodies, but it was important that selection should be efficient for a successful career in these callings. Piano tuning and teaching were the most usual openings for those who had been to the Royal Normal College.[4] In general, it was agreed that it was not so much the

---

[1] It was estimated that more than half could not get employment in workshops.
[2] Wages earned in large institutions in the first week of March 1914 were quoted as follows: men's wages averaged a little under 14s., women's a little over 6s., whereas the wages in fact paid were 19s. and 10s. respectively. There was general adoption of the trade union rate for the district.
[3] Some local authorities as well as voluntary institutions provided manual training in preparation for one of these trades, e.g. the L.C.C. was noted by the Departmental Committee to make special provision for blind children at the age of fourteen to go to schools where manual training was available.
[4] A number also became church organists.

SOCIAL POLICY IN THE PIONEER PHASE

finding of new openings that was needed, but more careful placement, and better marketing of products. This was particularly important for the home workers, many of whom worked in isolation. The onus was put upon the voluntary organisations for establishing a co-ordinated scheme. In so far as Government intervention was admitted it should be directed 'mainly to the securing of administrative efficiency': this 'would not affect prejudicially the flow of charitable funds for the blind'.

The Departmental Committee was also concerned with the incapable blind, some 9,000 of whom were having relief under the Poor Law. The attitude towards 'pauperisation',[1] and the concern with worthiness, are brought out clearly in the following quotations: 'We have had under consideration the question whether the incapable blind, who are generally so afflicted through no fault whatever of their own, should be allowed to become paupers.... In our opinion every incapable blind person who is worthy should be secured an adequate pension; and it will be necessary for the State to provide additional funds for this purpose, which should be distributed with due regard to the pensions already paid from charitable sources'.

One further point of special interest in the comprehensive report is the reference to the fact that ophthalmia neonatorum had only recently become compulsorily notifiable,[2] in spite of the strong recommendations of the Royal Commission. Consequently there had been no appreciable diminution of blindness due to this cause in the last twenty-five years. The proportion of cases of blindness due to ophthalmia neonatorum to the total number of blind persons was calculated to be more than 10%. There was also a considerable amount of preventable occupational blindness. The Committee drew attention to the fact that with one exception,[3] there was no compulsion on employers to provide protective goggles, in trades where mechanical injuries were common.

The Committee, although obviously sympathetic to voluntary organisations, made several references to shortcomings, due not only to financial needs, but to their dependence upon so much voluntary help. This had, for example, restricted the comprehensive work planned by the seven Unions of England and Wales. Home teaching societies were even more affected since they were not organised, like the Unions, but usually worked in isolation. Special reference was made to the *London Home Teaching Society*, the largest in the country, which employed

---

[1] It should be remembered that all persons on outdoor relief were disfranchised unless they received medical relief only. The Committee endorsed the view of the Royal Commission of 1889 that 'the well conducted blind should receive a liberal outdoor relief, if they have friends to live with, ... otherwise accommodation in a special ward or home as at Bradford and Manchester ...' should be provided, instead of the workhouse (*op. cit.*, p. 43).
[2] Notifiable compulsorily in 1914, but no statistics available by 1917.
[3] Aerated water bottling.

fifteen paid blind visitors. Other societies needed to have more paid visitors if they were effectively to keep up registration, and make frequent and regular visits.

The Advisory Committee and the Registration of the Blind. Voluntary–Statutory Co-operation

When the Departmental Committee reported in 1917 there was considerable interest. The war had made the public aware of the needs of blind ex-service men, and blindness ranked high in the disabilities for which a pension might be claimed. Support for further efforts was now assured. The recommendation of the Departmental Committee to set up a statutory advisory committee was acted upon without delay, while a special department of the Local Government Board was established to deal with blind welfare. It should be noted that membership of the Advisory Committee was drawn largely from those already experienced in the field of voluntary effort, so that co-operation between statutory and voluntary agencies was the accepted procedure at the centre. The Advisory Committee proved to be a vigorous and energetic body, and 1917 marked the beginning of a partnership which was to have considerable influence on the development of blind welfare.

One of the first issues of practical importance for progress was the compilation of a register. It was vital to know the incidence of blindness. The central authority therefore required not only an approved register of institutions, societies and agencies to which voluntary societies were invited to apply, but a register of all blind persons, to be compiled from information collected by local authorities and voluntary bodies. Although it took many years to perfect this national scheme for the registration of the blind[1] it has roused such widespread interest that it is worth noting the methods adopted at its institution. The information required was detailed and comprehensive, including particulars of age,[2] sex, name and address, marital and family condition, cause and degree of blindness, date of onset, place of training, ability to read Braille or Moon type, occupation before and after blindness and ability to live on income and earnings. In this vast effort to secure a reliable and comprehensive register all available help was needed, and the new department urged voluntary and statutory officers, whether health visitors, members of district nursing associations, or others who had entry to the home, to co-operate in the important work of ascertainment. Thus, not only in

[1] It should be noted that for many years registration suffered from a serious weakness: medical evidence of blindness might be given by any doctor. His knowledge in this sphere might well be limited. See p. 244, below.

[2] Information on the ages of those registered as blind was available from 1923 onwards. It resulted in the compiling of useful records. One of the most striking trends has been the fall in the proportion of infants and children in the blind population and the sharp rise in the proportion of the elderly, particularly those over 70 (registrations 1948-50 showed that 61·2% of the blind population were over 70 years of age).

SOCIAL POLICY IN THE PIONEER PHASE

the composition of the Advisory Committee at the centre, but in the day-to-day work in local government areas, the pattern of co-operative effort had official approval. Although no special Act for the welfare of the blind was passed in the first phase of development, a new vitality was infused into existing services, and effective administrative machinery was introduced. The stage was set for a forward move in the post-war era in which both statutory and voluntary agencies could participate.

XVII

THE EXPANSION OF SOCIAL POLICY BETWEEN THE TWO WORLD WARS

THE years following the end of the First World War marked a new phase in statutory responsibility for the welfare of the blind. The Ministry of Health had replaced the Local Government Board, and in 1919 it received the first report of its Advisory Committee. There followed an important circular,[1] announcing that an estimate had been laid before Parliament for grant-aid for a number of services for the benefit of the blind. In the same year there was also in preparation a draft bill which would cover other services not, so far, possible under existing legislation.

The new grants, available for both statutory and voluntary agencies, made a closer relationship possible, and the Minister pointed out that the regulations 'were drawn up with as much elasticity as is consistent with the efficiency of the services for which grants will be payable, and it will be observed that room is left for local initiative'. Schemes to be submitted to the Minister might include applications for grants towards (i) workshops for the blind; (ii) provision of assistance to home workers; (iii) homes and hostels for the blind; (iv) home-teaching; (v) book production; (vi) the work of counties associations and (vii) certain miscellaneous projects. A valuable advance was the statement of the Minister that under the last heading he would particularly welcome any considered schemes for research into new industries for the blind, or for work in connection with the prevention of blindness.[2]

The Minister was determined to ensure high standards,[3] and his circular included a number of detailed suggestions of a practical nature for the guidance of local authorities and voluntary organisations in the

---

[1] Ministry of Health: Ref. 106/19. Circular 7 B.D., 7/8/1919.
[2] See the later work of the Union of Counties Association, p. 219, below.
[3] The Advisory Committee reported the withholding of a grant to the S. Wales Association because it was 'not showing activity in its proper work' (*op. cit.*, 1919–20).

submission of schemes. For example, in extending the home teaching service 'the Minister would be glad to see one teacher for every 50 blind persons in an urban area and for every 30 in a rural area'.[1] In the formulation of schemes for home workers, 'while the Minister is of the opinion that, wherever practicable, employment in workshops is preferable to provision of assistance to workers in their own homes', ... where home work was necessary the needs might be met as follows: (*a*) the supply and maintenance of a full complement of tools and equipment necessary for executing the work satisfactorily; (*b*) the supply and delivery of materials at the lowest market prices; (*c*) assistance in making and finishing articles, and their inspection; (*d*) advice on current prices; (*e*) marketing the finished article, including advertising; (*f*) arrangements for periodic returns as to output. In every case of grant-aid the Minister would require that the organisation had a properly constituted committee, and duly appointed officers.

A number of suggestions were made concerning workshops. The influence of trade unionists was traceable in the requirement that the recognised standards of the trade should be observed in workshop employment, the Minister of Labour to determine the issue in any question arising. Of particular interest to our study is the statement that 'the Minister would be glad, in the interest of the blind themselves, to see more co-operation between the several agencies, more particularly in regard to workshops, and it will be observed that one of the general conditions of the grant is that services to be aided must be co-ordinated so far as is practicable'. Some agencies indeed preferred to forfeit a grant rather than comply with these conditions.[2]

Finally, the Minister referred to the 'large amount of valuable work done on behalf of the blind by the voluntary agencies interested in their welfare ... among the larger problems in this field of work is that of arriving at satisfactory arrangements for relieving the lot of the unemployable blind living in their own homes. For this there is no pecuniary provision in these regulations for the reason that none such is possible until suitable legislation has been passed'. A promise was made to lay proposals before Parliament as soon as possible. Meanwhile, now that grants were available in many other spheres of blind welfare, it was possible to exert influence not only through official regulations, but by personal contact with a special staff of inspectors. Many of these inspectors were known for their long experience in the field of voluntary blind welfare, and some of them were in fact drawn from amongst the first members of the Advisory Committee.

[1] It was suggested that the employment of more educated blind persons should be considered for the Home Teaching Service. It is interesting to note the low case load then considered desirable. Subsequent recommendations, recently reaffirmed, were 100 and 80, respectively.
[2] E.g. in South Wales where co-ordination was notoriously difficult to achieve.

THE WELFARE OF THE BLIND

The Blind Persons Act, 1920, and the Relationship with Voluntary Organisations

These and other regulations which followed marked a definite stage in the acceptance of statutory responsibility for the encouragement of local initiative, whether by local authorities or by voluntary organisations. Important duties were laid upon local authorities, if they were to qualify for grant-aid, not least that of compiling a register of blind persons in their area. This was strengthened when, in 1920, the first Blind Persons Act was passed. Any scheme submitted to the Minister must include arrangements for keeping an accurate register. In addition local authorities[1] now had a duty to make arrangements, satisfactory to the Minister of Health, for providing for the welfare of blind persons ordinarily resident in their area.[2] Not only were public funds, distinct from the Poor Law, available for blind welfare, but the necessitous blind were to be eligible for an old-age pension[3] at the age of fifty. The registration of charities for the blind was another important provision, following the useful experience gained from the operation of the War Charities Act of 1916.

The policy of the Minister on the question of the statutory–voluntary relationship was evident in his new circular to local authorities.[4] He felt sure that they would 'cordially co-operate with him and with the voluntary agencies in the development of assistance to the blind'. The Advisory Committee was to emphasise this point still further: 'the fostering of the voluntary side of the work', whereby the local authorities would 'aid and supplement the effort of the efficient voluntary agencies which, prior to the passing of the Act, had borne practically the whole charge of caring for the blind in this country'.[5] The new Act was thus firmly based on the principle of statutory–voluntary partnership foreshadowed in the 1919 regulations, but the implication was that statutory schemes were to be 'minimum': voluntary enterprise was to take first place, whenever possible.

Considerable discretion was given to local authorities in working out their schemes for blind welfare. Few authorities chose to make direct provision. The majority preferred to take advantage of the opportunity to work through existing voluntary organisations, particularly the home teaching societies, already in the field. In some areas the voluntary organisations acted as agents for certain services while the local autho-

---

[1] I.e. councils of counties and county boroughs.
[2] The use of the test 'ordinarily resident', instead of the hated 'settlement and removal' provisions of the Poor Law, was a welcome administrative simplification, later to be incorporated in the National Assistance Act, 1948.
[3] I.e. a non-contributory old age pension under the Old Age Pension Acts of 1908–19 by which pensions might be claimed, normally at the age of seventy, after certain conditions regarding needs, nationality and residence were satisfied.
[4] Circular 133, 25.9.1920, Ministry of Health.
[5] See Third Annual Report of the Advisory Committee 1921–22.

EXPANSION BETWEEN THE WARS

rities made direct provision in other spheres.[1] The pattern varied considerably from area to area. In some large towns the local authority was active in promoting more efficient service. In London, for example, the L.C.C. saw the need for co-ordination if a full partnership between public and voluntary enterprise was to be established. It took the initiative, in 1921-22, by setting up a Central Council for the London Blind, bringing together representatives of some nineteen societies, national and local, to serve with the L.C.C. representatives. In the same year the Minister of Health invited the National Institute for the Blind to be responsible for a home workers' scheme for an area covering the metropolitan district south of the Thames and the counties of Kent, Surrey, Sussex and Hants. They in turn immediately consulted the county and county borough councils within the area.

Some idea of the variation in the administrative pattern from area to area can be gained from the account given by the Advisory Committee,[2] some five years after the passing of the Blind Persons Act of 1920, on the provision made for the unemployable blind in four areas. In one the town council undertook full responsibility, but authorised the voluntary agency to make the initial enquiries, and to arrange for augmentation of the incomes of single blind persons up to 16s. 6d., and of married couples up to 25s. a week. The council then reimbursed the voluntary agency. The council also paid for the cost of blind persons in Poor Law institutions.

In the second area the Boards of Guardians were asked by the town council, with the agreement of the voluntary agencies, to relieve all 'difficult and destitute cases', while the voluntary agency undertook to assist all others. The first group received relief at the rate of up to a maximum of 15s. a week for a single person, the second assistance up to a maximum of 20s.

In the third area a different pattern had emerged: the local authority delegated to the voluntary agency its work of administering relief, but made no direct grant for this specific service; it gave a general grant, however, sufficient in amount to cover the agency. The policy of the voluntary organisation included the administration of relief on a scale covering a variety of needs (e.g. whether applicant was widowed, married, or single; whether living alone or with relatives). While the average range was from 15s. to 25s. the maximum might be higher if there were exceptional need.

In the last area chosen for illustration the county council made a specific grant of £500 a year to the voluntary agency to cover assistance to any in the unemployable group who were not permanently destitute.

---

[1] A very few local authorities ran their own municipal workshops; a few others provided their own home teaching service, relying on voluntary organisations for certain welfare services, such as convalescence or holiday homes.

[2] Sixth Annual Report, 1924-26, pp. 13-14.

The latter were to be left to the boards of guardians. The voluntary agency usually tried to supplement incomes to reach a maximum of 19s. a week in urban, and 15s. a week in rural areas.[1]

The Advisory Committee was still noting with satisfaction that as a general rule the scheme of local authorities provided for the fullest use of voluntary agencies. At the same time they found it encouraging that there was an increasing tendency for local authorities to take a more active part in the actual work and management of the voluntary agencies.[2] The post-war economic difficulties strengthened the practice in many areas of relying largely upon voluntary enterprise. So much depended upon the presence or absence of a vigorous and enterprising voluntary society that the Advisory Committee could report in 1928–29 that 'it is generally true to say that in those areas where progress is not yet satisfactory (i.e. under the Blind Persons Act, 1920) the voluntary organisation is weak and ineffective'.

One element which may be specially stressed is the interest taken by the Advisory Committee in any experiments to help the blind worker to lead a more normal life. Considerable encouragement was given by the announcement, for example, that the Ministry of Health would consider extending grants to hostels primarily intended for sighted persons, but with some blind residents. 'This would help the blind to take part in normal social life.'[3]

Effect of the Local Government Act, 1929

1929 marked a new development in statutory schemes for blind welfare. The Local Government Act of that year gave power to local authorities to declare that domiciliary assistance to the blind should no longer be given under the Poor Law but under the Blind Persons Act.[4]

---

[1] When a sub-committee on the unemployable blind, set up by the Advisory Committee, reported in 1935, they still found wide differences in the scales of financial assistance, varying from 15s. for a single adult to 27s. 6d. weekly. An analysis shows:

Payment per week to single adult, Shillings	Number of county councils	Number of county boroughs
Under 20s.	17	9
20s. to 24s.	3	24
25s. to 30s.	8	28
According to circumstance, or 'no regulation'	34	23
TOTAL	62	84

Cf. 1939 when the total expenditure per head on blind welfare by county councils and county borough councils ranged from £6 to £33 in county councils and £12 to £50 in county borough councils. See *Voluntary Social Services*, ed. A. F. C. Bourdillon, p. 64, and *Social Security*, ed. W. Robson, p. 179.

[2] See Sixth Annual Report, 1924–26.

[3] See the Seventh Annual Report of the Advisory Committee on the Welfare of the Blind, p. 18.

[4] More than 50% made declarations.

EXPANSION BETWEEN THE WARS

Even if local authorities did not elect to make such a declaration, the blind would benefit from the transference of the administration of the Poor Law from Boards of Guardians to the local authorities. The same authority was now responsible for assistance, for health, and for blind welfare. A third important change which affected the blind was the new method of financing the social services. The major local authorities[1] were to receive general exchequer contributions out of which various social services were to be assisted. The supervision of voluntary agencies and the payment of contributions towards their work were to be the responsibility of the local authorities, and not directly, as before, of the Minister of Health. Once more the Minister safeguarded the position of the voluntary organisations. Contributions to voluntary associations were calculated, so that they should be no worse off than when the Ministry made direct grants. Provision was also made for variation and expansion. The outcome was a considerable transfer of responsibility to the local authorities, the Minister of Health keeping a close watch on the schemes, which had to be submitted for scrutiny.

The Local Government Act led, on the one hand, to a closer relationship between local authorities and voluntary organisations who already carried out services on their behalf; on the other hand, there was an increasing tendency for statutory bodies to provide their own schemes after 1929. In the bigger towns, where large sums of public money were involved, it was natural that direct control should be assumed. Many were finding the machinery cumbersome when a voluntary association did the work under the supervision of the council. In areas where political opinion in favour of statutory intervention was strong this tendency was most marked.[2] In some areas, however, local authorities could scarcely discharge their obligations, and many of them were ready to accept the assistance of voluntary associations which, so recently freed from some of their financial commitments, willingly turned their energies to the provision of welfare schemes in some of the poorly served districts.

The Minister of Health suggested lines of development in the preparation of statutory schemes,[3] and full scope was given for both local authority discretion and for voluntary agency participation. Such a scheme might include provision for (*a*) registration; (*b*) children under school age; (*c*) education and training of (i) children, and (ii) young persons and adults; (*d*) employment, (i) in workshops, and (ii) through

[1] I.e. county councils and county borough councils.
[2] London took over direct control of many of the services following upon the change in the political complexion of the council. (The new scheme to operate from 1st April, 1935.) It should be noted that in spite of the L.C.C. change of policy, the London workshops remained as a voluntary enterprise, and the services of the Metropolitan Society were retained for special cases. In the north a number of labour councils preferred direct management of such activities as workshop employment and home teaching.
[3] Memorandum 27/B.D., of 25th September, 1920, was still applicable under Section 2 of the Blind Persons Act, 1938.

home workers' schemes; (*e*) augmentation; (*f*) hostels for blind workers; (*g*) homes; (*h*) home teaching; and (*i*) necessitous blind. A scheme generally included co-operation with voluntary organisations in the provision of workshops, home workers, home teaching and registration.[1]

In London there was by now a tradition of voluntary work for the blind in all these spheres. Table IX shows how much the L.C.C. relied

TABLE IX

Total Expenditure by the L.C.C. on Welfare of the Blind and Grants to Registered Charities for the Blind, 1924–39*

[Source: London Statistics; Accounts of Registered Charities and Accounts of the L.C.C.]

Year	A Total expenditure by the council	B Grants to charities by the council	B as % of A (Grants to charities as % of total expenditure)
	£	£	
1924–45	no data	4,342	—
1925–26	no data	7,456	—
1926–27	10,367	12,274‡	100
1927–28	15,005	18,582‡	100
1928–29	17,555	16,538	94
1929–30	41,602	33,506	80
1930–31	77,567	71,823	92
1931–32	85,446	86,298‡	—
1932–33	90,687	90,748‡	100
1933–34	98,351	97,804	99
1934–35	112,862	111,776	99
1935–36	149,417	32,899†	22
1936–37	149,607	33,207	22
1937–38	155,810	34,236	22
1938–39	224,424	32,340	14

* I am much indebted to the L.C.C. for checking these statistics and for providing additional information where necessary.

† From 1.4.35 most of the services for the welfare of the blind in London were operated directly by the Council.

‡ The discrepancies in the figures for total expenditure and grants to charities noted at † are due to the fact that the financial year of charitable organisations does not always coincide with that of the L.C.C. (31st March 'London Statistics' figures for grants to charities are taken from the published accounts of those charities in respect of their accounting year).

on charities until the change of policy in 1935. Even then the Council decided to operate many of the services directly although they continued to co-operate with voluntary organisations for special purposes, and to make substantial grants. From Table X, which shows payment to a

[1] See Handbook on the Welfare of the Blind, Ministry of Health Advisory Committee, 3rd edition.

EXPANSION BETWEEN THE WARS

TABLE X
Payments by the L.C.C. to Voluntary Associations for the Welfare of the Blind, 1937-38

Name of institution	H*	I*	W*	M*	Total
Barclay Workshop for Blind Women	—	—	1,192	—	1,192
Catholic Blind Asylum.	—	300	—	—	300
Cecilia Home for Blind Women	—	202	—	—	202
Church Army (Hostel).	—	50	—	—	50
Devonport and W. Counties Association.	—	216	—	—	216
Glynn Vivian Home of Rest.	—	14	—	—	14
Inc. Ass. for Promoting General Welfare of the Blind	—	—	4,439	—	4,439
Indigent Blind Visiting Society	—	1,127	—	—	1,127
London Assn. for the Blind.	—	1,547	4,483	—	6,030
Manchester and Salford Blind Aid Society	—	38	—	—	38
Metropolitan Soc. for Blind Occ. Centres.	—	—	—	793	793
N.I. for the Blind	4,177	698	266	—	5,141
Lond. Soc. for Teaching and Training.	3,232	7	5,228	—	8,453
N. Libr. for the Blind.	522	—	—	—	522
Provision, etc., Lit. and Music	—	—	—	838	838
N. London Homes for the Blind	—	2,174	—	—	2,174
Royal Assn. in Aid of Deaf and Dumb	—	—	—	60	60
Royal Schools for the Blind.	—	1,700	6,325	—	8,025
S. Regional Ass. for the Blind	—	—	—	50	50
S. London Inst. for the Blind	—	19	—	—	19
Workshop for the Blind, Greater London.	—	—	1,559	—	1,559
Sundry Assns.	—	20	—	—	20
Paid direct by M.H. to N.I.B. deductable from General Exchequer grant to L.C.C.	—	—	—	1,072	1,072
St. Dunstan's	—	—	—	—	—
TOTAL.	7,931	8,098	23,492	2,813	42,334†
Percentage of Total	19	19	55	7	100

* NOTE: H—Home Worker.   W—Workshops
           I—Institutions   M—Miscellaneous
† This total differs from that in Table IX by the amount paid to Institutions.

variety of voluntary societies in the year 1937–38, several interesting points emerge: (1) the associations benefiting include national and regional organisations as well as local societies; (2) half the total payments went to organisations providing workshops, while most of the remainder went to home workers and institutions in equal proportions; (3) under the heading 'miscellaneous' the largest single payment was made to the N.I.B. by the Ministry of Health, and deducted from the general exchequer grant to the L.C.C.

Causes and Prevention of Blindness. The Blind Persons Act, 1938, and Other Relevant Legislation

Meanwhile, statutory action had been taken in certain other fields. In 1920 a Departmental Committee[1] was set up to consider the causes and prevention of blindness, and it laid great stress, as others had done before it, on the importance of early action.[2] It also reported upon industrial diseases and accidents which affected the eyes. Advance was made possible in 1925 with the passing of the Public Health Act.[3] The major local authorities were now given powers 'to make such arrangements as seem desirable',[4] to assist in the prevention of blindness, and to provide facilities for treatment. These preventive powers, together with powers under the Maternity and Child Welfare Act of 1918, were consolidated in the Public Health Act of 1936. Throughout the 1930's the general pattern of statutory-voluntary co-operation held. Local authorities continued to have a large measure of discretion and the variation in provision continued to be a feature of blind welfare.

The Government felt that the time was now ripe for a more comprehensive scheme, and the second Blind Persons Act was passed in 1938. The permissive 'declarations' of the 1929 Act were superseded by an obligation placed upon all major local authorities to provide domiciliary assistance under the Blind Persons Act. Moreover, there was a duty to consider the needs of dependents when a blind person needed assistance. Another important provision was the reduction of the age of eligibility for an old-age pension (non-contributory) from fifty to forty. There was now a complete separation from the Poor Law of those who needed assistance, other than medical assistance, in their own homes. The methods of calculating need were also based on the more generous provisions familiar under the Unemployment Act of 1934, where certain assets were disregarded in considering means. The Blind Persons Acts of 1920 and 1938 thus gave local authorities full financial responsibility for the domiciliary assistance of blind persons and their dependents, and placed upon them a general duty and certain specific powers to provide for the welfare of blind persons in their area. Financial aid to the blind was now almost entirely statutory.[5] The Minister of Health no longer required local authorities to submit schemes for his approval, but should

[1] It reported in 1922.
[2] We have seen that the first step for the compulsory notification of ophthalmia neonatorum was taken in 1914, after several progressive local authorities had proved its value: it had resulted in considerable reduction of blindness in infants.
[3] Public Health Act, 1925, Part VII, Sec. 66 (i).
[4] With the approval of the Ministry of Health.
[5] A relatively small amount in cash payments continued to be paid by voluntary societies administering charitable pensions schemes.

they not fulfil their obligations, he had the ultimate sanction of a reduction of the block grant. The Ministry retained its general advisory function, and was responsible for the revision of the payments to be made by local authorities to voluntary agencies for each fixed-grant period. The Ministry was also the Court of Appeal for any dispute which might arise between a local authority and voluntary agency.

To complete the legislative framework of the inter-war years it remains to mention the provision of the Education Acts of 1918 and 1921 which re-enacted and expanded the Acts of 1893 and 1902 relating to the education and training of the blind. The Board of Education continued to support, by grant-aid, the many residential schools provided by voluntary organisations, and to encourage local authorities who were concerned with education and training. A further step forward had been taken under the Education Act, 1918, when local authorities were empowered to give maintenance grants to adults who were undergoing training, thereby fulfilling a valuable recommendation of the Royal Commission.

Various Acts were also passed to assist blind persons to enjoy the amenities of civilised life and the rights of citizens. Such were the Wireless and Telegraphy (Blind Persons Facilities) Act of 1926, and the Blind Voters Act of 1933,[1] and the Post Office (Amendment) Act of 1935. Blind persons might now have a wireless set, as well as a guide dog, without paying for a licence.[2] The provision of the dogs and the wireless sets continued to give opportunity for charitable effort.[3]

By the end of the inter-war years England could claim to have one of the most comprehensive schemes of blind welfare in the world. Its system of registration was certainly the envy of many countries. The service recognised the value of encouraging self-help and independence while securing assistance and certain amenities for those who needed them. Its achievements had resulted from a combination of public and private effort which, though far from perfect, was reaching out towards a closer statutory and voluntary partnership.

The voluntary organisations played a vigorous part in the pioneer phase, and they continued to take a large share after the State had accepted responsibility for blind welfare. What their special contribution was in the second phase of development should now be considered in more detail.

[1] This Act extended the Ballot Act of 1872 by giving a blind voter the alternative of using the services of a companion of his choice instead of having to rely on the Returning Officer.
[2] The permission to have a guide dog without a licence had been given as early as 1878. See footnote 3, p. 194, above. Wireless licences, on the other hand, must be applied for, but exemption from payment is given upon proof of registration as a blind person.
[3] E.g. the British Wireless for the Blind Fund, and the Guide Dogs for the Blind Association. Many local associations also helped towards the cost of maintenance of the wireless sets.

XVIII

VOLUNTARY ORGANISATIONS AND THEIR RELATIONS WITH STATUTORY AUTHORITIES BETWEEN THE TWO WORLD WARS

THE immediate expansion of the voluntary organisations after the passing of the first Blind Persons Act was remarkable, considering that the country was passing through a period of economic stringency. We learn from the Advisory Committee[1] that in three years there were set up three new workshops, that there were considerable extensions to six other workshops, while three new residential homes were opened, and one new hostel established and one extended. The Board of Education had recognised eight new centres and four new hostels for training purposes. The whole quality of the service had also improved, and we find the Advisory Committee in the following year noting with satisfaction that the service was now more a social welfare service than a 'commiserating and comforting undertaking'.

Meanwhile, the National Institute for the Blind expanded its services for the provision of embossed literature, music and magazines, and it was continually on the look-out for new ideas for the production of special apparatus. Its research and appointments department was active,[2] and it had succeeded in demonstrating the value of placements in ordinary factories and workshops.[3] The N.I.B. also helped to raise the status of professional workers by founding a school of massage where the students were trained to the standards required for the examination of the Chartered Society of Massage and Medical Gymnastics.[4]

---

[1] Fourth Report of the Advisory Committee, 1922–23.
[2] See p. 224, below.
[3] Although the number so placed was still small. It was in this field that local authorities were now urged to use their powers to co-operate in schemes for the augmentation of wages.
[4] Originally set up in 1915, it was later extended until, in 1931, the Eichholz Clinic of Massage and Physiotherapy was opened.

RELATIONS WITH AUTHORITIES BETWEEN THE WARS

The foundation of the first grammar school for blind girls[1] was another of the developments in direct line with the teaching of Edward Rushton, Dr. Armitage, Francis Campbell and other pioneers. They had always insisted on two things: that the blind must be efficiently educated to reach high standards, and that, wherever possible, they must take their place among sighted persons in ordinary activities of the community; they must not look upon themselves as belonging to a special class.[2]

After the war the N.I.B. welcomed the opportunity to co-operate with local education authorities in the rehabilitation of blind men and women who had lost their sight in later life, and who were now eligible for maintenance grants.[3]

One of the services which a national voluntary body is specially equipped to give is the prolonged care of those suffering from multiple handicaps. A special school for mentally retarded blind children was one of the first of such residential schools established in the inter-war years by a voluntary society.[4] It is interesting to find the Ministry of Health circularising voluntary agencies in 1923 to ask how much support might be expected for a proposal by the N.I.B. to open a home for the physically defective blind.[5] The National Institute was to increase the range of its services in all these directions and to include the provision of many amenities which made life for the blind happier, and more nearly approaching the normal. Such were a school journeys centre, and a holiday home for boys and girls, hostels for students, and, finally, with the help of St. Dunstan's, the manufacture and distribution of talking books for the blind.[6] The N.I.B. had sufficient funds to be able to step in when disaster threatened another organisation; such was the case when it took over financial responsibility for Worcester College for Boys in 1936.[7]

The National Library for the Blind, too, had a fine record of service. Since the loan of books was free of cost to blind readers, and since postal concessions were increasingly generous, the circulation reached a

[1] Chorley Wood College for Girls, opened in 1921.
[2] It was in accord with this principle that one voluntary society questioned the insertion in the Blind Persons Act, 1938, of the section giving old age pensions to the blind at forty. Was it not in fact doing them a disservice since it suggested that they were too old at forty?
[3] This was part of a developing after-care service in line with the suggestions of Dr. Armitage in the pioneer years.
[4] *The Servers of the Blind League* was commended by the Advisory Committee in their Reports 1922–24 for the opening of a school for mentally deficient children under seven and another for those seven to sixteen.
[5] A residential school for children of both sexes at Court Grange, Abbotskerswell, was opened as a school for retarded blind children in 1932. It was later, 1947, transferred to Condover Hall as a school for Blind Children with other handicaps. Grange Court was used as a Sunshine Home after 1949. See p. 247, below.
[6] Initiated in 1935.
[7] See N.I.B. Bulletin 7 (revised edition), p. 6. It was to take over the work of the Servers of the Blind League in the mid-20th century.

high level.[1] By 1937–38 it not only employed 115 blind copyists, but had the services of 600 voluntary writers, all of whom were specially trained.

There were many other organisations, local, regional and national, which were alert to new needs and showed fresh vitality as the social services expanded. Some of them, like the Jewish Blind Society, were of long standing. It has only been possible, however, to select a few for the purpose of illustration. One development is worth special note: the inter-war years saw the extension of associations of blind workers. The long-established National League of the Blind, having gained its objective of State responsibility for blind welfare, kept its special interest in the blind worker in industry. No longer in open conflict with other national bodies, it took its place as one of many groups serving the interests of the blind,[2] although it still kept its political association with the Labour Party, and its trade union affiliation. By contrast, the *National Federation of the Blind*,[3] whose function was similar, that is, to protect the interests of blind workers and to improve their status, claimed to be a non-political body. It was specially concerned to watch for opportunities for qualified blind workers in local government service. The inter-war years saw the expansion of another well-established society, namely the College of Teachers of the Blind, which had considerable success in improving standards of teaching and raising the professional status of teachers of the blind.[4] In this period too, blind welfare was enriched by the foundation, after much tribulation, of the *Association of Workshops for the Blind* in 1929. But comments on this Society will be more appropriately considered in the later section on the struggle for co-ordination of blind welfare.[5]

Another of the valuable activities which a voluntary association can perform is to see that statutory authorities make full use of their powers and duties. In no field of blind welfare was this more fruitful than in that of the prevention of blindness. It was here that the Regional Associations took an active part.

The Prevention of Blindness

The opportunity for constructive action for the prevention of blindness came with the passing of the Public Health Act, 1925, when a valuable voluntary–statutory partnership was built up with the

[1] In 1937–38 the circulation was 345,868 volumes.
[2] It is interesting to note that the General Secretary of the National League was one of the seven members of the Working Party on the Employment of Blind Persons, 1951.
[3] Formerly the *National Union of the Professional and Industrial Blind*, it changed its name to 'National Association of Blind Workers', and then, after the Second World War, was reconstituted as 'The National Federation of the Blind'.
[4] The Advisory Committee in its 1928–29 report, stated that the College had started a correspondence college on the lines of one in the U.S.A.
[5] See p. 225, below.

encouragement of the Ministry of Health. That so little was so far known of the causes of blindness was largely the result of failure to get accurate information about those who were registered. There was no requirement for medical evidence of blindness, and registration was still somewhat amateurish.

In 1922 a Departmental Committee had reported on the causes and prevention of blindness,[1] but there was need for a more comprehensive enquiry. The *Union of Counties Associations* took action in 1929 by setting up a standing committee to examine the whole question.[2] It found itself 'faced with the lack of any scientific data of two essential kinds; first as to the prevalence of the actual defects of the eye determining blindness, and secondly, as to the various causes of these defects.'[3] Their contention that the first step in prevention was the requirement that certification should be undertaken by doctors qualified[4] by special experience in ophthalmology was accepted by the Minister of Health.[5] The Union produced a form for use in the certification of blindness which was officially sanctioned, and its standing committee continued its study of causes and prevention until its work was finally taken over by the Ministry of Health in 1938.[6] In the previous year the Minister had issued an important circular[7] calling the attention of local authorities to the valuable recommendations of the Prevention of Blindness Committee of the Union of Counties Association for the Blind.[8] Some account of the main recommendations of the committee is called for since it gives an idea of how much remained to be done for the prevention of blindness, even as late as 1936. Their findings were summarised by the secretary of Gardner's Trust[9] as follows:

[1] Departmental Committee on the Causes and Prevention of Blindness, 1922 (Chairman, G. H. Roberts).
[2] The standing committee was supported by contributions from the N.I.B. and from the Clothworkers' Company. It issued a series of reports on the Certification of Blindness and Ascertainment of Causes (1931), on Hereditary Blindness (1933), the main report on Causes in 1936, on Cataract in 1937, and an analysis of a Preliminary Classification of Causes in 1938.
[3] N.I.B. Bulletin, No. 7, p. 30 (1934 edition).
[4] See circular 1086, 1930, for the first suggestion by the Ministry to local authorities of the desirability of this measure.
[5] The Advisory Committee on the Welfare of the Blind, reporting in 1928-29, drew attention to some of the difficulties. 'It has been represented to us that in their work for the prevention of blindness, voluntary agencies have been hindered owing to the difficulty of getting the eyes of an uninsured person examined by an ophthalmic surgeon, excepting as a private patient and on payment of full fees, which, on occasions, has caused real hardship.'
[6] In this year the Minister set up an Advisory Committee on Blindness which was to carry on the work on Prevention.
[7] Circular of 6th August, 1937.
[8] The Advisory Committee in its Sixth Annual Report, 1924-26, had already paid a handsome tribute to voluntary societies for their propaganda and other measures for the prevention of blindness.
[9] See *C.R. & D.*, 1938.

THE WELFARE OF THE BLIND

Report of Standing Committee on Prevention of Blindness, Union of Counties Association, 1936

The recommendations included:

1. Investigation of part played by faulty nutrition in producing dangerous form of myopia.
2. More regular ascertainment of precise ocular complications occurring in cases of measles.
3. More exact details of congenital cataract cases.
4. Possible desirability of some modification of present form of report and certification and need to refer to expert committee.
5. Examination of arrangements made by Local Authorities for prevention of blindness under Section 176 of the Public Health Act, 1936, and for dissemination of knowledge.
6. The setting up of an authoritative standing committee.

'A number of local authorities approve and are endeavouring to carry out these recommendations,' was a heartening comment.

The 1938 Report of the Standing Committee made an analysis of causes of blindness amongst 67,521 blind persons registered in England and Wales. They examined 5,290 cases, and found:

Percentage	Causes
24·97	Primary cataract
11·09	Glaucoma
10·96	Congenital, hereditary and developmental
10·24	Myopia
5·97	Local infection of coats of eye
5·12	Syphilis, congenital
2·83	Syphilis, acquired
4·91	Ophthalmia neonatorum
1·39	Individual trauma and disease
22·52	Other categories
100·00	

It is, perhaps, convenient here to anticipate a later section by reference to a scientific enquiry[1] carried out under the auspices of the Ministry of Health some ten years later. The incidence of causes of blindness operative in the elderly—cataract, glaucoma and the senile macular lesions—

[1] Advanced work on the Causes of Blindness was carried out by Professor Arnold Sorsby and published by the Medical Research Council. See Memorandum, No. 24, 1950. It was done with the close co-operation of the Southern Regional Association for the Blind. See p. 244, below.
A further report was published by the Ministry of Health in 1953: 'The Causes of Blindness in England 1948–50' (Arnold Sorsby). It is good to see that the Chief Medical Officer, in an introduction, states that 'arrangements are being made to keep this important subject under continual review by including reference to it in the annual report of the Ministry of Health'.

showed a proportionate increase, reflecting the drastic redistribution of ages within the blind population. There was a corresponding decrease in the causes operating earlier in life. One of the notable changes was the fact that ophthalmia neonatorum and congenital syphilis contributed less than 1% of cases. Yet Professor Sorsby left no doubt that more effective means for early diagnosis and more intensive investigation into congenital and hereditary factors were necessary if the incidence of blindness was to be further reduced.[1]

In the same year in which the Minister had first set up his Advisory Committee on Blindness, in 1938, the National Institute for the Blind also decided to set up its own committee to work closely with local authorities on the prevention of blindness. The Ministry of Health had also encouraged local authorities to grant-aid the N.I.B. for its provision of 'Sunshine Homes' for Babies, a further link in the search for causes, as well as a constructive step in progressive education from an early age to adult life. The co-operation of statutory and voluntary agencies at the national level was now so close that it is difficult to consider them apart in a study of the development of blind welfare in the inter-war years.

Voluntary–Statutory Partnership

The relationship between the statutory agencies, both central and local, and the voluntary organisations, played so prominent a part in the development of blind welfare in the inter-war years that it is worthy of more detailed study.

In the first place there is no doubt that the Minister was glad to avail himself of the experience of voluntary societies. The composition of his Advisory Committee bore witness to this fact. He also did much by his circulars, and through his inspectors, to urge local authorities to co-operate with voluntary organisations. Soon after the passing of the first Blind Persons Act it was suggested to local authorities that they might with advantage let the actual work of compilation and maintenance of a register, for which they were ultimately responsible, be undertaken by voluntary agencies 'who had considerable experience'.[2] The Advisory Committee also encouraged local authorities to co-operate with voluntary agencies in their work for the unemployable blind. Comparison between various areas was one of the well-tried methods used to stimulate activities.[3] Local authorities were urged to co-operate, too, whenever augmentation of wages, under suitable safeguards, was called for.[4] When the National Association of Workshops reported on methods of

[1] *Op. cit.*, p. 29.
[2] Ministry of Health Circular, 1922.
[3] See pp. 209–210, above, for examples. Cf. this method used by the Board of Control in work for the mentally defective.
[4] Ministry of Health Advisory Committee on the Welfare of the Blind, 1928–29.

payment of wages in 1931, it was suggested that there should be joint consultation with the National League of the Blind.[1]

The central authority sometimes found opposition to co-operation, for the triple partnership was not welcomed everywhere. We find the Advisory Committee reporting with regret that 'in some quarters, so much attention is concentrated on the financial assistance of the blind and the elimination of voluntary effort, to the neglect of other considerations which must be borne in mind if the blind are really to be assisted in overcoming their handicap'.[2] They were, on this occasion, advising the Minister that they were opposed to clauses in the Blind Persons Bill, which would, in their opinion, 'rob the blind of incentive and undermine their morale'.[3]

Some disquiet had been felt on the effect of the Local Government Bill on the finance of voluntary agencies, but far from recommending the elimination of voluntary effort the Advisory Committee did its best, when the Bill came before Parliament, to urge the Minister to do all he could to avoid imperilling the position of the voluntary agencies. They hoped indeed that 'the Act as finally passed will considerably strengthen the position of voluntary agencies'.[4] In the result the voluntary agencies found that they were to be generously treated. A somewhat unexpected opportunity for co-operation was also given by the withdrawal of H.M. Inspectors, who, under the Act, were available only upon application when difficulties arose. Some of the newly responsible local authorities turned to the experienced voluntary agencies for assistance. Such was the case when, in the north of England, 'a considerable number of local authorities' asked the Northern Counties Association to appoint a knowledgeable and experienced inspector to act for them in the inspection of voluntary agencies.

Another important feature of the partnership was the influence exerted by the statutory authority in keeping up standards and in encouraging greater efficiency. Several examples of intervention in the sphere of education and training may be cited. The central authority decided that the examination for home teachers should be made obligatory and the College of Teachers for the Blind drew up a special syllabus and regulations at the request of the Minister.[5]

[1] The Advisory Committee had reported, 1923–24, that since larger numbers of blind persons were being trained as a result of the operation of the Blind Persons Act, 'it is gratifying to note that the voluntary agencies are making a serious attempt to cope with the increased demands that are being made upon them for workshop accommodation' (*op. cit.*, pp. 7, 8 and 9).
[2] Eighth Annual Report of Advisory Committee, 1928–29, p. 8.
[3] There had been uneasiness over the method of augmentation of wages and considerable dislike of granting old age pensions (non-contributory) at fifty, now to be reduced to forty years of age. They also pointed out that the suggestions for a greatly increased local authority responsibility, to include not only monetary assistance to blind persons but provision of workshops, hostels, homes and similar places, would be very costly. Cf. W. McG. Eager in *Social Security*, ed. W. Robson, p. 178.
[4] Eighth Annual Report, 1929, pp. 7–8.
[5] See Ministry of Health Circular 369.

RELATIONS WITH AUTHORITIES BETWEEN THE WARS

The need for higher standards of training was emphasised when the Minister called upon the College of Teachers of the Blind to institute a national qualifying examination for blind piano-tuners. It had been reported that there were too many mediocre workers in this field which was so well suited to selected blind persons of proved efficiency.[1]

A more difficult and knotty problem was the relation between education, vocational training and entry to employment.[2] There was some difference of opinion on this issue between the Ministries concerned and the voluntary bodies. The workshops, for example, felt that they could provide the best craft training under conditions similar to those in which the trainees would later be employed, while the Minister of Education insisted that pupils at the age of sixteen should attend special training institutions, preferably attached to schools, so that continued education could be combined with vocational training. The Minister of Health supported the Minister of Education in the effort to secure greater co-ordination between training and employment. The somewhat strained situation was eased as good preventive work reduced the number of blind adolescents, and as 'open industry' offered further opportunities.[3]

In the third place the central authority acted from time to time as an intermediary. The Advisory Committee seems to have maintained a judicial and objective attitude, on occasions correcting the too active enthusiasm of partisan bodies. We find it, for example, reminding the National League for the Blind, which was pressing for the preferential appointment of blind persons as home teachers, that the needs of each area must be judged separately and the best men appointed, whether blind or sighted.[4] The voluntary workshops had, in their turn, urged the exemption of their employees from payment of contributions to the Unemployment Insurance scheme, but the Advisory Committee disagreed with their claim that there was little risk of unemployment in workshops for the blind, or that the workshops should be in a privileged position as charitable undertakings.[5] At the same time the Committee was willing to reverse its own decision if good reasons were given, as it

[1] Joint Memorandum by the Board of Education and the Ministry of Health with a circular letter, 1403, of 1.7.29.
[2] See Ministry of Health Circular No. 387, 24.4.23. The Minister drew attention to the unco-ordinated efforts in training blind boys and girls without 'any carefully administered system of after-care'. He went on to suggest ways of co-operation with a view to securing continuity of education and training and to keeping in touch with employing bodies.
[3] At a later stage voluntary organisations and the Ministry were to combine more readily in a new experiment to bridge the gap between education, further training and employment. (See 'Hethersett", p. 247, below.)
[4] Fourth Annual Report of Advisory Committee on Welfare of the Blind, 1922–23, p. 12. A generation later the Ministry was still emphasising the need for home teachers with a personal qualification of a high order and urging appointing bodies to throw open their vacancies to both blind and sighted applicants. See Ministry of Health Circular 1/47, 7.1.47.
[5] Fifth Annual Report of Advisory Committee on Welfare of the Blind, 1923–24.

THE WELFARE OF THE BLIND

did in the case of an appeal for the amendment of the Act concerning blind voters.[1]

A valuable part was also played by the central authority in its readiness to encourage new ventures, and to enlighten local authorities about the opportunities offered by the voluntary organisations. An excellent example of this practice is to be found in a series of reports where attention is called to the advisability of employing blind persons in 'sighted workshops'. In the first instance the Advisory Committee itself carried out a small enquiry into prospects,[2] and suggested that local agencies might follow this up. By 1924–26 they are reporting with satisfaction that the N.I.B. had opened a Research Department 'to explore, *inter alia*, the possibility of opening up new lines of employment'. The following year the Committee congratulates the N.I.B. upon its co-operation with the *National Institute of Industrial Psychology* in its investigations into suitable employment, and urges all local agencies, both statutory and voluntary to do all in their power to help. They remind local authorities, in 1928–29, that 'local authorities can materially help by augmenting, where necessary, under suitable safeguards, the earnings of those blind persons who are provided with employment in ordinary factories and workshops'. In 1930 the Committee is advising local authorities and voluntary societies to study the published report of the N.I.B. on its research, while suggesting to the N.I.B. that they should offer to place at the disposal of local bodies the accumulated experience of the placement committee and their officers.[3]

Perhaps one of the most fruitful results of co-operation at a national level was the Minister's active encouragement both of the experimental work of the voluntary agencies,[4] and of their propaganda to educate and prepare the public for advances in the field of blind welfare.

Finally, the Ministry can be said to have acted to some extent as co-ordinator in a field where independent action was still strong. The part played by the Inspectorate in helping the three partners to work together amicably can be gathered from the last report before the Minister's Inspectors handed over their duties to the local authorities[5] under the Local Government Act of 1929. Their claim that they had done much to encourage and advise voluntary bodies was certainly true, and they were justified in adding, 'In this way the Department was a real unifying and developing force.'[6] The Advisory Committee, indeed, expressed some regret, shared by many of the voluntary agencies and, as

[1] Tenth Annual Report of the Advisory Committee on the Welfare of the Blind, 1931–32, p. 16.
[2] Fourth Annual Report, p. 13.
[3] Ninth Annual Report, pp. 16–17.
[4] The Minister gave tangible evidence, e.g. the 'addition to grants' for the period 1937–42 provided for an annual grant of £500 in respect of 'talking-books' (Circular 1605, 30.3.37).
[5] As from 1.4.30.
[6] Advisory Committee Ninth Annual Report, 1930, pp. 8–9.

we have seen, by some of the local authorities, that the Ministry's inspectors would be available only upon application, to advise either voluntary societies or local authorities in matters of special difficulty. The Minister, and his Advisory Committee, continued to watch with considerable interest, and to encourage to the limit of their power, any attempt made to co-ordinate the work for the welfare of the blind. It had hitherto proved to be an uphill task. So much effort went into it, and so considerable a resistance was shown that it deserves separate treatment.

The Difficulties of Co-ordination. Problems of Administration and Representation

There were two requirements before success could be achieved; one, co-operation between statutory and voluntary agencies, and two, co-operation between the voluntary agencies themselves. Although the principle of co-operation between statutory and voluntary agencies was nationally accepted in 1917 and made explicit in the first Blind Persons Act, 1920, the form the combined effort was to take was not made clear; nor, as we have seen, were local authorities always convinced of the merits of voluntaryism. Co-operation was non-existent in some areas, and informal in many others, even although the Advisory Committee might claim that the 'public evidently approve the triple partnerships of State, local authority and voluntary agency'.[1] Not all had taken to heart the advice of the Minister: 'It may be desirable that the Council should be represented on the governing body of the agency, and such representation will, it is believed, be cordially offered and welcomed.'[2] The Advisory Committee had also suggested that local authorities might with advantage offer representation to the local voluntary organisations.

The full effect of the goodwill of the central authority towards voluntary organisations[3] could not, however, be felt until the organisations themselves achieved a greater measure of co-operation. One of the greatest stumbling blocks was the strong spirit of independence shown by certain groups, particularly by the workshops. They had, as we have seen, achieved a measure of federation amongst themselves, but they were suspicious of any attempts to induce them to co-operate outside their own sphere of marketing and collective bargaining. The eventual formation of an association affords an interesting example of joint statutory–voluntary effort to break down the barrier to co-ordination.

---

[1] Report of Advisory Committee, 1924–26, p. 5. Cf. also report for the year 1923–24, p. 19, 'The triple partnership has been abundantly justified'.

[2] *Op. cit.*, Circular 1920. 'Cordiality' was the last word to apply to the distant relationship existing in some areas.

[3] One of the ways in which the Minister encouraged Counties' Associations was by the offer of grant-aid to the extent of £20 for every 100 blind persons registered by them.

THE WELFARE OF THE BLIND

In 1929 a conference was called, convened by the National Institute for the Blind, at the instigation of the Advisory Committee, with the strong support of the Minister of Health. Representatives of the workshops for the blind were invited, in the first place, to consider the technicalities of management. At length, after much hard work by the Advisory Committee, an *Association of Workshops for the Blind* was formed 'to foster co-operation among workshops, to promote research in problems connected with the employment of the blind, to facilitate united action, and to raise the standard of efficiency in workshops by the interchange of information and the encouragement of new methods and ideas'.[1]

Other obstacles had still to be overcome. It had been hoped that co-operation in various fields of blind welfare would be strengthened by the Blind Persons Act, 1920, particularly by the requirement for registration of charities and in the regulation of appeals.[2] The question of appeals for public support was a notoriously difficult problem since the local agencies felt aggrieved that the national societies were appealing over their heads and collecting, in their view, a disproportionate amount of money. In spite of the face that the Vice-Chairman of the Advisory Committee, who was also Chairman of the Union of Counties Association, used his personal influence to form an independent committee to work out a scheme,[3] there were several years of frustration before a satisfactory solution was found.[4] The N.I.B. was anxious to break down the suspicion of local societies, and with this in view it invited them to enter into agreements for the unification of collections. Many of them did so, and the N.I.B. offered either to organise the collections and give an acceptable proportion to the local society[5] or to leave the area free for local effort and to receive a percentage of the proceeds for its own funds and for the National Library for the Blind.

Co-ordination was more immediately welcome when it came from below upwards. The various counties associations which had early combined to form unions, and then a union of unions, were to achieve an even greater measure of success as regional associations. Their closer

[1] N.I.B. Bulletin, No. 7, p. 25.
[2] No public appeals might be made by an unregistered charity, and local authorities had power to refuse registration if they were satisfied that its objects were adequately attained by a charity already registered under the Act. Blind Persons Act, 1920, Section 3 (3).
[3] Known as the Decentralisation Scheme. See Sixth Annual Report of the Advisory Committee, 1924–26, pp. 20–23.
[4] The N.I.B. reported its satisfaction that, in 1924, a scheme, approved by the Minister of Health, for the notification of collections and the limitation of appeals had been prepared (see Annual Report, N.I.B., 1929–30), but in 1926 we still find the Minister sending a covering letter to all voluntary agencies for the blind, enclosing the scheme for the unification of voluntary collections (see Circular 682/1926) while the Advisory Committee, in its 1928–29 report, reveals itself as mediator in the settlement of difficulties standing in the way of such unification.
[5] 75% was paid over, and 25% kept for National expenses. See also p. 228, below.

amalgamation and growth in status belongs properly to the third phase of development, however, and will be considered later.

Meanwhile, the N.I.B. had reorganised its executive council, offering nearly half the membership to the Minister of Health.[1] The Local Government Act had strengthened the partnership with local authorities,[2] and they in turn sought to have a common policy by forming a *Joint Blind Welfare Committee*.[3] The result was a request to the Minister to use his influence to secure 'a greater combination of effort, preferably under the aegis of the National Institute for the Blind'. The N.I.B. was willing to accept the role, and a scheme was worked out by the Joint Committee and the N.I.B.[4] It proved acceptable to the Union of Counties Associations and resulted in a general reorganisation at a national and regional level.

The position was, however, not entirely satisfactory, for complete co-ordination was not yet achieved. A few national organisations, like St. Dunstan's, preferred to make their own appeals, although they were ready to work closely with the N.I.B. and to accept representation on its executive council. Neither were all local authorities prepared to co-operate fully, and it was noted with regret that the L.C.C. which had such a fine record of work for the welfare of the blind, refused representation on the executive council of the N.I.B. Co-operation with a regional body, depending as it must upon consent, was not always acceptable to some individual local agencies. There was a tendency for some large institutions to remain aloof. It has been suggested,[5] too, that questions of prestige, with the representatives regarding themselves as delegates for sectional interests, sometimes tended to emphasise 'municipalisation *versus* voluntaryism' instead of fostering the partnership of voluntary and statutory agencies in the general interest of the blind.

A closer examination of the composition of two national committees will reveal the steps by which a more democratic basis of representation was achieved, at the same time reflecting the changing attitudes towards public responsibility in the development of blind welfare. The two committees selected for illustration are those of the Advisory Committee on the Welfare of the Blind, and the executive council of the N.I.B.

The changing composition of the statutory Advisory Committee is of special interest as it resulted from the legislative changes which gave wider powers and duties to local authorities. At first the central authority seems to have appointed members of the Advisory Committee as

[1] 17 out of 36 places were offered to nominees of the Ministry.
[2] The Act made local authorities responsible for grant-aiding voluntary organisations out of the new block grant which had replaced the old percentage grant system.
[3] I.e. a committee representing the County Councils Association and the Association of Municipal Corporations.
[4] A scheme was published in April 1936. See *Voluntary Social Services*, Bourdillon, p. 68.
[5] By J. F. Wilson, *Voluntary Social Services, op. cit.*, p. 70.

individuals, and not as representatives of particular groups, although most of them were, in fact, closely connected with well-known voluntary organisations. But when the committee was reconstituted in 1921, the first Blind Persons Act had been passed, and representation was given to councils of counties and county boroughs and Boards of Guardians, as well as to voluntary agencies for the blind. The proportion of voluntary to statutory membership was now 5:12.[1] The Board of Education and the Ministry of Health both sent inspectors as assessors.[2] The acceptance by local authorities of their responsibilities in relating health and blind welfare is reflected in the appointment in some instances of the Medical Officer of Health as their representative.[3] In 1924 the committee was enlarged to include a representative of the National Union of Professional and Industrial Blind, and of the National League of the Blind, a reflection of the changed political temper of the time. A second change in composition occurred in 1930 when the statutory authorities[4] were given the responsibility for nominating representatives. The Minister also doubled the number of persons appointed by himself as having special experience of work amongst the blind.[5] In addition to the nucleus of men and women with long connection with voluntary welfare, the Minister appointed councillors and aldermen who were in close touch with the newer statutory development. These administrative changes do not seem to have affected the policy of the Advisory Committee which continued to exert its influence towards the co-operation of statutory and voluntary agencies. It remained a representative body which took a lively interest in every development in blind welfare.

The second example is taken from the committee of the National Institute for the Blind. Founded by a group of blind men, it was, in its early years, governed solely by blind or partially-sighted men.[6] In its vigorous growth during the First World War it tended to concentrate on national issues and to overlook the claims of the well-established local counties associations. Its contact with blind welfare agencies was usually direct, and, as we have seen, it was sometimes accused of riding roughshod over local sentiment, particularly in the matter of appeals for public support. It was on this issue that negotiations were instituted with regional and local groups, and a measure of agreement achieved, in 1926. In the same year the N.I.B. offered 17 of the 36 places on its

[1] Excluding the Chairman who was an M.P., the Vice-Chairman who was a Doctor of Law and the Secretary.
[2] Dr. Eichholz represented the Board of Education for a great many years, and was appointed a member for 'his experience' after his retirement.
[3] E.g. in 1923 the Medical Officer of Health for Hampshire.
[4] The Association of Poor Law Unions was now excluded since it ceased to exist with the transfer of the functions of the board of guardians to the counties and county borough councils.
[5] This followed upon the Local Government Act, 1929, when much of the responsibility was passed on to the local authorities, particularly for inspection.
[6] See p. 180, above. About 25% of the members of the Executive Council were blind in the later history of the Institute.

executive council to nominees of the Minister of Health, and in 1931 it opened its doors still further to include representatives of the County Councils Association and the Association of Municipal Corporations. By 1938 its basis was broadened to include regional bodies, 31 seats; national members,[1] 21; associations of local authorities, 20; voluntary agencies, 12; organisations of blind persons, 12. The regional and local groups were now in a strong position at the centre, and local authorities were well represented. The N.I.B. had by this time fully appreciated the benefit to the whole movement arising from 'this intimate connection between the Minister of Health, local authorities and voluntary agencies'.[2]

Further opportunity for breaking down any barriers of resentment which existed between voluntaryism and officialdom, or between central pressure and local independence might have followed from the new Blind Persons Act. By 1939, however, when the outbreak of the Second World War made tremendous demands on all the social services, the new machinery for blind welfare was only just getting into working order.

A Summary of the Roles of Voluntary Organisations and Local Authorities

A summary of the practical roles of voluntary organisations and local authorities may complete the picture of the development of blind welfare in the inter-war years. The main cost of financial assistance to the blind devolved upon the statutory authorities either through the Treasury, by payment of old-age pensions and war disability pensions, or through local authorities, by payment of domiciliary assistance, or payments for special education and training. A small proportion of monetary assistance was given by voluntary agencies who administered blind pension schemes.[3] The cost borne by local authorities included payments to voluntary agencies either as fees, or as grants for various purposes, since many of the services under blind welfare schemes were provided by the voluntary organisations by arrangement with the authorities. The contribution of voluntary organisations included provision of the majority of the elementary schools,[4] and of all schools for higher education. Education for children with other disabilities was a special service in which voluntary societies did some excellent work. This was so far accepted as a proper sphere of voluntary influence that

[1] This was a nucleus of the original national voluntary group.
[2] The N.I.B. had accepted this in 1929, see Annual Report, N.I.B., 1929–30, p. 9.
[3] In the early 1940s estimated expenditure by statutory authorities was Treasury £1,604,000, local authorities £2,185,000, total approximately £3,789,000. Voluntary pensions schemes accounted for £75,000. (This was part of an estimated total expenditure by voluntary organisations of £809,000.)
[4] In the proportion of about 16:11. Of the 16 provided by voluntary agencies the majority were larger schools than those normally provided by local authorities. The L.C.C. in 1937–38 decided to close its three special day schools for junior boys and girls, and to send them to residential schools.

we find the central authority, during the Second World War, holding it as a matter of reproach that voluntary agencies were not doing more for 'the misfits', such as the delinquent blind. The voluntary organisations had already made special provision for mentally defective and retarded blind children, and for the deaf-blind,[1] together with some provision for blind epileptic children. Residential nursery schools in the form of Sunshine Homes for blind babies, and schools for children up to the normal school entering age, were also under voluntary auspices. With one or two exceptions, sheltered workshops for the blind had been traditionally under voluntary control: although a few local authorities ran their own municipal workshops,[2] the number employed was a small proportion of the total.[3] 'Tangible and continuing service' to home workers[4] was given almost entirely by voluntary agencies, even in areas where there was a municipal workshop. Local authorities usually accepted responsibility for the home teaching service, staffed by paid workers who had the certificate of the College of Teachers of the Blind, which was a voluntary agency. Many local authorities left the general welfare schemes to a voluntary agency.[5] The provision of homes and hostels was also mainly a voluntary effort,[6] although there was a good deal of reciprocity—the local authority paying capitation fees and sometimes maintenance grants for approved boarders ('inmates', as they were normally still called in official language). An example of the close relationship which existed in some areas was provided by Portsmouth which built and equipped a home, and asked the voluntary organisation to accept and administer it.

We have seen that in much of their work voluntary organisations acted as agents for local authorities and received appropriate payment. In the sphere of training and employment there might be a scheme of grant-aid to the organisation and augmentation of wages to their employees. In workshops and home workers schemes some local authorities went so far as to meet all trading losses. Indeed, an increasing proportion of the income of voluntary organisations came under the

[1] Work for the deaf-blind is specially worthy of notice since it included ascertainment as well as the establishment of special residential homes.

[2] Luton later afforded an interesting example of the transfer of a municipal workshop to voluntary management (in 1941), but this was largely due to the exigencies of war time.

[3] In the early years of the Second World War the total number employed in some 52 workshops was approximately 3,580, of whom 490 (in municipal workshops) were local authority employees.

[4] This was the official requirement before a voluntary organisation was recognised by the Ministry of Health as a supervisory agency, and given grant-aid. Only 38 out of 1,686 home workers were supervised, etc., by local authorities.

[5] L.C.C. was one of the exceptions, having its own staff for this purpose. It was glad, however, to accept the services of the Metropolitan Society for the Blind for the distribution of various amenities such as wireless sets, clothing, white sticks and fireguards.

[6] About 3 out of a total of 42 were directly managed by local authorities in the early war years.

heading of 'payments for services', and a large share of such payments came from local authorities.

Unfortunately statistics are not available to illustrate the strength of this trend over the country as a whole. The most inclusive returns are those to be found in the C.O.S. *Annual Charities Register and Digest*,[1] but these are deficient in two respects: they are not comprehensive, since the Charity Organisation Society had to depend on the voluntary co-operation of the societies concerned: the number of charities for the blind who supplied information fluctuated considerably from year to year; secondly, the series ended in 1927:[2]

A useful indication of the trend is given, however, in a series of statistics published annually by the L.C.C. after 1924, until the Second World War made such detailed analysis impossible. The following diagrammatic presentation of the total income of charities for the blind registered with the L.C.C., showing the proportions received from various voluntary and statutory sources, illustrates several significant points: (1) In the decade preceding 1935, the statutory grants showed a steady increase, while the proportion of such grants to the total income rose from 6% to 22%. (2) A sharp fall in statutory grants occurred in the year 1935–36. This was largely due to the changing policy of the L.C.C., the largest statutory contributor.[3] (3) In spite of the general trend noted in (1) above, subscriptions, donations and legacies, together with income from investments, still accounted for the greater part of the total income of charities for the blind.

To complete our summary we should add that, at the national level, under voluntary auspices, schemes were worked out for the provision of embossed literature,[4] talking books, and special apparatus available to any blind person. Some of these ventures attracted small grants from the Ministry of Health, but the N.I.B. depended chiefly upon voluntary subscriptions for its experiments and research. Perhaps one of the spheres in which the national voluntary effort had achieved most was in the establishment of a principle: its particular contribution was its insistence that the blind were not a class apart, but that, given suitable opportunity, they could take their place in the community in much the same way as sighted persons. The repeated effort to open normal employment to the blind and the increasing opportunities afforded for

---

[1] Returns were made annually from 1904. They were regularly quoted in 'London Statistics'.

[2] An attempt was made to revive the records in 1936 and again from 1948 onwards, but comparatively few organisations responded.

[3] An analysis of the statutory grants for the year 1934–35 gives the allocation as follows: from government grants £996; from L.C.C. grants £111,776; other local authorities £82,948. Of the L.C.C. grant £81,731 was given to the Metropolitan Society for the Blind for domiciliary relief and administration as agents of the L.C.C., i.e. some 73% of the total grant from the Council. The following year the L.C.C. carried out this work direct.

[4] At considerably less than cost price.

THE WELFARE OF THE BLIND

COMPOSITION OF INCOME OF CHARITIES FOR THE BLIND REGISTERED WITH THE L.C.C. FOR THE YEARS ENDING MARCH 31ST, 1925–1937

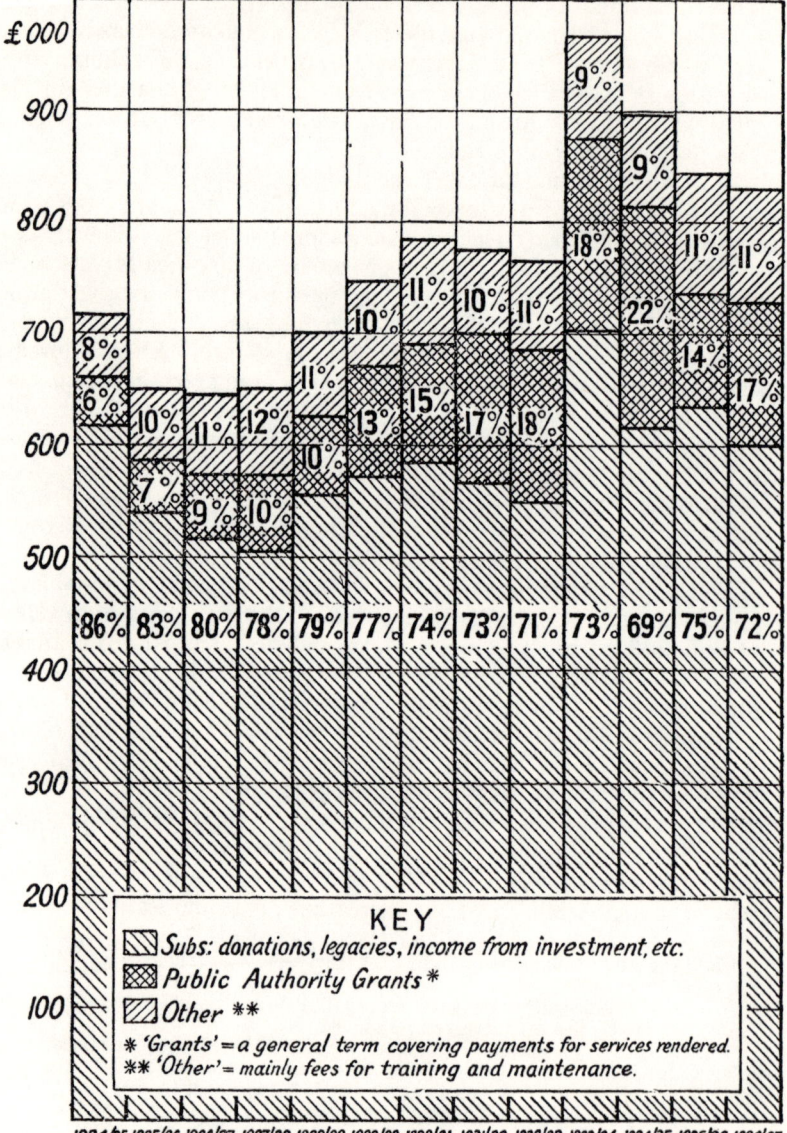

Year	Subs: donations, legacies, income from investment, etc.	Public Authority Grants*	Other**
1924/25	86%	6%	8%
1925/26	83%	7%	10%
1926/27	80%	9%	11%
1927/28	78%	10%	12%
1928/29	79%	10%	11%
1929/30	77%	13%	10%
1930/31	74%	15%	11%
1931/32	73%	17%	10%
1932/33	71%	18%	11%
1933/34	73%	18%	9%
1934/35	69%	22%	9%
1935/36	75%	14%	11%
1936/37	72%	17%	11%

KEY
- Subs: donations, legacies, income from investment, etc.
- Public Authority Grants*
- Other**

* 'Grants' = a general term covering payments for services rendered.
** 'Other' = mainly fees for training and maintenance.

training in trades and professions bore rich fruit in the emergency of a Second World War.

Such a summary gives only the bare bones of the complex relationship in this voluntary–statutory partnership. A social worker in the field, whether employed by a voluntary agency or local authority would be in constant touch with whatever body, public or private, could meet the personal needs of the individual blind boy or girl, man or woman, with whom she was concerned. Since the majority of blind persons were elderly and beyond working age,[1] much of the friendly visiting and general welfare service could appropriately be given by voluntary agencies, once any financial needs had been met by the statutory authority. Yet most of the constructive work of voluntary agencies had been with the young and the employable, and it was in this sphere that they were to offer their special experience to meet the demands of the war and post-war years.

[1] In 1936 about 80% of the registered blind in England and Wales were classed as unemployable.

XIX

DEVELOPMENTS DURING THE SECOND WORLD WAR: THE POST-WAR PERIOD

Rehabilitation: The Tomlinson Report and the Disabled Persons Employment Act

THE war naturally focused attention on the use of man power, and there was a quickening of interest in the question of the placement of disabled persons in industry. In 1941, the Ministry of Labour and National Service announced an interim scheme for the training and resettlement of disabled persons[1] whether members of the Fighting Services, the Civil Defence Services, civilians injured through raids, or through accidents in factories, etc. 'It is in the interest of the country as well as of the disabled citizen that he should get back to suitable employment as soon as possible—not to any employment, but to the most skilled work of which he is capable.' It was agreed that not only were these measures a contribution to the winning of the war, but that the whole question of rehabilitation was a matter of concern for the future. Consequently, at the end of the same year the *Tomlinson Committee*[2] was set up (*a*) to make proposals for introduction at the earliest possible date of a scheme for the rehabilitation and training for employment of disabled persons not provided for by the interim scheme, (*b*) to consider and make recommendations for introduction as soon as possible after the war of a comprehensive scheme for (i) the rehabilitation and training of, and (ii) securing satisfactory employment for, disabled persons of all categories; (*c*) to consider and make recommendations as to the manner in which the scheme proposed for introduction after the war should be financed.

---

[1] See PL/1941, Ministry of Labour and National Service.
[2] *Inter-departmental Committee on the Rehabilitation and Resettlement of Disabled Persons.*

DEVELOPMENTS DURING THE SECOND WORLD WAR

The following summary of the Committee's broad conclusions shows how strongly they reflect the experience gained by those who had been working on behalf of the blind,[1] the only group of handicapped persons for whom there were, as yet, comprehensive voluntary and statutory schemes:

I. Rehabilitation in its widest sense is a continuous process, partly in the medical sphere and partly in the social or industrial sphere.

II. Close co-operation between the health and industrial services is necessary throughout the whole process.

III. Ordinary employment is the object and is practicable for the majority of the disabled.

IV. A minority of the disabled will require employment under sheltered conditions.

The Tomlinson Committee drew attention to the one important factor in which the blind differed: there existed a relatively large number of blind persons who were unemployable. Leaving aside those under sixteen and over sixty-five (42,000 out of a total register of some 83,000), only about 9,000 of the remainder were in employment. 'Of the remaining 32,000 in the sixteen to sixty-five age group, a considerable number have mental and physical defects which make them practically unemployable.'[2]

The N.I.B. which set up a special committee[3] to examine the Tomlinson Report, together with the *Beveridge Report*,[4] in relation to blind welfare, gave a general welcome to the main recommendations. They endorsed the principle which they themselves had long accepted, that the blind could be helped to take a fuller part in ordinary industry to the enrichment of themselves and the community, but that many others required sheltered conditions of work. They particularly shared the view that there should be assurance not only of financial support but of 'occupation under conditions which approximate as nearly as possible to the normal'. They felt, however, that there was a tendency in the Tomlinson Report to think of the blind as 'a race apart from other men, whereas the true interests of the blind are best served by bringing them as fully as possible into the main stream of national life'.[5] In any

[1] See, for example, St. Dunstan's and the N.I.B. It should be noted, too, that firms like Vauxhall Motors had been experimenting in the employment of physically handicapped men and had designed special apparatus in some cases.

[2] *Op. cit.*, p. 35. Compare these estimates with those given in the Report of the Working Party on the Employment of Blind Persons, 1951, p. 2. Of some 87,000 registered blind persons in Great Britain, some 36,400 were between 16 and 65. Of these about 11,000 were in employment or undergoing training. As a result of a close scrutiny of the registration, particularly of the remaining 25,000, the Working Party concluded that a further 3,000 blind persons would be capable of employment if they were given the opportunity.

[3] See N.I.B. Bulletin No. 15, *Blind Welfare after the War*. (Now out of print.)

[4] *Social Insurance and Allied Services.*

[5] *Op. cit.*, p. 6.

preferential treatment in the field of employment, e.g. in the provision of sheltered workshops, they welcomed the suggestion that it should be co-ordinated with the general proposals for such employment for the handicapped. It is in line with the principle long accepted by the N.I.B. that they 'recognised their privileged position since the passing of the Blind Persons Act, 1920', but privileged 'only in the sense that certain things have been done for them that might well have been done for others'.[1]

The Disabled Persons (Employment) Act which followed in 1944, did much by its wide definition of disablement to make provision for the employment needs of all those who were 'substantially handicapped'. The newly appointed Disablement Resettlement Officers were often glad to avail themselves of help offered by experienced workers in blind welfare, and they were encouraged by the Ministry to do so.[2] The Ministry of Labour and National Service was now made responsible for the training of blind people over the age of twenty-one, and in this field also co-operation was welcomed.[3]

Working Party on the Employment of Blind Persons

The Ministry's continued interest resulted in the appointment, in 1948, of a representative *Working Party*[4] 'to investigate the facilities existing for the employment of blind persons in industry and in public and other services and to make recommendations for their development'. The Working Party, which reported in 1951, considered evidence from a wide range of organisations and local authorities, and issued a valuable report. They reviewed what had been achieved, and made recommendations for developing what had proved to be useful methods of training, employment and after-care. Special attention was paid to

[1] Quotation from *The New Beacon*, April 1942. This principle did not prevent the N.I.B. from seeking certain concessions on behalf of the blind, e.g. they tried, unsuccessfully, to get exemption from purchase tax for apparatus and appliances for the blind (1940–41). *N.B.:* the special work done for the Government in censorship of 'blind packets' during the war. The N.I.B. received 'a pleasant surprise' when they were awarded a gratuity of 500 guineas for this service (1945–46).

[2] In August 1948 the Minister outlined the machinery for consultation 'for purposes of assuring the closest co-operation between the interested parties'. See Report of Working Party on the Employment of Blind Persons, 1951, p. 34.

[3] The continuity of the work on Rehabilitation was assured by the establishment by the Ministry of Labour and National Service of a 'Standing Committee on the Rehabilitation and Resettlement of Disabled Persons'. This Committee issued a series of reports. Its composition was inter-departmental, including representatives of the Ministry of Health, Ministry of Education, Ministry of Labour and National Service, Department of Health for Scotland, Government of Northern Ireland, Ministry of National Insurance, Scottish Education Department and Ministry of Pensions.

[4] Apart from the chairman and secretary who were from the Ministry of Labour, of the seven members one was an Inspector of Blind Welfare Services in the Ministry of Health, one a personnel manager of a large industry, and the rest were closely connected with blind welfare organisations. See Report of the Working Party on the Employment of Blind Persons, 1951, Ministry of Labour and National Service, p. ii.

DEVELOPMENTS DURING THE SECOND WORLD WAR

the development of placing services. There was an appreciation of the extent to which both voluntary agencies and local authorities had contributed: the N.I.B. had had long experience of research into employment in open industry, and St. Dunstan's had investigated such possibilities on behalf of those blinded in the war,[1] while the London County Council and Essex County Council had their own schemes.[2]

The N.I.B. had also co-operated with the Ministry of Labour and National Service, and with Local Authorities, in various war-time measures to help the blind to play their full part in the community's economic efforts. In Greater London, for example, the N.I.B. investigated the possibilities of employment for the civilian blind, and reported on the various suitable jobs in a number of industries. The Ministry, in turn, passed on to local authorities and voluntary agencies any applications from employers for these particular jobs inviting them to recommend suitable blind persons. Although during the war more employers realised that blind workers could give good service, and the idea of employment in open industry was gaining ground, the methods of training and placing were not entirely acceptable. It was recognised that many employers had neither the time nor the facilities to give the individual attention needed by the blind employee entering upon a new process, and he was not always able to settle down. In this, of course, he was like many sighted employees faced with unaccustomed work. The N.I.B., looking to future peace-time requirements, decided to increase the number of special placing officers who would each be responsible for one area and have more time to give to selection and guidance.[3] Many of the local authorities and some of the regional voluntary bodies asked the N.I.B., which was co-operating closely with the Ministry of Labour and National Service, to carry out their placement service.[4] Some effective schemes were worked out on a regional basis.[5] The special placing officers were able to give more individual attention to each blind person, discovering his potentialities, finding a suitable job, training him, often in the factory itself, and keeping in touch with him and his employer afterwards to see that all was going smoothly. The intention behind this careful work was to make sure that a full week's work could be done

[1] See also the account of the efforts of the *Birmingham Royal Institution* and other regional schemes (*op. cit.*, p. 30).
[2] The L.C.C. had established a special placing service in 1944 and the Essex County Council in 1947.
[3] By 1951 the N.I.B. was spending something like £10,000 on this service alone (*op. cit.*, p. 35).
[4] With the exception of the L.C.C., the counties covered by the Birmingham Royal Institution for the Blind, and Essex County Council, the N.I.B. were responsible for appointing the placing officers; and in most areas for operating the service (*op. cit.*, p. 31).
[5] An interesting scheme of co-operative effort was worked out in the North where the *North of England Industrial Employment Service for the Blind* was responsible. The North Regional Association for the Blind and the National Institute for the Blind were represented and the latter appointed all the placing officers.

for a full week's wages. It was, in fact, to be an economic and altogether sound undertaking for employer and employee alike, with no tinge of the eleemosynary.

The placing officers, since they were experienced in discovering work suitable for the blind, necessarily undertook a great deal of direct enquiry, but they were glad to avail themselves of the specialised knowledge of local industries of the disablement resettlement officers. It was intended that there should be close partnership at both the national and local level with the Ministry of Labour and National Service. The Working Party later recommended that the placing officer should be called in to advise the blind adolescent about his future employment, at the appropriate stage of his training. He should also be available, they suggested, when the local authority interviewed a newly registered blind person to advise on questions of rehabilitation and training. He should certainly be consulted before a blind person was classified as unable to work. It was also recommended that the system of 'follow-up visits', already known to voluntary agencies as after-care, should be extended. They recognised the value of having someone ready to discuss problems, should they arise, with both employee and employer, and someone, who, from experience in a wide field, would be ready to make suggestions for more effective service.[1]

It was realised that some local authorities needed to be reminded of their responsibilities: 'Where the N.I.B. or other voluntary agency provides this service for local authorities, we consider that some firm arrangement should be made to ensure that the whole cost of the service does not fall on voluntary funds.' Local authorities were strongly recommended to review their arrangements for providing employment for the blind in their areas, for there was considerable room for development and expansion: 'where they are not already providing a placing service of the comprehensive character we have described, they should consider doing so either themselves or by arrangement with the N.I.B. or other competent voluntary agency'.[2]

The Ministry of Health and the Ministry of Labour and National Service followed up the report by issuing a joint circular[3] calling attention to the recommendations of the Working Party, which they fully supported. They urged every local authority to examine its own provision to see how far its services for the welfare of the blind were effective, and they suggested that regional conferences might be called for this purpose.[4] Two illustrations may be given of the response to these

[1] The Working Party referred to instances of suggested improvements, designed originally for the blind, which proved to be of value to sighted workers also.
[2] It was in connection with this point that the Working Party called attention to the heavy expenditure of the N.I.B., namely, £10,000, in its placing service.
[3] Joint Circular 8/52, 15th April, 1952.
[4] It is interesting to find the suggestion that this should be a fully representative group to include the Welfare Authorities, the two Ministries, and the Youth Employment Service.

DEVELOPMENTS DURING THE SECOND WORLD WAR

stimuli, in areas where there were different backgrounds of welfare policy. In Wales[1] a conference of representatives of local authorities and voluntary agencies was called to discuss arrangements for the rehabilitation, training and employment of registered blind persons in the principality. A spokesman of the Welsh Board of Health pointed out that, so far, very little had been done by local authorities in Wales to carry out their duty to find employment, although certain voluntary bodies had accomplished something. After hearing a representative of the N.I.B. describe the value of rehabilitation, it was resolved to recommend county and county borough councils in Wales to avail themselves of the specialised service provided by the N.I.B. and to make such contribution as might be agreed upon towards the costs.

The second example comes from an area where there had already been fruitful co-operation and where industrial placement had yielded some good results. A conference[2] of representatives of the statutory and voluntary bodies in the West of England met to discuss the Joint Circular of the Ministry of Health and the Ministry of Labour. Strong support was given to the conference by all three members of the triple partnership.[3] After full discussion it was recommended that the N.I.B. placement service should continue to operate in the West Region, that the number of placement officers be increased, and that further research be undertaken by these officers. The service was to be put upon a firm business footing by the further recommendation that financial arrangements to be made between local authorities and the N.I.B. should be negotiated between the County Councils' Association, the Association of Municipal Corporations and the N.I.B.

It should be noted that while the two Ministries concerned called special attention to the placing service in open industry as the spearhead of advance, they also drew attention to the importance of considering the needs of all blind workers capable of employment, whether in open industry or sheltered workshop, in the public services or as home workers. The statutory authorities were now in full agreement with the principles accepted by the national societies: if opportunities were given they must be of such a kind that the blind person is able to give efficient service; he must have appropriate backing both from his own family and from public resources: it would be useless sending out blind piano tuners, for example, unless they had an efficient repair service behind them, or to provide materials for home workers unless their goods were marketable. Occupations such as poultry farming might be excellent

---

[1] See *The New Beacon*, 5th July, 1952.
[2] See *ibid.*, 15th August, 1952.
[3] The Conference, presided over by the Chairman of the Welfare Services Committee of a County Council, was addressed by representatives of the Ministry of Health, Ministry of Labour and National Service and the N.I.B.

for selected blind persons, but members of their family, or friends, must be willing to assist them.[1] There might be an extension of the shop and kiosk schemes, successfully tried out by the N.I.B. and St. Dunstan's, so long as there were adequate supervision in the early days, and adequate help with accounts.

The General Welfare of the Blind: Social Policy and Voluntary Action

The question of the social welfare of those who were either too old or too handicapped to earn a living, whether in the open market or in a sheltered workshop, was under close consideration in view of the powers and duties of local authorities under the National Assistance Act.[2] The Act marked an important stage in the development of services for the handicapped.[3] The newly constituted welfare authorities were given comprehensive powers and duties, firstly to make arrangements for those who were in need of care and attention, and, secondly, to promote the welfare of handicapped persons. These provisions were valuable in encouraging experimental schemes in which statutory and voluntary bodies could combine.[4] The Minister of Health lost little time in making certain permissive sections of the Act mandatory,[5] and in issuing outline schemes for the guidance of local authorities on the Welfare of the Blind, and Partially Sighted Persons. Once more the privileged position of the blind was manifest and the welfare services for other handicapped persons had to wait upon more propitious times.[6] It was clear both from the Act and from the Minister's circular that ample provision was to be made for co-operation with voluntary organisations. The following extract from a scheme submitted by a local authority is typical: 'The Council shall continue to promote the general social welfare of blind persons by the provision of all necessary services either directly or by arrangement with the County Association for the Blind or other registered voluntary associations as the Council may from time to time decide'.

Home teachers played an important part in carrying out social policy on general blind welfare, and the Minister was concerned, with interested voluntary organisations, in improving standards in this field. There had long been a requirement that uncertificated teachers should pass a

[1] Cf. the experiments of St. Dunstan's in the First World War. See p. 189, above.
[2] See Sections 21, 26, 29 and 30, National Assistance Act, 1948.
[3] We should note the special rates of assistance provided for the blind (and for the tuberculous), above those for other persons in need.
[4] See p. 246, below, for examples.
[5] See Section 29 (2), and the direction by the Minister in para. 58, circular 87/48.
[6] In August 1951 (circular 32/51) the Minister was prepared to consider other schemes for which he issued some guidance but he made it clear that 'he had no intention at present of giving any similar direction' (i.e. as for the blind and partially sighted). No general direction has yet been given except in the case of the blind; but a number of local authorities have submitted schemes on behalf of the handicapped and have had them approved; they are, therefore, under an obligation to carry them out.

qualifying examination within two years of appointment. They must now pass a selection Board of one of the recognised Regional Associations before they could be admitted to a course. This principle had emerged from a co-ordinated effort on the part of the College of Teachers of the Blind and the several Regional Associations. The Minister now went further, suggesting that 'Welfare Authorities may wish to consult the appropriate Regional Association as to the possibility of the Selection Board being able to express an opinion on the suitability of a particular applicant for the post of uncertificated home teachers before he or she is appointed'. There was also approval by the central authority of the Working Party's recommendation that, to get the best results, both sighted and blind home teachers should be appointed to work in co-operation. The concern over the recruitment of home teachers was growing, in view of the shortage of supply, and both the central authority and the voluntary societies were planning to attract suitable applicants.[1] The purely administrative work of many home teachers was lightened when the National Assistance Board took over responsibility for the actual payment of financial assistance to the necessitous blind and their families. Until then assessments and payments had been undertaken by home teachers in many areas. They were now released for their proper work of teaching and advising and it was anticipated that many more blind persons would be able to read Braille or Moon, or to enjoy handicrafts.

As an extension of home teaching as a medium of rehabilitation, it was suggested by the Ministries that welfare authorities might wish to co-operate with the N.I.B. by sending the newly-registered blind, or others in need of rehabilitation, to one of the voluntary homes such as The Queen Elizabeth Homes of Recovery in Devon. The authorities would be well advised, it was suggested, to consider this as part of their duty 'to make arrangements to promote the welfare of blind persons.'[2]

Before we leave the account of social legislation which affected the welfare of the blind we should note the developments possible under the Education Act, 1944. Wide powers on behalf of handicapped children, and facilities for further education and training of handicapped persons gave fresh opportunities to local authorities and voluntary organisations to take part in experimental schemes which held promise for the future.[3] The National Health Service Act, 1946, also improved opportunities for treatment and research. Although voluntary hospitals and certain homes were taken over by the Regional Hospital Boards,

---

[1] In 1952 we learn that steps were being taken to this end by the Regional Associations for the Blind, the College of Teachers of the Blind and the N.I.B.

[2] The Ministers pointed out that it was more appropriate to do this under Section 29 than under Section 26 of the National Assistance Act.

[3] E.g. Part VII of the School Health Service and Handicapped Pupils Regulations, 1953, under which Hethersett is approved. (See p. 247, below).

there was still room for co-operation with the voluntary organisations in the development of special schemes.[1]

It is early yet to evaluate the effect of the new social legislation as a whole on the relationship between statutory and voluntary services for the welfare of the blind. We know that ample provision was made for the participation of all three partners, i.e. the central authorities,[2] the local authorities and the voluntary agencies, and for consultation between all interested parties 'for the purpose of assuring the closest co-operation'. There is no doubt that at the national level general agreement was reached on the principles of blind welfare and on the desirability of close co-operation.

At the local level there was still considerable variation. Some authorities preferred to keep responsibility in their own hands, although this did not rule out the possibility of contact with voluntary organisations for special purposes. The motives which led a local authority to take over direct provision of blind welfare, when there was a tradition of service by voluntary organisations, were mixed. Only a special enquiry in each area could reveal the influences which led to the Council's decision. From particular instances which have come to light it would seem that changes in administration have affected the position. It was, perhaps, a natural reaction for some Poor Law Officers, reinstated in 1948 as Chief Welfare Officers, to seize the opportunity to justify their position. Blind welfare gave them the chance to develop a new scheme, and they were not always concerned to review the role of voluntary organisations in the process. In some cases the difficulties of adjustment between the welfare officers and the medical officers of health influenced the pattern of development. Sometimes the M.O.H. found that the resources of the voluntary society gave him so much greater elasticity, that he was willing to offer every opportunity for co-operation; sometimes he himself acted as honorary secretary.

In many areas the development from voluntary to statutory responsibility was no more than the continuation of a trend already discernible in other spheres of local government. A study of *Directories of Agencies for the Blind* reveals some significant changes. If we take the last year before the outbreak of the Second World War and compare it with the situation ten years later we find that while, in 1938, 33 statutory authorities were making direct provision of 'general blind welfare', voluntary organisations were carrying out the work in 109 areas; by 1948 the numbers were 56 and 86 respectively. The most recent figures, contained

---

[1] See examples, p. 246, below.
[2] The Central Authorities concerned with the blind included the Minister of Health, under the National Assistance Act and the National Health Service Act; The National Assistance Board; the Minister of Labour and National Service, under the Disabled Persons Employment Act; the Minister of Education was responsible for most of the education, although certain technical education was the responsibility of the Minister of Labour.

DEVELOPMENTS DURING THE SECOND WORLD WAR

in the Directory for 1954, show that this trend continued. By now 82 statutory authorities were making direct provision, those served by voluntary organisations falling to 60. In some areas a close partnership was welcomed, but, whatever the local situation, nearly all schemes submitted to the Minister made some provision for co-operation. Most local authorities, for example, relied on voluntary societies to provide social activities, whether in a specially equipped social centre or otherwise. Some who organised their own home teacher service looked to voluntary agencies to supervise the home workers. Throughout the country the voluntary organisations continued to provide most of the workshops, training departments, schools, nurseries, residential homes and hostels.

Yet statistics from a Directory of Agencies cannot give the whole of the picture, and may even, on occasions, be misleading. Middlesex, for example, operated a scheme by direct provision, but they appointed as their chief administrative officers social workers experienced in voluntary organisation. In some areas co-operation to-day is so close and relations are so cordial that it becomes almost irrelevant to consider whether a service needed for a blind client is provided by a voluntary or a statutory agency.

Regional Associations: An Essay in Co-operation

In the development of a smooth relationship between local authorities and voluntary organisations, the regional associations have made a valuable contribution. From the pioneer days of the unions, their committees had been representative: statutory and voluntary bodies were constituent members of the regional associations. The threat of a second world war and the disturbed conditions following its outbreak emphasised the need for still closer co-operation. The amalgamation of three large associations to form a Southern Regional Group[1] was followed later by an Inter-Regional Committee covering all four regions of Great Britain. The immediate occasion of this final effort to take a comprehensive view of questions affecting blind welfare had been the discussions held in common to prepare a joint memorandum for the Beveridge Committee. They could now go on to consider further proposals for comprehensive changes in the social services.[2] In their new role they could more easily combine with the N.I.B. and other national societies like the *British Council for Rehabilitation.* Moreover, the several Ministries concerned with blind welfare recognised that their practical knowledge of local conditions, and their close contact with a

[1] The Eastern Counties, The Midland Counties and the London and Eastern Counties Associations' amalgamation resulted in the reduction from seven to four Regional Associations to cover England, Scotland and Wales.
[2] Joint deputations with the N.I.B. to the Ministries concerned were organised to discuss matters of special concern to the blind, e.g. to consider National Insurance benefits, and National Assistance allowances.

THE WELFARE OF THE BLIND

wide range of agencies made the regional associations a unique source of information. They were in an excellent position to suggest experienced workers to man the many advisory committees, national, regional and local, set up as a result of the new social policy. Above all, the Minister of Health welcomed the detailed and accurate work done by the regional associations in building up a classified register of the blind and the partially sighted.[1] Such statistical returns, based on information sent in on prescribed forms by the constituent bodies, not only gave knowledge of the incidence of blindness, but supplied essential data for further research into causes.[2] The regional associations found their opportunities increasing and their prestige growing with the development of the statutory social services. A summary of some of the activities of the Southern Regional Association will illustrate the renewed vitality of these voluntary organisations.

Efficient examination for proper certification of blindness was a service which ranked high in the aims of the Association. For some years they had operated an ophthalmic referee service, and they had been prepared to pay the fee for the additional examination. They had, in 1945, set up a special certification committee in consultation with the Faculty of Ophthalmology[3] to press for a ruling that certification should only be undertaken by qualified ophthalmic surgeons. These persistent efforts were finally rewarded when, in 1955, the Minister of Health issued a circular[4] to all local authorities recommending that they should amend their scheme to provide that only ophthalmologists of consultant status should examine and certify applications for admission to the registers.

It was during the war years that experiments were made to institute Home Teachers' Training Courses.[5] In spite of many difficulties they succeeded in instituting some short courses, and plans were made to extend them after the war. By 1947-48 both the Ministry of Labour and National Service, and the Ministry of Education were recognising a full

---

[1] Allowance was made in the estimates for additional expenditure, e.g. for additional staff for the registration section.

[2] Research of this nature had always been a cherished project; the S.R.A.B., and later other regional associations, welcomed the opportunity to co-operate with Prof. Sorsby, of the Royal Eye Hospital, in his investigations into the causes of blindness. His researches were later published under the auspices of the Medical Research Council, see p. 220, above. There was much goodwill between the hospital and the association, and home teachers and welfare officers were indebted to the staff of the hospital for the weekend course held there each year.

[3] See the Annual Report of the S.R.A.B., 1945-46, for the detailed preparatory work necessary.

[4] See Circular 455, 2nd March, 1955.

[5] The S.R.A.B. reported in 1939, 'The haphazard way whereby a prospective home teacher in the past has gained her knowledge and experience have left a very great deal to be desired.' Both the Southern and the Northern Regional Associations provided courses. Another valuable course was started later in co-operation with the Jewish Blind Society which was holding training courses for its matrons and welfare officers. By 1954 the S.R.A.B. was running an independent course for matrons of homes for the blind.

year's course. It is relevant to note how careful the Association was to work in close co-operation with the established College of Teachers of the Blind who were the recognised examining body, and how much this effort to raise the status and qualifications of the home teacher was welcomed by local authorities and by the teachers themselves.[1] Before long the S.R.A.B. was accepting a few trainees from overseas, and in 1950-51 consultations took place between the Inter-Regional Committee, The College of Teachers of the Blind, the N.I.B., and the Colonial Office on the possibility of setting up a special type of training for overseas students to fit them for undertaking administrative duties in the development of blind welfare in their own countries.

During the War the S.R.A.B. had become increasingly useful to their constituent members, whether in bulk buying and distribution of materials for pastime occupations at a time of rationing and short supply, or in acting as consultant on the many problems confronting voluntary societies and local authorities at a time of stress. One example of their function as adviser, after the war, will illustrate the continued need for an information service: their journal *Regional Review* was available for all constituent members, but when a special report on Homes was included the demand was so great that a reprint was necessary. This occurred in spite of the policy of the S.R.A.B. in maintaining that the provision of residential homes was the responsibility of the local bodies, since it needed local experience and initiative.[2] The S.R.A.B. seems to have shown much wisdom in their relations with their constituent members, both voluntary and statutory: while respecting the independence of local groups they recognised the importance of maintaining close contact, and their secretary undertook visiting, attending conferences or speaking at meetings, as an important part of her responsibility.

Finally we should note another valuable result of the co-operative spirit in which the Association worked. Its readiness to combine with other groups in matters of common interest had already brought it into close touch with the N.I.B., and this led naturally to a better understanding between this powerful national organisation and local agencies. In the words of the annual report for 1942-43 joint action had led to the removal of 'small disagreements and misunderstandings'. When, some years later, the N.I.B. was petitioning for a Royal Charter, the S.R.A.B., although critical on one or two issues, hastened to correct 'an inaccurate impression' that it was not in sympathy as a whole. After representations had been made by the regional associations on specific points, it was decided to support the petition, in the belief that it would be 'in the best interest of blind welfare'. That they had much in common was

---

[1] Home teachers had been stimulated by the refresher courses and annual conferences arranged by the S.R.A.B., which had 'rescued them from their isolation'.

[2] The Welsh Regional Association preferred to provide the Homes to serve their constituent members.

already evident in the various schemes for the deaf-blind,[1] and in their joint interest in developments overseas. There was friendly contact between the headquarters staff of both organisations, and there was no doubt that, in the mid-century, there was closer co-operation between all concerned with blind welfare than ever before.

The welcome given to the work of the Regional Associations by the Ministry is illustrated by the large proportion of their income received from public funds.[2]

Examples of Voluntary Enterprise: Local and National. Co-operation with statutory authorities

The fear that voluntary organisations might find less opportunity once the war was over and the new social legislation in operation was certainly not realised in the field of blind welfare. A few further examples will show the vitality of both local and national organisations. New projects were started by counties associations in many parts of the country to meet exceptional needs, such as the flatlets for able-bodied men and women at Swail House, provided by the London Association for the Blind, or the nursing homes for those with varying degrees of infirmity run by the Essex County Association, or the special occupation centre for blind children who were backward but not certifiable. All such experiments were welcomed by the statutory authorities concerned.[3] The R.N.I.B. again demonstrated its readiness to pioneer and it was successful in establishing a good relationship with voluntary and statutory bodies at all levels. The general public had an opportunity to see the progress made in the technical field when the Louis Braille centenary was celebrated in 1952, for example: the electro-mechanical printing machine using plastic ink, the electronic sensing fingers, infra-red drying methods, and the Du Platt Taylor map-making machine. Much was hoped from the new Braille printing technique, the result of research carried out at the instigation of the R.N.I.B.'s Scientific Development Committee.[4] The Institute was also able to develop its 'Talking Books' with a substantial grant from the Nuffield Trust.[5]

Several new trends were discernible in experiments in rehabilitation. The earliest projects had been concerned with ex-service men, and later ones with civilian war casualties, leading on to the industrial rehabilita-

---

[1] A special survey of the deaf-blind was undertaken by the Association and the results submitted to the Minister of Health. At the same time the S.R.A.B. was giving a warm welcome to the experiment of the N.I.B., in starting a small research unit in its new home for children with multiple handicaps. When the Ministry published its report on the Welfare Needs of the Deaf-Blind, 1951, a special subcommittee was set up to consider it.
[2] See Table XII, p. 250.
[3] See p. 248, below.
[4] Several plastic manufacturers were consulted in order to get the best plastic for the purpose. At the moment this is still in the experimental stage.
[5] £50,000 was given for this purpose.

tion of the newly blinded in the Homes of Recovery at Torquay (Manor House and America Lodge), all of which had concentrated upon young and able-bodied men and women to fit them for return to employment. A new venture in 'social rehabilitation' was started at Oldbury Grange, near Bridgnorth, where a course was now offered to older people, especially women, to help them in the daily round of their own homes. The group also included those likely to be unemployable through some physical or temperamental defect.

A second project reflected the modern concern with the family and the role of the parent. A parents' unit was opened in the grounds of a Sunshine Home at Court Grange, Abbotskerswell; it was essentially a family house, the mother staying with her blind child[1] while becoming familiar with the methods of training in the Home, the father coming down for weekends whenever possible. The co-operation of parents was also invited by the formation of parents' groups at the R.N.I.B. headquarters. Parents from London and the Home Counties learned that they were not alone in facing their child's handicap; they could meet home teachers, and experts in various fields of blind welfare, and discover how to share more intimately some of the children's interests, e.g. by learning Braille. Both the Parents' Unit and the Parents' Groups filled a valuable need as consultation and discussion centres, helping parents to adjust themselves to the problems raised by their children's handicap, and giving them greater confidence and hope.

A third project was essentially an extension of earlier ventures. Condover School, near Shrewsbury, an Elizabethan house maintained as a building of historic interest, was opened in 1948 for children with multiple handicaps. A nucleus of 30 children from Court Grange, Devon, was soon increased by the addition of children who were 'educationally blind', with various other handicaps. By the addition of a special unit for deaf-blind children in 1952 it was hoped also to add to the data for research in this field. Two points are of special interest for our study: that the project was undertaken at the request of the Ministry of Education, and that the board of governors included not only representatives of the R.N.I.B.'s education committee but also members of Birmingham University, in addition to local men and women.

One further recent experiment should be noted for it, too, was started at the invitation of the Ministry of Education, following a recommendation of the Working Party.[2] Hethersett, near Reigate, was opened in 1956 as a pilot centre for blind adolescents, in a further attempt to

---

[1] The visit, lasting normally 7 to 10 days, can include as many of the family as the parents wish to bring. The mother has her main meal with the teaching or nursing staff and spends some time in the school groups.
[2] *Op. cit.*, Chapter X.

discover how best to bridge the gap between education and employment,[1] and to prepare a boy or girl who has spent a large part of school life in a residential institution, for normal life in the community. Emphasis is laid upon further education and training, particularly social training; opportunities are to be taken to assess the abilities and wishes of the trainee for his future employment and vocational training, and there will be a fresh effort to stimulate and encourage research into new fields of employment.

In all these schemes local authorities, too, have an important part to play: in keeping up to date with the various fresh opportunites for rehabilitation or training, in selecting and recommending applicants, and in making grants, or paying fees in accordance with their wide powers under the new social legislation.

Finally, some examples of the financial relationship between the voluntary organisations which provide residential establishments of various kinds, and statutory authorities which use them, will illustrate one important aspect of the partnership established in the mid-20th century.

Miscellaneous examples of financial relationships

(1) The Ministry of Labour meets the cost of fees of trainees at the Homes of Recovery concerned with industrial rehabilitation.

(2) The Ministry of Education sanctions the payment by local education authorities of the fees for training at the experimental Adolescent Centre.[2]

(3) The L.E.A. is responsible for grants for children of nursery school age at the Sunshine Home; voluntary organisations providing residential schools normally received some 50% of the cost from statutory sources. In the case of schools for children with multiple handicaps, voluntary bodies have to find only 15%.

(4) The Welfare Authorities can meet various needs under Section 21 of the National Assistance Act which makes them responsible for those in need of care and attention. In those cases they may 'make arrangements with voluntary organisations' or they can use their powers

---

[1] It is interesting to note that applications for admission are made to the R.N.I.B., which provides and manages the Centre, by the L.E.A. after consultation with the school attended by the candidate. 'The Minister hopes that the department of the county or county borough responsible for the provision of welfare services under Section 29 of the National Assistance Act, 1945, will be kept fully informed...'

[2] The fees approved by the Ministry of Education for this pilot scheme are high, £475 per annum; L.E.A.'s were reminded that they would be recognised for main grant under the Education (L.E.A.) Grant Regulations, 1953. In the subsequent training of those who enter a workshop or course of training approved by the Ministry of Labour, the Ministry of Labour would accept financial responsibility. Training in any recognised establishment for further education or in training establishments or schools recognised by the Ministry of Education would be the responsibility of the appropriate local education authority.

DEVELOPMENTS DURING THE SECOND WORLD WAR

as welfare authorities concerned with the promotion of the welfare of the blind and other handicapped persons, when voluntary organisations can be 'employed as their agents' (Sec. 29). It is useful to note the wide interpretation allowed in the use of Section 29 of the National Assistance Act: for example help may be given to a blind baby under this section, by meeting the cost to parents of attending the Parents' Unit.

(5) Residents in a number of homes for the able-bodied elderly blind, including those in the special flatlets mentioned above, receive allowances from the National Assistance Board to cover maintenance fees and pocket money.

(6) A County Association is under contractual arrangement with the Regional Hospital Board to accept patients in one of its nursing homes for infirm blind persons.

Table XI shows the changes in the expenditure on the welfare of the Blind and grants to Charities by the largest local authority in the country. It is of interest to note the increase in the grants to charities after 1947 in contrast to the lean years which followed the outbreak of war.

TABLE XI

Total Expenditure by the L.C.C. on Welfare of the Blind and Grants to Registered Charities for the Blind, 1939–55

[Source: London Statistics; Accounts of Registered Charities and Accounts of the L.C.C.]

Year	A Total expenditure by the council	B Grants to charities by the council	B as % of A (Grants to charities as % of total expenditure)
1939–40	242,486	21,947	9
1940–41	259,493	27,826	11
1941–42	285,164	14,145	5
1942–43	342,725	18,065	5
1943–44	347,997	22,117	6
1944–45	329,682	25,856	8
1945–46	339,895	24,972	7
1946–47	296,178	24,633	8
1947–48	269,572	37,242	14
*1948–49	155,060	41,043	27
1949–50	103,204	42,117	41
1950–51	112,773	47,213	42
1951–52	123,136	50,112	41
1952–53	206,737	58,427	28
1953–54	219,628	61,401	28
1954–55	230,570	62,477	27

* After the passing of the National Assistance Act, 1948 (July), the L.C.C. was no longer responsible for domiciliary assistance.

THE WELFARE OF THE BLIND

Finally, Table XII, showing the sources of income of the S.R.A.B., illustrates the dependence of the Regional Associations upon statutory grants: until 1948 almost entirely from local authorities, and since 1948 jointly from the Ministry and local authorities, together with a nominal sum in affiliation fees.

TABLE XII
Southern Regional Association for the Blind
[Annual income, 1940–55, to the nearest £]

Year	Total income	Grants from local authorities	Grants from Ministry of Health (general)	Grants from Ministry of Health (research)	Affiliation fees
1940	3,521	3,470	Small fluctuating amounts received from subs. and donations, and sundry other sources, to complete the balance.		
1941	3,408	3,331			
1942	2,581	2,471			
1943	3,447	3,294			
1944	3,421	3,294			
1945	3,463	3,294			
1946	3,442	3,294			
1947	3,457	3,294			
1948	3,677	3,444			
1949	4,617	2,649	1,602	175	162
1950	5,433	2,500	2,509	175	153
1951	5,532	2,611	2,614	175	189
1952	5,828	2,736	2,736	175	171
1953	7,028	3,320	3,320	175	193
1954	7,169	3,318	3,318	175	187
1955	7,380	3,519	3,519	175	190

Between 1949 and 1955, sundry payments were received from training fees, and there were occasional subs. and donations, usually of quite small amounts.

If all local authorities were fully aware of their statutory powers and appreciated the opportunities offered by voluntary organisations, or if all were prepared to have more effective liaison between their own officers, the services for the welfare of the blind could be generally improved. Even to-day there are many areas where contacts between the several statutory departments concerned with blind welfare are faulty,[1] or where the contribution of voluntary agencies is not understood. In spite of much general progress there is still need for an efficient information and public relations service to ensure that every blind person, of whatever age or capacity, is able to take advantage of the facilities available to meet his special requirements. The history of blind welfare has shown what excellent results can be achieved when statutory and voluntary bodies recognise their complementary roles.

[1] E.g. between the Welfare and Health Departments, and the Welfare and Education Departments. Note the conference held by the S.R.A.B. to study the link between welfare officers and others concerned with the education and welfare of blind children, (S.R.A.B. Annual Report, 1952–53).

PART V

Reflections on the Changing Role of Voluntary Organisations and their Relations with Statutory Bodies

XX

PERSISTENCE AND CHANGE IN SOCIAL ATTITUDES AND THEIR EFFECT ON SOCIAL RELATIONS

OUR study of three selected services has shown the influence of changes in the economic and social structure upon the development of voluntary organisations; it has illustrated the changing relationship between voluntary and statutory bodies as the community gradually accepted responsibility for the social services, and it has brought to light the corresponding shift in emphasis in the functions of voluntary societies which necessitated the working out of new forms of organisation, involving the co-ordination of voluntary action, and closer co-operation with statutory authorities.

Two features, in particular, separate the period before and after the First World War: firstly, the pace at which changes occurred, and secondly, the social attitudes towards such changes. During the 19th century social reformers had had to be content with the slow accumulation of legislation in limited fields. In spite of numerous reports of Select Committees and Royal Commissions, there was strong resistance to statutory action unless it could be shown conclusively that the community needed protection, as in public health measures, or that the beneficiaries might be considered as a special case by reason of their immaturity or low status, as in factory legislation. Somewhat paradoxically the same period saw the multiplication of voluntary organisations, and an increasing emphasis on the need for charitable action. Yet this, in fact, did no violence to Individualism but tended rather to strengthen it: voluntary enterprise was a substitute for state aid. As industrial, social and demographic changes high-lighted poverty and distress, morality and religion combined to encourage private philanthropy. At the same time the class structure determined the pattern within which the well-to-do should become the benefactors of the 'lower orders'.

CHANGING ROLE OF VOLUNTARY ORGANISATIONS

In spite of much 'shortness of thought' and some obscurantist opposition to the development of social policy, voluntary organisations, nevertheless, made a notable contribution to social reform. In face of the apathy and indifference of the majority throughout the 19th century, they persisted in their efforts to meet a variety of needs. They stood for a principle which is generally accepted to-day, that social service is an essay in human relations. For good or ill the form and content of the pioneer voluntary experiments have left their mark on the development of the public social services.[1]

The advance of Collectivism in the late-19th century, and the Liberal regime of the early 20th, gave new impetus to statutory action, but it was the upheavals of the First World War which precipitated vast changes in social policy. Class distinctions became blurred, and the patronage of the rich towards the poor was no longer an acceptable attitude in an increasingly democratic society. Voluntary organisations had to adjust themselves to the new conception of statutory responsibility, and some of them had to reconsider their relationship to their clients.

Persistence and Change

The acceptance in the mid-20th century of full statutory responsibility for the provision of social services, with opportunity for voluntary co-operation, was a policy not won without a struggle. Throughout the last fifty years examples can be multiplied of the influence of traditional ideas and attitudes, some of which persist to the present day. The early history of the three selected services illustrates the strength of the individualism which baulked social reformers as they endeavoured to enlist public support. Opposition to the first efforts to secure compulsory notification of births was based on the fear of undermining family influence. Reluctance to weaken the rights and duties of parents also accounted for the failure of several attempts to introduce a Mental Deficiency Bill. The sanctity of the family is still a cherished ideal, and legislators have hesitated to introduce measures to meet the needs of children neglected in their own homes, preferring to rely mainly upon the efforts of a voluntary society.[2]

The liberty of the individual, so strong a principle in 19th-century political philosophy, was at the root of the requirement for the certification of lunatics: they must be protected from wrongful 'custody' in

---

[1] The inclusion of voluntary schools within the public system of education, and the combined service for the rehabilitation of the handicapped are outstanding modern examples.

[2] I.e. the N.S.P.C.C. The new interpretation of 'in need of care or protection' in the Children and Young Persons Amendment Act, 1952, goes some way to modify this. The importance of safeguarding the child from over-zealous attention, and of preserving parental rights are, nevertheless, still regarded as fundamental; any infringements may be challenged in the Courts.

asylums. That the emphasis on such legal aspects of care may adversely affect medical treatment is a problem with which the community is faced to-day.

In the early 20th century, so great was the fear of weakening the sense of individual responsibility that several moderate liberal reforms were opposed on principle by the Charity Organisation Society: increasing statutory aid might create for the recipients 'no end to expectation'. Voluntary organisations have found it difficult, in some politically conscious areas, to live down the hostility aroused by this early attitude to statutory intervention. Yet even a modern Fabian can have qualms about the tendency to regard the State as a 'a kind of penny in the slot machine',[1] and discussion is active to-day on the need to strengthen the acceptance of obligations as well as rights in a responsible 'Welfare State'.

But while similar problems may exercise men's minds, there is often a difference of emphasis, and sometimes a complete change of attitude. The theme of a recent International Conference, 'Promoting Social Welfare through Self-Help and Co-operative Action', would have been an appropriate title for a memorandum by the C.O.S. in the 1870's, but the content was certainly different.[2]

Perhaps no better example of the change of attitude can be found than in the development of case work. The need to respect the individual rather than to treat him as an item in a category was a principle of case work strongly urged by the C.O.S. and now accepted by voluntary and statutory bodies alike. But whereas the Charity Organisation Society of the past made a plan for the applicant, the Family Welfare Association of to-day works out a solution with the client. Herein lies the essence of the change from the old individualism to the new understanding of human dignity. The value placed by case workers on personal relationships is now accepted as an integral part of social policy. It lies at the heart of the new child-care service established in 1948. Yet, however enlightened social policy may be, public administrators know that action may be vitiated if relations between the individual citizen and the statutory representative are strained. It is a lesson which has constantly to be relearned. As late as 1954 civil servants were being reminded that 'the citizen has a right to expect, not only that his affairs will be dealt with effectively and expeditiously, but that his personal feelings no less than his rights as an individual will be sympathetically and fairly considered'.[3]

One of the most significant changes has been in the moral attitude towards the beneficiaries of the social services. In the past much

[1] See W. A. Robson, *Social Security*, 1st ed., p. 26.
[2] See the report of the International Conference on Social Work held in 1954.
[3] Quoted in a letter to *The Times*, 5th September, 1954, from a report of the Prime Minister's Committee on Crichel Down.

charitable work was concerned with character training, while the statutory Poor Law always had a strong disciplinary element. Even in the field of maternity and child welfare in the early 20th century infant mortality was seen as a moral problem. To-day, while training for parenthood is as strongly urged as in the first phase of the movement, it is advocated as a part of health education, not as a question of morals.[1] Yet redemptive action is still thought necessary in several fields of social welfare, and character training is a strong ingredient. Perhaps what most distinguishes voluntary organisations working in this sphere from their Victorian prototypes, is the desire to avoid a claim to virtuous superiority. We no longer tolerate a 'League of Well-doers', working for the 'betterment of the poor'. The Salvation Army may preserve its well-known title, but it is in the 'Mayflower Home' that it carries out its new work for the training of 'neglectful mothers'. The Church of England Moral Welfare Council, offering help of many kinds to mothers and babies, and carrying out educational work amongst men and women, sometimes finds its traditional name an embarrassment. The uninitiated have to be convinced that the element of condemnation, often associated with moral welfare in the past, has given way to the 'casework approach'. The modern age has been noted for its search for new names for old services, whether statutory or voluntary, to give expression to the changing attitudes to human needs.

We may note, too, the persistence of religious influence in the work of voluntary societies. Many of the voluntary social services still have a religious basis; the churches show renewed vitality in many spheres of social welfare, while a number of organisations which pride themselves on their scientific approach at the same time attach value to religious influence. We can see this illustrated in two recent reports of the National Association for Mental Health, that for 1953–54 which announced 'two important events', one of which was a Service of Intercession for Mental Health Workers,[2] and the other a paper read at the International Congress of the World Federation for Mental Health on 'Mental Health and Spiritual Values', by the chairman of the Research Committee of the Mental Health Research Fund, reported 1953–54.

In spite of ponderous titles, and aims couched in language appropriate to the age in which they were founded, pioneer voluntary organisations led the way towards a constructive attitude in several fields of social service. Blind welfare offers an outstanding example of the early recognition of the principle that the disabled could be helped to take part in

---

[1] Yet the authors of *Our Towns* referred to the moral aspects of evacuation problems during the Second World War.

[2] The service was well attended, not only by a large number of workers in the field, but also by friends and relatives of patients in hospital, and by a group from the National Association of Parents of Backward Children. The Minister of Health read the lesson.

the normal life of the community.¹ The institutions for the blind demonstrated the value of training for responsible work in the industrial field, while schools for blind boys and girls showed how these children could be helped to enjoy most of the activities open to the sighted. Similarly, when a small voluntary society for mental health discovered that finding employment made a valuable contribution towards the recovery of a patient discharged from the asylum, they were taking the first steps towards the modern conception of rehabilitation. When the Charity Organisation Society and the Settlements urged the need for professional training, if social work was to be given its rightful status, they were anticipating questions which are lively issues to-day.² Even the new voluntary organisations, said to be characteristic of the modern age, the so-called consumer groups such as the National Association of Parents of Backward Children or the Infantile Paralysis Fellowship³ had their forerunners in the societies founded by blind men and women in the 19th century.

But while we recognise the constructive approach to social questions in several fields of voluntary action we have also to acknowledge that older conceptions of the function of voluntary societies have sometimes tended to hold up developments in statutory responsibility. Such was the conviction that voluntary bodies, by virtue of their pioneering activity, had acquired the right to continue to play the major role. Even when the need for a wider range of statutory provision was more generally accepted, it was for long maintained that State action must be supplementary only. As late as 1920 it was the declared official policy in the welfare of the blind 'to aid and supplement voluntary effort'. In 1935 the Board of Control was affirming, in relation to mental health, that there were limits to the extent to which Central Departments can, or ought to, influence public opinion.

An essential element in the negative policy towards statutory responsibility was the strongly held belief that voluntary action had inherent virtues denied to statutory aid. Voluntaryism had, therefore, to be protected from any threat of intervention. One of the early arguments against a measure of statutory responsibility for the welfare of the blind was that it would react unfavourably upon voluntary effort.

When social policy was extended in the first decade of the 20th century, the new services were burdened with theories from the past. Poverty and worthiness were the first tests,⁴ whether for school meals

---

¹ Protests against treating the disabled as a class apart, first voiced on behalf of the blind, have now spread to include other groups, e.g. the mentally defective.(See the evidence given by the N.A.M.H. before the Royal Commission on the Law relating to Mental Illness and Mental Deficiency, 1954.)
² See Prof. J. M. Smith, *Professional Education for Social Work in Britain*, and the Introduction by Prof. Titmuss (1952).
³ The National Spastics Society is an interesting recent example. Not less than two-thirds of the executive committee must be either spastics or parents of spastics.
⁴ The education services and maternity and child welfare were in a slightly different category, but they, too, were influenced by this approach.

reserved for necessitous children, or for old age pensions limited to the aged respectable poor. Voluntary aid was pre-eminently for those who could, with temporary help, be set upon the road to self-support, or for those so severely handicapped that assistance could not be thought of as a reward to folly. The strength of the belief in the intrinsic value of voluntary aid is evident in the recommendation of the Royal Commission on the Poor Laws[1] that voluntary organisations should have a privileged position in the administration of public assistance.

The voluntary organisations were the first to accept the principle that a higher status demanded the acceptance of responsibilities. *Noblesse oblige* underlay the statement of the National Institute for the Blind that its relations with Boards of Guardians would not be impaired by a more generous allowance of relief to blind paupers nor would it 'relieve the Institute of its obligations'. Acceptance of the same principle is implied in the suggestion made by the Central Authority during the Second World War that voluntary organisations had failed in their responsibilities by not making special provision for delinquent blind children.

The particular virtues of voluntary effort were often expressed in the inter-war years as a special capacity for offering personal service, a capacity denied to a statutory body concerned with the provision of uniform services to whole classes or groups of citizens. This was implicit, for example, in the recommendation of the Royal Commission on Lunacy and Mental Disorder in the mid-1920's that after-care 'should not be part of the official machinery'. Later, when trained professional social workers were appointed both by statutory and voluntary bodies this assumption was challenged. The social case work of the probation officer, the hospital almoner and the psychiatric social worker did not differ in essentials, whether it was done for a statutory or a voluntary agency, or whether in connection with institutional treatment or community care. With the introduction of the comprehensive social services of the mid-20th century, the responsibility of a statutory authority for the appointment of skilled social workers was given full acknowledgment. The capacity of statutory authorities to enter the field of personal service could no longer be denied.[2]

Development of Social Policy and the Changing Relationship with Voluntary Bodies

Our study of three selected services illustrates several broad trends in the changing relationship between statutory and voluntary agencies in the provision of social services, as the community as a whole accepted

[1] The Majority Report. This was opposed by the signatories of the Minority Report.
[2] A Working Party has since been set up, July 1955, to examine the need for social workers in the health and welfare services of local authorities.

greater responsibility for the welfare of its citizens. Let us look first at the chief difference in their relative position in 1900 and 1950. When the 20th century opened, with the one exception of Lunacy Law, there was no responsible social policy on Mental Health, Maternity and Child Welfare, or the Welfare of the Blind. A strictly disciplinary Poor Law might offer relief to any 'pauper' within these categories, but destitution was the test for statutory aid. At the same time, welfare was the accepted sphere of voluntary enterprise. By the mid-century the hated Poor Law had disappeared, and statutory social security and social welfare schemes were designed to meet the needs of the whole community, not merely the impoverished or handicapped groups, though special consideration was to be given to them. Voluntary societies still played an accepted part but their role was now secondary. Whereas, fifty years before, the state made a reluctant entry to supplement voluntary action, it was now fully responsible, leaving voluntary societies to co-operate in a relatively small though still important sphere.[1]

One result of changing conditions was that many voluntary organisations, instead of depending upon charity for financial support, began to look to payments for services for a substantial part of their revenue. Many such payments were drawn from public funds. The nature and extent of grant-aid, whether received for specific services or for general purposes, depended increasingly upon local authorities after 1919, more especially after the Local Government Act of 1929, when direct financial responsibility was given to local authorities.

The trends from the beginning of the century may be illustrated from the accounts of charities recorded in the *Charities Register and Digest* issued annually by the C.O.S.[2] The amounts received as 'payments by or on behalf of beneficiaries' rose from some £765,000 in 1904 to £4,277,000 in 1927. As a proportion of total receipts such payments increased from 12% to 28%.[3] Although there was a decided increase in voluntary contributions at the end of the First World War, reaching an average of £6 million by the mid-20's, the proportion of this source of income to total receipts fell by 7%: 'Payments' had risen even more.

While we can recognise general trends it is important, at the same

[1] There are many indications of an actual increase in voluntary action. It is only in relation to the vast expansion of the public social services that it takes a secondary place.
[2] It should be remembered that only those charities which chose to send in returns were included. Fewer societies did so after 1927, and the C.O.S. decided to discontinue the series. Several later attempts were made to revive the tables, e.g. in 1936, and again from 1948, but the number of charities participating were many fewer.
[3] What is, perhaps, surprising is that this proportion averaged as much as 26% between 1909 and 1914, and that charitable contributions in the first phase of development, in 1904-18, fluctuated very little, varying only between £3,383,000 and £3,805,000.

time, to note the wide differences between societies.[1] To take two of our selected services as examples: organisations for the blind continued to draw a large proportion of their income from charitable sources even though the increase in 'Payments' was in line with the general trend. By contrast, charities concerned with mental health had always depended largely upon payments for services, to the extent of 58% of the total income in 1904. This proportion increased to 76% by 1927. The difference in their command of charitable support is emphasised again if we compare the amounts received from donations, legacies and investments. While in the case of organisations for the blind this combined source yielded £148,000 in 1904, rising to £557,000 in 1927, that for mental health societies actually fell in the same years from some £100,000 to £49,000. When we consider the change in the value of money in this period we realise what an immense loss this represented. It should be emphasised that these accounts are not comprehensive:[2] the C.O.S. itself excluded the so-called 'spiritual organisations' from their list, although it recognised that many churches were doing charitable work. Indeed the churches were preparing to undertake new responsibilities, for example in the new housing areas. There were many signs that voluntary action, widely interpreted, was showing fresh vitality. The National Council of Social Service, representing a great variety of voluntary organisations, bore witness to this fact as it extended the range of services offered to all sections of the community. Nevertheless the C.O.S. accounts indicate a trend; statutory responsibility for the social services had resulted in increasingly heavy expenditure from public funds, and it was now generally recognised that the State must bear by far the larger financial burden. There was no longer any doubt that voluntary organisations were now the junior partner in the provision of the social services. This process was taken still further by the social policy of the 1940's, when new statutory bodies were created, and the community accepted a still heavier financial burden for the organisation of its social services. At the same time the traditional pattern of a voluntary–statutory partnership held as provision was made for co-operation in the comprehensive schemes for social security and welfare. But voluntary societies were now dependent upon the goodwill of local authorities if they wished for support from public funds.[3] Some of the

[1] C. Braithwaite in *The Voluntary Citizen* used the accounts as a basis for a statistical analysis. She pointed out that between 1908 and 1927 the total receipts for all charities rose by 77%, but this was only just sufficient to balance the rise in the cost of living. She also noted that the share of blind charities in the total receipts rose from 4·0% to 6·8% while their share of charitable contributions increased from 1·9% to 5·4%.

[2] The difficulty of getting information was later emphasised by the Nathan Committee (Report on the Law and Practice Relating to Charitable Trusts, 1952). They pointed out that although it was known that there were some tens of thousands of charitable trusts in this country 'accessible records do not exist'.

[3] Many of the remaining direct grants from central authorities to voluntary organisations came to an end, although support from Exchequer to Regional and National Associations for special work was still an accepted sphere of public aid.

older voluntary organisations who continued to cherish their financial independence were finding it increasingly difficult to raise money. Many of those who derived their income from both private and public sources found that charitable donations formed a decreasing proportion of the total: payments from clients towards the cost of a service, whether from the client's own resources or, as often, from his statutory benefits, became an important source of revenue.

The changing pattern of social policy was reflected in the changing functions of voluntary organisations, or, more accurately, in the changing emphasis placed upon their various functions. In the pioneer phase direct provision of services was the main concern of most voluntary organisations, many local societies concentrating upon finding or providing institutional accommodation. The selection of candidates for residential homes of various kinds was a characteristic feature of their work. Many of the large national organisations, meanwhile, were combining direct provision of services with active participation in propaganda for social legislation. In the early 20th century education and training schemes were important additional functions. After the First World War experiments in direct provision were intensified, and the range and variety of services offered by voluntary organisations were considerably extended. But in the years between the wars statutory provision caught up with, and then rapidly passed, that of voluntary bodies. We have seen that public expenditure on the social services outstripped that of private philanthropy. Voluntary societies now placed increasing emphasis on research, information and advisory services, and a close scrutiny of new statutory powers and duties. Supplementary training and education schemes were expanded, but no considerable change occurred in the general pattern worked out in the first creative period.

There was, however, one important exception: a number of experiments in co-ordination were made, not only between kindred voluntary societies, but between voluntary and statutory bodies. It was in this period that the National Council of Social Service was founded to act both as a central co-ordinating body and as general consultant. This interaction between groups is so important a development that further consideration will be given to it later.

In the third phase, with the introduction of the comprehensive social services of the 1940's, the role of direct provider was weakened still further,[1] but that of consultant and adviser became of even greater importance. In the complexities of the new social legislation of the mid-20th century, information services were a valuable asset, and the experience and knowledge of the voluntary societies were in demand.

[1] There is an important exception to this generalisation: the provision of residential homes of various kinds continued to be a welcome function, and demands were intensified after the Second World War.

Although such general trends may be discerned in the changing functions of voluntary organisations, there are differences in the extent to which each of the three selected services have fitted into the pattern. In the new comprehensive health and welfare schemes the voluntary maternity and child welfare centres have been largely absorbed by the statutory system,[1] the national organisations[2] remaining essentially consultative and advisory bodies.[3] The Royal National Institute for the Blind, on the contrary, is still taking a large and active part in direct provision of services, while retaining its research and advisory functions. The associations concerned with mental health would seem to hold a mid-way position, acting mainly as consultative and advisory bodies, but still prepared to experiment in direct provision and to maintain a variety of residential homes.

Types of Inter-Action: 1. *Statutory–Voluntary Partnership*

For sociologists the study of voluntary organisations in relation to social policy affords some interesting examples of inter-action, both in the relationship between public and private agencies in the provision of social services and in the inter-action of groups of kindred voluntary societies.[4]

Let us consider first the nature of the relationship between statutory and voluntary bodies. That achieved during the 19th century was mainly of two kinds. The first is illustrated by the education service, where a partnership was evolved, developing steadily from the first small grant of public money to two voluntary societies in 1833, to the acceptance of joint responsibility under the first Education Act of 1870. Throughout the 19th century the voluntary organisations remained the senior partner, and even when, in the 20th, their status was reversed, 'dual control' continued to be an integral part of the national system of education. The Education Act of 1944 reflects the force of history in its incorporation of the voluntary principle.

The second type of relationship was the recognition of respective spheres of influence, worked out in the assistance services to paupers

---

[1] If they have kept their voluntary character they have been heavily subsidised from public funds. Whichever course has been followed the centres continued to welcome voluntary helpers.

[2] The National Association for Maternity and Child Welfare was now renamed—Maternal and Child Welfare. The National Baby Welfare Council was mainly concerned with 'the education of public opinion'.

[3] The provision of mother and baby homes, homes giving 'recuperative holidays' to nursing and expectant mothers and children under five, and other maternity and child welfare services still played an important part in the local voluntary services, and were usually grant-earning. See Table XIII, p. 293.

The extension of 'amenity services' through such bodies as the Red Cross or the W.V.S. in hospitals and other institutions offers further illustration of the value placed on voluntary service.

[4] A further set of relationships, that between individuals and groups in the social service setting, has been indicated in an earlier section (see p. 258 *et seq.*).

and non-paupers respectively. The Poor Law Board, later the Local Government Board, was only too glad to leave to voluntary organisations the respectable and helpable poor, while they carried out a disciplinary regime fitting to Victorian ideas on the treatment of the destitute. It was a negative form of partnership and its machinery received some shocks during the Boer War, and barely survived the First World War. That it continued in existence at all, until the post-war economic depressions forced a new solution to meet the needs of the unemployed, bears witness to the strength and persistence of 19th century Individualism. Some attenuated forms of the 'spheres of influence' theory may still be discovered in some local interpretations of the role of voluntary organisations.

A partnership of a different kind, begun in the 19th but carried out mostly in the 20th century, was made in the field of infant welfare when local authorities sought the co-operation of voluntary organisations in building up a new health service outside the hated Poor Law. Knowledge and goodwill were happily combined as the newly appointed Medical Officers of Health saw the advantage of enlisting local voluntary societies in the campaign to reduce infant mortality through the health and social education of the mothers, and the provision of milk for the children. Public and private bodies were alike active in discovering new ways of contributing to the welfare of mothers and children, and the first decade of the 20th century saw the foundation of a combined movement which was not only national in scope, but which from the beginning had close links with developments overseas. Unfortunately, the central statutory authority, the Local Government Board, took little interest in the new schemes until the movement was well under way. It was the more active Board of Education which gave all the encouragement in its power as it grant-aided 'Schools for Mothers', and other training efforts.

The mental deficiency service affords a similar example of co-operation, but in this case the initiative came from the central statutory authority, in consultation with an existing national voluntary organisation which had combined with others to press for legislation on behalf of the mentally defective. When the Mental Deficiency Bill became law in 1913, a new national association was founded on the basis of combined representation from local authorities and voluntary organisations. It had hardly time to do more than work out plans for a wide range of activities, and to institute its first education course, when the First World War broke out. This was a severe setback for a new and less popular service, and a hard test for the voluntary organisation. That it survived, and came through the ordeal with renewed energy, was largely due to the firm basis of statutory–voluntary co-operation, and the determination of its affiliated local societies to support this policy by combined action with their local authorities. The national organisation was always careful to consult both voluntary and statutory bodies before starting a new venture. The Board of Control encouraged this attitude, and did much to stimulate the Central Association for Mental Welfare to try out experiments in the lean years, while the Board of Education took an active interest in the supplementary training courses giving grant-aid whenever it was in its power to do so.

In both the maternity and child welfare and the mental health services a three-fold partnership of central authority, local authority and voluntary organisation was built up, although it was not effective in every area. Since one of the main objects of the foundation of the national societies in both movements had been the encouragement of public responsibility, it was to be expected that the inauguration of the National Health Service would be accepted as the logical consummation of this principle. The inclusion of provisions in the new social legislation for co-operation between local authorities and voluntary organisations was a tribute to the early experiments in combined action. The traditional pattern of voluntary enterprise side by side with public responsibility was officially acknowledged in the comprehensive social service schemes of the mid-20th century.

2. Kindred Groups of Voluntary Organisations

With one or two exceptions the 19th century was characterised by individualism in the field of philanthropy as in that of industry. The outstanding features of most voluntary organisations were isolation and independence. Although certain kinds of national organisation were acceptable, such as those formed to secure specific legislation, for example the Anti-Slavery League, or those founded to provide direct services thought inappropriate for statutory action, for example the National Society and the British Society with their schools for poor children, such organisations pursued their particular aims with little reference to kindred societies, unless, indeed, it was to compete with them for public favour.

A new feature of national organisations established in the late 19th and early 20th centuries was their appreciation of the need to seek contact with like-minded organisations, although it was long before some national societies accepted the role of co-ordinator. The National Institute for the Blind, for example, never sought to become a federating body, and took little interest in the formation of local societies. Co-ordination of allied services within blind welfare depended largely upon the enterprise of the Regional Associations. The chief concern of the N.I.B. in the pioneer phase was the production of embossed literature and the securing of postal concessions, although they were also closely associated with experiments in education and training.

Some limited efforts to make contact with other societies were made in the 19th century. Such was the action of the After-care Association for the Female and Friendless Convalescent . . ., as it sought the help of various societies for women and girls to provide 'associates' in different parts of the country. Since such societies were widely scattered, it was not easy for a voluntary staff of workers to maintain contact, and similar attempts at inter-relationship were not developed. More successful, though limited geographically, were the experiments made in Liverpool and London in the late 60's and the 70's of the 19th century. The C.R.S. and the C.O.S. realised that, not only would co-operation bring strength, but it would concentrate effort upon the most helpable, and raise the standard of voluntary organisation. Neither society was able to achieve full co-ordination, but each made a valuable contribution to the organisation of charities and, to a lesser degree, to the establishment of a working agreement with statutory authorities. The production of an annual *Charities Register and Digest*, together with reviews of contemporary social questions, is not the least of the fruits of the early experiments by the C.O.S. The knowledge of the work of kindred societies thus made available did much to facilitate co-operation between social workers in the field.

Over the country as a whole, however, there was little attempt to co-ordinate services either functionally or geographically. Local voluntary societies continued to spring up to meet a variety of needs. Some had but a short existence as, ill organised, without a standing committee, they sought to meet an immediate and temporary crisis. Others survived to take a continuous part in a specific service such as the provision of a home for the aged, or the establishment of a visiting society for the indigent, or a mission for the deaf. It was the realisation of the advantage of bringing together workers in these fields and officers in the statutory services, which led to the foundation of Councils of Social Service, or Guilds of Help,[1] in a number of industrial centres in the early 20th century. An attempt to unite such scattered groups was made with the formation of the British Council of Social Service in 1904, but success was limited and the membership small.

The impetus towards more effective co-ordination came from the urgent need to make the fullest use of both voluntary and statutory effort during the First World War. Co-operation, achieved through practical experiments in combined action, led the Central Statutory Authorities to encourage the Councils of Social Service, the Charity Organisation Society, and similar groups to unite in the foundation of the National Council of Social Service, in 1919. This new national voluntary organisation was more broadly based than any of its predecessors. It represented both voluntary and statutory interests; it was concerned with social services in both industrial centres and rural areas; it welcomed contacts with a variety of kindred organisations overseas; and

[1] A variety of titles covered similar work in a number of towns. Another common title was 'Personal Service League'.

it built up a widespread federal organisation which could speak on behalf of voluntary societies as a whole. Such growth was not achieved without opposition from some voluntary bodies, and the suspicion of some statutory authorities. The N.C.S.S. proceeded gradually, however, to build up confidence by the development of local and regional associations, and by a policy of encouragement of local initiative, supported by an active central advisory service.[1] One of its most valuable functions was to bring together a variety of national organisations, many of which were federating bodies, for consultation upon specific issues. At the same time its active participation in national and international conferences, attended by members of both voluntary and statutory bodies, made a further important contribution towards strengthening inter-relations.[2]

In spite of such experiments there were still to be found many local and national societies who preferred to work independently, while others remained so isolated that they were unaware of developments in other parts of the country. One of the outstanding problems to-day is the need for an effective method for co-ordinating the activities of those who work in allied fields of social service. The joint committee or the standing conference have been tried by councils of social service, community councils and similar bodies in various parts of the country. They have been found useful in offering a forum for the discussion of common problems and, sometimes, for decisions on joint action. A modern development at a local level, has been the recognition of the value of the 'case conference' both as a source of strength to administrators and social workers faced with a difficult problem, and as a means of preventing overlap, and the risk of over-visiting. It is a device which goes far to meet the difficulties inherent in a situation where there is too great specialisation amongst social workers, or too great departmentalism amongst public administrators.

Relationships within the Three Selected Groups of Organisations

Meanwhile, the more specialised societies, of which our selected national bodies may be taken as illustrations, were making their own attempts to establish a relationship with societies working in allied fields. The national societies within the Maternity and Child Welfare Service were seeking in various ways to work more closely with the many 'comparable organisations' in their field. At first sight there seemed to be considerable overlapping, but in practice these several organisations with similar aims were all helping to spread knowledge of a new movement which became increasingly popular. In the early phase of develop-

[1] It could speak from detailed knowledge since it not only had specialist organisers in various parts of the country, but it sponsored a number of investigations (see for example, 'Our Towns', or 'Over Seventy').
[2] It produced some valuable reports of these conferences e.g. that on 'The Family'. [See The British National Conference on Social Work, held at Bedford College, April, 1953.]

ment mutual aid was characteristic as, for example, when a more wealthy society helped in the production of the reports and periodicals of its struggling contemporaries. There was also much cross representation upon committees, a practice which is common amongst a variety of voluntary organisations to-day. In the inter-war years there were constant attempts at federation: occasionally it was an outside body, such as a charitable trust, which precipitated changes in organisation, leading to the amalgamation of comparable societies, or even to the liquidation of a national society whose work was found to be adequately covered by some of its own affiliated bodies. In spite of a bewildering multiplicity of voluntary organisations within the maternity and child welfare movement, a common underlying purpose, helped no doubt by the popular nature of the activities, led to considerable success in the achievement of a smooth relationship in all its parts.

Attempts to co-ordinate activities within the sphere of blind welfare met with greater difficulties. Although, early in the 20th century, local and regional efforts to secure co-operation within limited fields led to the successful formation of a Union of Unions, later efforts by the National Institute for the Blind to bring together such diverse groups as local societies and the scattered workshops for the blind met with fierce resistance. Local loyalties and a traditional independence tended to foster suspicion of an increasingly powerful national society. This attitude was reinforced by the potential threat to the long-established methods of raising funds by local appeals. It was not until a statutory blind welfare service had been established, and a second world war threatened, that co-ordination received fresh impetus. By this time an acceptable basis had been agreed upon for the distribution of funds resulting from financial appeals.

With the outbreak of war the experience of national organisations was in demand, and rivalries tended to disappear in the common effort to meet urgent needs. A new pattern of combined action was emerging, strengthened by the further co-ordination of the regional associations. With the formation of the Inter-Regional Committee it was not surprising to find them co-operating closely with the N.I.B. and other national organisations on matters affecting blind welfare as a whole. At the same time they kept in close touch with their constituent members, ready to interpret locally decisions taken at the national level, whether by the Minister of Health or by the N.I.B. Their role as consultant and interpreter did much to smooth the way for a better understanding between small local groups and large centralised bodies. The regional associations, after some fifty years' experiment in co-operation, helped to remove the last remnants of suspicion inherited from the isolation of the past.

The Central Association for Mental Welfare, a 20th-century organisation without the traditional attitudes which sometimes tended to hamper relationships between national and local groups in blind welfare, was more successful from the outset in securing the support of existing local societies. At the same time it pursued an energetic policy for the establishment of new local associations, so that it became a highly organised federating body. The C.A.M.W., followed by the N.A.M.H., was able to offer a variety of services to its constituent bodies, and the contact between local areas and headquarters in London was close and friendly.

But while co-ordination within the mental deficiency branch achieved a high degree of success, the history of the mental health services as a whole shows how difficult it was to make contact between the various specialised branches. A concerted effort to secure amalgamation of the national voluntary organisations was not made until the years immediately preceding the Second World War, although a number of successful local associations had long been active in the several departments of mental welfare. The abstention of the oldest of the national societies, when co-ordination was all but completed by the formation of the National Association for Mental Health, illustrates the strength of a tradition which had its roots in the 19th century. The desire for freedom and independence, and the dislike of sinking its identity, and its funds, in a new association, outweighed the advantages of co-ordination for this pioneer society. However, the three national organisations which combined to form the N.A.M.H. found that they received new vitality, each group bringing experience which gave added strength and wider vision to meet the demands of the war and post-war years.

From the point of view of the statutory authorities and the charitable trusts, amalgamation was to be welcomed as they sought for the most appropriate channel for the distribution of financial aid. Diversity had much in its favour, but it sometimes added to confusion. Public bodies had for this reason exerted pressure from time to time to secure co-ordination when the individualism of voluntary societies made negotiation impossible. At the same time, it should be remembered that, while co-operation and co-ordination may be useful methods for achieving good relationships and efficiency of service, the form and extent must vary with the social situation. Co-operation may not be essential in certain contexts. Co-ordination may not be desirable at the expense of initiative and variety. Unification can be achieved at too high a price.

To sum up: the study of the several selected social services emphasises the need for great care if a right relationship is to be established and co-operation maintained. The history of the Royal National Institute for the Blind illustrates the difficulty of breaking down suspicion and reducing conflict before the co-operation of local and national agencies could be achieved. The development of the Central Association for Mental Welfare shows that, in spite of the advantage of a constitution based on co-operation between voluntary and statutory bodies, success depended upon local acceptance. Progress was slow in some areas, and propaganda to arouse public interest had to be correspondingly intense. Even in the field of maternity and child welfare, with its history of co-operative effort and popular appeal, co-ordination was never fully achieved, and it remains to-day one of the urgent problems to be solved in a comprehensive health scheme.

One of the lessons to be learned from the more successful ventures is that representation by the statutory authority on the working committee of the voluntary agency cements a good relationship. Conversely when local authorities co-opt members of voluntary organisations on to the relevant statutory committees, or when a Central Authority secures representatives of voluntary societies to serve on advisory committees, good public relations are encouraged. The co-operation between the C.A.M.W. and Middlesex illustrates the success of such representation at the local level. The composition of the Advisory Committee on the Welfare of the Blind is an example of excellent relationship at the national level. The changing balance of the statutory–voluntary membership of the Advisory Committee is an interesting reflection of the increasing acceptance of social responsibility for the welfare of the blind. At the same time the gradual infusion of democratic principles into a largely authoritarian body is shown to advantage in the changing composition of the executive committee of the National Institute.

Yet, however representative the organisation, and however strongly supported by the Central Statutory Authority, the history of the three selected services shows that the proffered help was not always acceptable, nor could the voluntary organisations hope for much success when public interest in the administration of the social services of an area was weak. If well-ordered societies sometimes failed to win a response, the position was even less hopeful when voluntary agencies were too ill-organised to seek co-operation or to invite confidence. Sometimes the goodwill of an authority was lost in this way. Occasionally a statutory body which appreciated the advantages of combined action, but found no voluntary society in its area to respond, itself took the initiative in seeking the intervention of a national organisation to create the conditions necessary for a partnership. The great Charitable Trusts could also, as we have seen, play an effective part in stimulating initiative and promoting co-ordination.

XXI

INFLUENCES AFFECTING THE RELATIONSHIP

Diversity in the Provision of Social Services

THE mid-20th century was faced with the problem of reconciling the principle of co-operation embodied in the new social legislation with the fact of considerable diversity in practice up and down the country. The opportunities for combined action varied from one area to another, and the attitude towards voluntary–statutory co-operation depended largely upon local tradition. How great a drive was made in the years between the wars to reduce the difference between the progressive and the backward areas is seen in the efforts of both voluntary and statutory bodies in the field of mental health. The Board of Control and the C.A.M.W. worked together to stimulate the poorly served areas. Whether through apathy or poverty a local authority failed to carry out a service, the Minister of Health welcomed the intervention of a voluntary society to make good the deficiency, in so far as its resources allowed. In some fortunate areas local interest and initiative inspired both statutory and voluntary bodies to fine achievement. In others indifference affected all agencies, and the result was a meagre and impoverished service. Consequently, citizens to-day may be well- or ill-served according to the tradition of the locality in which they chance to live.

Among the many influences determining to which of the existing patterns a local area conforms, the initiative of 'men of sense and publick spirit'[1] has stood high. Since the social services with which we are concerned are essentially personal this is, perhaps, not surprising. Even more important is the fact that, in spite of an impression to the contrary,[2] a combined role as philanthropist and as participant in statutory

---

[1] Footnote 2, p. 31. This descriptive phrase occurs in an essay written in 1748 by Dr. Wm. Cadogan of the Foundling Hospital.
[2] Mr. S. Mencher seems to suggest that this combined role belongs to the past. Cf. footnote 1, p. xi, above.

activities is by no means uncommon to-day. Many a voluntary society founded in the 20th century has looked to salaried administrators and local councillors for active membership. Alternatively, many local councillors have come to take an interest in public work through their participation in voluntary service; many have been selected as candidates for public office by reason of their known activities with voluntary organisations. The recent increase in the number of statutory advisory committees has given further opportunity to members of both voluntary and statutory bodies to share a common interest. At the same time traditional forms of service persist: members of local authorities are still to be found acting as trustees for charitable trusts, and mayors are usually ready to sponsor public appeals for special causes. Our study of three selected services has given ample illustration of the fact that many men and women have a foot in both camps, and are ready to give service whether in the field of public or private enterprise. For them there is no problem of opposition between voluntary and statutory action.

One of the points of great interest emerging from a study of the membership of *ad hoc* committees of enquiry in the three selected services, is the active part taken by professional men and women, particularly by many Medical Officers of Health, in the work of voluntary organisations. The professional element has been extended of recent years to include trained social workers, and this has led to a further strengthening of the bond which unites those working in the field of social service.

But professional workers, or laymen with wide interests, are not to be found in every locality, nor are local administrators always interested in activities beyond their immediate duties. Councillors may be wholly absorbed in party loyalties and exacting committee work. An M.O.H. may be interested mainly in infectious diseases. Indifference to voluntary–statutory co-operation may give way to hostility in certain circumstances. The reasons for this attitude need further study at the local level, but certain factors emerge from a general review of the development of the social services.

There is no doubt that some of the antagonism has its origin in the social and economic influences which shaped the early development of the voluntary societies, while some of the difficulties have resulted from the upheavals of war, and the changing social structure of recent times. The history of blind welfare shows that the independence and conservatism of some of the voluntary societies could be serious stumbling blocks. In the mental health services both voluntary and statutory agencies were to be found reacting strongly at times against intervention from the centre. Local loyalty and parochialism were not always distinguishable. Recent trends have shown that encroachment by a central statutory authority in fields hitherto claimed as local preserves have been resented as a blow to prestige. Curtailment of work in these spheres has made local authorities the more ready to use their remaining powers to the full rather than to accept voluntary organisations as their agents. This policy has sometimes reduced co-operation to the minimum.

Much hesitation on the part of local authorities is undoubtedly due to an increasing sense of responsibility for the use of public funds as the social services develop in range and scope. But it is also true that absence of co-operation, in some cases, is the result of the misunderstanding of the function of voluntary organisations, or to ignorance of the part which they are in fact playing. The example is not isolated of the medical officer of health who denied that a family case work agency in his area had any useful function to perform, only to be confronted with unassailable evidence of the frequent use of this agency by his own health visitors.

Active conflict in the past seemed to be closely related to the political complexion of the local authority, where the tendency to see all the virtues in statutory services and none in voluntary societies led to a refusal of financial aid for voluntary effort. There are still some areas where a political alignment holds. In many of the newer services, however, no such clear-cut division emerges, for example, in the provision of Citizens' Advice Bureaux, or in the services for the welfare of old people. The extent of co-operation would often seem to depend rather on the personality of the chairman of the relevant committee, or on the temperament of the chief administrator, than on political bias. An ambitious officer may be tempted to push ahead in a sphere in which his authority has hitherto had little experience, regardless of the traditional contribution of voluntary societies. Sometimes a lack of cordiality is due to the desire of the public administrator for a controlled and ordered service which runs according to rule. He is intolerant of the voluntary organisation which does not fit tidily into his schemes. If such is the case his own social workers may well be in closer sympathy with the voluntary bodies than with the statutory authority which employs them.

It seems to some workers in the field that the hierarchy of officials and the routine of committee procedure freeze all human warmth. 'We can't move County Hall' is a cry which tends to break the spirit, while a sense of frustration impedes the worker who thinks that her seniors, all administrators, have no interest in case work. Administrators, on the other hand, sometimes complain that social workers have little or no understanding of an administrator's responsibility to his committees, nor of the constant need for careful scrutiny of the expenditure of public money. Above all, the need to keep within the statutory powers and duties is, in their view, often too little appreciated by the social worker intent on her own interpretation of what is best for the client. A greater knowledge of each other's function, a better understanding of the special responsibilities, of the particular skills, and of the limits within which each must work, would not only reduce friction but allow

INFLUENCES AFFECTING THE RELATIONSHIP

both the administrator and the social worker to make the contribution necessary for the full development of the service.

Since the social services are essentially services on behalf of individuals, dependent in the last resort upon human relationships, the attitude of those who administer them is crucial to their success. Policy must be interpreted at the local level both by administrators and by field workers. This principle applies alike to statutory and to voluntary services. If public administrators have sometimes failed to appreciate the importance of the interaction between individuals and groups, voluntary organisations have sometimes been guilty of carrying over from the past attitudes inconsistent with modern aims. Any element of condescension or patronage is properly resented in an age which rejects class barriers, while a cold official aloofness or an authoritarian approach are equally out of place in a community which values personal relationship, especially in a social service which offers help according to need. Furthermore, the very term 'social service' has been broadened to include services available for the whole community, with individual choice rather than need as the test of use, so that these attitudes have become even more outmoded.

It is important to remember that our evidence has been drawn largely from a study of three well-organised national societies, two of which were founded on a co-operative basis. We have seen that not all voluntary organisations have had similar records of willingness for combined action, nor have they all impressed their local authorities by the quality of their service. We have learnt the danger of making exclusive claims for voluntary societies. By the same token it is unscientific to make general denunciations of the nature of their contribution.

Some Criticisms of Voluntary Societies

It is perhaps advisable to consider here some of the charges made against voluntary societies.[1] Amongst the most frequent are the following: that they are concerned only with palliatives, that they are uninterested in causes, and that they are unscientific in their approach, and unbusinesslike in their methods. The contrast is sometimes drawn between philanthropists concerned only with relieving distress, and political reformers working for changes in social policy. It is argued that voluntary organisations have worked within the existing social structure while political reformers have sought to change it.

It is difficult to justify this last claim when we remember how many of the Victorian pioneers were both philanthropists and social reformers. Nor can we ignore the activities of those national voluntary

---

[1] Cf. E. Cohen, *op. cit.*, p. 74, where she charges the voluntary movement with showing little interest 'in radical preventive work', and suggests that 'the scientific approach made no appeal'. She adds, even more surprisingly, that 'propaganda has fallen to the lot of official bodies'.

organisations which carried out urgent propaganda for social legislation, nor of the many others which helped to pave the way for changes in social policy by demonstrating new ways of meeting individual needs.

Our study has shown, too, that no rigid line can be drawn on the question of participation in research. In mental health and blind welfare, voluntary organisations pioneered in investigating causes and in discovering preventive measures, often in close co-operation with the statutory authorities. It was the Central Authority which asked the voluntary organisations to undertake an inquiry into the causes of blindness; voluntary societies and local authorities worked together in a study of neonatal mortality: local authorities, in several instances, co-operated as their medical officers or administrators acted as skilled advisers to a committee of enquiry set up by a voluntary body in the mental health service. The C.O.S. embarked on a number of fact-finding enquiries before organising its propaganda campaigns, setting an example in method followed by a number of responsible organisations. The practice of the C.A.M.W. in promoting accurate ascertainment and in insisting upon the keeping of proper records by their affiliated associations belies the charge that voluntary organisations are necessarily unbusinesslike.

Even more questionable is the assertion, sometimes made, that voluntary organisations have had no concern for education and training, nor for the instruction of the general public. In my view, one of the most valuable contributions made by the three selected organisations is their educational and advisory work. The supplementary training courses of the C.A.M.W., and of its successor, The National Association for Mental Health, whether for teachers, doctors, magistrates or social workers, have put the experience gained in a largely unknown field at the command of busy workers in a variety of callings, who nevertheless, come frequently into contact with problems of this specialised nature. Similarly, the advisory work of this organisation was essentially educational, as occupational organisers, speech therapists or psychiatric social workers went about the country, offering their services to local authorities and voluntary bodies alike.[1] We have seen that both in blind welfare and in maternity and child welfare educational and advisory services also played an important part, while propaganda for the education of the public was a service common to all three national organisations.

In some parts of the country the memory of the patchwork nature and eleemosynary character of certain forms of voluntary enterprise is stronger than the recognition of the work of other more dynamic and constructive societies, some of whom have taken an active part in a progressive social policy. Perhaps prejudice dies hard amongst some of

[1] Or as workers in Child Guidance Clinics helped parents to understand their children's behaviour problems.

the politically conscious who cannot forget old social attitudes, and who, consequently, tend to reject the work of all voluntary societies as 'palliative'.

If the denigration of voluntary societies is sometimes carried too far, it is equally a mistake to make too great a claim for voluntary action. It has, for example, been commonly argued that voluntary organisations are more flexible and better able to take risks than are public bodies. To-day, however, the financial position of many societies is so precarious that they have been forced to concentrate their resources upon limited objectives, often devoting much of their energy to the more circumscribed agency functions. Others, who still prefer to keep their independence, have had to curtail some of their existing services, and to give anxious thought to any suggestions for embarking upon new projects. It is a considerable temptation to hard-pressed voluntary bodies to concentrate upon those services which may attract financial support rather than upon others which may be of greater value but less spectacular in their appeal. This trait is not peculiar to voluntary societies, however, since statutory authorities must also keep a close watch upon popular favour.

Few societies are to-day in a position to carry out large-scale enterprise. Perhaps blind welfare offers an exception, for substantial funds enable the national organisation to produce embossed literature and to experiment in technical equipment as a major enterprise.

Most voluntary organisations, however, are less generously supported by the charitable public, and are not in a position to carry out so extensive a service nor to employ so large a salaried staff. Not many, to-day, command sufficient funds to have more than a few qualified staff in key positions. Where they have been able to appoint a professional of high standing, as in the medical directorship of the N.A.M.H., they have not always found it possible to maintain this policy in full.[1]

Social legislation has incorporated the principle that public money may be made available for private enterprise in the social services. In the first place voluntary societies, as charitable or social welfare organisations, benefit from a number of concessions[2] such as the consideration of claim for relief from taxation and from rating. The public is encouraged to support them by covenanted subscription or by bequests, by devices for the refund of taxation or exemption from death duties under certain conditions. Entertainment tax may also be remitted where the purpose is the raising of funds for charity. Secondly, voluntary

[1] During the war the clinical experience of the Medical Director was needed for the After-Care Scheme. After the war it was more difficult to attract a consultant to full time work which was educational rather than clinical. An 'honorary panel' under a distinguished chairman took over the advisory work and, in the spring of 1955, a member of the panel agreed to act as regular part-time Medical Adviser, the panel continuing to serve as Honorary Medical Consultants.

[2] This is sometimes referred to as the 'hidden subsidy'.

societies may benefit from grants and other payments by statutory bodies, sometimes directly from the Exchequer, more often by arrangement with local authorities or regional bodies. Organisations which co-operate with statutory authorities may have financial support from public funds in several ways: they may receive *per capita* payments for services rendered as they act as agent for the Authority, or they may receive grants in aid of specific services within their competence, or contributions for the society's general purposes. This latter form of financial help is of special value since it gives greater freedom for spontaneous action.

To what extent local authorities use such powers must depend upon the particular needs of the area in relation to public resources, and to the quality and extent of the voluntary activity available. In the last resort it is for the voluntary organisations to prove that they have a service to offer which, combined with existing statutory facilities, will enrich the life of the community. They have the task of encouraging the enthusiasm and interest which have sustained pioneer experiments in the past, without resort to pressure which may lead them to 'oversell a speciality'. It is the responsibility of the local authority to take account of the total needs of the neighbourhood and to make full use of all available resources, both statutory and voluntary.[1]

What may be offered through voluntary action, in combination with statutory schemes for social welfare, may perhaps be usefully summarised at this juncture.

Characteristics of Voluntary Action in Relation to Social Policy

Since our study has emphasised the diversity in quality and range of service of both voluntary and statutory bodies, it follows that we cannot distinguish a clearly defined voluntary or statutory sphere of action. Nor can we properly speak as though each were an entity having its own distinctive agreed attitude to social questions. Yet it may be possible to point to certain features of voluntary action which have been dominant in the past and which suggest fruitful forms of co-operation in the future development of the social services.

The tendency of voluntary organisations to throw up experiments in

---

[1] A recent example of the official recognition of the need for a comprehensive view is given in the Joint Circular issued from the Home Office, Ministry of Health, and Ministry of Education on Children Neglected in their own Homes. 'The Ministers are convinced that it is by means of co-ordination that this complex question can best be dealt with.' To this end the local authorities were asked to make special arrangements for designating an officer who should hold regular meetings of officers of the local authority and other statutory services, and of local representatives of the voluntary organisations. It should be his task to enlist the interest and to secure full co-operation among all the local services. (Circular issued July 1950, to Councils of Counties and County Boroughs for action, and to the Councils of Metropolitan Boroughs and County Districts for information. Quoted in Appendix IX, in the Sixth Report on the Work of the Children's Department, 1951.)

various forms of social service has persisted in spite of radical changes in social policy. Recent legislation, while enlarging the sphere of statutory responsibility, has given opportunity for voluntary enterprise and combined action.[1] The relationship may be that of a voluntary body testing an idea and calling attention to its applicability in wider spheres appropriate for statutory action. On the other hand, a statutory body may suggest to a voluntary society that it might experiment in a direction not yet within the powers of a statutory body, in the hope that if the activity were found suitable it might lead to the granting of further powers. We still find examples of both approaches. We also find the central authority grant-aiding experiments which could not in existing circumstances be carried out directly by a statutory body. Marriage counselling is one of the more recent examples of such co-operation.

If experimental work is one of the best known and more obvious functions of voluntary societies inherited from the pioneer phase, it must be remembered that statutory bodies have sometimes sought special powers to pioneer, while recent legislation has allowed further opportunities for experiment in various fields. The several types of health centre, and the new comprehensive schools are evidence of this spirit. Voluntary organisations can make no exclusive claim. The main difference lies in the requirement that statutory bodies work within an agreed social policy, and a comprehensive framework. Voluntary organisations have greater freedom to choose the field of experiment and to select the beneficiaries of their schemes. They usually begin with small projects, gradually adding to the number as the value becomes apparent, or, alternatively, encouraging others to imitate them. Such was the history of occupation centres, or, more recently, of 'meals on wheels'. In all these spheres voluntary–statutory co-operation has been a marked feature as the service developed.

The small-scale venture giving opportunity for personal service, characteristic of so much voluntary effort, brings us to a consideration of a second quality which has been recognised in modern times as valuable in the relationship between public and private enterprise in the social services. Voluntary societies had long demonstrated the need for a concern for the personal welfare of the individual in the administration of a social service, but full recognition had to await a more enlightened public attitude. The stimulus came largely from the pressure of events, but, when the time was ripe, the discerning took note of small private experiments in many fields and used them effectively for the advantage of the wider community. The recognition of the need for personal as distinct from environmental services is one of the characteristic features of the development of social policy in the 20th century, and it is here

[1] An interesting recent example is that of support given to a Family Service Unit by joint action from the Health Department, the Children's Department and the Education Department of a Local Authority.

that a good relationship between statutory and voluntary agencies has been particularly fruitful.

The voluntary agency is often better able to spend time and money on one individual or one family who may, by reason of special circumstances, require prolonged help. Although statutory bodies are increasingly able to extend their welfare services both by using the substantial 'discretionary' powers of recent legislation, and by appointing, in certain branches, professional social workers, yet there are practical limits of finance and personnel within which they must act, and they must always act consistently.[1] While these conditions hold they are often glad to welcome the co-operation of voluntary societies who can do more intensive case work. The family case work agency, where it exists, is often used for 'referrals' whether by hospital almoners, child care officers, probation officers or health visitors.

It remains true, even in the improved social conditions of to-day, that the State cannot meet every contingency: some actions are *ultra vires;* some individuals do not fit the usual categories; voluntary organisations may step in to perform services needed by the minority but beyond the powers of a statutory body to perform. It is no unusual occurrence for a two-way traffic to exist between co-operating agencies in certain areas, the voluntary body referring its clients to the statutory authority for available benefits, while itself offering additional assistance beyond the scope of the authority. Alternatively, and increasingly often since the new social legislation became effective, the initiative comes from the statutory authority who, after fulfilling its obligations, refers its clients to the voluntary organisations for the help it is itself debarred from giving. An interesting example of the official recognition of this type of relationship is to be found in the National Assistance Act, 1948, where the provision of meals and of recreation for old people is an accepted function of voluntary organisations within the comprehensive welfare services for which statutory bodies are responsible.

Such co-operation may be welcomed by the statutory authority interested in offering a full service to its applicants. There have been occasions, however, when a voluntary society has had to use much of its resources in drawing attention to the need, and in creating a demand. We have seen that the central authority and its staff of inspectors have often welcomed the co-operation of voluntary agencies in helping to rouse the local authorities in the backward areas. While local government continues to be organised on the basis of discretionary powers in addition to statutory duties, there are bound to be differences in the quality and range of services. Voluntary organisations may still be welcomed by the central authorities to help in the task of implementing social policy by encouraging the full use of statutory powers.

[1] E. Cohen suggests that one of the merits of voluntary service is that there is no obligation to be consistent. See *English Social Services*, p. 155.

INFLUENCES AFFECTING THE RELATIONSHIP

But there are abundant indications that voluntary organisations have a more positive part to play in the making of social policy. Whatever advances have been made in recent times there can be no doubt that the 'Welfare State' has not been able to meet the high expectations raised by the Beveridge Report. Those working in the field, whether for statutory or voluntary bodies, are building up experience of new services, noting not only their achievements but their shortcomings. While statutory advisory bodies, experts in their various spheres, may be in close touch with the general problems, there is need for all who are knowledgeable about particular services to scrutinise existing legislation and to offer suggestions. The long-standing voluntary organisations can do this the more readily since they can work both within and without the statutory framework. Their evidence is recognised by Royal Commissions and other committees of enquiry as of value in the total assessment of the situation as it affects the users of a service. By virtue of their specialised knowledge they are also able to offer suggestions in the preparation of legislation, or to brief their supporters in Parliament on amendments which they believe to be desirable when a Bill is under consideration.

It has been characteristic of the three selected voluntary organisations that they put education and training high amongst their aims. From the beginning the maternity and child welfare societies made parentcraft the basis of their propaganda, and schools for mothers were later merged into the general advisory work of the centres. Supplementary training courses took a regular place in the services offered by the Central Association for Mental Welfare, while its successor, the N.A.M.H., continues to offer a variety of such courses to professional workers; in addition to the scheme for selecting educational psychologists for training at various approved centres it organises the only recognised diploma course for those working as home teachers or on the staff of occupation centres or the children's department of mental deficiency hospitals. The long-established College of Teachers of the Blind, in co-operation with the regional associations, plays an essential role in the training and examination of home teachers in blind welfare, and its professional qualification is still demanded by the appointing statutory authorities.

It is one of the virtues of voluntary agencies that they early appreciated the need for trained social workers, whether salaried or voluntary. The C.O.S. were amongst the first to demand that their workers should have training either by attendance at organised courses or by training 'on the job'. Another outstanding example of the success of this principle was offered by the L.C.C. Child Care Service, a co-operative venture in statutory–voluntary enterprise. In this case the organisers were fully-trained and salaried workers, while the voluntary workers received 'in-training' and were required to give regular and knowledgeable service if they were to be acceptable. The need for training volunteers, as well as salaried workers, in the various social services is at last receiving more general recognition.

To-day, statutory authorities are making increasing use of trained professional social workers, most of whom have had practical experience with both voluntary and public bodies, and are therefore in a good position to foster good relations amongst field-workers in both spheres. But the demand is still greater than the supply, and many public bodies are glad to co-operate with voluntary societies who can attract large numbers of men and women of good will as volunteers. It is characteristic of such groups as Red Cross Societies, Old Peoples' Welfare Committees, or the Women's Voluntary Services, that they help to foster good public relations in the social services.

It is significant that the W.V.S. was founded under official auspices,[1] and that it was concerned not only with the direct provision of services but with the important modern function of interpreting statutory demands and official duties in human terms. In the words of the History of the Second World War, it was the link between officialdom and the public 'with mutual benefit to both sides'.[2] The W.V.S. is in a class by itself and does not properly come within our definition of a voluntary organisation. It is of interest in this connection, however, for the public recognition of the importance of the interpretative function, and of the mutual benefit to be derived from voluntary–statutory co-operation.

The continuation to-day of Citizens' Advice Bureaux, originally founded like the W.V.S., to meet an emergency, bears witness to the need for information centres to deal with the general enquiries of the citizen in face of the complexities of modern legislation.

The use of specialised organisations as consultants is a similar service of great value. Their contribution to a satisfactory relationship between voluntary and statutory bodies is evident in a period of instability and change. Local authorities undertaking new powers and duties have often been glad to turn for help and advice to an experienced organisation. Not only in a transition stage, however, are such contacts welcomed, for throughout the period of development we find the national voluntary societies ready to give advice on intricate and difficult problems, whether to officers of public bodies, to social workers in voluntary organisations, or to individual citizens.

As consultants and advisers these societies are naturally brought into touch with a wide range of problems. They are in a good position, therefore, to assess needs and to investigate possibilities for further developments. Research has been, and still remains, an important contribution to community service. In this field, too, close co-operation with statutory

---

[1] Founded in 1938 as part of the organisation for Civil Defence, after consultation with the national voluntary organisations.
[2] *Civilian Health and Medical Services*, p. 233.

INFLUENCES AFFECTING THE RELATIONSHIP

bodies is essential. Some of the most fruitful results in the past have been the product of joint voluntary–statutory investigations.

One of the main developments in combined action in the inter-war years was the use of voluntary organisations as agents of statutory bodies. An advantage of this arrangement was the effect upon the standard of service. If voluntary societies sometimes helped to improve the services offered by local authorities, there is much evidence that statutory authorities, through their inspectors, have encouraged improved standards from voluntary agencies. In the last resort grants depended upon the quality of service.

The use of a voluntary organisation by a group of local authorities when the demand has been insufficient to justify direct provision by any one authority, is of particular value in any consideration of the agency functions of voluntary societies. A specialised service such as a residential home for handicapped children is an example of a customary service of this kind.

Mutual benefit is also apparent when combined action leads to service on a wider scale than would be possible if it were dependent upon the resources of voluntary or statutory bodies alone. Maternity and child welfare schemes were an early example. Schemes for the welfare of the aged offer a modern illustration.

One of the outstanding contributions made by voluntary organisations has been in sustaining interest, in times of upheaval and financial stringency. The mental deficiency service, during the First World War and the subsequent economic crises, gives evidence of the strenuous work of voluntary societies to revive waning enthusiasm. The inscription over the entrance to Staunton Harold church may aptly be applied to the organisations working in this field:

> Whose singular praise it is
> To haue done the best things in ye worst times,
> And
> hoped them in the most callamitous.

It is notorious that in prosperous times public sympathy tends to wane, while periods of stress or disaster will often bring greater understanding. An era of economic expansion may be an age of limited vision, while a large-scale catastrophe opens men's eyes to wider needs. The community has been more ready to appreciate the need for constructive services when its standards and way of life have been threatened; much important social legislation has been passed during and immediately after a World War. It is the needs of a minority, particularly a less vocal minority, which are sometimes overlooked in the waves of enthusiasm for broad measures of reconstruction. Voluntary organisations have done useful service both in prodding the complacent in the good times, and keeping alive the needs of special groups in times of difficulty. Enlightened local authorities have sometimes welcomed the help of voluntary organisations in rousing and sustaining interest in a project which has no immediate popular appeal.

Another of the interesting features of voluntary enterprise has been the development in the methods of case work. Voluntary societies were among the first to protest against the labelling of human beings in categories such as 'the destitute' or 'the disabled'. They demonstrated that a client suffering from a disability was, above all, a person, able to share in many of the normal activities of life. A blind boy or girl was first and foremost a child: an old-age pensioner was a person and a citizen. Each individual was unique. Psychology has endorsed this view and extended our knowledge of 'individualisation', to use the modern jargon. To-day this principle is embodied in social policy, but much has yet to be done to create an enlightened public opinion. Perhaps schemes for rehabilitation are amongst the more recent expressions of the new approach to human needs. It is in this sphere, too, that voluntary and statutory bodies can most usefully combine to ensure that a handicapped person is helped to take part in all the services and amenities available, in so far as he is able to do so.

If voluntary societies have been specially concerned with the individual, they have also widened their scope to include interests overseas. Each of the three organisations studied in detail had early contacts with pioneers abroad. To-day the R.N.I.B.[1] has far-reaching international contacts, while each of the other selected societies has created a consultant service for overseas visitors which is making increasing demands upon their resources. Again, close contact with statutory authorities is essential, for enquiries are concerned with the social services as a whole. Special interest is always shown in the relationship built up in this country between governmental and non-governmental services, while the several committees of the United Nations bear witness to the acceptance of this pattern in the social services.

Finally, we may refer to certain values associated with a democratic society. Co-operation between voluntary and statutory societies gives greater opportunity for consideration of the minority point of view. It allows room for diversity and initiative when the trends are all in favour of centralisation and unification, and insists on the value of individual effort in an era of large-scale organisation. It helps to spread interest in the social services amongst a wider section of the community, many of whom may not have a bent for service on statutory committees.

If we agree, with T. H. Marshall, that welfare is concerned with the enrichment of human relations, then all available sources of co-opera-

[1] See, particularly, the foundation of the British Empire Society for the Blind, following upon an investigation in 1946 by the R.N.I.B. and the Colonial Office.

tion are to be welcomed. The community has need of the enthusiasm and faith of those who are prepared to go on, in spite of indifference, to create a demand, whether as social reformers in the political field, or as workers in voluntary organisations discovering by empirical methods new forms of service.

Experience suggests that there is urgent need for further development in good relations between voluntary organisations and local authorities. If generous use could be made of the power to grant-aid voluntary organisations for general purposes,[1] in addition to payments for specific services, combined action could secure elasticity and experiment, together with efficiency and maintenance of standards. It could infuse the administration of the social services with the objectivity desirable in a comprehensive scheme and the warmth of personal interest essential to the individual approach.

In the first flush of enthusiasm for the 'Welfare State' many were led to believe that the days of voluntary organisations were numbered. Since 1948, however, when the new social policy came into action, events have shown that in spite of the intention to inaugurate 'a comprehensive scheme of social security and social welfare', weaknesses have appeared in the range and quality of many of the services, and, most conspicuously, in the administrative machinery for carrying them out. There has been ample scope for voluntary action to help meet the problems which have become manifest. We have also to remember that, in spite of full employment, the international situation has made the period since the war particularly difficult for carrying through a vast scheme of reconstruction in the social services. The demands of rearmament and the perils of inflation have led to reluctant restrictions and curtailment. Once more voluntary societies have found their services welcome to meet unexpected needs.

It would be unfortunate, however, if this aspect of the work of voluntary organisations were too much stressed. Their function is more positive than that of acting as a stop-gap in times of failure or crisis.

Our study of voluntary action in relation to social policy leaves no doubt that the voluntary principle has not only been a valuable asset in the past, but that voluntary organisations have a constructive part to play in the development of the social services in the future. The higher the standards of social welfare set by a democratic community, the greater the need for offering full scope for voluntary action. The combination of statutory responsibility with voluntary effort is essential for a creative approach to the satisfaction of human needs.

[1] 'In general it would be true to say that it is the modern societies best fitted to meet the needs of to-day which are the shortest of funds and which suffer most from lack of popular appeal'. (Report of the Committee on the Law and Practice Relating to Charitable Trusts. Cmd. 8710, December 1952.)

CHANGING ROLE OF VOLUNTARY ORGANISATIONS

EPILOGUE

Current Problems and Trends

Most of the foregoing study was made in the early 1950s and it may be well to see whether (Summer 1956) there have been any special developments which indicate future trends.

Two aspects seem to me to have received special stress: a greater appreciation of the value of education and training, and a better understanding of the link between psychological and social questions.[1] Each of these has significance for the relationship between voluntary and statutory bodies. One of the most interesting developments in the field of education and training is the recognition of the need 'to educate the educators', to offer further opportunities for acquiring skills and techniques. There are examples in almost every field of social work, both voluntary and statutory. The C.O.S. were amongst the first[2] to recognise the need for the training of supervisors as they shared with the Institute of Almoners the experiment of bringing over an American caseworker to teach supervision and case consultation.[3] The N.A.M.H. also looked to America as they secured the services of a Fulbright scholar to conduct a group of seminars for their experienced caseworkers. Another development of great interest was the secondment by the National Assistance Board of officers to take the new 'generic course' at the London School of Economics, where experience and a recognised qualification were the conditions of entry. Here, too, there was a strong emphasis on supervision in casework.[4] There is considerable discussion at the present time about the training of health visitors in order to strengthen their educational role within the family. An indication of the same trend is seen in the changing emphasis in the organisation of the traditional 'Exhibition' arranged by the National Baby Welfare Council. No longer a travelling exhibition attracting, in the main, parents and schoolgirls, it is now established in London for 'student observation' to help in the training of nurses, health visitors, doctors and others concerned with the education of parents in child welfare.

The efforts to bring parents more closely into touch with training schemes is worth special note. Within blind welfare, the parents' unit project and the parents' discussion groups are recent illustrations.[5] In

---

[1] It is interesting to find the *British Journal of Psychology* now containing as many articles on community care as on clinical work.
[2] The Tavistock Clinic was also early in the field as it offered special courses for senior caseworkers.
[3] C.O.S. courses were attended by a number of senior workers from other fields: e.g. senior probation officers recommended by the Home Office and health visitors released by local authorities.
[4] A group of workers experienced in various fields, including a distinguished caseworker from America, supervised this training.
[5] See p. 247, above.

INFLUENCES AFFECTING THE RELATIONSHIP

the field of maternity and child welfare 'parentcraft' has had a long tradition. It is now officially recognised by the special appointment of 'parent advisors' and, at the international level, by conferences and publications which reflect the new emphasis on the emotional relationships between parent and child.[1] The publicity given in the inter-war years to the psychological development of the child was not always wisely conducted and much recent propaganda has been designed to restore parents' confidence and to give assurance on the wide range within which the child's development is normal.[2] The maternity and child welfare organisations have been a little chary in the past of anything labelled 'psychiatry', although preventive advisory work has always had an important place in their scheme.[3] Recent suggestions that voluntary workers helping in a centre would be useful members of a team in 'group discussions', when problems have been encountered, show an appreciation of modern educational methods, while overtures from the N.A.M.H. to the National Association for Maternal and Child Welfare have been warmly accepted.[4] They had much in common since the child guidance centres have had a generation of experience in team work where the training of parents in an understanding of the child's emotional needs has taken a prominent part.

We should note, too, the recognition of the need to go further back in preventive work, to the parents' own problems. One example of official interest in this question is the policy of grant-aiding national organisations concerned with marriage counselling,[5] and 'family discussion'. These and other bodies concerned with educational and advisory work are instances of the modern recognition of the importance of psychological and social adjustment.

Greater awareness of the link between psychological and social questions has led to developments not only in projects on behalf of emotionally disturbed parents or maladjusted children, but also in the training and appointment of social workers in many fields. In the sphere of mental health such a link had already been firmly established, and the role of the psychiatric social workers, whether in the child guidance clinic or the mental hospital, is now recognised as essential. Her place in

[1] E.g. Prof. Bowlby's study 'Maternal Care and Mental Health' (W.H.O. Monograph Series 2, 1951).
[2] Note the pamphlet sponsored by the Ministry of Health prepared from broadcast talks by a doctor closely associated with the N.A.M.H. where this approach is emphasised.
[3] See an interesting article in *Public Health* (the Journal of the Society of Medical Officers of Health),Vol. LXVIII, No. 4, Jan. 1955.
[4] See also the Report of the Committee on Maladjusted Children (Ministry of Education) which recommends a close link between child welfare centres and child guidance clinics.
[5] The F.W.A., one of the three organisations receiving grants, has, as an experienced case work agency, offered training courses for the other workers in this field, while its own 'Family Discussion Bureau' has for several years been engaged on a research project.

community care[1] is, however, only just beginning to be appreciated by statutory authorities. Although several of the larger local authorities[2] had already included a few P.S.W.s on their staff after a period of experiment in co-operation with voluntary organisations, only a very small proportion throughout the country have so far made such appointments.[3] In view of the shortage of trained social workers, the N.A.M.H. is urging the acceptance in principle of the need to provide short training courses for the various mental health workers who have been appointed to carry out the duties of the local health authority. The organisation has sent deputations to the Minister of Health and has itself offered to co-operate in providing such courses, so far without positive result. The situation is still fluid as the Minister awaits the final reports of the statutory committees considering related questions. The necessity for psychiatric consultation has also been accepted by a number of family casework agencies. It is now becoming a recognised pattern for a consultant psychiatrist, or a P.S.W., to be either a full-time member of staff or to be available for regular consultation on a part-time basis.[4] This new emphasis has arisen from the growing awareness of the problems of social adjustment which lie behind so many applications for help. The relationship between such voluntary organisations and the statutory bodies has been strengthened by this development in skill; many of the 'referrals' from the National Assistance Board, disablement resettlement officers, health visitors, hospital almoners, and other workers in the field are connected with the clients' need for psychological and social support rather than for material help.[5]

Two recent reports have stressed the importance of psychological factors in family relationships within the community: *An Enquiry into Health Visiting*[6] suggests that in addition to their essential function of health education and social advice, health visitors 'should be able to take account of psychological factors' in their 'important if unspectacular role in relation to mental health'. The *Report of the Committee on Maladjusted Children*[7] makes special reference to prevention, and the promotion of mental health, and pays tribute to bodies like the N.A.M.H. in helping to bring about the changed outlook which

[1] It is of interest to note that the Association of Psychiatric Social Workers has just formed a branch of P.S.Ws. doing community care.
[2] E.g. Middlesex County Council and the London County Council.
[3] See a notice in *Mental Health*, Vol. XV, No. 3, Summer 1956: Of 447 qualified P.S.Ws. employed in the mental health field 182 were in hospitals, 138 in child guidance clinics, 95 in other types of work and only 32 employed by local health authorities.
[4] The F.W.A. has appointed an experienced P.S.W. to its H.Q. staff, and psychiatrists are available for consultation in various districts.
[5] See an article in *The Medical Officer*, 94, 351–353, 16/12/1955.
[6] The report (1956) of a Working Party appointed by the Ministry of Health, the Department of Health for Scotland and the Ministry of Education.
[7] Report, 1955, Ministry of Education.

encourages the development of an environment, and attitudes of mind conducive to mental health.

This brings us to a current problem of some difficulty. The need to consider the family as a whole is now recognised by all social workers, yet the desire to make full use of skilled workers, many of whom are specialists in their branches of social service, is equally strong. We must note, too, that local authorities have a statutory duty to visit under certain conditions. If overlap and overvisiting of particular families are to be avoided much thought has to be given to the question of the co-ordination of effort. Some of the voluntary societies had already been trying out the idea of the 'case conference', bringing together for discussion all those concerned with the family in question. This method has now been officially accepted in principle,[1] and consideration is being given to the possibility of forming a composite casework unit, principally in New Towns where an experiment might well be carried out. But there are outstanding difficulties to be faced in practice, not least the education of any untrained workers involved, in the professional attitude towards confidential information. Close co-operation between various local authority departments concerned with the same family, and between statutory and voluntary agencies is equally vital.[2] When questions of policy are under discussion public and private effort are often usefully combined in the standing conference or joint committee, whether through existing groups such as community associations, or by the setting up of *ad hoc* bodies. Organisations like the National Council of Social Service continue to play a valuable part in fostering such developments. The N.C.S.S. also offers a forum for the discussion of questions of common interest to a large number of local authorities and voluntary organisations. This is closely related to the need, increasingly recognised to-day, for the administrator and the social worker to understand each other's point of view and to work in closer harmony.

Trained social workers can often help considerably to foster good liaison work. While qualified workers are in short supply it is of the greatest importance to see that they are well placed in key positions to act in the capacity of consultant or supervisor. Where a psychiatric social worker appointed by a county health authority receives clients referred by the National Assistance Board, hospital almoners, general practitioners or workers in a citizens' advice bureau, we have a practical demonstration of her value in this role.[3] When less highly trained officers are helped to detect a need, guided in coping with minor problems, and

[1] See recent circulars from the Ministry of Health in which this method receives favourable mention.
[2] Reference is made earlier in the text to discussion of the lack of liaison between the welfare and the health and education Departments of some local authorities (see Southern Regional Association for the Blind), p. 250, above.
[3] Cf. *The Medical Officer*, 16th December, 1955 (94, 351–353), article by Eugene Heimler: 'Psychiatric Social Work with National Assistance Board Cases'.

advised when to refer those requiring special skill, the role of supervisor is seen to be of the utmost value. These results are being achieved to-day in only a few areas. More such 'key appointments' would go far towards meeting the acute shortage of social workers in community care.

One unresolved and closely related issue is the place of the 'all purpose visitor'. It has come to a head in consideration of the new demands for the welfare of the physically handicapped. Those who have long been concerned with special groups, such as the blind, have built up skills and techniques, and they resist the suggestion that a general social worker could take the place of a qualified home teacher. They argue that even if she were capable of recognising a need she would not have the special skill to meet it. On the other hand, there is a suggestion[1] that the training of the higher-grade feeble-minded might well be carried out within the framework of the general social services, rather than through a special mental deficiency service. The achievement of unity and coherence in administration would be matched by the absorption of this group into the community without the need for certification and the attachment of a label which links them with idiots and imbeciles. Obviously a good deal of thought will have to be given to the right deployment of special skills to see that services which have reached a high degree of efficiency are not allowed to deteriorate. At the same time the public is now aware of other groups, long neglected, whose claims must receive attention. It is no easy matter to achieve a true balance.

The situation is further complicated by a recent tendency to form sectional groups amongst the physically handicapped, cutting right across the movement towards amalgamation worked out by the older voluntary societies. In demanding new services it is the sufferers themselves, or their parents, the 'consumer groups', who have been most urgent. The National Spastics Society, for example, founded in 1952, was essentially a parents' movement. Grimly determined to bring the needs of this little-known disabled group before the public eye, they pursued a vigorous campaign and launched large, successful appeals for funds. But they did it without reference to the British Council for the Welfare of Spastics which had been working since 1946 on scientific lines[2] to promote research and to act as an advisory and co-ordinating body: its activities were too slow-moving for the parents anxious to see immediate results. If the experience and professional knowledge of the one could be united with the enthusiasm and flair for publicity of the other, combined action would make for an enlightened public opinion and an effective service.

[1] See article in *Mental Health*, Vol. XV, No. 3, Summer 1956, 'The Mental Deficiency Services To-day and To-morrow', by J. Tizard.
[2] The British Council for the Welfare of Spastics represented professional interests, both medical and educational.

INFLUENCES AFFECTING THE RELATIONSHIP

Several attempts have been made by more experienced organisations to bring together all those concerned with the handicapped, and there are signs that the first impatience with traditional methods may be lessening. One group which has received less publicity is that of 'The National Association of Parents of Backward Children'. They have shown their appreciation of the work of the National Association for Mental Health by asking them to manage on their behalf a special home for which they provided the funds. The N.A.M.H. has been fortunate, too, in securing the co-operation of another new society, the Mental Health Research Fund. In this instance there is close liaison through cross-representation on committees, and through a happy arrangement whereby the N.A.M.H. has been able to offer offices in the same building.[1] Occasionally the movement has been in the opposite direction, when an older society has itself suggested a splitting off. This occurred when the N.A.M.H. agreed that, with the advance of medical knowledge on the treatment available for epileptics, the *British Epilepsy Association* should no longer be kept under the mental health umbrella. The N.A.M.H. was still prepared to co-operate if advice on the mental health of a patient were needed.[2]

There is no sign that the older organisations are preserving a rigid attitude, content to rest on their laurels. With the financial backing of the great trust funds many new projects have been started. Some of them have been suggested in the first instance by the central authority; all of them have the active encouragement of the Ministries concerned. Some are supported by local authorities.[3] Most are in the nature of pilot experiments, such as the two five-year projects of the F.W.A.,[4] or the scheme for blind adolescents at Hethersett.[5] Interest in research continues to be characteristic of large foundations, such as the Carnegie and the Pilgrim or, more recently, the Nuffield Trusts. Voluntary organisations, by virtue of their traditional interest in experimental work, are natural vehicles for the use of grants from these sources; such combined action would seem to be an established pattern in the development of the social services.

The early interest of the great national societies in development overseas has considerably expanded. The linking of the British organisations

---

[1] The two societies recently shared the proceeds of a joint flag day appeal.

[2] In the same way the Family Discussion Bureau moved, by agreement, from the aegis of the F.W.A. to become an activity of the Tavistock Institute of Human Relations.

[3] E.g. the enquiry 'Over Seventy', sponsored by the N.C.S.S., with the support of the Halley Stewart Trust, had the full co-operation of the Hammersmith Metropolitan Borough Council.

[4] One concerned with questions of marital disharmony—carried through by the Family Discussion Bureau—the other seeking to arrive at an understanding of 'problem families'. A further three-year scheme is concerned with the welfare of West Indian immigrants.

[5] See p. 247, above.

with World Federations, the establishment of international seminars to supplement conferences, the new emphasis in journals concerned with social welfare on problems in other countries, the readiness to welcome an increasing number of overseas enquirers[1] are features of recent growth. Whereas pioneer British workers brought back ideas from abroad, as they launched their new movements early in the century, recent developments in the social services and the unique partnership built up between statutory and voluntary agencies in Great Britain have in turn attracted wide attention from all parts of the world. Interest has been so far stimulated that some of the voluntary organisations would be relieved if extra funds were available to meet this welcome but exacting part of their responsibilities.[2] One comment on this use of voluntary organisations is worth making. Not only have the national and regional associations continued to emphasise their consultative function but they have been aware of the need to keep their feet on the ground if the value of their advisory work is to be preserved. Their close relationship with statutory bodies depends upon their active participation in schemes for the development of the social services: only so can they speak from experience and invite confidence.

In this study we have been particularly concerned with the development of care within the community as distinct from institutional care. Voluntary bodies, together with an increasing number of local authorities, have established their claim that it is in this field that the roots of preventive work lie. To-day, the preventive aspects of health are an issue of some urgency, and it is increasingly realised that only with adequate community care can breakdown be avoided or the risk of relapse minimised. It is difficult to prove statistically that an increase of expenditure on community care is more than met by a saving in the cost of institutional accommodation, but progressive areas, like Birmingham for example, believe that this is true.[3] The shortage of social workers creates a real problem as new uses for their services are realised. The situation is aggravated as experienced local government officers, like some of the old relieving officers, reach retiring age.[4] There is, therefore, even more need for the provision of introductory courses and supplementary training courses such as those offered by many of the experi-

[1] Including many serious students for whom planned programmes of observation are arranged.
[2] The Ministries concerned also do much to answer such enquiries, but they are glad to be able to refer their visitors to the voluntary organisations for more detailed information.
[3] Cf. the recent experiment in the care of old people within the community and the consequent saving of beds in hospital wards, or the licensing of patients from institutions to do useful work under guidance, as in the wartime agricultural hostel experiments.
[4] The relieving officer, in spite of shortcomings due to the traditional Poor Law background, brought a wealth of experience to his tasks. Newer appointments are being made in some instances, when neither qualification nor experience can be commanded.

enced voluntary bodies, in addition to 'training on the job' on which most have to rely to-day.

The voluntary organisations have much to give as they co-operate in the development of social policy, but some of them have to work under constant strain to meet their financial commitments. Grants from trust funds are usually on a short-term basis, for an experimental period; payments from statutory bodies are dependent on the goodwill of the authority; the public is not always enlightened in its charitable giving and some of the less spectacular work has no immediate appeal. It is notoriously difficult to raise funds for general purposes connected with family casework or mental health, though the public may respond generously to specific appeals such as those on behalf of the blind or the spastic child.[1] It is a traditional part of the work of voluntary associations to educate public opinion, but it is sometimes difficult to combine publicity for appeal purposes with the pursuit of sterner interests. There is no doubt that voluntary effort, both in personal service and in charitable giving, is still active to-day. One of the main problems is to direct the flow of financial aid where it is most needed. Another is to persuade all local authorities that voluntary societies have a useful and complementary part to play: that they are in fact 'an essential part of the British social services'.

This study suggests that there is urgent need to strengthen the financial relationship. It has shown that, although the principle of co-operation is officially acknowledged, there are still areas where joint action receives little or no support; there are a number of voluntary societies of proved worth which are struggling against heavy odds to make their full contribution[2]: already increasing costs and reduced income have forced some of these to limit their activities. If individual citizens have cut down their charitable donations in view of their own increased commitments, or under the impression that social legislation has now made adequate provision for social needs, it is all the more necessary for the community, collectively, to see that social policy on voluntary-statutory co-operation is carried out, and that the wide powers given to local authorities to grant-aid voluntary organisations are wisely used.

There are encouraging signs of greater readiness on the part of local authorities to use these powers. Some final tables of the expenditure of the L.C.C., both directly and through voluntary organisations, will illustrate the extent to which a large and powerful statutory body has

[1] It is significant that a recent broadcast appeal on behalf of the physically handicapped produced ten times the amount received in a similar appeal for the mentally handicapped.
[2] It is worth quoting again from the Nathan Report: 'In general it would be true to say that it is the modern societies best fitted to meet the needs of to-day which are the shortest of funds and which suffer most from lack of popular appeal' (*The Law and Practice Relating to Charitable Trusts*, p. 13).

CHANGING ROLE OF VOLUNTARY ORGANISATIONS

continued to value co-operation with voluntary societies. It will be seen from these tables that the payments made to voluntary organisations were still substantial after 1948, although many had feared that such societies would be redundant once the National Health Service was in operation. In the case of services for the physically handicapped, and to a lesser extent in the mental health services, the amounts so paid increased both absolutely and relatively to the direct expenditure of the Council. On the other hand, the L.C.C.'s own services for mothers and children expanded considerably, and there was some contraction in the payments to voluntary associations. Voluntary maternity and child welfare services[1] were, however, still heavily subsidised, and these payments, together with those to moral welfare organisations, showed an increase.[2]

Not all local authorities have responded in this way. It has been characteristic of the development of social policy that initiative should be encouraged. Central authorities have been eager to see that social legislation should not be too tightly drawn.[3] If flexibility has resulted in diversity, creating wide differences between progressive and backward areas, it has also had the advantage of offering opportunities for experiment. Some of the greatest of these have been undertaken in co-operation with voluntary organisations.

---

[1] These included well-known centres such as the Violet Melchett which remained under voluntary management.
[2] It was the mothers' and babies' homes and the organisations arranging recuperative holidays which lost most.
[3] E.g. the practice of placing local authorities under an obligation, not 'to provide' a service, but 'to secure the provision of' a service: or, again, the power 'to make arrangements for the purpose of...' as in Part II of the National Health Service Act. See the Nathan Report, pp. 159–160, for a discussion of this point.

TABLE XIII

Expenditure by the L.C.C. on Services for Mothers and Children
[Directly and through Voluntary Associations]

Year	I Total expenditure under Sec. 22, N.H.S. Act (excluding day nurseries and child-minders)	II Payments to Voluntary Associations (included in I)							III Expenditure incurred directly by the Council (I less II)	IV II as % of III
		a Family planning	b Mother-craft in-patients	c Mother and baby homes	d Maternity and child welfare	e Moral welfare	f Recupera-tive holidays†	Total a–f		
	£	£	£	£	£	£	£	£	£	
1948–9*	369,728	—	—	21,608‡	23,703	4,710	19,603	69,624	300,104	23·2
1949–50	588,756	33	—	15,862	42,285	7,245	32,429	97,854	490,902	19·9
1950–51	626,154	1,087	—	13,238	46,758	7,200	33,957	102,240	523,914	19·9
1951–52	602,525	559	121	13,772	37,103	9,160	30,083	90,798	511,727	17·7
1952–53	611,651	465	—	12,489	42,901	9,285	18,010	83,150	528,501	15·7
1953–54	563,899	461	—	14,629	45,891	8,635	12,620	82,236	481,663	17·1
1954–55	597,698	345	—	10,845	48,320	9,550	9,739	78,799	518,899	15·2

* Nine months only.
† For children under five, nursing and expectant mothers.
‡ For whole year.

TABLE XIV

Expenditure by the L.C.C. on the Mental Health Services
[Directly and through Voluntary Associations]

Year	I Expenditure under Sec. 51, N.H.S. Act		II Expenditure under Sec. 28, N.H.S. Act‡		III Expenditure incurred directly by the Council (Col. Ia, less Ib)	IV Expenditure through voluntary associations§ (Col. IIa+b and Ib)	V IV as % of III
	a Total	b† On guardian-ship cases	a Care and after-care	b Recuperative holidays			
	£	£	£	£	£	£	
1948–9*	64,586	11,836	638	—	52,750	12,474	23·6
1949–50	122,926	12,933	12,575	—	109,993	25,508	23·2
1950–51	133,799	11,748	14,465	1,253	122,051	27,466	22·5
1951–52	140,234	12,195	16,739	945	128,039	29,879	23·3
1952–53	155,496	12,939	19,740	2,475	142,557	35,154	24·7
1953–54	179,873	14,126	21,485	2,180	165,747	37,791	22·8
1954–55	188,146	15,009	24,246	3,237	173,137	42,492	24·5

* Nine months only.
† Payments principally, but not entirely, to voluntary organisations.
‡ All payments to voluntary associations.
§ It should be noted that this unavoidably includes a small amount spent directly by the Council. See (1).

INFLUENCES AFFECTING THE RELATIONSHIP

TABLE XV

Expenditure by the L.C.C. on Services for the Welfare of Handicapped Persons (including the Blind)
[Directly and through Voluntary Associations]

Year	I Expenditure incurred directly by the Council*					II Expenditure incurred through voluntary Associations				III
	a Domiciliary assistance†	b Maintenance of residents in small houses‡	c Pastime, occupation and social centres	d Miscellaneous	Total (a+b+c+d)	a Maintenance in residential accommodation (handicapped including blind)	b Payments re blind in workshops and home workers	c General welfare§	Total (a+b+c)	II as % of I
	£	£	£	£	£	£	£	£	£	
1948–49	50,042	18,534	3,037	1,478	130,680	16,547	39,148	1,894	57,589	44
1949–50	—	16,171	2,284	4,215	100,137	35,350	40,352	1,765	77,467	77
1950–51	—	18,165	3,993	4,732	112,205	38,102	45,526	1,687	85,315	76
1951–52	—	18,348	4,691	4,200	123,136	45,886	48,234	1,777	95,897	78
1952–53	—	19,411	6,248	4,271	148,426	60,069	56,111	2,316	118,496	80
1953–54	—	17,332	6,748	4,122	154,937	65,334	59,354	2,047	126,735	81
1954–55	—	20,034	5,095	6,370	164,861	70,885	60,660	1,817	133,362	81

* These figures do not include central administrative expenses or the salaries etc. of home visitors and guides, which are not available.
† Ceased from 5th July, 1948.
‡ A certain number of blind persons were maintained in public institutions, general and mental hospitals prior to 5th July, 1948, and since that date there have been blind and other handicapped persons in Council large homes and other small homes for whom no reliable assessment of cost can be made.
§ E.g. provision of music, literature, etc.

BIBLIOGRAPHY

For Publications of Societies see p. 298.
For Government Publications (a) Acts of Parliament see p. 299.
  (b) Reports of Royal Commissions, etc. see p. 300.
  (c) Annual Reports, etc. see p. 302.

ANSON, P. F.: *The Call of the Cloister*, 1955: 12 n.
ASHDOWN, M., and BROWN, S.C.: *Social Service and Mental Health*, 1953: 116 n., 121 n., 150 n.
BALLANTYNE, Dr.: *Manual of Ante-Natal Pathology and Hygiene*, 1902: 37 n.
BELL, G. K. A.: *Randall Davidson*, 1938: 9 n., 18 n.
BELL, E. MOBERLY: *Life of Octavia Hill*, 1942: 15 n.
BEVERIDGE, LORD: *Voluntary Action*, 1948: xi n., 21 n.; *see also* Statutory Committee's Reports.
BLACKER, C. P.: *Neurosis and the Mental Health Services*, 1948: 98 n.
BOOTH, CHARLES: *Life and Labour of the People of London*, 17 vols., 1889–1902: 5 n., 20 n., 24.
BOOTH, W. (General): *In Darkest England*, 1890: 11, 12
BOURDILLON, A. F. P. (ed.): *Voluntary Social Services*, 1945: 186 n., 188 n., 210 n.
BOWLBY, J.: *Maternal Care and Mental Health*, 1951: 75 n., 285 n.
BRAITHWAITE, C.: *The Voluntary Citizen*, 1938: 54 n., 260 n.
BURT, Dr. CYRIL: *The Young Delinquent*, 1944: 116 n.
CADOGAN, Dr.: *Enquiry into Infant Mortality. An Essay upon Nursing and the Management of Children from their Birth to Three Years of Age*, 1754–60: 31 n.
CARPENTER, S.C.: *Church and People*, 1933: 8 n.
CHURCH, M. C. (ed.): *Life and Letters of Dean Church*, 1894: 9 n.
COHEN, E. W.: *English Social Services*, 1949: 100 n., 273 n., 278 n.
CONNOLLY, Dr.: *Enquiry Concerning the Indications of Insanity . . .*, 1844: 93
CROWTHER, Dr.: *Practical Remarks on Insanity* 1811: 90, 91 n.
EAGER, W. McG.: contrib. *Social Security*, 1943: 222 n.
FERGUSON, S. and FITZGERALD, H.: *Civilian Health and Medical Services*, 1954: xi n., 66 n., 159 n., 280 n.
Feversham Committee: *Voluntary Mental Health Services*, 1939: 112 n., 122 n., 126 n., 167 n., 168 n.
FORSTER, E. M.: *Marianne Thornton*, 1956: 24 n.
FRAZER, W. M.: *A History of English Public Health*, 1950: 32 n.
GEORGE, M. D.: *England in Transition*, 1931: 7 n.
HAWKINS, Rev. H.
  A Plea for Convalescent Homes, 1871: 93 n.
  'After Care', 1879 (*Journal of Mental Science*: papers): 93 n.
HEIMLER, E.: 'Psychiatric Social Work with N.A.B. Cases' (*The Medical Officer*, Dec. 1955): 287 n.
JONES, K.: *Lunacy, Law and Conscience*, 1955: 5 n., 82 n., 91 n.
LINDSAY, W. L.: *The Theory and Practice of Non-Restraint . . .*, 1878: 93 n.
LOCH, C. S.
  3000 *Years of Social Service*, 1910: 19 n., 20 n., 192 n.
  Contribution to *Charities Register and Digest*: 199 n.
LOMAX, Dr.: *The Experiences of an Asylum Doctor*, 1921: 112 n.
London County Council: *London Statistics*: 212 n., 231 n., 249

BIBLIOGRAPHY

McCleary, Dr.
The Early History of the Infant Welfare Movement, 1933: ix, 33 n., 34 n., 35 n., 36 n., 38, 39, 41 n., 61 n.
The Maternity and Child Welfare Movement, 1935: 38 n.
The Development of British Maternity and Child Welfare Services, 1945: 38 n., 62 n., 63 n., 64 n., 74 n.
Mencher, Samuel: *Relationship of Voluntary and Statutory Agencies...*, 1954: xi n., 270 n.
Mess, H. A.: *Voluntary Social Services*, 1948: xi n.
Newman, Dr.: *The Health of the State*, 1913 ed.: 32 n., 38, 67 n.
Nuffield Foundation: *Voluntary Social Services*, ed. Bourdillon, A. F. P., 1945: xi n., 186 n., 188 n., 210 n.
Odlum, Dr. Doris: *You and Your Children* (Ministry of Health Pamphlet), 1946: 74 n.
Peck, W. G.: *Social Effects of the Oxford Movement*, 1933: 9 n.
Petty, Miss R. F.: *The Education of the Blind under the London School Board*, 1902?: 183 n.
Peyser, Dr. D.,: *The Strong and the Weak*, 1951: 24 n.
Pinsent, Dame E. F.: *Mental Health Services, Oxford,* etc.: 103 n.
Raven, C. E.: *Christian Socialism*, 1920: 11 n.
Raverat, G.: *Period Piece*, 1954: 24 n.
Robson, W., ed.: *Social Security*, 1943: 210 n., 222 n., 255 n.
Rogers, B.: 'The Social Science Association 1857-1886', *The Manchester School of Economics,* XX, No. 3, 1952: 7 n.
Rooff, M.: *Youth and Leisure*, 1935: 14 n.
Simey, M. B.: *Charitable Work in Liverpool*, 1951: 10 n., 13 n., 24 n.
Smith, Prof. J. M.: *Professional Education for Social Work in Britain*, 1952: 257 n.
Soddy, Dr. K.,
'Mental Health Community Care' (*British Medical Bulletin* Vol. 6 No. 3, 1949):
'Some Lessons of War-Time Psychiatry' (*N.A.M.H. pamphlet*): 150 n.
Sorsby, Prof. A.
Causes of Blindness (Memo 24, 1950, Medical Research Council) 220 n.
Causes of Blindness in England (Ministry of Health, 1953): 220 n., 221, 244 n.
Southern Regional Association for the Blind: *Regional Review*: 245
Thomas, R., *see* N.A.M.H. advisory pamphlets: 163 n.
Thurnam, Dr.: *Statistics of Insanity*, 1845: 84 n.
Tiffany, F.: *Life of Dorothea Lynde Dix*, 1891: 92 n.
Tillotson, K.: *Novels of the Eighteen Forties*, 1954: 7 n.
Titmuss, Prof. R.
Problems of Social Policy, 1950: 150 n.
Introduction to J. M. Smith, *Professional Education for Social Work,* 1952: 257 n.
Tizard, J., *see Mental Health*, Vol. XV, No. 3, 1956: 288 n.
Tredgold, Dr. R. F. (ed.): *Mental Health*: 163 n.
Trevelyan, J.: *Voluntary Service and the State* (N.C.S.S., 1952): xii
Tuke, S.: *The Retreat*, 1813: 92 n.
Webb, S. and B.: *English Local Government*, Vol. VIII, 1927: 15 n.
Wilson, H. J. (contributor): *Charities Register and Digest*, 1899 *et seq*: 177 n., 185 n., 186 n., 187 n.
Wilson, J. F. (contributor): *Voluntary Social Services*, 1945: 186 n., 191 n.
Young, A. F. and Ashton, E. T.: *British Social Work in the Nineteenth Century*, 1956: xi n.
Zilboorg, G. and Henry G.: *A History of Medical Psychology*, 1941: 90 n., 92 n., 93 n., 97 n., 116 n.

BIBLIOGRAPHY

PUBLICATIONS OF SOCIETIES

British Journal of Psychology: 284 n.
British National Conference on Social Work, 1953: *The Family*: 266 n.
Central Association for Mental Welfare
   Memo. on *The Care of the Mentally Deficient after the War*, 1917?: 107
   Report of *Enquiry into the Care, Training and Employment of Epileptics*, 1936: 132
Charity Organisation Society, *see also* Loch, C. S.
   Charities Register and Digest: 85 n., 89 n., 100 n., 101 n., 102 n., 104 n., 177 n., 180 n., 185 n., 186 n., 187 n., 188 n., 192 n., 195 n., 196, 197 n., 199 n., 219 n., 231, 259, 265
   Report on *The Education and Care of Idiots, Imbeciles and Harmless Lunatics*, 1875: 100
Gardner's Trust: *The Blind*: 182 n., 183 n., 184 n., 195 n.
International Conference on Social Work, Report: *Promoting Social Welfare through Self-Help and Co-operative Action*, 1954: 255
International Journal of Psycho-Analysis: 116 n.
Joint Committee of Royal College of Obstetricians and Gynaecologists and the Population Investigation Committee: Report on *Maternity in Great Britain*, 1948: 30 n., 69 n., 71 n.
The Medical Officer: 74 n., 286 n., 287 n.
National Association for Maternal and Child Welfare
   Maternal and Child Welfare: 39 n., 74
   To Mothers and Fathers: 68
National Association for Mental Health
   Mental Health: 137 n., 150 n., 155 n., 163, 286 n., 288 n.
   Annual Reports: 154 n., 256
   Advisory pamphlets: 163 n.
National Baby Welfare Council: *Mother and Child*: 59 n., 73
National Council of Social Service
   Social Service: 105 n.
   Over 70, 1954: 266 n., 289 n.
   See also Women's Group on Public Welfare
National League for Health, Maternity and Child Welfare: *Health Visiting in Rural Areas*, 1911 (pamphlet): 43 n.
National League of the Blind: *The Blind Advocate*; 179
Royal National Institute for the Blind
   Bulletin 7, 'A History of Blind Welfare': 181 n., 226 n.
   Bulletin 15, 'Blind Welfare after the War': 235 n.
   N.I.B. *Annual Reports*: 200 n., 229 n.
   A Guide to the Institutions and Charities for the Blind, 1884: 176 n.
   Directory of Agencies for the Blind: 242 n.
   The New Beacon: 236 n., 239 n.
Society of Medical Officers of Health: *Public Health*; 285 n.
Union of Counties Associations: Reports on
   Certification of Blindness and Ascertainment of Causes, 1931
   Hereditary Blindness, 1933
   Causes, 1936
   Cataract, 1937
   Analysis of Classification of Causes, 1938: 219 n.
   Prevention of Blindness: 220
Women's Group on Public Welfare (N.C.S.S.): *Our Towns: A Close Up*, 1943: 29 n., 64 n., 68, 256 n.
World Federation for Mental Health: *World Mental Health*: 164

BIBLIOGRAPHY

GOVERNMENT PUBLICATIONS
ACTS OF PARLIAMENT

Ballot Act, 1872: 215 n., 224
Blind Persons Act, 1920: 22 n., 186 n., 208–10, 216, 221, 222 n., 225, 226 n., 228, 236
Blind Persons Act, 1938: 186 n., 211 n., 214, 217 n., 229
Blind Voters Act, 1933: 215, 224
Children and Young Persons Act, 1933: 152 n.
Children and Young Persons (Amendment) Act, 1952: 254 n.
Choice of Employment Act, 1910: 184 n.
Contagious Diseases Acts, 1864, 1866, 1869: 15
Customs and Inland Revenue Act, 1878: 194 n.
Disabled Persons (Employment) Act, 1944: 159, 160, 236
Education Acts, 1870, 1876: 4, 18, 32 n., 195, 262
Education Act, 1902: 18, 86 n., 102 n., 182, 197
Education Act, 1918: 49 n., 107, 215
Education Act, 1921: 22 n., 152 n.
Education Act, 1944: 143 n., 159–61 *passim*, 241, 262
Elementary Education (Blind and Deaf Children) Act, 1893: 23 n., 32 n., 181, 192 n., 196, 215
Elementary Education (Defective and Epileptic Children) Act, 1899: 32 n., 86, 88 n.
Elementary Education Act, 1914: 115
Factories Acts, 1801 *et seq*: 31 n.
Franchise Act, 1867: 4
Huddersfield Corporation Act, 1906: 36 n.
Idiots Act, 1886: 85
Infant Life Protection Act, 1872: 31 n.
Insane Persons:
    An Act to regulate the Care and Treatment of Insane Persons in England, 1828: 84 n.
Labour Bureaux (London) Act, 1902: 184
Labour Exchanges Act, 1909: 102 n., 184 n.
Local Government Act, 1888: 22 n.
Local Government Act, 1894: 15 n.
Local Government Act, 1929:
    transference of functions of Poor Law Guardians: 21 n.; added responsibility of local authorities: 52, 211, 228 n., 259; responsibility for inspection: 55 n., 211, 222, 224
    effect of Local Government Act: on M.D.s in institutions: 110 n., 115; on pauper lunatics: 113
    co-operation, voluntary-statutory, affected by: 192 n., 211, 227; local authorities and domiciliary assistance: 210, 214, 222; pressure from voluntary societies: 60, 61 n., 137
    effect on finance of voluntary organisations: 52, 117, 124 n., 211, 222, 259
Local Government Act, 1948: 14 n.
London (General Powers) Act, 1908: 39
Lunacy Act, 1890: 79, 82 n., 85, 89, 112, 113, 116 n., 118 n., 140, 148, 155 n., 158 n., 259
Lunatic Asylums:
    An Act to Amend the Laws for the Erection and Regulation of County Lunatic Asylums, etc., 1828: 84 n.
    An Act for the Provision and Regulation of, 1845: 85 n.
Lunatics: An Act for the Regulation of the Care and Treatment of, 1845: 85 n.
Maternity and Child Welfare Act, 1918: 22 n., 49, 53, 55, 70 n., 214

BIBLIOGRAPHY

Mental Deficiency Acts, 1913 and 1927: 22 n., 79 n., 88–9, 100 n., 103, 104 n., 107–08, 110, 114 n., 124, 136, 140, 143, 153 n., 163 n., 263
  effect on foundation of C.A.M.W.: 103, 263; effect of Local Government Act: 22 n.; certification under M.D. Acts: 79 n.; provisions of the M.D. Act, 1913: 88–9, 104 n.; amendments, 1927: 114, 124; classification of M.D.: 100 n.; effect of war on 1st M.D. Act: 114; indifference of local authorities to: 100, 115; influence of voluntary societies on: 103, 107–8; consultation on amendments: 136; further co-operation: 140, 143–4, 153 n., 163 n.; co-operation in Cambridge: 147–8; recognition of Diploma Course under M.D. Act: 154 n.; need for training of duly authorised officers: 155 n.
Mental Treatment Act, 1930: effect of M.T. Act: 79; voluntary patients, etc.: 82 n., 85, 89 n.; further powers under M.T. Act: 113; responsibilities of local authorities: 117; co-operation with voluntary societies: 118, 144; C.A.M.W. influence on M.T. Bill: 136
Midwives Act, 1902: 33
Midwives Act, 1936: 33 n., 53, 55
National Assistance Act, 1948:
  effect in field of mental health: 155 n., 160, 161
  effect in field of blind welfare: 208 n., 242 n.; mandatory sections of: 240; Homes of Recovery under: 241 n.
  assistance for the handicapped: 160, 240, Table xv
  possibilities for co-operation in wide field: 248–9, 278
National Health Service Act, 1948: 30, 35 n., 69–72, 79, 80, 85 n., 126 n., 146 n., 153 n., 155, 156, 159–66, 241, 242 n., 294
  need for co-ordination: 30; role of health visitor: 35 n.; effect in field of maternity and child welfare: 69–72; mental health: 79, 80, 85 n., 126 n., 146 n., 153 n., 155, 156, 159–66 *passim*, Table xiv; blind welfare: 241–2
Notification of Births Act, 1907: 33, 34, 45, 51 n.
Notification of Births Act, 1915: 46, 70 n., 199
Old Age Pensions Act, 1908: 102 n.
Old Age Pensions Acts, 1908–19: 208 n.
Poor Law Acts, 1862, 1867, 1879: 194 n.
Poor Law Act, 1930: 55
Post Office Amendment Act, 1935: 215
Prevention of Cruelty to Children Act, 1889: 31 n.
Public Health Act, 1875: 22 n., 33, 34, 45, 199
Public Health Act, 1925: 214 n., 218
Public Health Act, 1936: 70 n., 214, 220
Public Health (Tuberculosis) Act, 1921: 22 n.
Statute of Charitable Uses, 1601: 3
Statute of Poor Relief, 1601: 3, 194 n.
Trade Boards Act, 1909: 102 n.
Unemployed Workmen Act, 1905: 19 n.
Unemployment Act, 1934: 214
Vagrancy Act, 1744: 83
War Charities Act, 1916: 208
Wireless Telegraphy (Blind Persons Facilities) Act, 1926: 215

REPORTS OF ROYAL COMMISSIONS, DEPARTMENTAL COMMITTEES, &C.

Blind, Deaf and Dumb: Report of the Royal Commission on The Blind, Deaf and Dumb, etc., of the United Kingdom, 1889: 86, 182, 184, 196, 201, 203, 215
Blindness, Advisory Committee on (Min. Health), 1938: 219 n., 221
Blindness, Causes and Prevention: Report of the Departmental Committee on the Causes and Prevention of Blindness, 1922 (Chairman, Roberts, G. H.): 214, 219

BIBLIOGRAPHY

Blindness, The Causes of, in England: Report by Arnold Sorsby to the Minister of Health, 1953: 220 n., 221

Blind Persons, Employment: Report of the Working Party on the Employment of Blind Persons, 1951 (Ministry of Labour): 184 n., 218 n., 235 n., 236–40, 241, 247

Blind Welfare: Report of the Departmental Committee on the Welfare of the Blind, 1914–17: 178 n., 188, 189 n., 192 n., 200–04

Charitable Trusts: Report of the Committee on the Law and Practice Relating to Charitable Trusts, 1952 (Chairman, Lord Nathan): xi n., 13 n., 14 n., 19 n., 260 n., 283 n., 291 n.

Education: Report of the Royal Commission on the State of Public Education in England and Wales, 1861 (Newcastle Report): 18 n.

Feeble Minded, Report of the Royal Commission on the Care and Control of the, 1908: 86–8, 100 n., 101, 102, 111, 114, 115, 131 n.

Health Visiting:
  Memo. on Visiting, 1916, Dr. Newsholme: 47 n.
  Report of the Working Party of an Enquiry into the Field of Work, Training and Recruitment of Health Visitors, 1956 (Ministry of Health, Department of Health for Scotland, and Ministry of Education): 35, 286

Infant and Child Mortality: Special Report to Local Government Board, 1910, by Dr. Newsholme: 32 n.

Lunacy and Mental Disorder, Report of the Royal Commission on, 1926: 113, 136, 258

Lunatic Asylums: Report of the Royal Commission on the Conditions of Lunatic Asylums in Scotland, appointed 1855: 92

Madhouses: Report of the Select Committee . . . for the Better Regulation of Madhouses in England, 1815: 84

Maladjusted Children, Report of the Committee on, 1955 (Ministry of Education): 165, 285 n., 286

Marriage and Divorce, Report of the Royal Commission on, 1956: 165

Maternal Mortality and Morbidity, Report of the Departmental Committee on: interim report 1930, final report 1932: 53

Mental Deficiency: Report of the Joint Committee of the Board of Education and the Board of Control (Wood Committee), 1929: 82 n., 100 n., 114–5

Mental Hospitals, Public, Report of the Committee on the Administration of, 1922: 112, 117

Midwives, Report of the Working Party on, 1948 (Chairman, Mrs. Stocks) (Joint Com. of the Ministry of Health, Dept. of Health for Scotland and the Ministry of Labour and National Service): 69

Physical Deterioration of the Race, Report of the Departmental Committee on the, appointed 1904: 20 n., 32, 43

The Poor Laws, Royal Commission on, 1909: 20, 83 n., 102, 192, 258

Population, Royal Commission on, 1949: 68 n.

Rehabilitation: Report of the Interdepartmental Committee on the Rehabilitation and Resettlement of Disabled Persons, 1943 (Tomlinson Committee): 165, 189, 234–5

Second World War, History of the: U.K. Civil Series:
  Problems of Social Policy, 1950: 150 n.
  Civilian Health and Medical Services, 1954: xi n., 66 n., 159 n., 280 n.

Sexual Offences against Young Persons: Report of the Departmental Committee on, 1926: 136

Social Insurance and Allied Services: Report by Sir Wm. Beveridge, 1942: 235, 243, 279

Social Workers in the Mental Health Services: Report by the Mackintosh Committee: 155 n.

Sterilisation, Report of the Departmental Committee on, 1933 (Chairman, Sir L. Brock): 137

BIBLIOGRAPHY

ANNUAL REPORTS, CIRCULARS, &C.

Control, Board of: Annual Reports, Circulars, etc.: 98 n., 126, 138 n., 139 n., 142 n., 143 n., 144 n., 145 n., 146 n., 169
Education, Board of:
  Annual Reports: 60 n.
  Joint memoranda with Ministry of Health: 35, 223 n.
  Reports of departmental enquiries, *see* above under subject headings, e.g. Maladjusted Children
Health, Ministry of:
  Annual Reports, circulars, etc.
  in field of maternity and child welfare: 29 n., 53, 55 n., 68 n., 71 n., 75 n.
  in field of mental health: 153 n., 159 n., 169; child development (pamphlet): 285 n.
  in field of blind welfare: 173 n., 182 n., 206 n., 219 n.–226 n., 238 n., 244 n., 276 n.; handbook on welfare of the blind: 212 n.; Joint memo. on training: 223 n.; Reports of Advisory Committee on Welfare of Blind: 206 n., 208 n.–210 n., 216 n., 218 n., 219 n., 221 n.–225 n.
  Reports of Central Health Services Council: 70 n., 74 n.
  State of the Public Health during Six Years of War, 1946: 67 n.
Home Office: VIth Report of the Work of the Children's Department, 1951: 276 n.
Labour, Ministry of:
  Joint circular on recommendations of Working Party on Employment of Blind Persons: 238 n.
  Reports of Departmental Enquiries, *see* above under subject headings, e.g. Rehabilitation
Local Government Board: Circulars, etc: 45 n.–51 n.

VOLUNTARY SOCIETIES AND PROFESSIONAL ORGANISATIONS

(1) MATERNITY AND CHILD WELFARE

Association for the Welfare of Women and Girls: 94
Association of Infant Consultations: *see* Association of Maternity and Child Welfare Centres
Association of Maternity and Child Welfare Centres: 42 n., 61, 61 n., 62 n.
  formerly
    (1) Association of Infant Consultations: 43
    (2) Association of Infant Welfare and Maternity Centres: 43, 57, 61 n., 62 n., 64
  See also National Association for Maternal and Child Welfare
Central Council for Health Education: 68 n., 73
Central Council for Infant and Child Welfare: *see* National Council for Maternity and Child Welfare
Child Welfare Association, Merseyside: 56
International Association for the Protection of Child Welfare: 74
International Union for Child Welfare: 75
Ladies Health Society of Manchester and Salford: 4 n. (*formerly* Manchester and Salford Ladies Sanitary Reform Association: 34)
London Federation of Infant Welfare Centres: 64
London Obstetrical Society: 33 n.
Manchester and Salford Ladies Sanitary Reform Association: *see* Ladies Health Society of Manchester and Salford
Maternal Health Committee (*formerly* Maternal Mortality Committee): 39
Maternal Mortality Committee: *see* Maternal Health Committee
Midwives Institute: 33 n., 61
Mothercraft Training Society: 65 n., 67 n.
National Association for Maternal and Child Welfare: ix, 39 n., 62 n., 63 n., 64 n., 67–74 *passim*, 262 n., 285 n.
  formerly
    (1) National Association for the Prevention of Infant Mortality and for the Welfare of Infancy: 42, 55 n., 57 n., 62 n.
    (2) National Association of Maternity and Child Welfare Centres and for the Prevention of Infant Mortality: 42 n., 62 n.
    (3) National Association for Maternity and Child Welfare: 42 n., 59 n., 62 n.
National Association for Maternity and Child Welfare: *see* National Association for Maternal and Child Welfare
National Association for the Prevention of Infant Mortality, etc.: *see* National Association for Maternal and Child Welfare
National Association for the Unmarried Mother and Her Child: 73 n., 163 n.
National Association of Maternity and Child Welfare Centres, etc.: *see* National Association for Maternal and Child Welfare; *see also* Association of Maternity and Child Welfare Centres
National Baby Week Council: 44, 48, 63 n., 284; *see* National Baby Welfare Council

VOLUNTARY SOCIETIES, ETC.

National Baby Welfare Council (*formerly* National Baby Week Council): ix, 59, 73, 262 n.
National Council for Maternity and Child Welfare (*formerly* Central Council for Infant and Child Welfare): 51 n., 58, 59 n., 63, 64 n.
National Council for the Unmarried Mother and Her Child: 62; *see* National Association . . .
National Health Society: 51
National League for Health, Maternity and Child Welfare: 43–4, 58, 59 n., 61
 formerly National League for Physical Education and Improvement *federated with*
   (1) National Association for the Prevention of Infant Mortality, etc.
   (2) National League for Health, etc.
   (3) Association of Infant Welfare and Maternity Centres.
National League for Physical Education and Improvement: *see* National League for Health, Maternity and Child Welfare
Royal College of Midwives: 73 n.
St. Marylebone Health Society: 39

(2) MENTAL HEALTH

After-Care Association for the Female and Friendless Convalescent: *see* Mental After-Care Association
Association of Psychiatric Social Workers: 286 n.
Brighton Guardianship Society: 103, 110, 131
Cambridgeshire Voluntary Association for Mental Welfare: 147–8, 163
Central Association for Mental Welfare (*formerly* Central Association for the Care of Mental Defectives): ix, 26, 103, 104–8, 109–11 *passim*, 113, 115 n., 120 n., 122, 123–48, 149–53 *passim*, Table VII, 264, 267–8, 269, 270, 274, 279; *see also* National Association for Mental Health
Central Association for the Care of Mental Defectives: *see* Central Association for Mental Welfare
Child Guidance Council: 118 n., 120-2, 134, 139, 148, 149 n., 152 n.; *see also* National Association for Mental Health
Joint Committee for the Passing of the Mental Deficiency Bill: 103 n.
Lancashire and Cheshire Society for the Permanent Care of the Feeble-Minded: 104 n.
London Association for Mental Welfare: 143 n.
Medico-Psychological Association: 93 n.
Mental After-Care Association: ix, 23, 93–6, 98, 109, 116–19, 145, 149, 150 n., 156, 157, Table VI, 264
 changes in title: 94 n.
Mental Health Emergency Committee: 149
Mental Health Research Fund: 256, 289
Mental Hospitals Association: 137
National Association for the Care of the Feeble-Minded: *see* National Association for the Promotion of the Welfare of . . .
National Association for Mental Health: ix, 74, 105 n., 119–22 *passim*, 137 n., 149–55, 156 n., 157, 161–5, Table VII, 257 n., 268, 274–89 *passim*
National Association for the Promotion of the Welfare of the Feeble-Minded (*formerly* National Association for the Care of the Feeble-Minded): 100–03 *passim*
National Council for Mental Hygiene: 120, 122, 139, 149 n.; *see also* National Association for Mental Health
National Special Schools Union: 106 n.
North-Eastern Council for Mental Welfare: 131, 148
Provisional National Council for Mental Health: 149 n., 167
World Federation for Mental Health: 164, 256

VOLUNTARY SOCIETIES, ETC.
(3) BLIND WELFARE

Association of Workshops for the Blind: 218, 221, 226
Braille Book Society: 185
British and Foreign Blind Association: *see* Royal National Institute for the Blind
British Empire Society for the Blind: 282 n.
British Wireless for the Blind Fund: 215
Central Council for the London Blind: 209
College of Teachers of the Blind: 181, 218, 222, 223, 230, 241, 245, 279
Guide Dogs for the Blind Association: 215
Home Teaching Society: 176, 178, 184 n., 201, 203
Incorporated Association for Promoting the General Welfare of the Blind: 178 n., 213
Indigent Blind Visiting Society: 176, 213
Jewish Blind Society: 218, 244 n.
Joint Blind Welfare Committee: 227
London Association for the Blind: 213, 246
London Home Teaching Society: 204
London Society for Teaching and Training: 213
Manchester and Salford Blind Aid Society: 213
Metropolitan Society for the Blind: 213, 231 n.
National Association of Workshops: *see* Association of Workshops for the Blind
National Committee for the Employment of the Blind: 202
National Federation of the Blind (*formerly* National Union of the Professional and Industrial Blind): 218, 228
National Institute for the Blind: *see* Royal N.I.B.
National League of the Blind: 179, 192, 199–200, 218, 222, 223, 228
National Library for the Blind: 178, 188, 190, 213, 217, 226
National Union of the Professional and Industrial Blind: *see* National Federation of the Blind
North London Homes for the Blind: 213
North of England Industrial Employment Service for the Blind: 237 n.
North of England Union of Institutions and Societies and Agencies for the Blind: 186, 198 n.
Northern Counties Association: *see* Regional Associations for the Blind
Northern Regional Association: *see* Regional Associations for the Blind
Regional Association for the Blind (*see also* Union of Unions)
   Southern: ix, 213, 220, 243–6, 250
   Northern: 222, 237 n., 244
   Welsh: 245 n.
Royal National Institute for the Blind (*formerly* (1) British and Foreign Blind Association, (2) National Institute for the Blind): ix, 26
   C.A.M.W. co-operation with: 130
   foundation of: 178; purpose of: 179–80, 186
   N.I.B. bulletin: *see* under authors
   relations with libraries: 185
   N.I.B. expansion: 188, 216
   membership of Advisory committee: 191, 269
   homeworkers' scheme: 209; grants from L.C.C.: 213
   relation with St. Dunstan's: 189–90, 217
   employment projects: 224, 231
   investigations and placement services: 237–240
   difficulties over collections: 226
   reorganisation to encourage co-ordination: 227, 228–9
   relations with regional organisations: 245, 267
   dependence on voluntary subscriptions: 231
   rehabilitation: 236–40, 246–7

VOLUNTARY SOCIETIES, ETC.

co-operation with College of Teachers of the Blind: 181, 241, 245
Royal Charter: 245
Louis Braille centenary exhibition: 246
new projects: Homes of Recovery, parents' units, social rehabilitation, schools for children with multiple handicaps, pilot centre for adolescents: 246-8
post-war activity in direct provision: 262
a non-federating body: 179, 264
international contacts: 282 (*see also* overseas)

Royal Schools for the Blind: 213
St. Dunstan's: 178, 189-90, 213, 217, 227, 235 n., 237, 240
Servers of the Blind League: 217 n.
Society for the Prevention of Blindness and for the Improvement of the Physique of the Blind: 177 n.
Southern Regional Association for the Blind: *see* Regional Associations
Union of Counties Associations for the Blind (*formerly* Union of Unions): 186, 187, 203, 219-20, 226, 227, 267; *see also* Regional Associations
Welsh Regional Association: *see* Regional Associations

(4) GENERAL

Anti-Slavery League: 264
Association for the Promotion of Social Science: 7
Association of Children's Officers: 163 n.
Association of County Medical Officers: 59 n.
Association of Municipal Corporations: 106 n., 227 n., 229, 239
Association of Nursery Matrons: 73 n.
Association of Sick Children's Hospital Nurses: 73 n.
Barnardo's Children's Homes: 11, 20, 63
British Council for Rehabilitation: 243
British Council for the Welfare of Spastics: 288
British Council of Social Service: 265
British Epilepsy Association: 289
British and Foreign School Society: 17 n., 264
British Legion, The: 155
British Medical Association: 74 n., 100, 136, 139
British Red Cross Society: xii, 15, 56, 58, 62, 75, 190, 262 n., 280
Central Council for the Care of Cripples: 56 n., 73 n.
Central Relief Society, Liverpool: 18 n., 265
Charity Organisation Society: *see* Family Welfare Association
Chartered Society of Massage and Medical Gymnastics: 216
Church of England Children's Society (*formerly* Waifs and Strays): 12 n., 62, 152
Church of England Moral Welfare Council: 62
College of Nursing: *see* Royal . . .
Council for the Promotion of Occupational Industries amongst the Physically Handicapped: 132, 133
Councils of Social Service: 22, 265, 266
County Councils Association: 139, 227 n., 229, 239
District Nursing Associations: 49, 54, 70, 204; Herts. D.N.A.: 56
Family Welfare Association (*formerly* (1) Society for the Organisation of Charitable Relief and Repressing Mendicity, (2) Charity Organisation Society): xi n., 18-21, 22, 26, 35, 255
change of name: 18 n., 21 n., 255
mental health: 85 n., 100, 102 n.
blind welfare: 177, 183, 188 n., 192 n., 199 n., 231
professional training: 19 n., 257, 279, 284
use of consultants: 286
co-operation: 18-19, 265

VOLUNTARY SOCIETIES, ETC.

enquiries: 18, 19, 26, 100, 192 n., 274
case work: 19, 255
propaganda: 19, 20, 85 n., 100, 192 n.
new projects: hospital almoners, I.C.A.A.: 19–20; Family Discussion Bureau: 285 n.; W. Indian immigrants: 289 n.; problem families: 289 n.
hospitals: 20, 21
school meals: 21
old age pensions: 21
Guilds of Help: 22, 265
Infantile Paralysis Fellowship: 257
Institute of Almoners: 284
Invalid Children's Aid Association: 20, 35, 63, 145
Jewish Board of Guardians: 12
Jewish Health Organisation: 121
King Edward's Hospital Fund: xii, 152 n.
League of Well-doers: 13 n., 256
London Diocesan Council for Moral Welfare: 73 n.
National Adoption Society: 73 n.
National Association for the Promotion of Social Science: 7, 100
National Association of Parents of Backward Children: 153, 256 n., 257, 289
National Children's Homes and Orphanages: 12 n., 63
National Corporation for the Care of Old People: 153
National Council of Social Service: ix, xii, 22, 29 n., 64 n., 68 n., 155 n., 260, 265–6, 287
  foundation of: 261, 265
National Council of Women: 64 n.
National Institute of Industrial Psychology: 224
National Old People's Welfare Committee: 153
  Old People's Welfare Committees: 280
National Society for Epileptics: 133
National Society for the Prevention of Cruelty to Children (N.S.P.C.C.) (*formerly* Society . . .): 20, 35, 254 n.
National Society for Promoting the Education of the Poor in the Principles of the Established Church: 17 n., 264
National Society of Children's Nurseries: 59 n.
National Spastics Society: 257 n., 288
Nursery Schools Association: 67 n.
Personal Service League: 265 n.
Royal College of Nursing (*formerly* College of Nursing): 73 n., 130
Royal Association in aid of the Deaf and Dumb (*formerly* Royal Association for . . .): 183, 213
Royal Society for the Assistance of Discharged Prisoners: 134
St. John Ambulance Brigade: 62, 75
St. Martin's Relief Committee: 133 n.
Salvation Army: 12, 20, Mayflower Home: 256; *see also* Booth, Wm.
Save the Children Fund: 73 n., 74 n.
Society for the Organisation of Charitable Relief and Repressing Mendicity: *see* Family Welfare Association
Society for the Prevention of Cruelty to Children: *see* National S.P.C.C.
Society of Medical Officers of Health: 59 n., 73 n., 285 n.
S.S.A.F.A. (*formerly* Soldiers and Sailors Forces Association): 22 n.
Temperance Societies: 13
Voluntary Sterilisation League: 137
Waifs and Strays: *see* Church of England Children's Society
Women's Co-operative Guilds: 15
Women's Institutes: 15
Women's Voluntary Services: xii, 15, 66, 75, 262 n., 280

INDEX

For Voluntary Societies and Professional Organisations see p. 303.

ACLAND, Sir A., 44
ADMINISTRATORS, 266, 271-4 *passim*, 280, 287, 290
ADVISORY SERVICES, *see also* Citizens' Advice Bureaux
  of Statutory Bodies, 25, 49, 66, 219 n., 221, 279; *see also* Advisory Committee on the Welfare of the Blind
  of Voluntary Organisations, 25, 261, 274, 280, 290
    maternity and child welfare, parent advisers, 67, 285; *see also* Health Visitors
    mental health: C.A.M.W., 7 *et seq.*, 10, 130 *et seq.*; Child Guidance Council, 122 n.; N.A.M.H., 155, 163, 262, 275 n.
    blind welfare, 262, 267, 282
    N.C.S.S., 266
    British Council for the Welfare of Spastics, 288
AGNES WESTON TRAINING CENTRE, 125, 129, 143
AGRICULTURAL HOSTELS, 151, 162, 290 n.
AGRICULTURAL WAGES COMMITTEE, 131
AGRICULTURE, MINISTRY OF, 138, 151, 162
AMERICA
  infant welfare, 41 n.
  mental health, 116, 121, 163 n.
  blind welfare, 198, 201, 218 n.
  case work, 19 n., 284
  sterilisation, 137 n.
  training, *see* Casework
  Fulbright Scholars, etc., xi n., 164
  work by D. L. Dix, 92
  work by E. Fox, 105
AMERICAN RED CROSS, 44 n.
ARMITAGE, Dr. (blind welfare), 178, 179 n., 180, 182, 201, 217
ARMSTRONG, Dr., 31
ARTS, 198
  C.E.M.A., 14; Arts Council, 14 n.
ASCERTAINMENT, *see* Table VIII
  of mental defect, 88, 104, 110, 114
    Royal Commission recommendation, 87
    Wood Committee and, 115
    variation between local authorities, 140-2
    in Cambridge, 147

C.A.M.W.'S work in, 274
  of blindness, 174, 204, 219, 220
  of epilepsy, 133
ASSISTANCE, *see also* Poor Law
  maternity and child welfare, 61
  mental health, 118, 132, 148, 161
  blind welfare, 16, 173, 175, 192, 195-200 *passim*, 209-14 *passim*, 229, 231 n., 243 n., 249
  for the handicapped, 258, 295
  for paupers, 262-3
Unemployment, 20 n., 148, 214
ATTLEE, Clement, 11 n.
AUSTRALIA, 201

BARNARDO, Dr., 11, 12 n., 20, 24
BATH, 99
BEDFORD, 131
BELGIUM, 134 n.
BELL, Mr. (National Society), 17 n.
BENTHAM, J., 4, 6, 17 n.
BIRMINGHAM, 52, 96 n., 100 n., 106 n., 111 n., 121, 128 n., 182, 185, 237 n., 290
BLIND WELFARE, 173-250; *see also* ix, xii, 22 n., 23, 26, 86, 130, 257-62 *passim*, 274, 275, 288, 295
  co-ordination, 267-8, 269, 271
BOARDS OF GUARDIANS, *see* Guardians, Boards of
BOGNOR REGIS, 132 n.
BOLTON, 197
BOND, Dr. H., 95
BOSANQUET, B., 4
BRADFORD, 106 n., 185, 203 n.
BRAILLE, Louis, 178, 246
BRIGHTON, 103, 103 n., 110, 131, 185, 197
BRISTOL, 106 n., 180 n.
BRITISH COUNCIL, 75, 164
BROADBENT, Alderman, 36
BRODIE, Dr., 7, 100 n.
BUDIN, Pierre, 41 n.
BURGOYNE, Mr., 200 n.
BURNS, John, 42 n., 42, 45, 188
BUTLER, Josephine, 15

CAMBRIDGE, 103, 128 n., 147-8, 163
CAMPBELL, Dr. F., 178, 180, 195, 217
CARLYLE, R., 7
CARNEGIE HOUSE, 63; *see also* Trust Foundations
CARPENTER, Mary, 7, 15
CASE CONFERENCE, 150, 266, 278, 282, 287

INDEX

CASE WORK
  C.O.S. and, 19, 21 n., 255
  family case work, 72 n., 272
  and psychiatric consultation, 286
  and the p.s.w., 121
  N.A.M.H. and, 163, 167–8 (Table XII)
  changing ideas and, 255–8 *passim*
  difficulty in arousing interest in, 291
  case workers from America, 284
CASHMORE, Hilda, 11 n.
CERTIFICATE of College of Teachers of the Blind, 181 n., 230, 241
CERTIFICATION
  mental health, 79, 82
    under Lunacy Act, 97, 113, 254
    under Education Act, 139 n.; removal of requirement, 160
    under M.D. Act, suggestion for removal of requirement, 288
    care of those not certifiable, 148
  blind welfare
    different requirements of Board of Education and Ministry of Health, 174
    certification by qualified doctors, 219–20, 244
CHADWICK, Edwin, 31
CHAMBERLAIN, Joseph, 19 n.
CHARITABLE TRUSTS, *see* Trust Foundations; *see also* Financial Aspects
CHARITY, 3, 18, 19, 25, 144, 176, 259; for Charity Organisation *see* Family Welfare Association
  Commissioners, 13 n.
CHARTISM, 4 n., 8
CHESHIRE, 101, 102, 104 n.
CHESTERFIELD, 55 n., 124
CHILD CARE SERVICE, 255, 276 n., 278; *see also* L.C.C. Care Committee
CHILD GUIDANCE, 116, 120–1, 150, 274 n., 285, 286 n.
  clinics and centres, 121, 152, 160, 161, 163, 274 n.
  Council, *see* Index of Societies
  Inter-Clinic Conference, 150
CHRISTIAN SOCIALISM, 11
CHRISTIE, Mr., 178, 180
CHURCH, *see* Religious Influence
CHURCH OF ENGLAND (Established Church), 8–10 *passim*, 18
  Moral Welfare Council, 256
  see also Voluntary Societies: C. of E. Children's Society
CITIZENS' ADVICE BUREAUX, 272, 280, 287
CIVIL DEFENCE, 149, 234, 280 n.
CIVIL SERVANTS, 255
CLASSES
  artisans, 4
  lower, 6, 8
  middle, 4, 5, 14

upper, 6, 24
  distinctions in, 6, 7, 19, 24
  attempts to bridge gulf, 10–11, 15, 24
  hostility to bishops, 8
  Consultation de Nourrissons, provision for three, 41 n.
  health provision for all, 79
  class structure, 253, 254, 273
CLOTHWORKERS COMPANY, 153, 219 n.
COBBETT, Wm., 7
COLCHESTER, 99 n.
COLLECTIVISM, 4 n., 20, 192, 254
COLONIAL OFFICE, 164, 245, 282 n.
COMMISSIONERS IN LUNACY, 85, 88, 93, 95, 104
COMMONWEALTH, The, 73 n.
COMMONWEALTH FUND, 121
COMMUNITY ASSOCIATIONS, 287
COMMUNITY CARE, xii, 258, 284 n., 288, 290
  mental health, 79, 80, 81, 90–8 *passim*, 102–4, 105–68 *passim*, 258, 275 n., 286, 294
  blind welfare (after-care), 182, 186, 188, 201, 236, 238; *see also* Welfare
COMMUNITY COUNCILS, 266
CONTROL, BOARD OF, *see also* Bibliography: Government Publications
  enlightened policy of, 85 n.
  function under M.D. Act, 88
  relations with Voluntary Societies, 104; with C.A.M.W., 108, 125, 133, 136, 264, 270; with M.A.C.A., 116–7, 157
  grant-aid, 107 n., 124
  Joint Committee with Board of Education, 114–5
  support for Feversham Committee, 122
  reports on occupation centres, 126; industrial centres, 127
  interest in C.A.M.W. schemes for mental patients, 133–4
  pressure from C.A.M.W., 137–9
  reasons for voluntary–statutory partnership, 140–4
  relations with Middlesex, 144–5
  support for N.A.M.H. diploma course, 154
  effect of National Health Service Act, 159, 165
  views on propaganda, 257
CO-OPERATION: voluntary–statutory partnership, xi, xiii, 13, 22, 23, 253, 259–61 *passim*, 262–4, 270–90 *passim*, 291–2
  maternity and child welfare, 30, 32, 34–40, 41, 46–53 *passim*, 54–7, 61–75 *passim*
  mental health, 81, 94–107 *passim*, 108–11, 116–69 *passim*
  blind welfare, 175, 180–3 *passim*, 191–228 *passim*, 230–3

INDEX

CO-OPERATION: workers' movement, 4 n., 8
CO-ORDINATION, 253, 261, 264–9, 276 n.
 maternity and child welfare, 30, 42, 64
 mental health, 122, 145, 149
 blind welfare, 186–7, 225–7, 243–6, 253
COVENTRY, 128 n.
CRICHEL DOWN, 255
CRIMINAL RESPONSIBILITY, 136
CURTIS COMMITTEE, 68 n.

DANNETT, Rev. H., 178 n., 180
DAQUIN, 93 n.
DARWIN, C., 6
DAVIS, Dr., 31
DEAF, 32 n., 86, 183, 196, 247, 265
 –BLIND, 181 n., 187 n., 230, 246, 247
DELINQUENT
 children, 7
 blind, 230, 258
DENTAL BOARD OF THE UNITED KINGDOM, 58
DERBY, 55 n., 143
DEVON, 100 n., 142, 241, 247
DICKENS, Ch., 7
DISABLED, 257 n.; *see* Handicapped
DISABLEMENT RESETTLEMENT OFFICERS, 160, 236, 238, 286
DISRAELI, B., 7
DIX, Dorothea Lynde, 85 n., 92
DOCTORS, *see* Medical Officers
DREW HARRIS, Dr., 41 n.
DUFOUR, Leon, 41 n.
DULY AUTHORISED OFFICERS, 155
DUNCAN, Dr., 85 n., 88, 99, 100 n.
DUNCROFT APPROVED SCHOOL, 152
DU PLATT TAYLOR, 246

EASTERN COUNTIES, 186 n., 243 n.
EBURY, Lord, 176 n.
EDINBURGH, 37, 180 n., 187
EDUCATION, 17, 262; *see also* Training; and Bibliography: Government Publications
 adult, *see also* Parentcraft
  Working Men's College, 11
  Adult School Union, 12
  settlements, 12
  women's, 14, 15
 of children, 6, 7, 8 n., 10, 17–8, 21, 32, 56 n., 67, 81, 86 n., 115, 254 n.
 of scholars, 3
 and the C.O.S., 19
 and religious bodies, 17–8, 256
 and the Government, 17; Newcastle Commission, 18
 maternity and child welfare, 30, 37, 53–72 *passim*, 253, 256, 263
  mental health, 86–9 *passim*, 106–16 *passim*, 120–2 *passim*, 127, 129–30, 143–52 *passim*, 164 n., 165, 274

blind welfare, 173, 178, 179, 180–4, 192 n., 194–201 *passim*, 211, 215, 221–4, 229, 241–50 n. *passim*, 264
EDUCATION, BOARD OF, *see also* Bibliography: Government Publications
 maternity and child welfare, 42–52 *passim*, 60, 74 n., 263
 mental health, 89, 121, 130, 137–9 *passim*, 151, 152, 263, 264
 blind welfare, 174, 181, 182, 187 n., 196, 198, 216, 228
EDUCATION, MINISTRY OF, 35 n., 154 n., 165; *see also* Bibliography: Government Publications
 blind welfare, 223, 236 n., 242 n., 244, 247, 248
 neglected children, 276 n.
 maladjusted children, 285 n.
EICHHOLZ, Dr., 187 n., 198 n., 216 n.
ELLICE, Mr., M.P., 92
ELY, Isle of, 124 n.
EMBOSSED LITERATURE, 185, 198, 216, 231, 264, 275
 Braille, 176, 178, 179 n., 185, 188, 189, 195, 204, 241, 246, 247
 Moon, 176, 178, 179 n., 195, 204, 241
EMPLOYMENT, 21, 115, 162, 283
 maternity and child welfare, Employment Bureau, 44, 61
 blind welfare, 173–87 *passim*, 189–90, 196–240 *passim*, 248, 257
 mental health, 95, 107, 125, 127, 138, 151, 160, 162
EPILEPTICS, 132–3, 152–68, 230, 289, Table VII n.
ESSEX, 132, 157, 237 n., 246
EVANGELICAL REVIVAL, 9
EVANGELICALS, 4, 10
EXHIBITION, TRAVELLING (Maternity and Child Welfare), 58, 73, 284
EX-SERVICE MEN (Table VII n.)
 and Maudsley Hospital, 98
 Ex-Services After-Care Scheme, 150, 157, 168
 St. Dunstan's, 189–90
 war disability pension, 204
 rehabilitation of, 246–7

FABIAN, 20 n., 25, 255
FAMILY DISCUSSION BUREAU, 285 n.
FAMILY RELATIONSHIPS, *see also* Parentcraft, Parent Groups, 285, 286, 287
FAMILY SERVICE UNIT, 277 n.
FEVERSHAM COMMITTEE, 112 n., 120 n., 122, 126, 146, 149, 167 n., 168 n.
 Report, 126 (Table III), 167 (Table VII n.), 168 (Table VII n.)

INDEX

FINANCE, STATUTORY POWERS:
early limitations of, 142-3; for research, 112; after-care, 113, 201; special home, 152; augmentation of wages or for embossed lit., 201-2; for unemployable blind, 207; effect of economy measures: in maternity and child welfare, 48, 52; in mental health, 114, 117, 124, 125, 128, 129, 138, 151; withdrawal of support, 70, 155; powers not used, 23, 124, 142, 181, 184, 199, 238; refusal of relief on purchase tax, 236 n.; wide variation in grant-aid, 173

effect of social legislation on powers of grant-aid, etc.
Elementary Education (Blind and Deaf Children) Act, 1893, 23 n., 196
Education Act, 1902, effect on technical educ., 182; on charitable funds, 203, 291; *see also* Education, Poor Law
Lloyd George's Budget, 1914, 23, 45
Maternity and Child Welfare Act, 1918, 50-4
Ministry of Health grants for blind welfare, 1919, 206
Blind Persons Act, 1920, 208; B.P.s Act, 1938, 214, 222
Local Government Act, 1929, 21 n., 52, 124 n., 210-11, 222, 259
Mental Treatment Act, 1930, 113
Education Act, 1944, effect on handicapped persons, 241
National Health Service Act, 1946, 69-72, 155, 241, 292
National Assistance Act, 1948, 161, 240, 248, 278, 292

FINANCES OF VOLUNTARY ASSOCIATIONS
almsgiving and appeals: 18, 19, 22, 23; maternity and child welfare, 43; mental health, 94, 115, 132, 289 n.; blind welfare, 174, 176, 178 n., 187 n., 226-7, 267, 291; spastics, 288, 291
other charitable sources: donations and subs., 103 n., from asylums, etc., 91, 148; the Colonies, 133; local authorities, 23, 73, 94, 156; library, 185 n.; Trust funds, 23, 52, 58, 60, 116, 152 n., 153, 155 n., 183, 246, 289; other funds for special purposes, 99, 163 n., 289; N.C.S.S., distribution of grants, 22; increased income for blind charities, 88 n., 191, 260 n.
unsatisfactory features of voluntary finance: 200, 203; limited resources, 261, 275, 290-1; for maternity and child welfare, 43; for M.A.C.A., 96 n.; for N.A.M.H., 164; for N.C.M.H., 120; for physically handicapped, 133; short-term basis of Trust grants, 291; 'window dressing', 275; need for generous aid, 283, 291; differences between charities, 260-1, 275

income part voluntary, part statutory: schools, 180-3 *passim*, 196-7, 215, 217; adult educ., 215; payments by or on behalf of beneficiaries, 23, 56, 103 n., 259, 261; special schemes: Orchard Dene, 153 n.; S. Wales boarding-out scheme, 134; Home for backward children, 289; Over Seventy investigation, 289, Hethersett, 247; Home for senile old people, 153; for maladjusted children, 153; Duncroft, 152; Ponds, 153.

earnings of patients, 103 n.
affiliation fees, 57 n.

statutory payments: on agency basis, 23; 281, mental health, 229; 100 n., 131, 147-8; blind welfare (registr.), 244 n.; grant-aid: homes, 53, 132; nursing ass., 54-5; parentcraft, 68; talking books, 224 n.; local authorities as channel of aid, 50, 52, 155, 260; new basis of aid, 206, 210 *et seq.*; subsidisation of maternity and child welfare centres, 262 n.

financial aspects of blind welfare: under Poor Law, 176, 194; changes in domiciliary assistance, 210, 214; effect on welfare, 222; gratuity to N.I.B., 236 n., L.C.C. and blind welfare, 212-3, 231-2; examples of variation in four areas, 209-10; expend. of N.I.B. on placement, 237 n., 238; negotiations with L.A.'s for payment, 239

hidden subsidies: death duties exemption, taxation and rating relief, bequests and covenanted subs., 275

FINANCIAL RELATIONSHIP BETWEEN VOLUNTARY AND STATUTORY BODIES, *see* Tables VI, IX-XV, diagram p. 232, and notes p. 248-9
in assistance services: 3, 19, 259, 278; summary of relationship in blind welfare, 229-33; in education services, 17-8; *see also* Schools
between voluntary organisations and local authorities: M.A.C.A. and L.C.C., 116, 143 n., 156; C.A.M.W. and Middlesex, 145; N.C.S.S. and Hammersmith M.B.C., 289 n.; between voluntary and statutory societies in Herts and Merseyside, 56-7, in Cambridge, 147-8; special schemes, 248-9, 277 n.

INDEX

FINANCIAL RELATIONSHIP BETWEEN VOLUNTARY AND STATUTORY BODIES—*contd.*
  financial support by central authorities: 277; Ex-Services After-Care Scheme, 150; agricultural hostels, 151; for maternity and child welfare, 23, 45–50, 60; for educational course (mental health), 130; for children with multiple handicaps, 247; for local assoc., 124; to assist defectives, 89 n.; for Homes of Recovery, 248; for Swail House, 249
FITCH, Mr. H. M. T., 196 n.
FOOD, MINISTRY OF, 191
FOX, Dame Evelyn, 105
FOUNDLING HOSPITAL, 31
FRANCE, 32, 37 n., 41, 41 n., 93, 99
FRASER, Sir Ian, 178, 189 n.
FRIENDLY SOCIETIES, 4 n.
FRY, Elizabeth, 12
FULBRIGHT: Scholars and Fellows, xi n., 164, 284
FURZEDOWN TRAINING COLLEGE, 106 n.

GASKELL, Mrs., 7
GERMANY, 97, 99
GHENT, 37
GILBERT, Elizabeth, 178, 182 n.
GLASGOW, 38, 39, 41
GORDON, Mrs., 37
GOSCHEN MINUTE, *see* Poor Law
GOVERNMENT, The, *see* Parliament
GREEN, T. H., 4
GREY, Dr. Asa, 9 n.
GREY, Sir G., 92 n.
GUARDIANS, BOARDS OF, 11, 15, 19, 20, 21 n., 22 n.
  maternity and child welfare, 32
  mental health, 82 n., 84, 94, 95, 100, 101, 106, 113, 119 n., 125, 130, 131, 140, 147
  blind welfare, 184 n., 190, 194–196 *passim*, 209, 211, 228
  Jewish, 12
GUARDIANSHIP, under M.D. Act, 88, *see* Tables IV, VIII, XIV
  substitute for institutional accommodation, 109
  Brighton Society, 131
  C.A.M.W. and, 145, 152
  effect of war on, 151, 164 n.
  effect of National Assistance Act on, 161
GUGGENBUHL, 99 n.
HAMPSHIRE (Hants), 67 n., 68, 209
HANDICAPPED, *see generally* The Mentally Handicapped, Part III; The Blind, Part IV

HANDICAPPED—*contd.*
  enquiries into needs of, 7
  residential accommodation for, 13, 281
  national organisations and children, 63
  modern concern for, 79
  promotion of industries for, 132–3
  services for those with multiple handicaps, 217
  employment of, 235 n., 236
  assistance to, 258–9
  attitude towards, 257 n., 282
  recent trends: spastics, 288; backward children and epileptics, 289
  financial aid to, 291–2, Table XV
  Disabled Persons Employment Act, 236
  Handicapped Pupils Regulations, 241 n.
HANWELL, 93 n.
HEALTH, 263, 290
  centres, 277
  National Service, xii, 30, 39 n., 47 n., 50 n., 292
  public, 5, 6, 10, 21, 23, 253
  maternity and child welfare, 21, 31–41 *passim*, 57, 60
  mental health, 130, 132, 169 n.
  blind welfare, 199, 211, 214, 220
  visitors, 34–9 *passim*, 45 n., 47, 51, 56, 69, 71, 72 n., 129, 130, 204, 272, 278, 284, 286
  Health Visitors (London) Order, 1909, 39
HEALTH, MINISTRY OF, *see also* Local Government Board and Government Publications
  Departments of Maternity and Child Welfare, Mental Health, Welfare of the Blind, ix
  approval of case work method, 287 n.; recognition of need for co-ordination, 70
  maternity and child welfare, 29 n., 30
  support for training of health visitors, 51; for model health centres, 52; for retention of local authorities' services and for co-operation with voluntary organisations, 53–75 *passim*
  mental health
    relationship with Board of Control, 140, 159
    attitude to sterilisation campaign, 137
    establishment of M.H. Emergency Committee, 149
    pressure from voluntary societies, 150
    establishment of special home: voluntary-statutory co-operation, 152–3
    no support for N.A.M.H. regional scheme, 155
    interpretation of new social policy, 161–2
    attitude to development of community care, 165
    short training courses, 286

INDEX

HEALTH, MINISTRY OF—*contd.*
  blind welfare
    definition of blindness, 174; Advisory Committee on Welfare of the Blind, 191, 204–10 *passim*, 219 n., 222 n., 222–8, 269
    encouragement of home-workers' schemes, 182, 230
    replacement of Local Government Board—new policy, 206–14
    interest in prevention of blindness, 218–21
    Advisory Committee on Blindness, 221
    voluntary–statutory partnership, 221–5, 242–3
    co-ordination, 225–9
    grant-aid small, 231
    Inter-Departmental Committee on Rehabilitation, 236 n.
    service for the handicapped, 240
    classified register, 244
    deaf-blind survey reported to, 246 n.
    co-operation with S.R.A.B., 250, 267
  neglected children, 276 n.
HEALTH, WELSH BOARD OF, 239
HERTS., 56, 148
HETHERSETT, 223 n., 247–8, 289
HILL, Dr., 93 n.
HILL, Octavia, 15, 20 n.
HOME OFFICE, *see also* Government Publications
  responsibility for child care, 68 n.
  relationship with N.A.M. & C.W., 73 n.
  pressure from C.A.M.W., 139
  co-operation with N.A.M.H., 152, 153, 154
  deputation to Home Secretary on behalf of blind, 200
  joint circular with Ministry of Health, 276 n.
  co-operation in training of senior case workers (C.O.S. course), 284 n.
HOMES, RESIDENTIAL, xi, 13, 261, 265; *see also* Waifs and Strays, National Children's Homes, Dr. Barnardo's Homes
  maternity and child welfare, 44, 50, 53, 56, 57 n., 61, 66–75 *passim*, 262 n., 281, 293
  mental health, 79, 94, 95, 100–03 *passim*, 110, 131, 132, 148, 151–7 *passim*, 289; Court Grange, 217 n., 247; Orchard Dene, 153; Ponds, 153 n.; Union of Homes, 101, 104, 105, 117–9 n. *passim*, 168 n., 169 n., 261
  blind welfare, 13, 153, 176, 177, 185, 201, 206, 209 n., 212–7 *passim*, 221, 222 n., 229 n., 230, 243, 244 n., 245, 295; Catholic Blind Asylum, 213; Cecilia Home for Blind Women, 213; Church Army (Hostel), 213; Condover Hall for Blind with other handicaps, 217 n., 247; Court Grange, Abbotskerswell, 217 n., 247; Glyn Vivian Home of Rest, 213; N. London Home for the Blind, 213, Oldbury Grange, 247; Queen Elizabeth, Torquay, 241, 247, 248
HOSPITAL(S), xi, 3, 13, 21, 262 n., 290 n.
  maternity and child welfare, 62, 70, 73 n., 75; Edinburgh Royal Maternity, 37; Glasgow Maternity, 38; Royal Free, 44
  mental health, 79, 80–4, 102 n., 114, 117, 121, 122, 143, 147–59 *passim*, 163, 169 n., 256 n., 285, 286 n.; Bethlem (Bedlam), 81, 83, 84, 90–1; Broadmoor, 134; Cell Barnes, 148; Chalfont, 149; Earlswood House, 99; Eastern Counties, 99, 132; Friern (Colney Hatch), 93 n.; Fulbourne, 147; Knowle, Birmingham, 100 n.; Lingfield, 133; Maudsley, 98, 112, 113, 118; Newcastle, 131; Park House, 99; Retreat, The, 84 n., 91–2; Royal Albert, Lancaster, 100 n.; St. Thomas', 97; Star Cross, Devon, 100 n.
  welfare of the blind, 190, 194, 241, 249
  Faculty of Ophthalmology, Royal Eye Hospital, 244
  almoners, 16, 20, 117, 156, 163, 258, 278, 279
  and link with other services, 30, 46, 51 n., 54 n., 55, 58, 62, 262, 286, 287
  Management Committees, 161
  Regional Boards, 70, 72, 153, 160–2 *passim*, 165 n., 241, 249
HOUSDEN, Dr., 67 n.
HOUSE OF COMMONS, *see* Parliament
HOUSING, 5, 115
  and class differences, 6; managers, 15 n., 16, 20 n.; C.O.S. and, 19
  and sanitary authorities, 35
  Town Planning, 79
  and blind welfare (Swail House), 246, 249
  and Churches, 260
  New Towns experiments, 287
HOWARD, John, 91
HUDDERSFIELD, 33 n., 36, 37 n., 41
HUMANIST, 3, 24, 25
HUMANITARIAN, 7, 9, 25
HUMANITY, 13

ILLEGITIMATE CHILDREN, 50, 53, 62, 73 n., 87
INDIVIDUALISM, 4, 5, 6, 253, 254, 263, 264, 268
INDUSTRIAL CENTRES, 126, 127, 144
INDUSTRIAL HOMES, 177
INDUSTRIAL HEALTH AND WELFARE, 5, 6

INDEX

INDUSTRIAL RELATIONS, 12
INDUSTRIAL WORKERS, 4, 5, 8
INDUSTRY
  expansion, 4, 5
  depression, 5
  settlements and, 11
INFANT MORTALITY (*see* National Assoc. for Prevention of), 5, 29–33 *passim*, 45, 56, 57 n., 59, 72 n., 256, 274
INSPECTORS
  influence in raising standards, 5, 281
  maternity and child welfare, 46, 52
  effect of voluntary-statutory co-operation on, 49, 55
  mental health, reports on training, 111
  blind welfare, reports on training and education, 186, 196; influence on development of welfare, 207
  influence on voluntary-statutory co-operation, 221–5 *passim*, 278
  members of working party, 236 n.
INSURANCE, MINISTRY OF NATIONAL, 161, 236 n.
  National Health Insurance, 139
  Unemployment Insurance, 223
  National Insurance benefits, 243 n.
INTERNATIONAL, *see* Overseas Interests

JAMIESON, Sir W., 68 n.
JOHNS, John, 10 n., 24
JONES, E., 116 n.

KENT, 128 n., 154 n., 165, 209
KINGSLEY, Charles, 11

LABOUR, MINISTRY OF, *see also* Government Publications
  co-operation with voluntary societies, 56 n., 236
  joint report with Ministry of Health on Midwives, 69 n.
  nursing appointments service, 70 n.
  workshops for the blind, the Minister's relation to employment issues, 207; schemes for training and resettlement, 234–6; appointment of working party on employment of the blind, 236; recommendations, 238–40; part-responsibility for technical education, 242 n.; and for home teachers' training, 244
  financial relationship with voluntary societies, 248
LABOUR PARTY, 200, 211 n., 218
LAISSEZ-FAIRE, 4, 6
LAMBERT, Dr. B., 56 n.
LANCASHIRE, 58, 101, 102, 104 n., 106 n.; Lancaster, 100 n.
LANCASTER, J., 17 n.
LEAGUE OF NATIONS, 74

LEATHERHEAD, 183
LEEDS, 155, 181 n., 185, 197, 201 n.
LEICESTER, 106 n.
LIBERAL GOVERNMENT, 20, 254
  Lloyd George's Budget, 23
LIBRARIES, 14
  Blind Welfare, 178, 185, 188, 190, 201, 217
LINCOLN, 93 n.
LISKEARD, 84
LITTLEHAMPTON, 131
LIVERPOOL
  Domestic Mission, 10, 24
  charitable work in, 10 n., 13 n.
  visiting societies, 13
  milk depot, 38 n.
  centres, 52
  Central Relief Society, 18 n., 265
  Food Association, 13 n.
  After-Care Committee, 106 n.
  education, 106 n., 129
  School for Indigent Blind, 177, 178, 180 n.
  residential schools, 197
LLOYD GEORGE, 23, 45, 48
LOCAL ASSOCIATIONS (SOCIETIES), 8, 13, 21 n., 22, 25, 261, 262, 265
  maternity and child welfare, 34–9 *passim*, 54–7 *passim*
  mental health, 101–03 *passim*, 111, 122–45 *passim*, 163, 165, Table VII, 168, 263, 267–8
  blind welfare, 173, 176–92 *passim*, 199, 207, 209, 215 n., 218, 226–9 *passim*, 240, 245, 246, 264, 267
  N.C.S.S. and, 266
LOCAL AUTHORITIES, xi, xii, 25, Table VIII; *see also* Co-operation
  see generally Maternity and Child Welfare, Part II and Table XIII; Mental Health, Part III, *see especially* Notes, p. 147–8, and Tables III, IV, XIV, XV; Blind Welfare, Part IV and Tables IX–XII, XV, diagram p. 232; and pp. 26, 259, 263, 270–3, 274, 276–83 *passim*, 287, 289, 290–2
  and appointment of social workers, 117, 258 n., 286 n., 287
  and interdepartmental relations, 227, 250, 287
  Joint Conference of, 131
  membership of, xii, 11, 25, 271
  parks, libraries, etc., 13
LOCAL GOVERNMENT, 4, 14, 15 n., 21 n., 22, 31, 52, 218, 278
  women's participation in, 14, 15
LOCAL GOVERNMENT BOARD, 19, 22, 263; *see also* Government Publications

314

INDEX

maternity and child welfare, 33, 34–52 *passim*
mental health, 101 n.
blind welfare, 188, 191, 194, 198, 200, 204, 206
LONDON, *see also* London County Council, Hospitals and Homes
  maternity and child welfare, 30 n., 47, 49 n., 64 n.; Battersea, 38, 41; Chelsea, 37; Finsbury, 38; Kensington, 15 n., 39 n.; St. Marylebone, 39; St. Pancras, 37, 41, 45; Shoreditch, 42; Westminster, 38, 43 n.
  mental health, 92, 96 n., 102, 103 n., 106 n., 118, 119, 125 n., 129, 132, 133, 148, 151 n., 268; Chelsea, 95; East London C.G. Clinic, 121 n.; Islington, 121; London C.G. Clinic, 121 n.; St. Pancras, 95; Wandsworth, 95
  blind welfare, 176, 180–9 *passim*, 195–203 *passim*, 209–13 *passim*, 237, 243 n., 246, 247
  Hammersmith, Over 70 Enquiry, 289 n.
  Juvenile Courts, 153; Obstetrical Society, 33 n.; School of Hygiene, etc., 64 n.; Visiting Societies, 13
LONDON COUNTY COUNCIL
  Department of the Comptroller, ix
  Care Committee, 22, 116, 279
  and M.A.C.A., 23, 116, 145
  maternity and child welfare, 43 n., 50 n., 51 n., 58, 62 n., 64 n., 67 n., 72, 73 n., 74 n.
  and mental health, 98, 105, 106 n., 112, 116, 118, 125, 128, 129, 143 n., 154 n., 156, 165 n., 166 n., 286 n.
  and blind welfare, 181 n., 183, 184, 201 n., 202 n., 209, 212–4, 227, 229 n., 231, 237; charities registered with, 232
  expenditure on blind welfare, Table XI, 249
  expenditure on mothers and children, Table XIII, 293
  expenditure on the mental health service, Table XIV, 294
  expenditure on services for handicapped, Table XV, 295
LONDON STATISTICS, Table IX, 212

MABERLY, Dr. Alan, 150 n.
MACADAM, Elizabeth, 11 n.
MACARTHUR, Mary, 39
MACDONALD, Mrs., 39
MAGISTRATES, 116, 129, 274
MALADJUSTED CHILDREN, 134, 148, 152, 153, 154 n., 160, 285
MALTHUSIAN THEORY, 3
MANCHESTER, 34, 35, 101 n., 129, 182 n., 187, 188 n., 203 n.

MARRIAGE COUNSELLING, 277, 285
MATERNITY AND CHILD WELFARE, 29–75; *also* ix, xii, 13, 14, 15, 21–6 *passim*, 104, 163, 199, 254–81 *passim*, 292, Table XIII
MAUDSLEY, Dr., 98
MAURICE, F. D., 11
MAYFLOWER HOME, *see* Salvation Army (Index: Societies)
MEALS ON WHEELS, 277
MEDICAL OFFICERS, 7, 271
  maternity and child welfare, 26, 33–74 *passim*, 263, 272, 284, 285 n.
  mental health, 90, 112 n., 117 n., 129, 130, 150, 152, 153, 155, 163, 274, 275, 287
  blind welfare, 204 n., 220 n., 228
  School Medical Service, 121, 129, 147
  Prison Service, 130
MEDICAL RESEARCH COUNCIL, 173 n., 220 n., 244 n.
MELCHETT, Violet, 39 n., 292 n.
MENTAL HEALTH, 79–169; *also* ix, xii, 7, 10, 13, 19, 22 n., 23, 26, 74, 185, 217, 235, 254–64 *passim*, 271–94 *passim*
  officers, 155, 286
  Research Fund, 256
MERSEYSIDE, 56
METHODISM, 12; *see also* Religious Influence
MIDDLESEX, 128, 129 n., 131, 144–5, 151 n., 156 n., 165, 243, 269, 286 n.
MIDDLETON, Mary, 39
MIDLANDS, 100, 140, 186 n., 243 n.
  Institution for the Blind, 182 n.
MILK MARKETING BOARD, 61, 138
MILL, J. S., 4 n.
MINISTRY: for the various Ministries *see* under respective name of Ministry, thus: Education, Ministry of, etc.
MITCHELL, Mr. G., L.C.C., 64 n.
MOON, Dr., 178
MOORE, Dr., 36
MORAL PURPOSE, 6, 30, 253, 255, 256
  of voluntary societies, 13, 19, 21, 263
  in maternity and child welfare, 30, 32, 35 n., 43, 256
  in blind welfare, 180, 203, 222
  in mental welfare, 102 n. (moral imbeciles, 88)
  in social legislation, 3, 17, 19, 257, 258, 259, 263
MORAL WELFARE, 12, 13, 53, 62, 71, 72, 145, 256; *see also* Josephine Butler
  L.C.C. and, 292, 293
'MORNING CHRONICLE'
  'London Labour and The London Poor', 7
MUNRO, Dr., 83 n.

INDEX

NATIONAL ASSISTANCE BOARD, 161, 241, 242 n., 249, 284, 286, 287
allowances, 243 n.
NATIONAL CONFERENCE, 55
First on Infant Welfare, 41
NATIONAL MILK SCHEME, 66
NEWCASTLE, 131 n.
NIGHTINGALE, Florence, 15, 43 n.
NORTHANTS, 106 n., 131
NORTHERN COUNTIES, 100 n., 131, 134, 186 n., 198 n., 200 n.
NOTIFICATION
maternity and child welfare, 33, 34, 45, 46, 51 n., 62, 70 n., 254
mental health, 88, 110, 138
blind welfare, 199, 203, 226 n. (of collections)
NOTTINGHAM, 55 n., 151 n., 182, 185
NURSERIES (RESIDENTIAL), see also Homes
maternity and child welfare, 66, 68, 72
mental health, 152
blind welfare, 185, 230, 243, 247, 248
NURSING ASSOCIATION, see District Nursing Association

OAKLEY, Mr., H. M. T., 196 n.
OCCUPATION CENTRES, 103–4, 114, 125–6, 129–54 passim, 163, 246, 277, 279
OLD AGE, 12, 13, 175, 176, 204 n., 220, 233, 247, 249, 265, 272, 290 n.
charity to aged, 3
almshouses, 12, 13; residential homes, 153
pensions, 21, 102 n., 177, 187, 200, 201, 203, 208, 214, 217 n., 222 n., 229, 258, 282
organisations concerned with aged, 153, 280
meals and recreation for aged, 278, 281
OPHTHALMIA, 188, 198 n., 199, 203, 214 n., 221
OPHTHALMIC SURGEON, 12, 174, 219, 244
'ORCHARD DENE', 153
OWEN, Robert, 7, 8, 24
OVERSEAS INTERESTS, 282, 284, 289–90
maternity and child welfare, xi, xiv, 37, 41, 45, 58, 73 n., 74–5, 263
mental health, 91, 92, 105, 150, 164
blind welfare, 182, 187, 188, 189 n., 191, 196 n., 198, 201, 245
N.C.S.S. and, 265, 266
International Conference on Social Work, 1954, 255
OXFORD, 103 n., 105, 142 n., 151 n.
OXFORD MOVEMENT, 9

PARENT GROUPS, see also Training, Schools for Mothers
maternity and child welfare, 284; see Parentcraft
mental health, 153, 155
blind welfare, 247, 249, 284
PARENTCRAFT, 30, 34, 37, 60, 67–8,. 72 n., 163, 256, 274 n., 279, 284, 285
PARLIAMENT, 17, 102; see also Bibliography: Acts of Parliament
maternity and child welfare, 45, 48, 52, 60, 64
mental health, 102, 137, 139, 161
blind welfare, 191, 200, 214
PEARSON, Sir A., 178, 188, 189 n., 200 n.
PENSIONS, MINISTRY OF, 98 n., 108, 130, 236 n.
PHYSICAL DETERIORATION OF THE RACE, COMMITTEE ON, 20 n., 32, 43
PINEL, 93
POLICE COURT MISSIONARIES, 13
POOR LAW, 3, 3 n., 5, 18–9, 21, 23, 34 n. 55, 82–9 passim, 258, 259, 290 n.; see also Workhouses, Boards of Guardians, Assistance, Schools
and pauper apprentices, 6
Goschen Minute, 18, 19
C.O.S., 19, 85 n.
Royal Commission, 20
effect of Local Government Act, 21
finance, 22
Statute of Poor Relief, 3
Public Assistance, see Assistance
poor relief and unmarried mothers, 88
and C.A.M.W., 105
and mental defectives, 110, 115, 169 n.
and mental patients, 113, 160
and the blind, 174, 176, 177 n., 184, 190–4 passim, 200–14 passim, 242, 256
and infant welfare, 263
Board, 263
PORTSMOUTH, 230
POSTMASTER GENERAL, 185, 198
POTTERIES, 199
PREVENTION, 273 n., 285, 290
maternity and child welfare, 33, 49, 67, 73, 74, 286
mental health, 80, 85, 97, 98, 102, 114, 120, 122, 165, 274, 286
blind welfare, 177 n., 179, 186, 187, 198, 199, 203, 206, 213, 218–21, 223, 274
PRISONS, 81, 87, 101, 102 n., 140
Holloway, 87 n.
Brixton, 130
Wormwood Scrubs, 134 n.
PROBATION OFFICER, 258, 278, 284 n.
PROBLEM FAMILIES, 289 n.

316

INDEX

PROFESSIONAL ATTITUDE, 287, 288 n.
PROPAGANDA, 19, 257, 261, 273 n., 274, 291
  maternity and child welfare, 42, 48, 58, 59, 64–73 *passim*, 262 n., 266, 279
  mental health, 81, 87, 90, 91, 95, 100, 103, 106, 120, 122, 136, 137, 144, 164 n., 165, 274
  blind welfare, 184, 186, 220, 224
  spastics, 288
PSYCHOLOGICAL MEDICINE, 79, 82, 90, 92 n., 93 n., 97–121 *passim*, 150, 152
  and psychiatrists, 155, 162, 285
PUBLIC RELATIONS, 64, 255, 257, 269, 280; *see also* Propaganda
PUBLIC TRUSTEE, 130

QUAKERS, 12; *see also* Tuke

RADICALS, Philosophic, 4
RATHBONE, Wm., 10 n.
RAYNER, Dr., 89 n.
READ, Andrew, 99
RECONSTRUCTION, MINISTRY OF, 23 n., 107
RECREATION, 14, 278, 295; *see also* Arts and Youth Service
REES, Dr. J. R., 164 n.
REGIONAL
  Advisory Service (N.A.M.H.), 155
  Associations, 187, 290
    for the blind, *see* Index of Societies: Regional Association . . . Union of Counties . . .
  Conference (maternity and child welfare), 60
  developments in blind welfare, ix, 173 n., 186–241 *passim*, 243–6, 266, 267
  Exchequer support to Regional Associations, 260 n., 276
  Hospital Board, *see* Hospitals
  Inter-Committee, 243, 245, 267
  N.C.S.S. and regional developments, 266
  psychiatrists, 162; psychiatric social workers, 150
REGISTRATION, 'Mutual register', 20
  maternity and child welfare, 33 n., 38, 42
  mental health, 111, 134, 148, 152 n., 154 n., 163, 167 n.
  blind welfare, 173–244 *passim*
REHABILITATION, 13, 56 n., 79, 254 n., 282
  mental health, 95, 96, 135, 160, 165
  blind welfare, 180, 217, 234–40, 241, 243, 246–8, 257
  Standing Committee (interdepartmental) on, 236 n.
RELIGIOUS CONTROVERSIES, 6
RELIGIOUS INFLUENCE, 8–12
  on individuals and groups, 9–13, 25, 253, 256, 260

  maternity and child welfare, 32, 35; of clergy in, 37
  blind welfare, 176; of clergy in, 178 n., 180
  mental health, 91, 92, 93 n., 196; of clergy in, 93 n., 94 n.
  and C.O.S., 19
Church and State 8–9, 17
RESEARCH, 20 n., 25, 43, 51, 261, 262, 274, 280, 289; *see also* Surveys
  mental health, 97 n., 112, 113, 120 n., 163
  blind welfare, 173, 186, 206, 216, 224, 231, 237, 243, 244, 246 n.
  spastics, 288
'RETREAT', The, *see* Hospitals
RHONDDA, 52, 128 n.
RHYL, 132 n.
ROBERTS, G. H., 219 n.
ROTARY CLUBS, 155
ROTH, Dr., 177 n.
ROTHERHAM, 128 n.
ROTTERDAM, 117 n.
ROYAL COMMISSION(S), 6, 253, 279; for reports of R.C., *see* Bibliography: Government Publications on Law relating to Mental Illness and Mental Deficiency, (sitting) xii, 165, 257 n.
ROYAL NORMAL COLLEGE FOR THE BLIND, *see* Schools
RURAL AREAS
  health visiting in, 43 n., 49
  midwifery in, 53
  district nursing in, 54–5
  welfare centre in, 68 n.
  incidence of mental defect in, 131 n.
  request to C.A.M.W. from, 142 n.
  encouragement by Board of Control, 144
  Ex-Services After-Care Scheme in, 150
  home teaching of blind in, 207
  N.C.S.S. in, 265
RUSHTON, E., 178, 180, 217
RUSSELL, Mrs. B., 37
RUTHERFORD, Mark, 7

SAEGERT, 99 n.
ST. HELENS, 38
ST. LEONARDS, 56
SALFORD, 34, 35 n.
SANDLEBRIDGE SCHOOLS AND COLONY, 104 n.
SAXONY, 182, 201
SCIENCE
  advances in, 5
  social, 7, 25, 150
  challenge to religion, 9
  C.O.S. and, 18, 19
  and Booth, Chas., 24
  Journal of Mental, 93
  blind welfare and, 246
  scientific attitude, 98, 137, 219, 256, 273

INDEX

SCHOOL(S), 18, 56, 147; *see also* Homes; Training Colleges
  associations, 101
  comprehensive, 277
  day continuation, 12
  for blind, 177, 180-3, 194, 195-8, 213, 223; Chorley Wood College for Girls, 217 n.; Worcester College for Boys, 180, 217; Royal Normal College, 178, 180, 182 n., 183, 195, 197, 202; Yorkshire School, 183 n.
  meals, 21, 257
  medical service, 22, 46, 56, 121
  special, 23 n., 86, 88, 101-10 *passim*, 129, 138
  for blind and mentally retarded, 217; open air, 43; *see also* Deaf-Blind and Epileptics
  for mothers, 34, 37, 44 n., 45, 46, 263, 279
  nursery, 68; *see also* Nurseries (Residential)
  Poor Law, 101
  secondary, for girls, 68
SCOTLAND, 85
SCOTT, Mr. Leslie (later Lord Justice), 105
SEAFORD, 131
SÉGUIN, 99
SETTLEMENTS, 11, 154
  and professional training, 257
SHAFTESBURY, Lord, 9-10, 81, 85, 94 n., 176 n.
SHARPE, Mr., H. M. I., 196 n.
SHUTTLEWORTH, Dr., 85, 100 n., 101 n.
SIMON, J., 31
SOCIAL INSURANCE, 21, 139, 161, 223, 236 n., 243 n.
SOCIAL SECURITY, 259, 260, 283
SOCIAL WORKERS, *see also* Training, Hospital Almoners, Case Work
  part-time, voluntary, 14-5, 22, 279; maternity and child welfare, 32, 36-7, 51, 71; mental health, 117; blind welfare, 176; child care, 116, 279
  professional, 16, 19, 152, 154 n., 163, 164, 258, 266, 272, 278, 279, 285
  in community care, 285-8
  in child care, 279
  maternity and child welfare, 58; *see also* health visitors
  mental health, 79, 80, 105, 116, 117, 129, 132, 134, 148, 149 n., 274
  C.A.M.W. travelling organisers, etc., 107, 124-9, 148, 274
  psychiatric social workers, 118, 120-2, 149 n., 274, 287; in regional scheme, 150; at Duncroft, 152; at Ponds, 153 n.; appointed by L.C.C., 156, 157 n., 286 n.; by Middlesex, 286 n.; American, 116, 163 n.

American case workers, 284
blind welfare, 233, 243, 288; *see also* Home Teachers
  appointment by local authorities; Working Party (Younghusband Committee), 258 n.
SOCIOLOGY, 25, 262
SOMERSET, 128 n.
SOUTHEND, 128 n.
SOUTHSEA, 197
STAFFORDSHIRE, 183, 201 n.
STATISTICS
  vital statistics, 7
  absence of, 33, 87, 192, 203 n.
  collection of, etc., by voluntary societies, 104, Tables VI, VII, 243, 244
  London Statistics, Table IX, 212
  statistical analysis of income by charities, 260 n.
  difficulty of statistical evaluation, 290
STAUNTON HAROLD CHURCH, 281
STERILISATION, 137
STOKE-on-TRENT, 128, 181 n., 197
SUFFOLK, 133 n.
SUNDERLAND, 124
SUPERVISION IN MENTAL HEALTH
  provision for in M.D. Acts, 88, 114
  needs of defectives, 99
  work of voluntary organisations, 111
  and link with occupation centres, 104, 125
  with guardianship, 110, 162, 164 n.
  in holiday homes, 132
  of patients from Broadmoor, 134-5
  variation between local authorities, 140-1
  of defectives outside M.D. Acts, 143-4
  in Cambridge and in other L.A. areas, 147-8, Table VIII
  effect of Local Government Act, 211
SURREY, 156, 209
  Reigate, 247
SURVEYS AND INVESTIGATIONS, 5, 6, 19, 20, 26, 281
  maternity and child welfare, 42, 43, 69 n., 71
  mental health, 85, 86, 100, 115, 116, 132, 154, 162
  blind welfare, 179, 219, 220, 225, 246 n., 274
  epileptics, 132-3
SUSSEX, EAST, 60 n., 110, 131, 153, 209
SWANSEA, 128 n.
SWEDEN, 201, 202
SWITZERLAND, 99
SYKES, Dr., 37

TAVISTOCK CLINIC, 74 n., 97 n., 121, 284 n.
TAVISTOCK INSTITUTE OF HUMAN RELATIONS, 289 n.

INDEX

TEACHERS, *see also* Training and child guidance, 121
  of blind with sighted children, 195
  maternity and child welfare, 60
  home teachers of mentally defectives, 151, 279
  of the blind, 176 n., 181 n., 201, 206–12 *passim*, 222, 223, 230, 240–6 *passim*, 288
  status of, 108
TEMPLE, Wm., 9 n., 11 n.
TERMS, USE OF, xiii
TOC H, 155
TORQUAY, Manor House and America Lodge, Queen Elizabeth Homes, 241, 247
TOWNSEND, Miss P. D., 101 n.
TRADE, BOARD OF, 59
TRADES UNIONS, 4 n., 8, 22 n., 200, 202, 207, 218
TRAINING, 7, 15, 19, 59, 97 n., 110, 111, 120, 129–30, 165, 234, 257, 261, 274, 279–80, 284–5, 290–1; *see also* Schools
  colleges, 17, 106 n., 129, 181; *see also* College of Teachers of the Blind
  for doctors, 60, 129, 130, 151; D.P.H. students, 130; medical students, 42, 120
  for health visitors, 30, 51, 60, 67, 129, 130
  for lecturers, 60
  for magistrates, 129
  for mental health officers, etc., 111, 129, 155, 160 n., 286
  for midwives, 42, 60 n., 67
  for nurses, 42, 56 n., 67, 130
  for psychiatric social workers, 112 n., 121
  for psychologists (educational), 121, 279; (medical), 112 n., 120, 121
  for social workers (short courses), 129, 130, 264, 279
  for students, social science, 19 n., 79, 105; 'generic' course, 284; mental health course, 121
  for supervisors of occupation centres, 125, 129, 143, 163; at Agnes Weston Centre, 125, 129
  for teachers, 60, 67, 110–11, 129, 130, 151, 181, 197, 240; home teachers' course, 244
  for voluntary workers, 15, 22, 117, 188, 213, 279–80
  for workers in hospitals, etc., and Homeworkers' Diploma Course, 154 n., 163, 279
  in infant welfare, 44, 58, 59, 60, 67 n.; post-certificate course, 55 n.
  of the blind, 173, 177, 180–4, 189–90, 198–243 *passim*; social training, 248
  of delinquents, 7; of epileptics, 132–3; of the handicapped, 234, 241; of mental defectives, 7, 79 n., 85, 86, 103, 104, 114, 125, 127, 128, 138, 144 n., 145 n., 147, 155, 188
  of parents, 131 n.
  Working Party on the recruitment and training of social workers, etc., (Younghusband Committee), 258 n.
TREASURY
  Chancellor of the Exchequer, 139, 211, 229, 260 n., 276
TRUST FOUNDATION, xi n., 13 n., 14 n., 23, 267, 268, 269, 270, 289, 290; *see also* Clothworkers' Company
  Carnegie, 14 n., 52, 58, 59, 63, 155 n., 189, 289
  Gardner's, 177, 183–4, 184 n., 187, 188, 195, 201, 219
  Halley-Stewart, 289 n.
  Henderson, 153
  Imperial Health Assocn. Fund, 60
  Mental Health Research Fund, 256, 289
  National Relief Fund, 190
  Nuffield, xi n., 246, 289
  Pilgrim, 60, 289
  Queen Adelaide's Fund, 23, 98, 116, 156, 166
  Queen's Scholarship, 180
TUCKWELL, Gertrude, 39
TUKE, S., and TUKE, D. H., 92 n.
TUKE, Wm. (and family), 12, 84 n., 91–2
TURNBULL, Dr. Jane, 62 n., 64 n.
TWINING, Louisa, 15, 93 n.

UNITARIANS, 12; *see also* Rathbone, Wm.
UNITED NATIONS, 164, 282
U.N.E.S.C.O., 164
U.N.I.C.E.F., 74; *see also* World Health Organisation
U.N.R.R.A., 74
UNIVERSITIES, 19, 36, 154, 178
  Birmingham, 247
  Leeds, 155
  London School of Economics, 121, 129, 284
  London School of Hygiene, etc., 64 n., 130
  Nottingham, 151 n.
  and psychology, 120
  and training of social workers, 79; C.O.S., 19 n.
  Extension and Tutorial Classes, 129 n.

VAUXHALL MOTORS, 235 n.
VIOLET MELCHETT CLINIC, 39 n., 292 n.

WAGES
  conditions of those with low, 8
  of defectives on farms, 138

INDEX

WAGES—contd.
supplementation (augmentation) of, blind workers, 177, 202, 209, 210, 212, 216 n., 230
methods of payment of, 221, 222 n.
full work for, 237
WALES, 128 n., 134
Pontypridd, 148
Aberdare, 148
Mountain Ash, 148
Monmouthshire, 148, 186 n., 206 n., 207 n., 239, 245 n.
WAR
women's opportunities in, 15
Boer War, influence on social services, 20, 21, 32, 263
First World War
a dividing line, 23, 25, 253, 254, 261, 263
impetus to co-ordination, 265
maternity and child welfare, influence of, 46–8
blind welfare, developments during, 188–93, 228, 240 n.; Departmental Committee, 201, 204
mental health, M.A.C.A., 96; on psychological medicine, 97, 98, 112; mental deficiency, 89, 108 et seq., 129; effect of post-war depressions, 115, 129; resilience of C.A.M.W., 281
Second World War
the Churches and religions in schools in, 18
maternity and child welfare, evacuation, 30, 48 n.; difficulty of supplies, 59; emergency measures, 66–75
mental health, amalgamation, 79, 120 n.; variety of response, 149–58; finance, 168; curtailments: mental testing, 130; work of C.P.O.I.P.H., 131; extensions, 138
blind welfare, 233; response to emergency, 234–50; co-ordination, 267; fostering of relationships, 280; influence on social legislation, 281
History of Second World War, xi n., 66 n., 150 n., 159 n.
WAR OFFICE, 98 n.
WARDLE, Mr., 200
WEBB, Beatrice, 25; see also Bibliography: Webb, S. and B.
WELFARE
of citizens, 259, 282, 283; see also blind, maternity and child, moral health and, schemes, 262
of the handicapped, 160, 173, 174, 240, 295
of old people, 272, 278

Authorities, National Assistance Act, 238 n., 240–1, 248–50 passim, 258 n.
Authorities, Maternity and Child Welfare Act, 53
officers, 160 n., 242, 244 n.
State, 4 n., 279, 283
WEST INDIAN IMMIGRANTS, 289 n.
WEST OF ENGLAND, 100 n., 103, 186 n., 239
WESTON-SUPER-MARE, 132
WHITE, The Misses, 99
WOLVERHAMPTON, 124
WOMEN, see Professional Social Workers; see also Women's Group on Public Welfare, and Women's Voluntary Services (Index of Societies)
emancipation of, 14–6
Co-operative Guilds, 15
Institutes, 15, 60, 155
on Boards of Guardians, 15 n., 32
in maternity and child welfare service, 32, 34, 35, 47
in mental health, 92, 93 n.
in blind welfare, 174, 178, 202
National Council of, 64 n.
W.R.N.S., 67
W.R.A.A.F., 67
A.T.S., 67
WORKERS' EDUCATIONAL ASSOCIATION, 154
WORKHOUSES (POOR LAW INSTITUTIONS), 20 n.
mental health, 81, 83, 84, 94, 95, 101, 102 n., 110, 132, 169
blind welfare, 194, 196, 201 n., 203 n.
WORKING MEN'S COLLEGE, 11
WORKING PARTY, for reports see Bibliography: Government Publications
(sitting) Younghusband Committee: on Recruitment and Training of Social Workers in the Health and Welfare Services, 258 n.
WORKSHOP
for epileptics, 133
for the blind, 177–213 passim (Barclay, 213), 216, 222 n., 223, 224, 225–6, 230, 236, 239, 243, 248 n., 267, 295
WORLD HEALTH ORGANISATION, 74, 75 n., 164

YORK, 39, 84, 91, 92 n., 186
YORKSHIRE, 103, 183 n.
School for the Blind, 183 n.
YOUNG WIVES FELLOWSHIPS, 155
YOUTH, service of, 13, 14
YOUTH GROUPS, Girls' Training Corps, 68; clubs for M.D., 126–7, 162 n.